Cast of Characters

The Knights of the True Cross

Rin Okumura

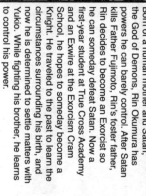

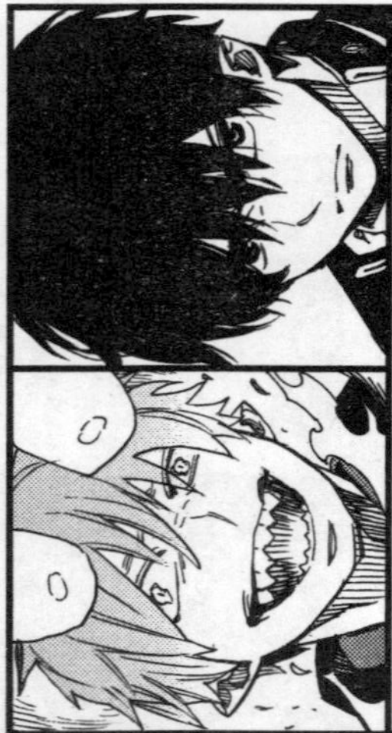

Born of a human mother and Satan, the God of Demons, Rin Okumura has powers he can barely control. After Satan kills Father Fujimoto, Rin's foster father, Rin decides to become an Exorcist so he can someday defeat Satan. Now a first-year student at True Cross Academy and an Exwire at the Exorcism Cram School, he hopes to someday become a Knight. He traveled to the past to learn the circumstances surrounding his birth, and now he is determined to settle matters with Yukio. While fighting his brother, he learns to control his power.

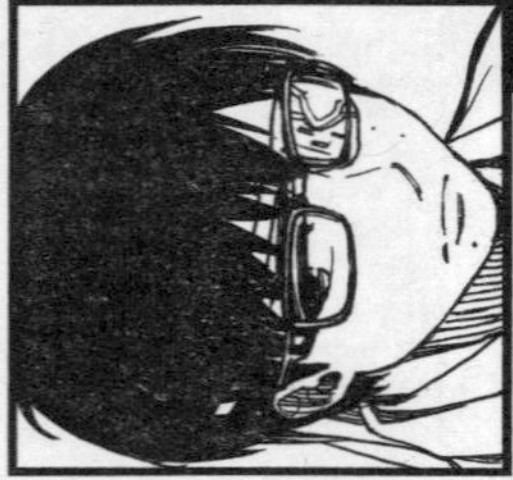

Yukio Okumura

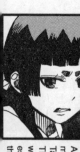

Rin's brother. He's a genius who is the youngest student ever to become an instructor at the Exorcism Cram School. While fighting his brother, he reveals his true feelings for the first time. In order to defeat Satan, who was occupying his left eye, he transfers the king of demons to a vessel for possession.

Shiemi Moriyama

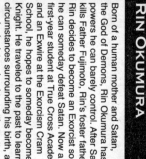

Daughter of the owner of Futsumaya, an Exorcist supply shop. She possesses the ability to become a Tamer and can summon a baby Greenman named Nee. After quitting the Exorcism Cram School, she went to a garden called El inside Vatican headquarters, where she began training.

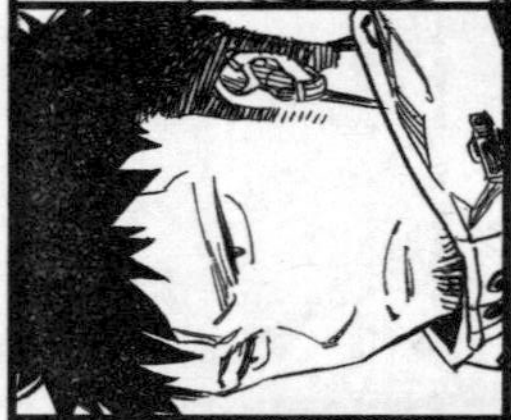

Ryuji Suguro

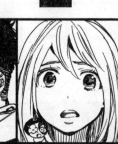

Heir to the venerable Buddhist sect known as Myodha in Kyoto. He wants to achieve the titles of Dragoon and Aria. He is Lightning's apprentice and they were conducting an investigation together.

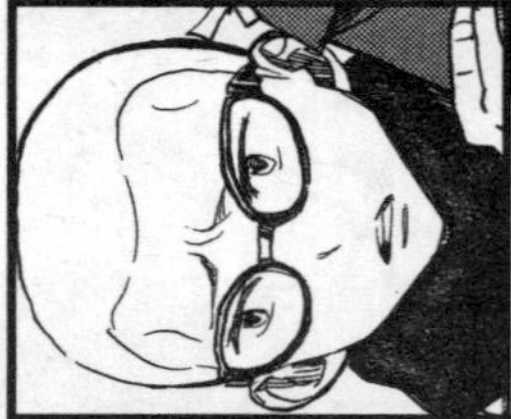

Konekomaru Miwa

He was once a pupil of Suguro's father and is now Suguro's friend. He's an Exwire who hopes to become an Exorcist someday. He is small in size and has a quiet and composed personality.

Izumo Kamiki

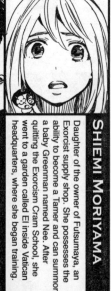

An Exwire with the blood of shrine maidens. She has the ability to become a Tamer and can summon two white foxes. The Illuminati had taken her captive, but with help from Rin and the others, she escaped and settled her grudge against the insane professor Gedoin.

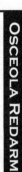

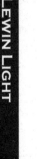

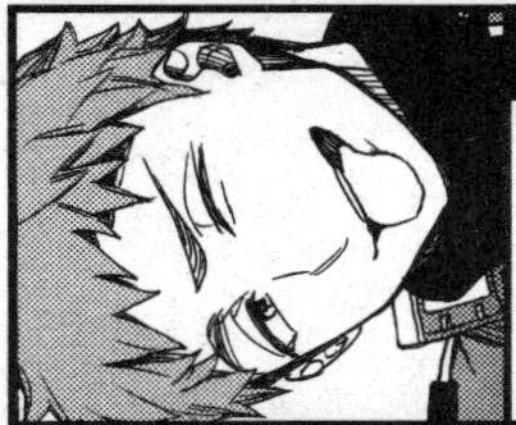

RENZO SHIMA

Once a pupil of Suguro's father and now Suguro's friend. Currently, he is a double agent providing information to both the Illuminati and the Knights of the True Cross.

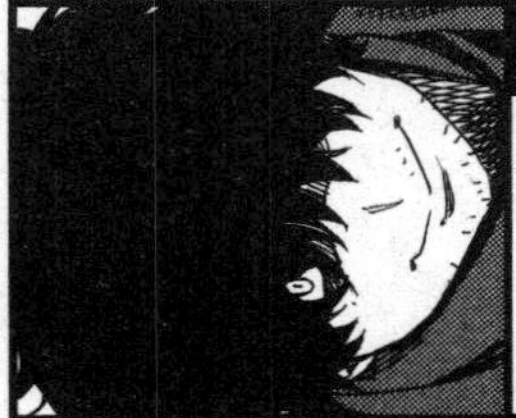

LEWIN LIGHT

An Arch Knight, he is Arthur's right-hand man as well as number two in the Order. An expert in Arias and summoning, he goes by the nickname Lightning.

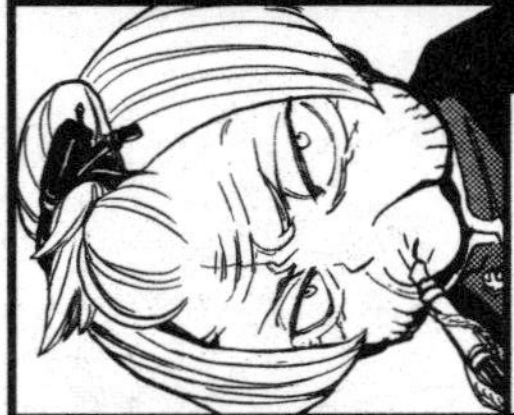

LUCY YANG

An Arch Knight from the China Branch.

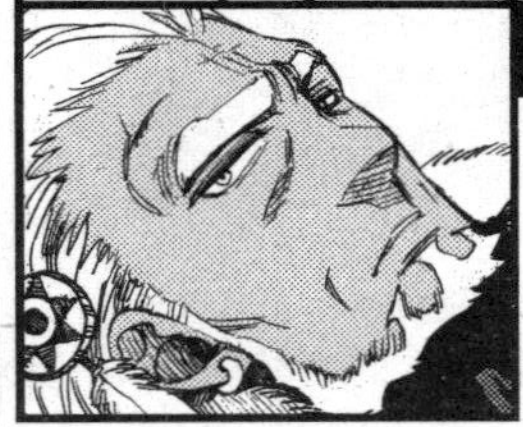

OSCEOLA REDARM

An Arch Knight from the Mexico Branch.

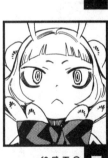

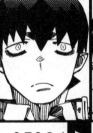

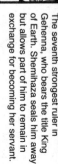

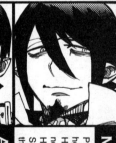

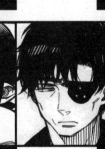

IGOR NEUHAUS

A Senior Exorcist First Class who holds the titles of Tamer, Doctor and Aria. Under orders from Mephisto, he was researching enhanced anti-demon compounds.

MEPHISTO PHELES

President of True Cross Academy and head of the Exorcism Cram School. He was Father Fujimoto's friend, and now he is Rin and Yukio's guardian. He's a high-ranking demon known as Samael, King of Time. He assembled the Anti-Satan Suppression Force.

AMAIMON

The seventh strongest ruler in Gehenna, who bears the title King of Earth. Shemihaza seals him away but allows part of him to remain in exchange for becoming her servant.

BEELZEBUB

One of the Baal and known as the King of Insects. She participates in the battle as part of the Anti-Satan Suppression Force.

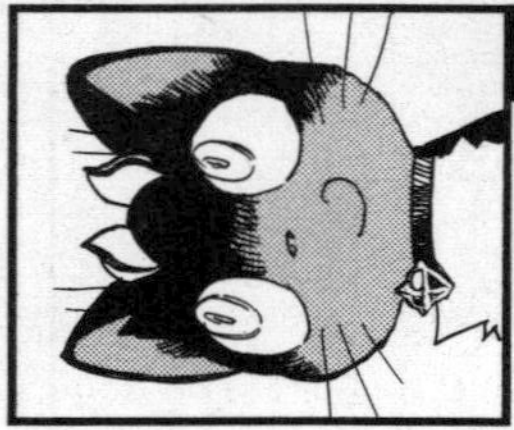

BLUE EXORCIST

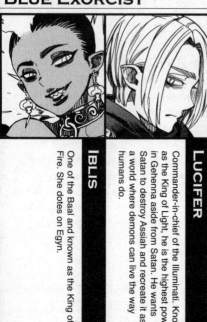

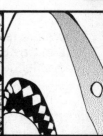

KURO

A Cat Sidhe who was once Shiro's familiar. After Shiro's death, he began turning back into a demon. Rin saved him, and now the two are practically inseparable. His favorite drink is the catnip wine Shiro used to make.

⦿ THE ILLUMINATI ⦿

LUCIFER

Commander-in-chief of the Illuminati. Known as the King of Light, he is the highest power in Gehenna aside from Satan. He wants Satan to destroy Assiah and recreate it as a world where demons can live the way humans do.

IBLIS

One of the Baal and known as the King of Fire. She dotes on Egyn.

EGYN

One of the Baal and known as the King of Water. Assistant director of the airborne research laboratory on *Dominus Liminis*. He participated in elixir research.

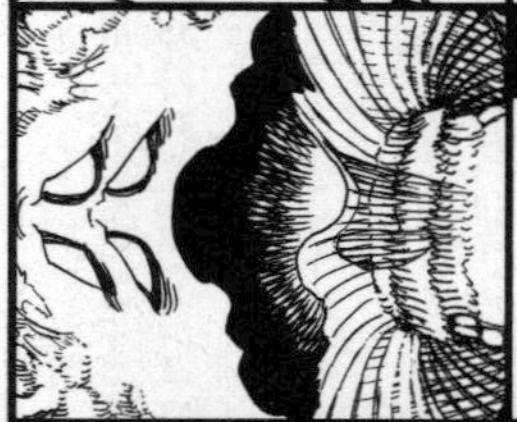

ASTAROTH

One of the Baal and known as the King of Rot.

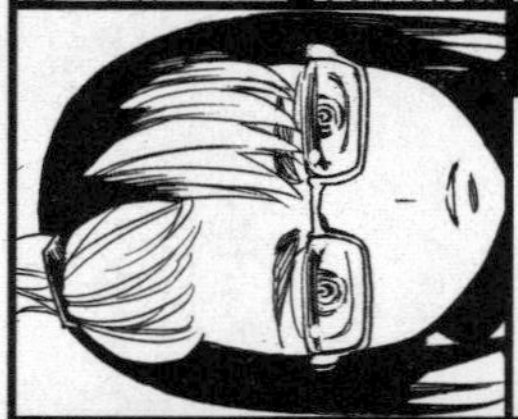

HOMARE TODO

Leader of Phosphorus, an organization of guards directly under Lucifer's command. She is Saburota Todo's daughter and Shima's superior officer, and holds a rank of Adeptus Minor or higher.

SATAN

Rin and Yukio's father. He is connected to and rules over almost all demons. He had occupied Yukio's left eye, but now he has taken physical form through possession.

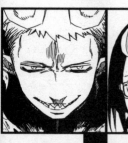

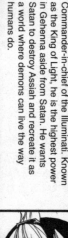

⚫ THE STORY SO FAR ⚫

BOTH HUMAN AND DEMON BLOOD RUNS THROUGH RIN OKUMURA'S VEINS. IN AN ARGUMENT WITH HIS FOSTER FATHER, FATHER FUJIMOTO, RIN LEARNS THAT SATAN IS HIS TRUE FATHER. SATAN SUDDENLY APPEARS AND TRIES TO DRAG RIN DOWN TO GEHENNA BECAUSE RIN HAS INHERITED HIS POWER. FATHER FUJIMOTO FIGHTS TO DEFEND RIN, BUT DIES IN THE PROCESS. RIN DECIDES TO BECOME AN EXORCIST SO HE CAN SOMEDAY DEFEAT SATAN AND BEGINS STUDYING AT THE EXORCISM CRAM SCHOOL UNDER THE INSTRUCTION OF HIS TWIN BROTHER YUKIO, WHO IS ALREADY AN EXORCIST.

RIN AND THE OTHERS SUCCEED IN DEFEATING THE IMPURE KING, AWAKENED BY THE FORMER EXORCIST, TODO. MEANWHILE, YUKIO FIGHTS TODO, AND AS THE BATTLE RAGES, HE SENSES THE SAME FLAME IN HIS OWN EYES AS HIS BROTHER.

LATER, MYSTERIOUS EVENTS BEGIN OCCURRING AROUND THE GLOBE ORCHESTRATED BY A SECRET SOCIETY KNOWN AS THE ILLUMINATI. FINALLY, THE JAPANESE GOVERNMENT PUBLICLY RECOGNIZES THE EXISTENCE OF DEMONS.

IN ORDER TO LEARN ABOUT SATAN INHABITING HIS LEFT EYE AND THE SECRETS SURROUNDING HIS BIRTH, YUKIO GOES TO JOIN THE ILLUMINATI. TRAVELING THROUGH THE PAST, RIN LEARNS HOW SHIRO AND YURI FELT ABOUT HIMSELF AND HIS BROTHER. THEN, RIN ONCE AGAIN APPEARS BEFORE YUKIO IN AN EFFORT TO BRING HIM BACK.

THE TWO VENT THEIR TRUE FEELINGS FOR THE FIRST TIME AND FINALLY COME TO AN UNDERSTANDING. COOPERATING WITH HIS COMRADES AND DETERMINED TO FIGHT, YUKIO EXPELS SATAN INTO A BODY FOR POSSESSION. NOW ALL-OUT WAR BETWEEN SATAN AND THE EXORCISTS BEGINS!!

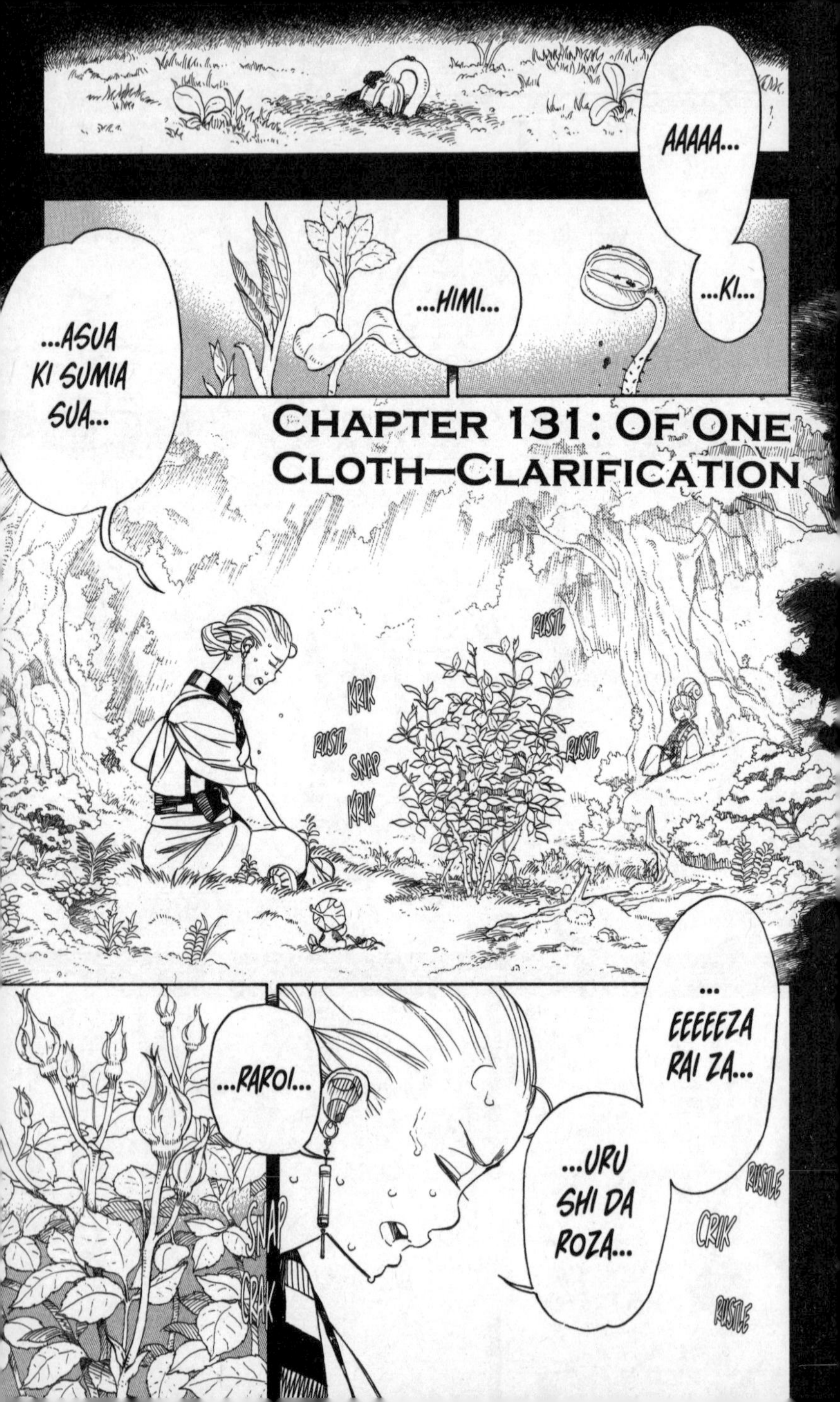
AAAAA...
...KI...
...HIMI...
...ASUA KI SUMIA SUA...
Chapter 131: Of One Cloth—Clarification
RUSTL
RUSTL
KRIK
RUSTL
SNAP
KRIK
...EEEEEZA RAI ZA...
...URU SHI DA ROZA...
RUSTLE
CRIK
RUSTLE
SNAP
CRAK
...RAROI...

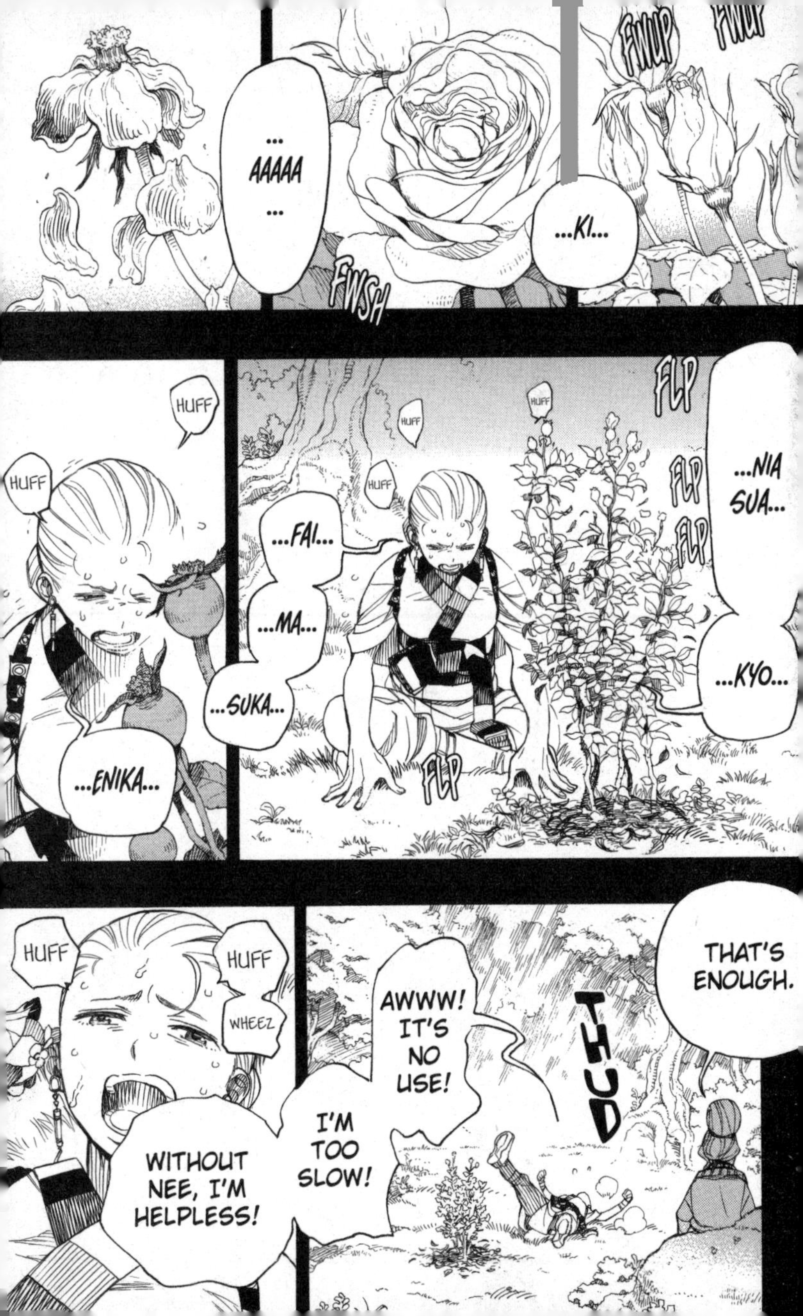
FWUP
FWUP
...KI...
...
AAAAA
...
FWSH
FLP
...NIA SUA...
FLP
FLP
FLP
...KYO...
HUFF
HUFF
HUFF
...FAI...
...MA...
...SUKA...
FLP
HUFF
HUFF
...ENIKA...
THAT'S ENOUGH.
THUD
AWWW! IT'S NO USE!
I'M TOO SLOW!
HUFF
HUFF
WHEEZ
WITHOUT NEE, I'M HELPLESS!

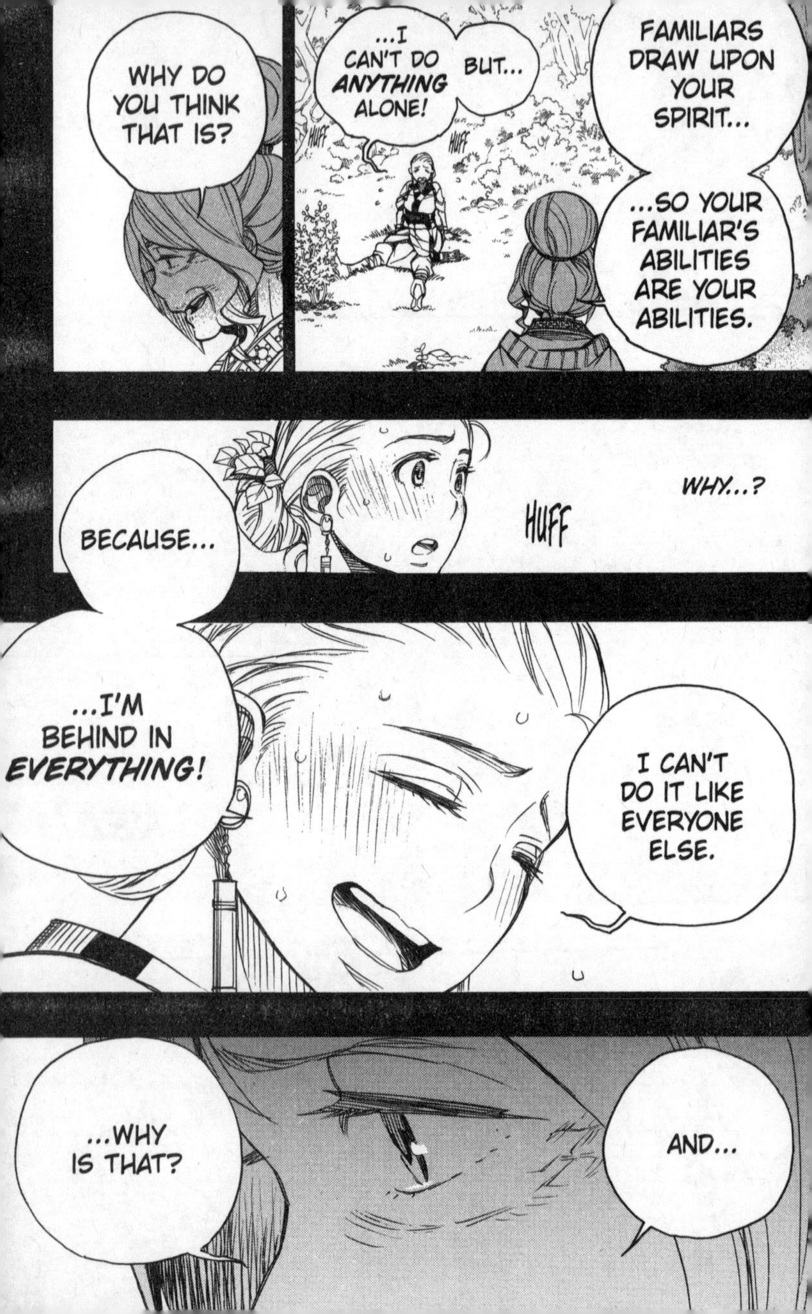
FAMILIARS DRAW UPON YOUR SPIRIT...
...SO YOUR FAMILIAR'S ABILITIES ARE YOUR ABILITIES.
BUT...
...I CAN'T DO *ANYTHING* ALONE!
HUFF
HUFF
WHY DO YOU THINK THAT IS?
WHY...?
HUFF
BECAUSE...
I CAN'T DO IT LIKE EVERYONE ELSE.
...I'M BEHIND IN *EVERYTHING*!
AND...
...WHY IS THAT?

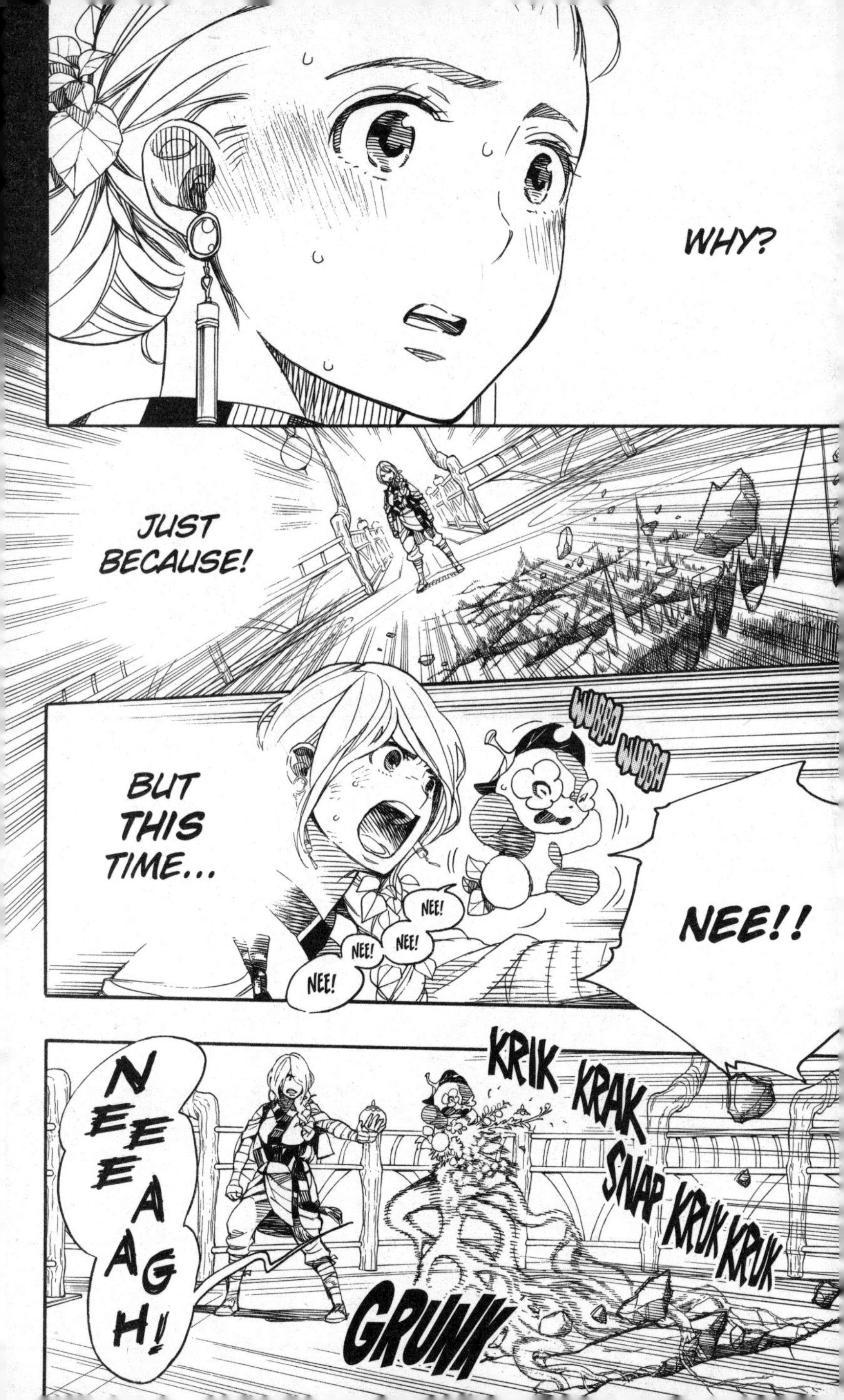

WHY?
JUST BECAUSE!
WUBBA WUBBA
NEE!!
BUT THIS TIME...
NEE!
NEE!
NEE!
NEE!
KRIK KRAK SNAP KRUK KRUK
GRUNK
NEEEEAAGH!

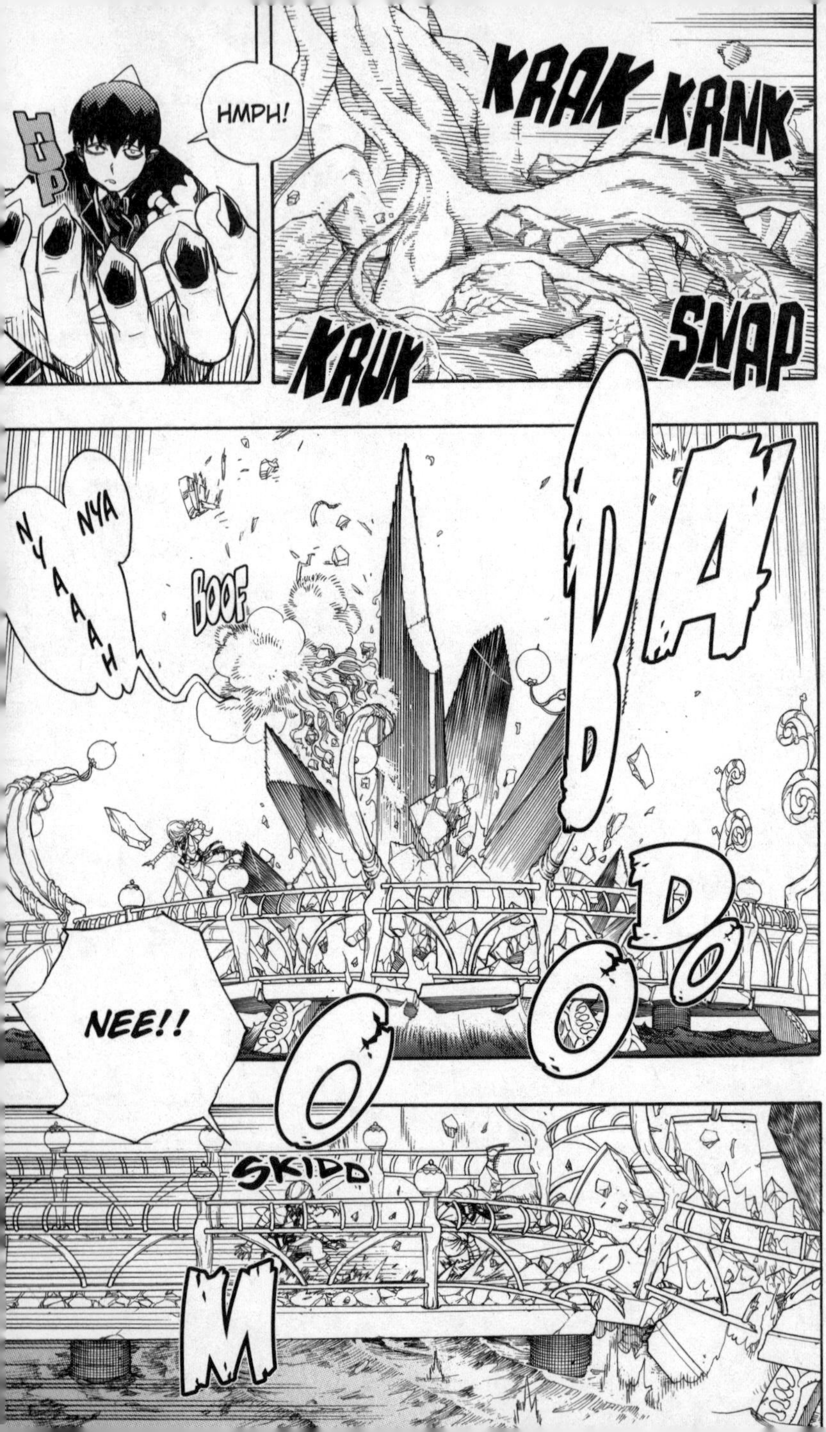

KRAK KRNK
SNAP
KRUK
HMPH!
DA
DOOO
BOOF
NYA
NYAAAAH
NEE!!
SKIDD
M

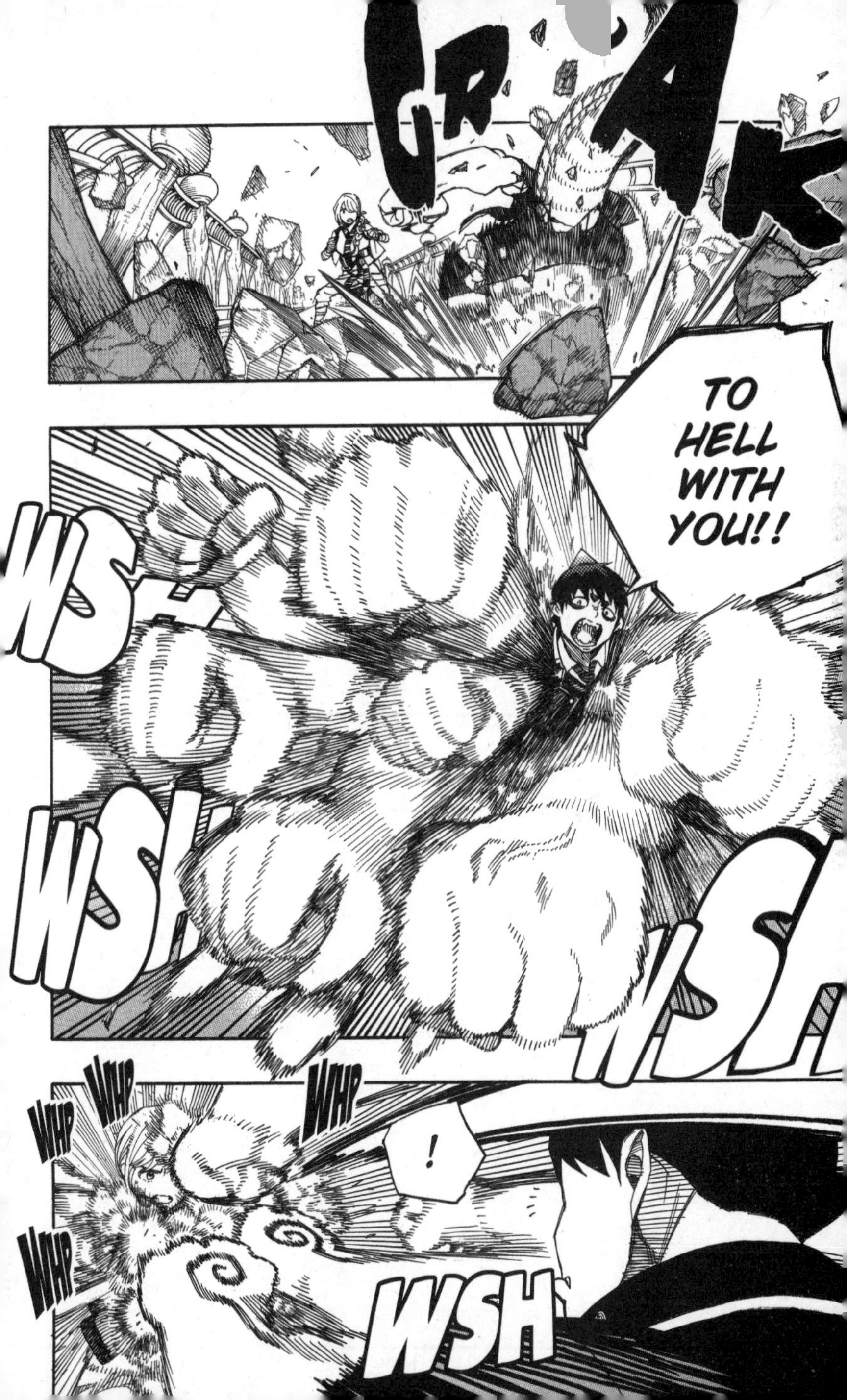
CRAAK
TO HELL WITH YOU!!
WSH
WSH
WSH
WSH
!
WHP
WHP
WHP
WHP

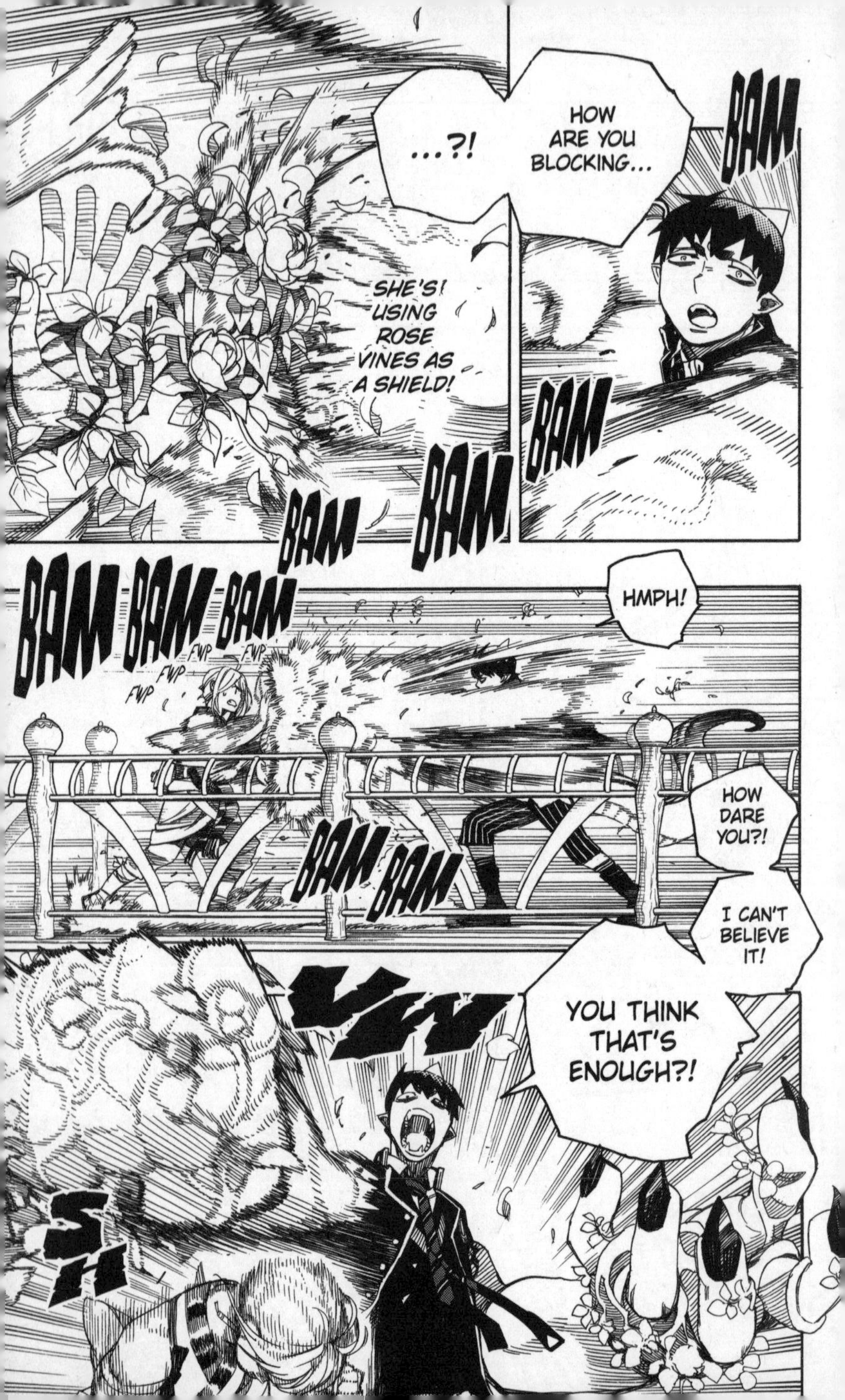
BAM
HOW ARE YOU BLOCKING...
...?!
BAM
SHE'S USING ROSE VINES AS A SHIELD!
BAM
BAM
BAM
HMPH!
BAM BAM BAM
FWP FWP FWP FWP
HOW DARE YOU?!
BAM BAM
I CAN'T BELIEVE IT!
YOU THINK THAT'S ENOUGH?!
VN
SH

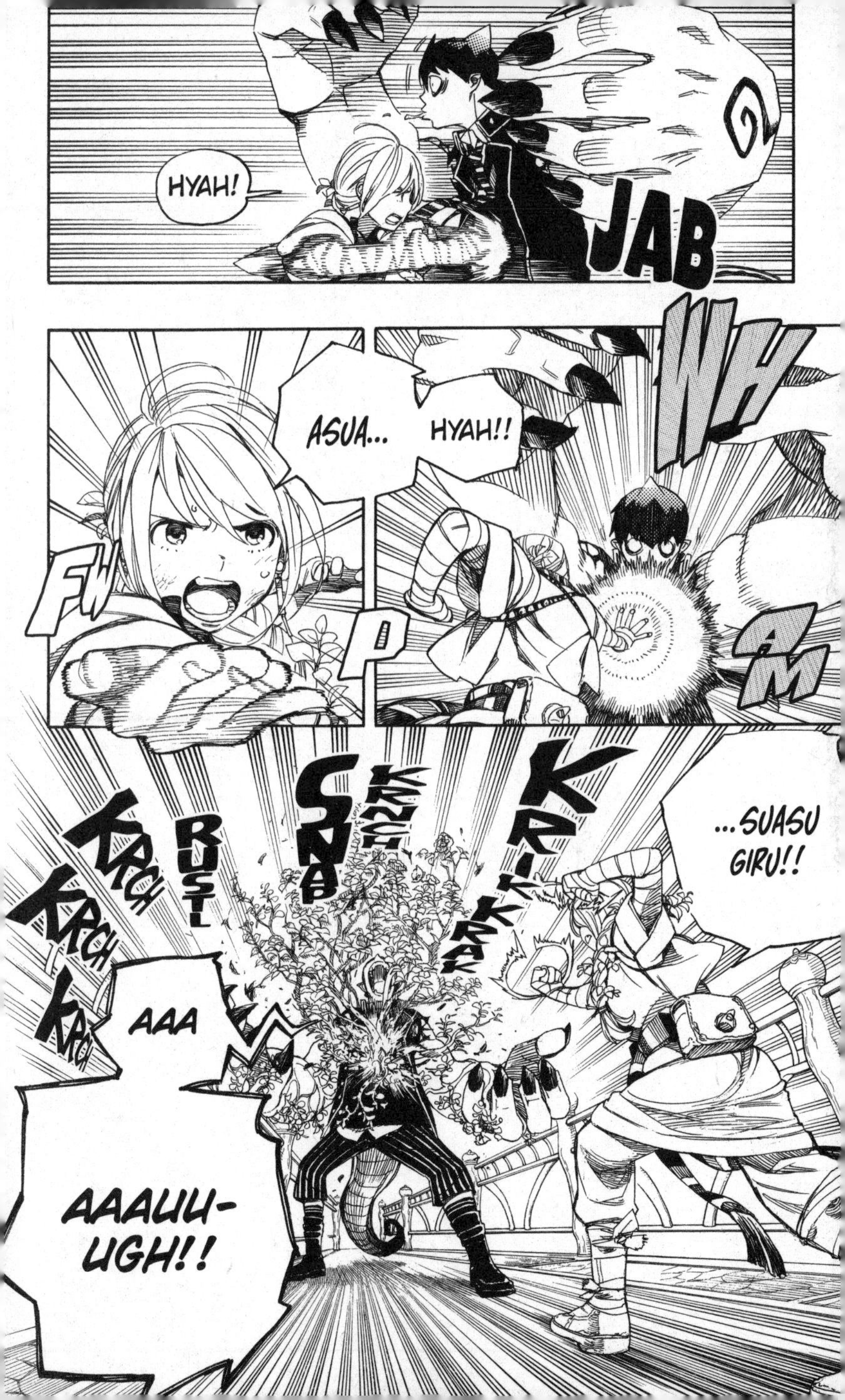

JAB
HYAH!
WH
ASUA... HYAH!!
AM
FW
P
...SUASU GIRU!!
KRIK KRAK
KRUNCH
SNAP
RUSTL
KRCH
KRCH
KRCH
AAA
AAAUU-UGH!!

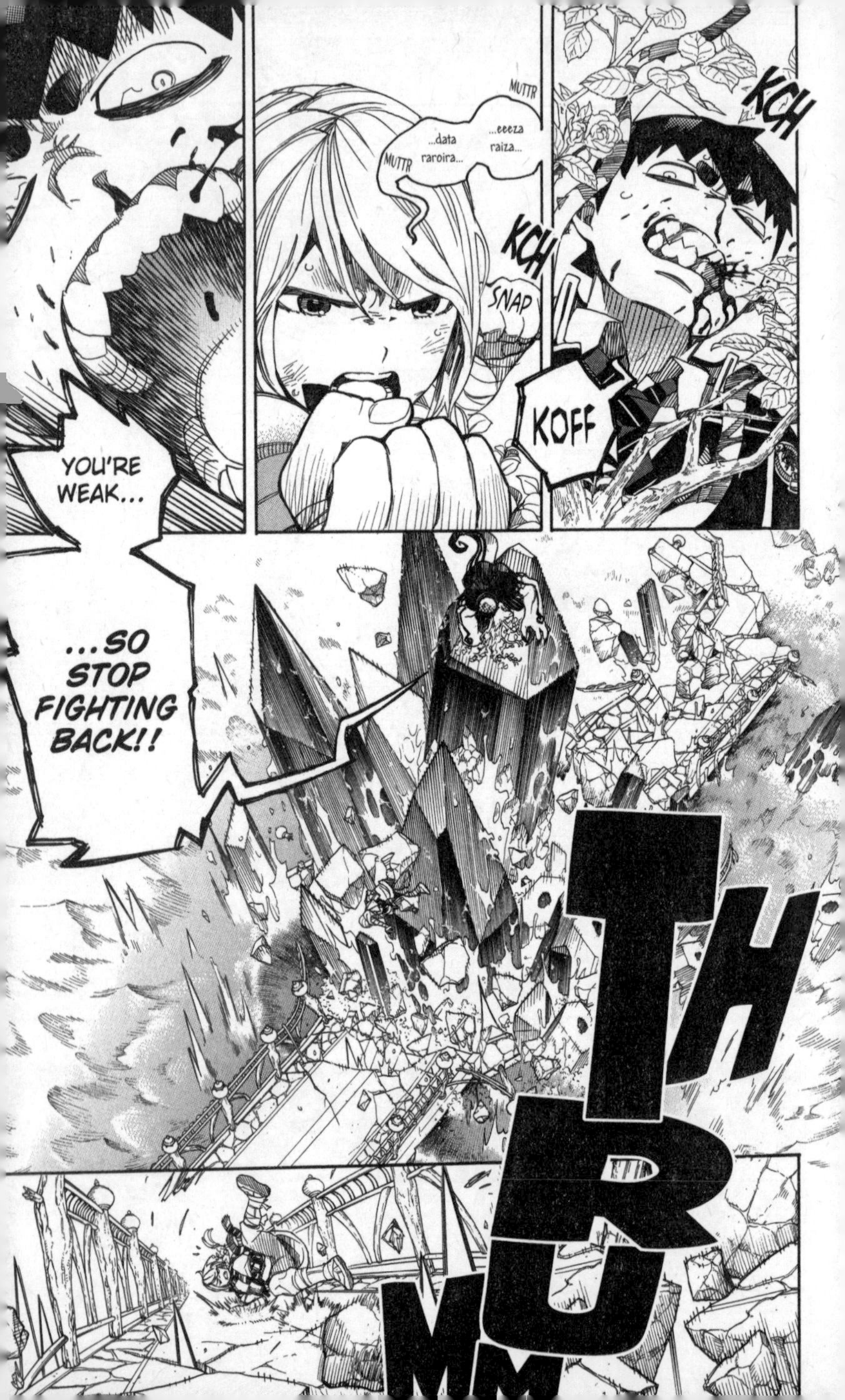
KCH
KCH
SNAP
KOFF
MUTTR
...eeeza raiza...
...data raroira...
MUTTR
YOU'RE WEAK...
...SO STOP FIGHTING BACK!!
THRUMM

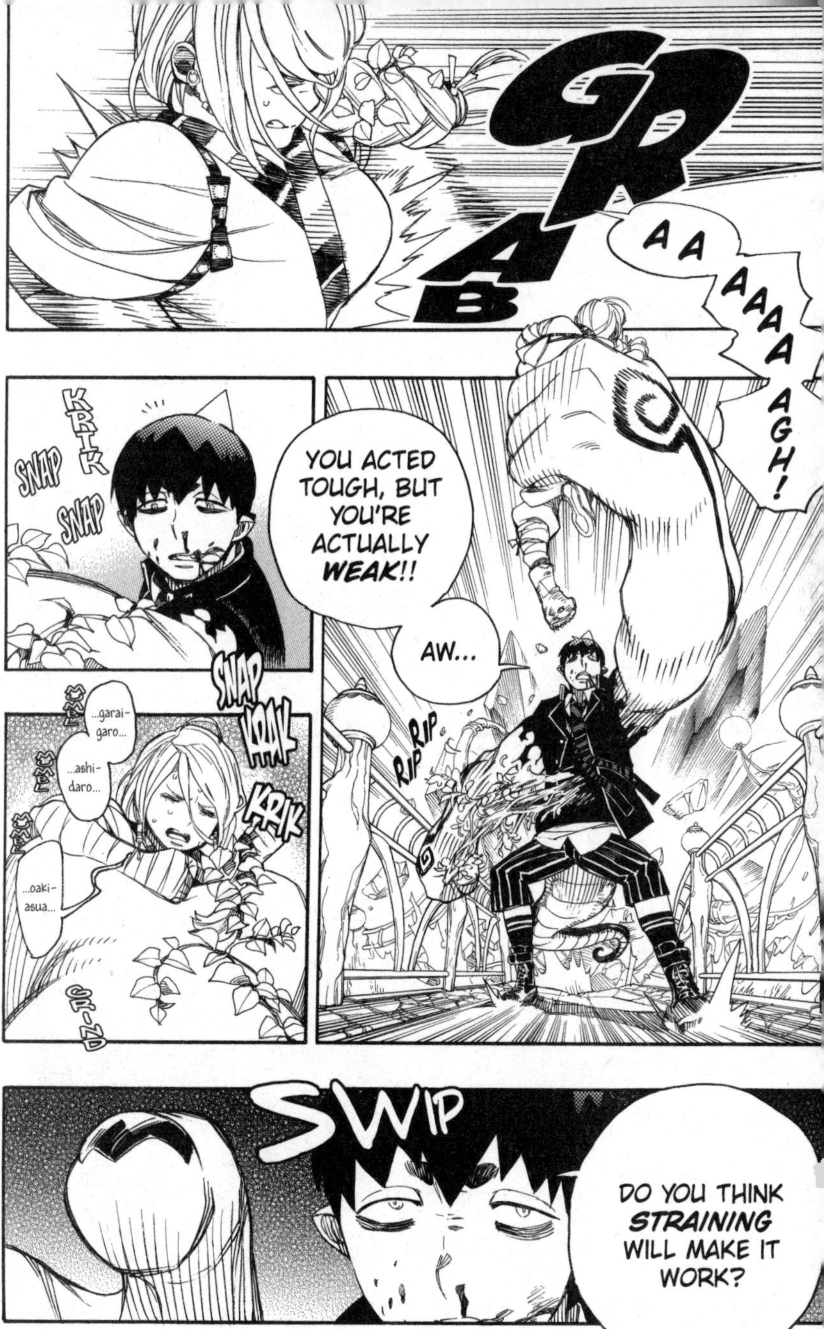
GRAB
AAAAAAAAGH!
YOU ACTED TOUGH, BUT YOU'RE ACTUALLY WEAK!!
AW...
RIP RIP
KRIK
SNAP
SNAP
SNAP
KRAK
KRIK
MMBL
...garai-garo...
MMBL
...ashi-daro...
MMBL
...oaki-asua...
GRIND
SWIP
DO YOU THINK STRAINING WILL MAKE IT WORK?

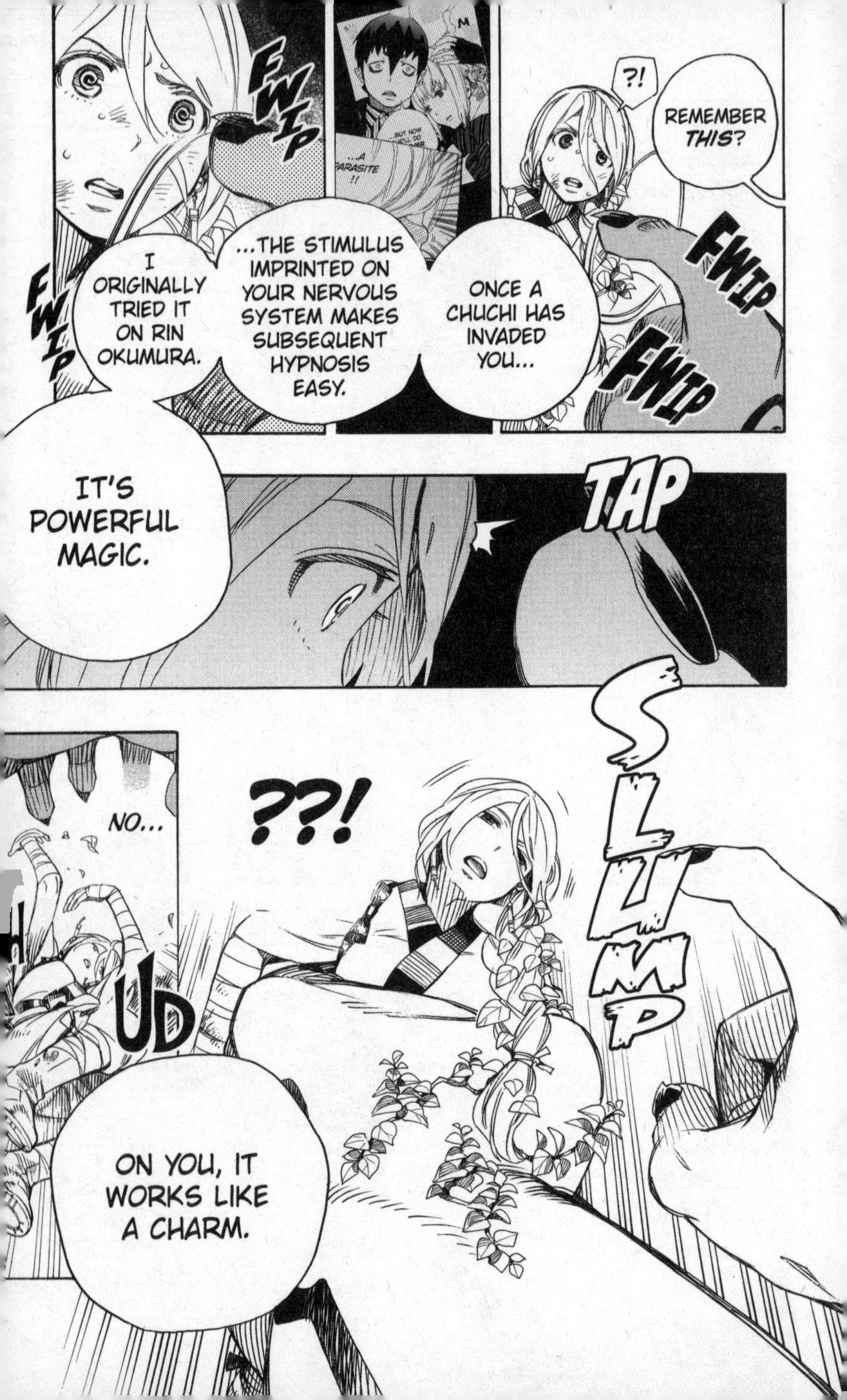
?!
REMEMBER THIS?
FWIP
FWIP
ONCE A CHUCHI HAS INVADED YOU...
...THE STIMULUS IMPRINTED ON YOUR NERVOUS SYSTEM MAKES SUBSEQUENT HYPNOSIS EASY.
...A PARASITE !!
FWIP
FWIP
I ORIGINALLY TRIED IT ON RIN OKUMURA.
TAP
IT'S POWERFUL MAGIC.
SLUMP
??!
NO...
UD
ON YOU, IT WORKS LIKE A CHARM.

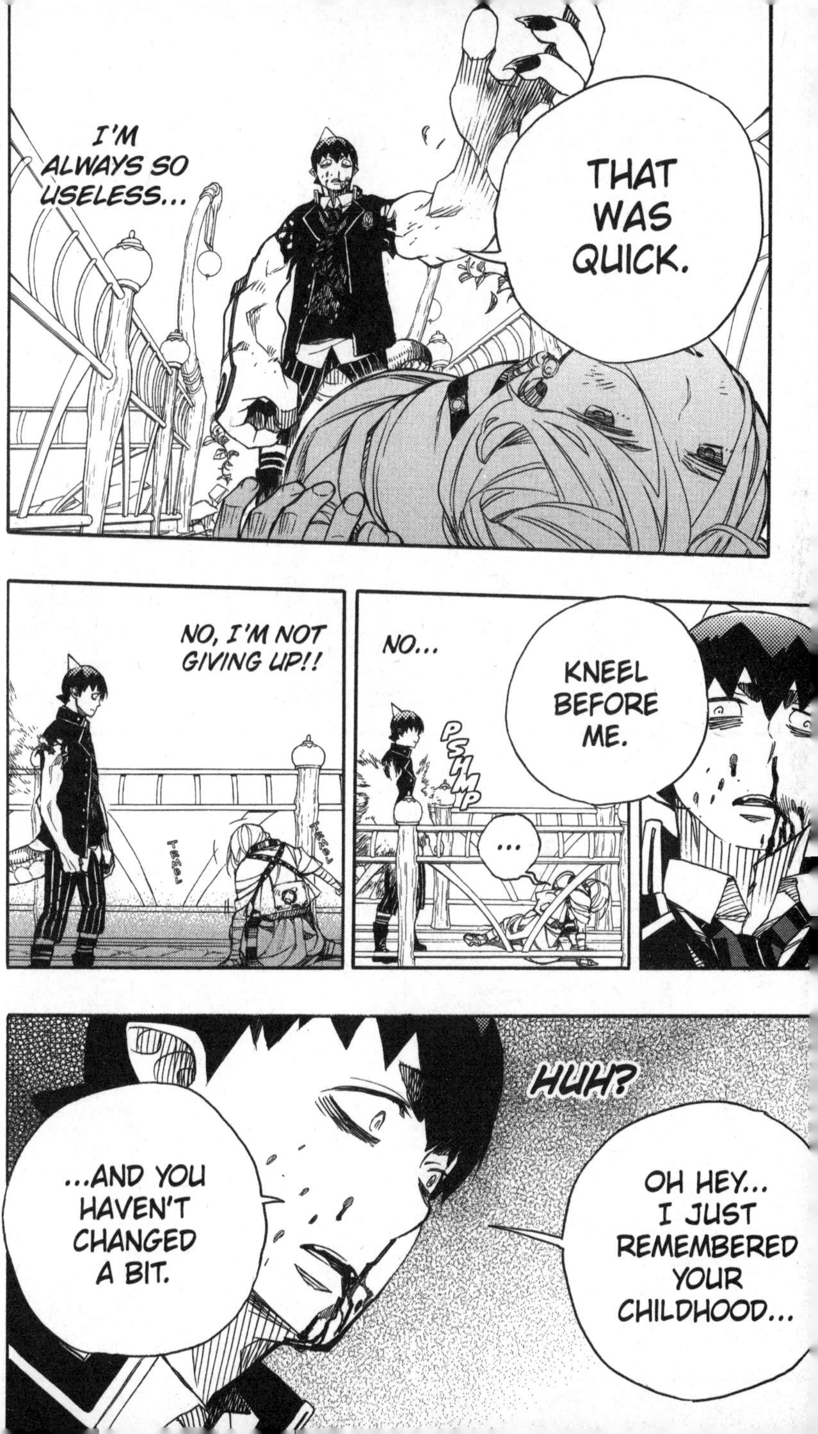
THAT WAS QUICK.
I'M ALWAYS SO USELESS...
KNEEL BEFORE ME.
NO...
PSHMP
...
NO, I'M NOT GIVING UP!!
OH HEY... I JUST REMEMBERED YOUR CHILDHOOD...
HUH?
...AND YOU HAVEN'T CHANGED A BIT.

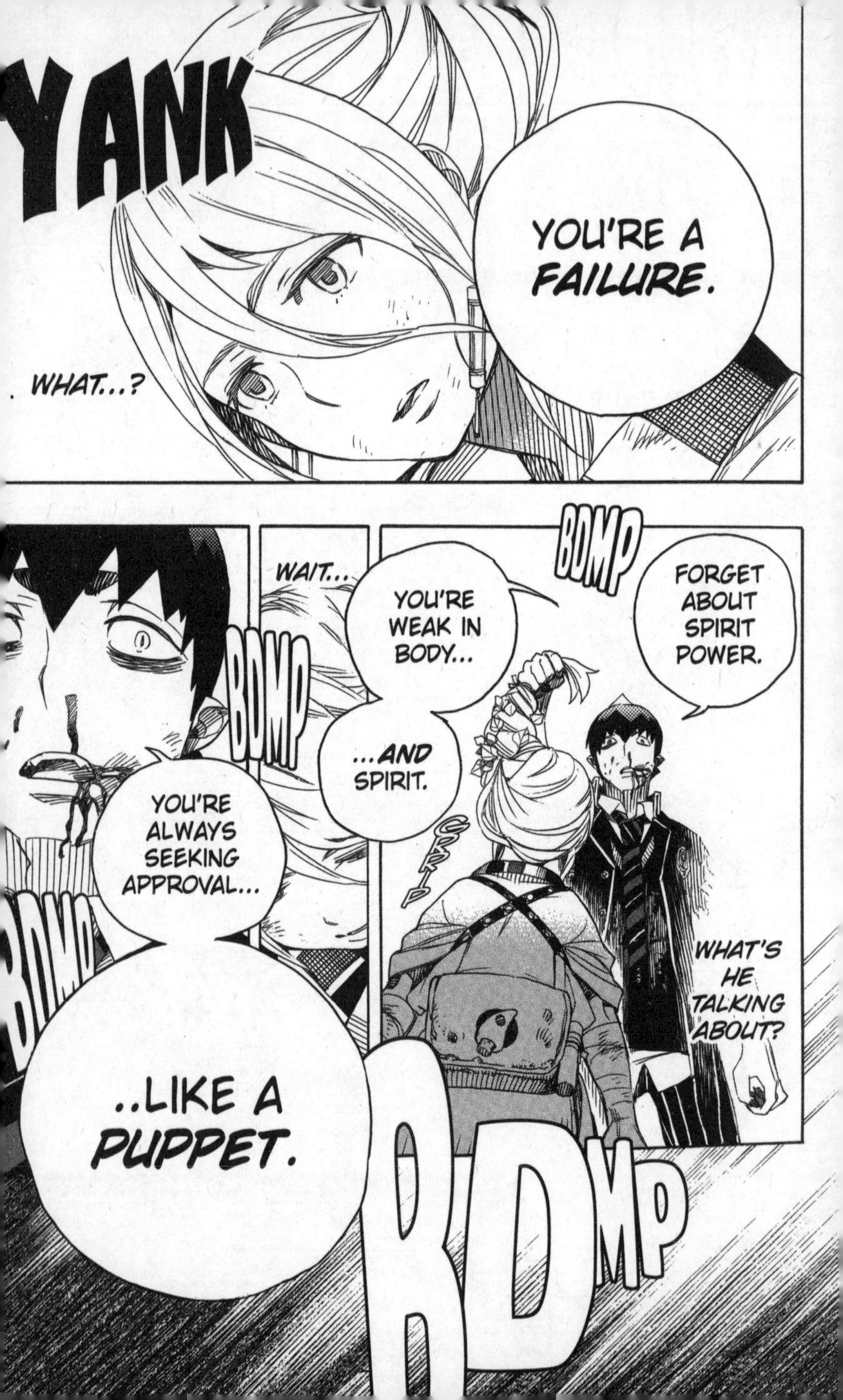
YOU'RE A FAILURE.
YANK
WHAT...?
BDMP
FORGET ABOUT SPIRIT POWER.
GRRIP
WHAT'S HE TALKING ABOUT?
YOU'RE WEAK IN BODY...
WAIT...
...AND SPIRIT.
BDMP
YOU'RE ALWAYS SEEKING APPROVAL...
BDMP
..LIKE A PUPPET.
BDMP

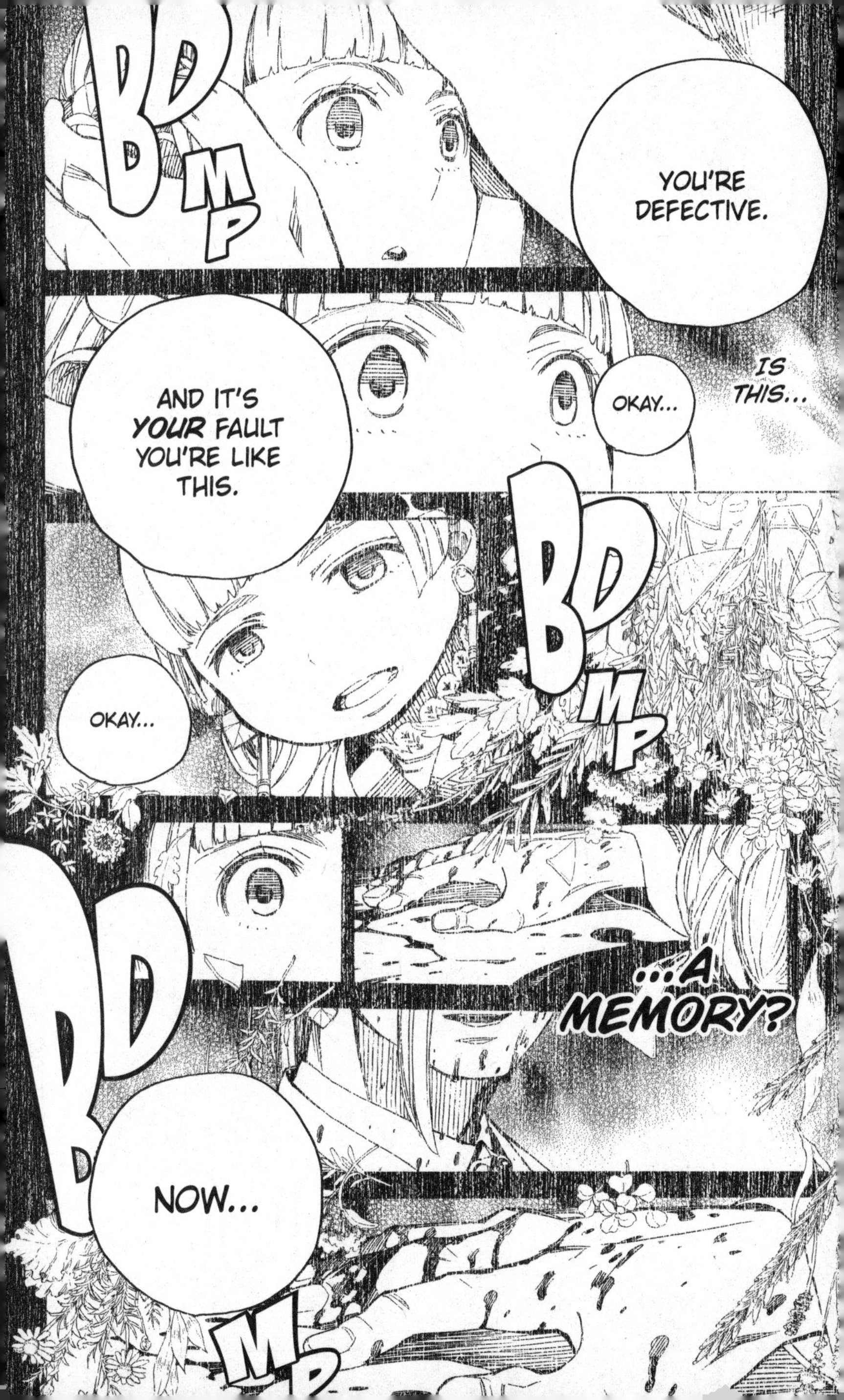
YOU'RE DEFECTIVE.
BDMP
IS THIS...
OKAY...
AND IT'S *YOUR* FAULT YOU'RE LIKE THIS.
BDMP
OKAY...
...A MEMORY?
BD
NOW...
MP

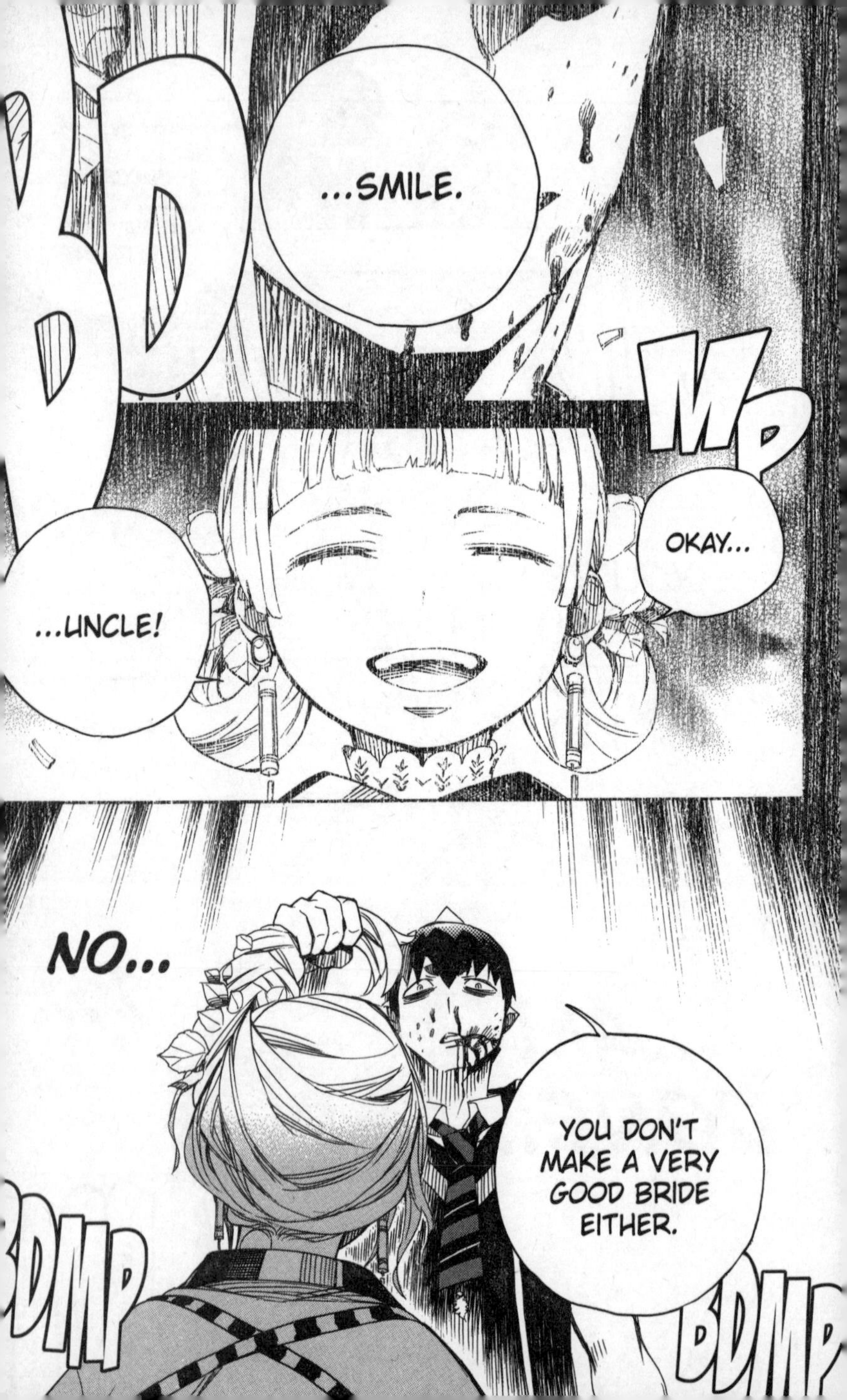
...SMILE.
MP
OKAY...
...UNCLE!
NO...
YOU DON'T MAKE A VERY GOOD BRIDE EITHER.
BDMP
BDMP

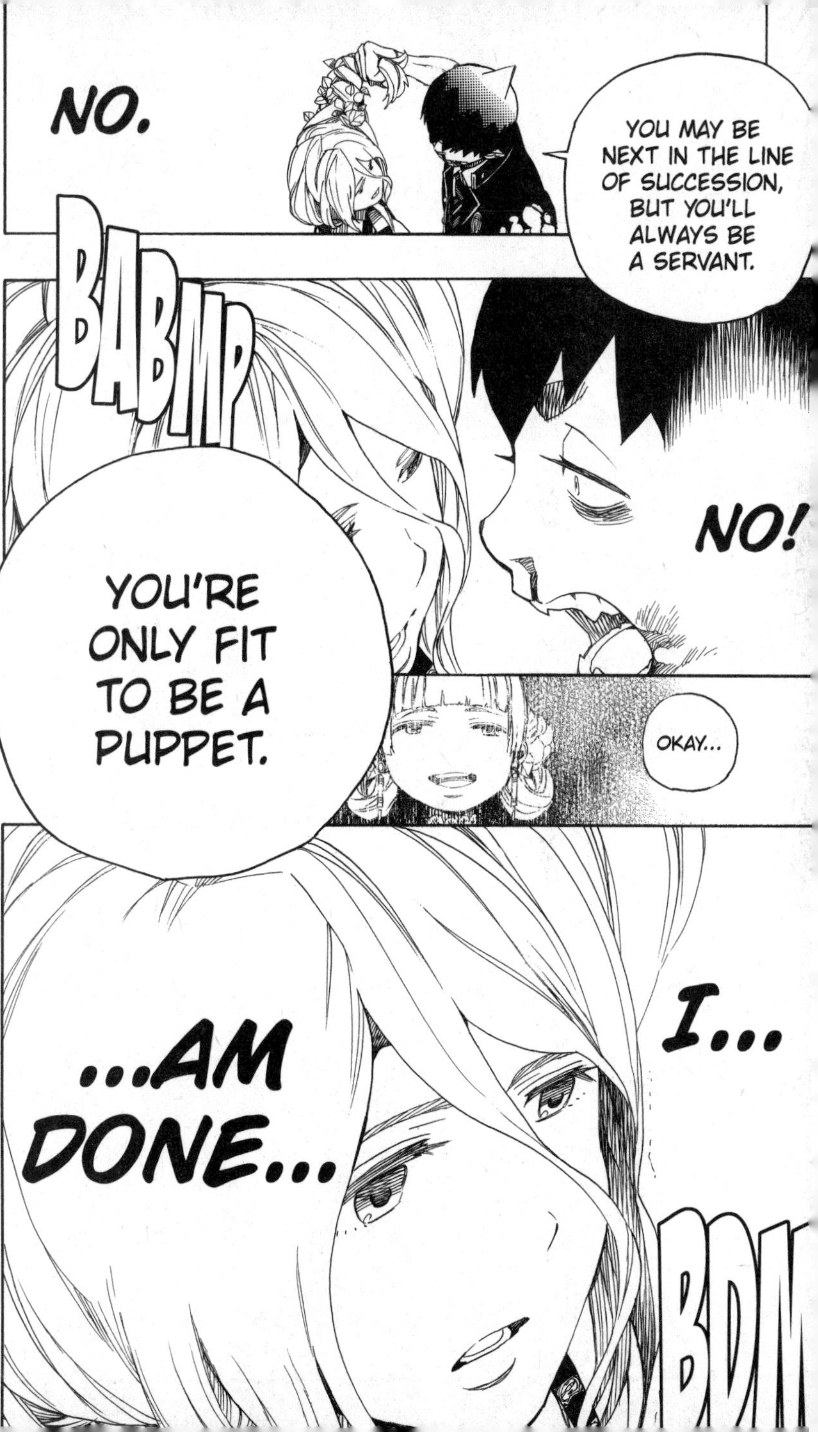
YOU MAY BE NEXT IN THE LINE OF SUCCESSION, BUT YOU'LL ALWAYS BE A SERVANT.
NO.
BABMP
NO!
YOU'RE ONLY FIT TO BE A PUPPET.
OKAY...
I...
...AM DONE...
BDM

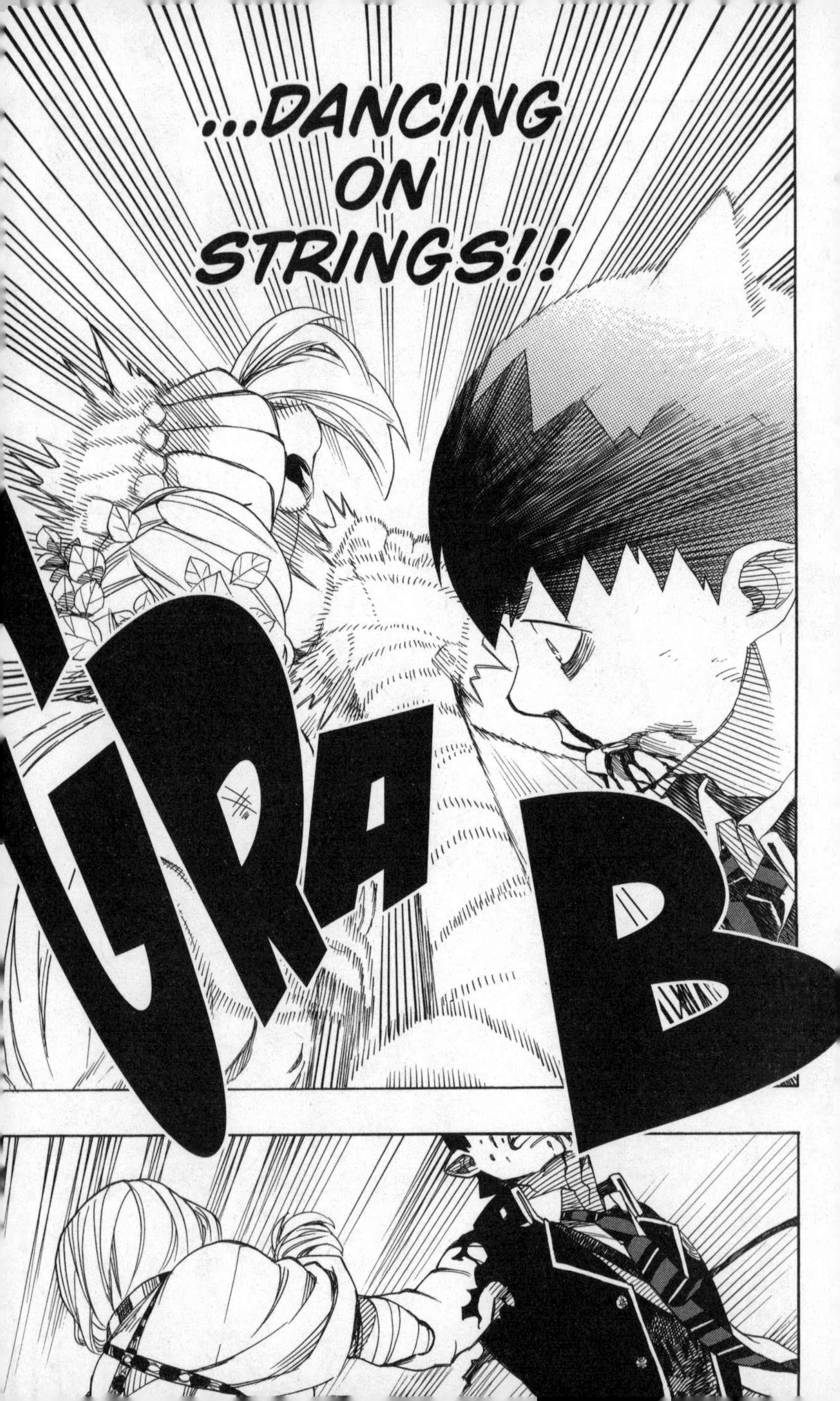
...DANCING ON STRINGS!!
GRAB

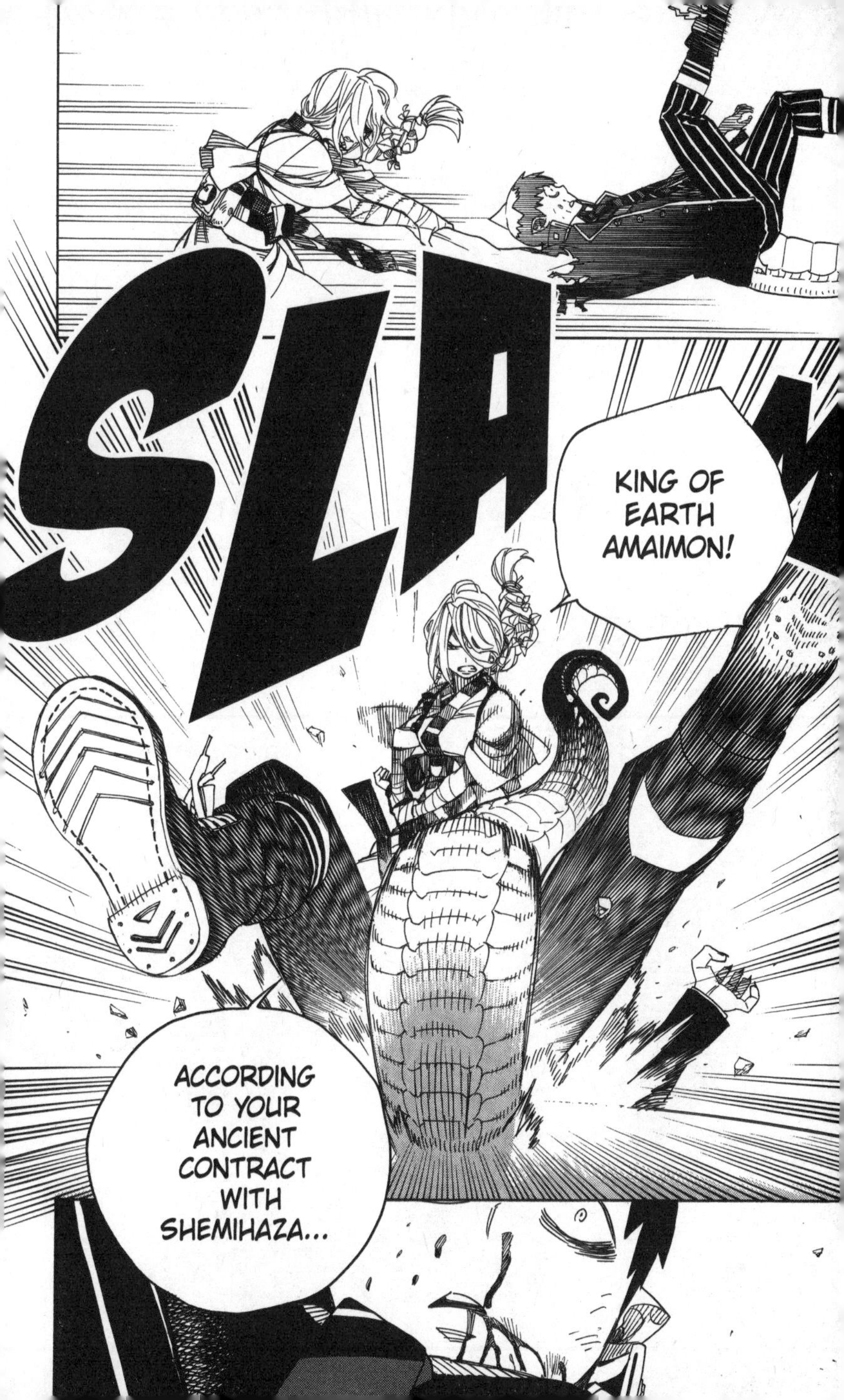
SLAM
KING OF EARTH AMAIMON!
ACCORDING TO YOUR ANCIENT CONTRACT WITH SHEMIHAZA...

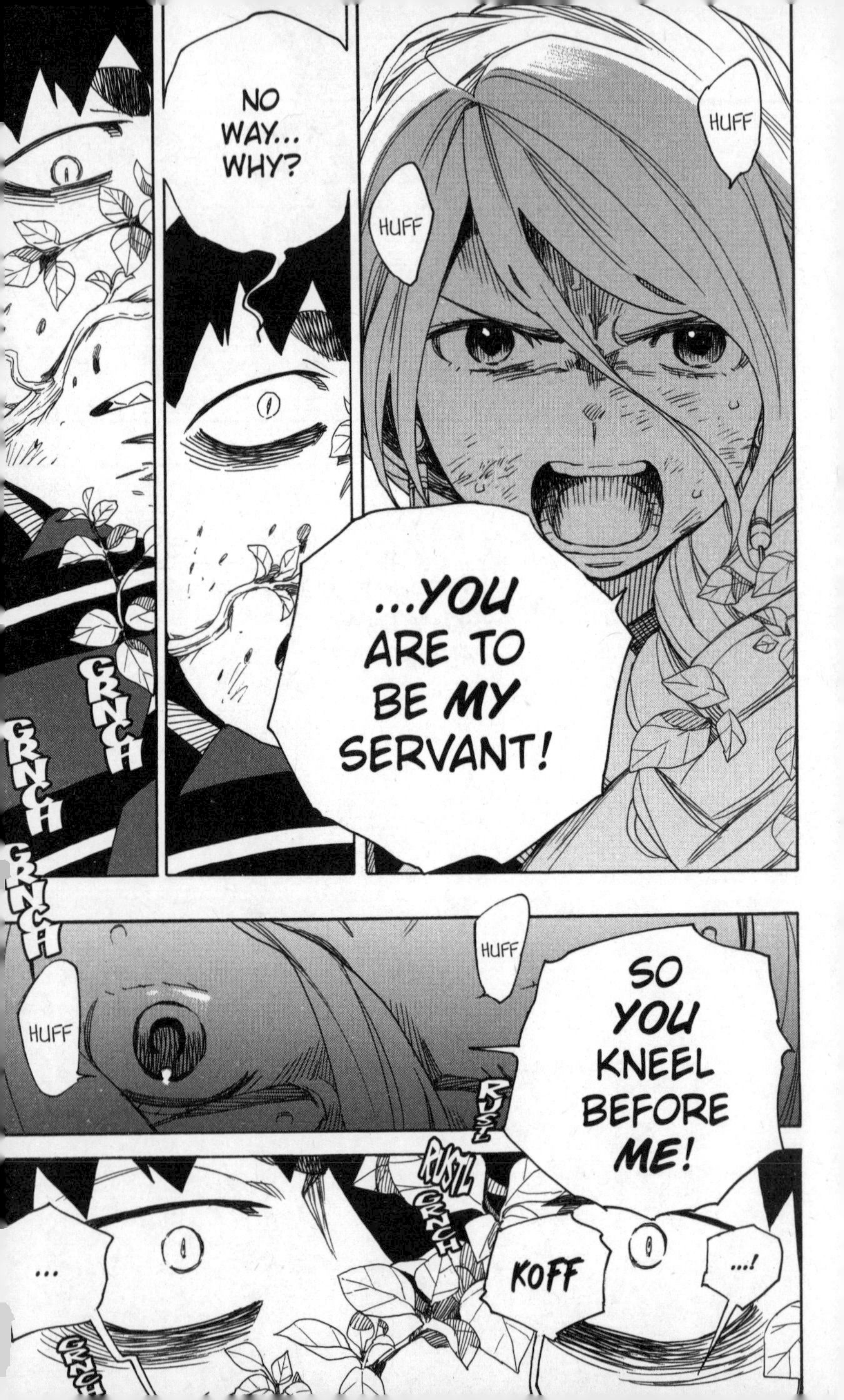
HUFF
HUFF
...YOU ARE TO BE MY SERVANT!
NO WAY... WHY?
GRNCH
GRNCH
GRNCH
GRNCH
HUFF
SO YOU KNEEL BEFORE ME!
RUSL
HUFF
RUSTL
GRNCH
...!
KOFF
...
GRNCH

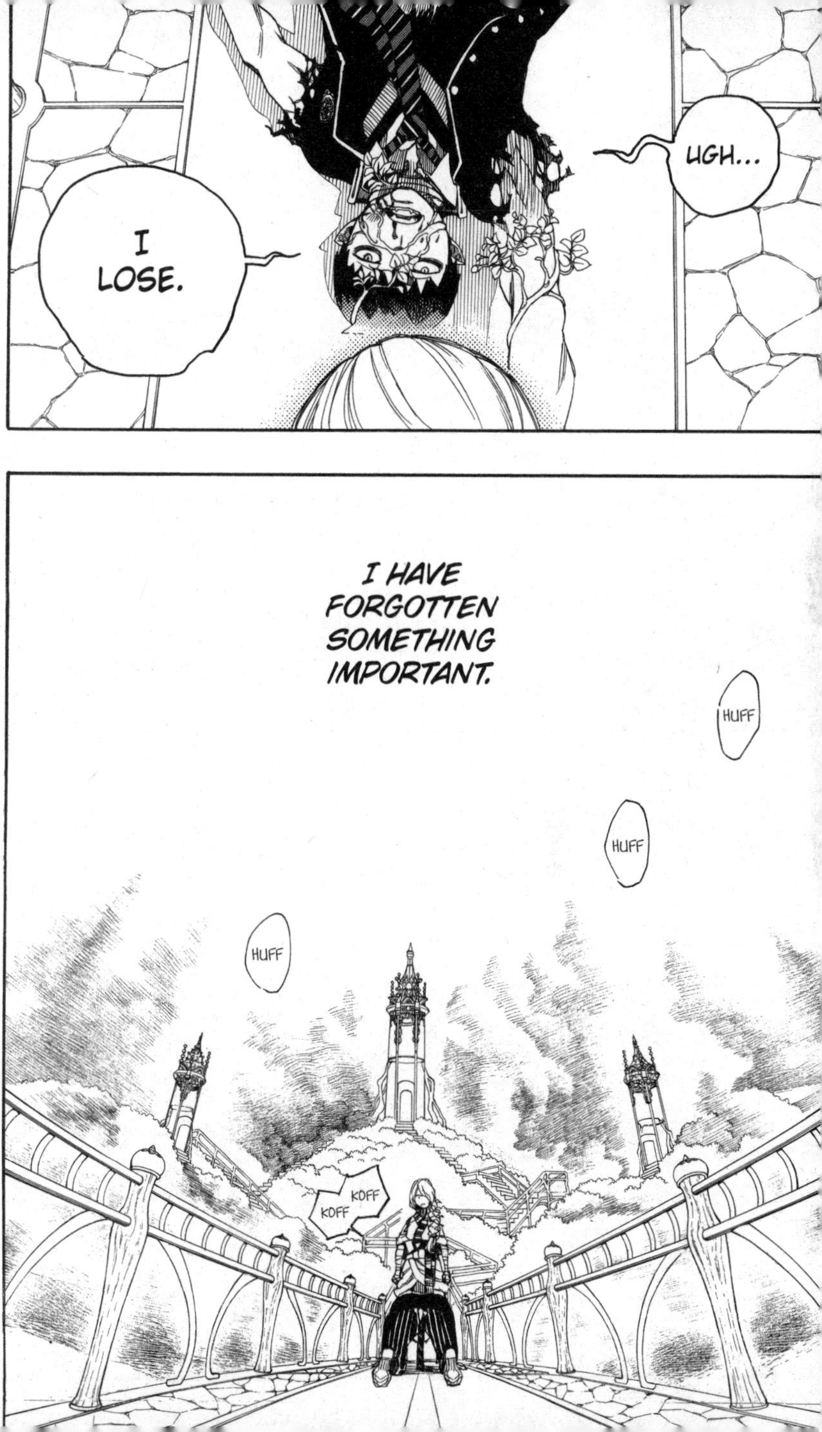
UGH...
I LOSE.
I HAVE FORGOTTEN SOMETHING IMPORTANT.
HUFF
HUFF
HUFF
KOFF
KOFF

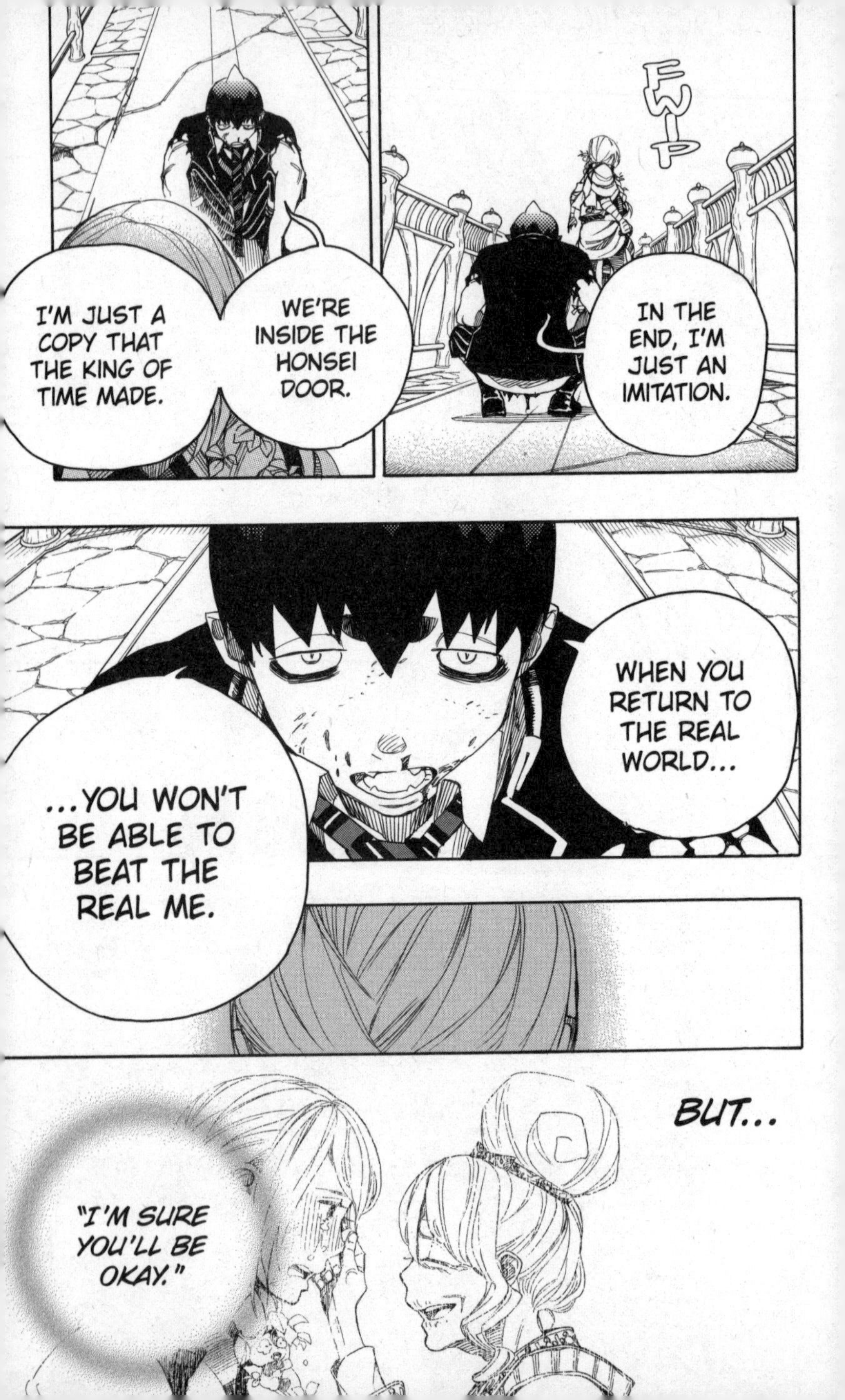
FWIP
IN THE END, I'M JUST AN IMITATION.
WE'RE INSIDE THE HONSEI DOOR.
I'M JUST A COPY THAT THE KING OF TIME MADE.
WHEN YOU RETURN TO THE REAL WORLD...
...YOU WON'T BE ABLE TO BEAT THE REAL ME.
BUT...
"I'M SURE YOU'LL BE OKAY."

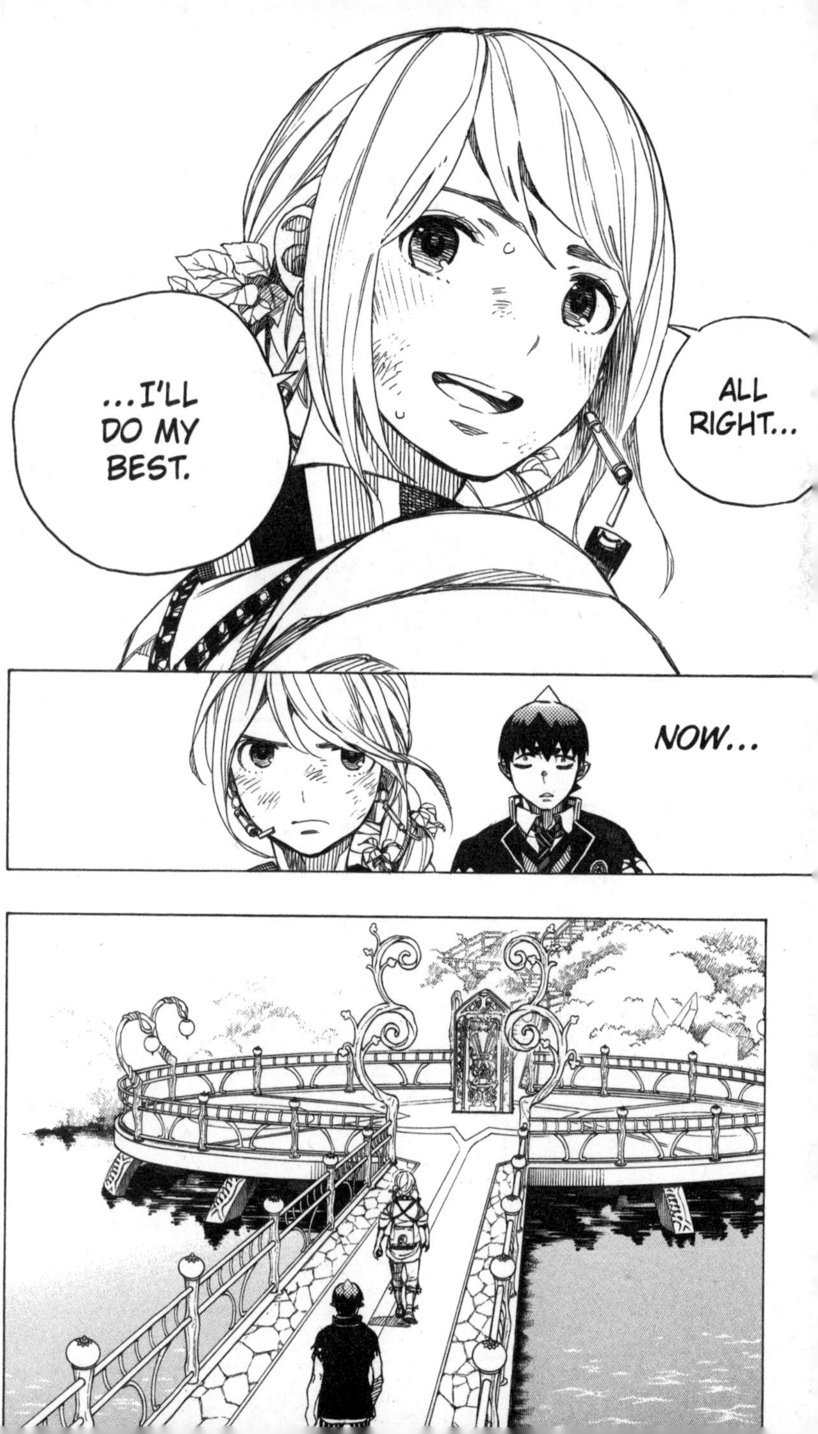
ALL RIGHT...
...I'LL DO MY BEST.
NOW...

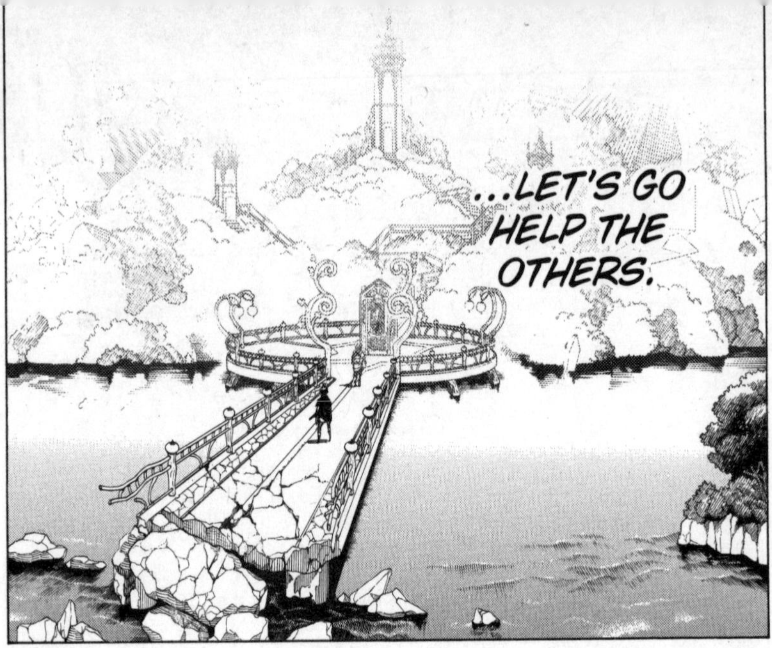
...LET'S GO HELP THE OTHERS.

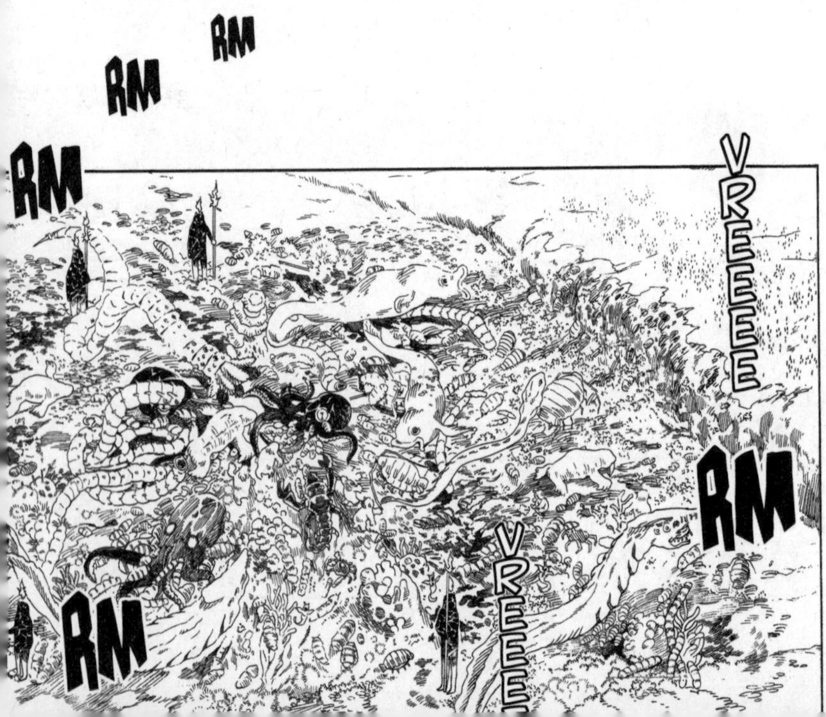
RM
RM
VREEEE
RM
RM
VREEE
RM

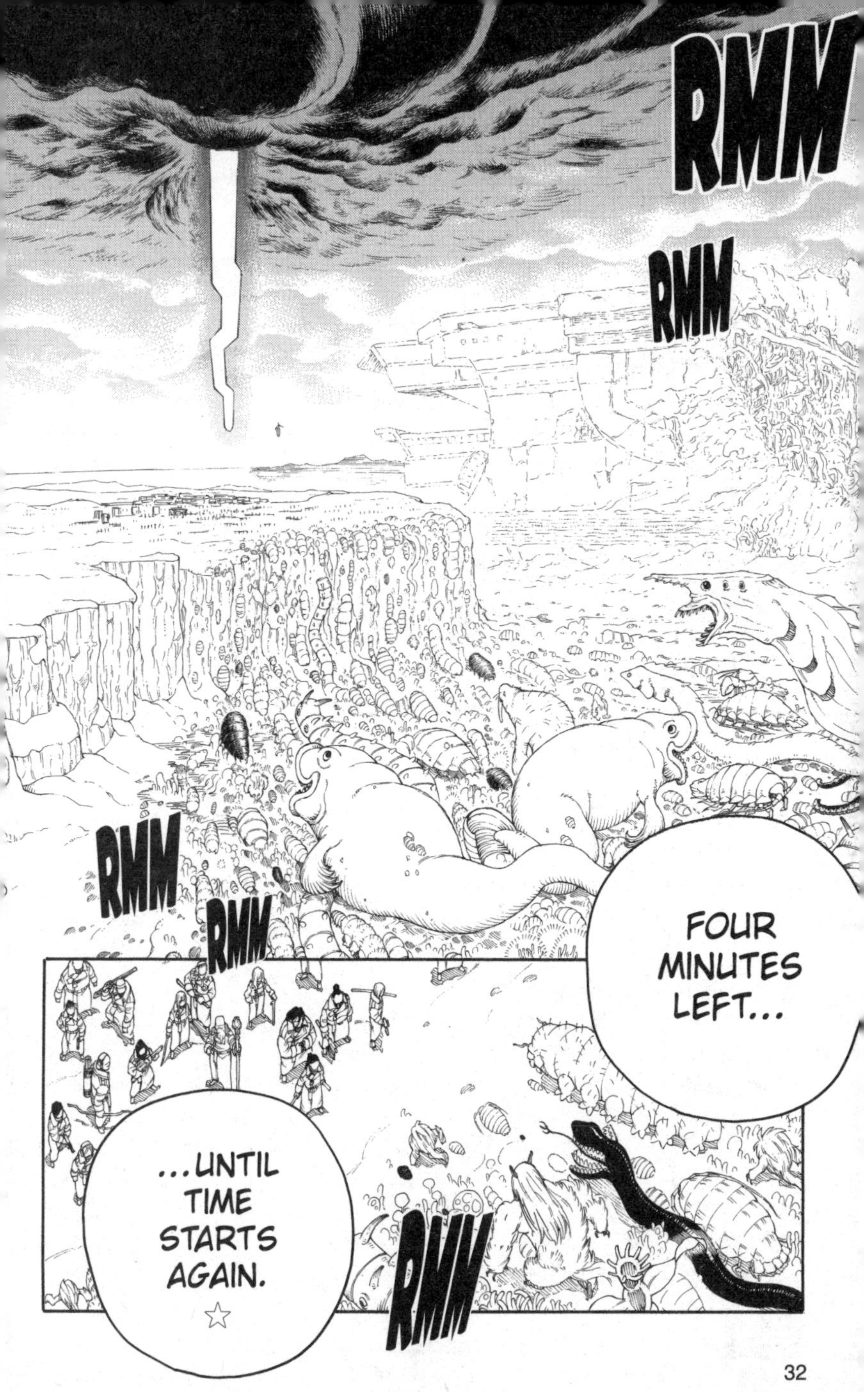
RMM
RMM
RMM
RMM
FOUR MINUTES LEFT...
...UNTIL TIME STARTS AGAIN. ☆
RMM

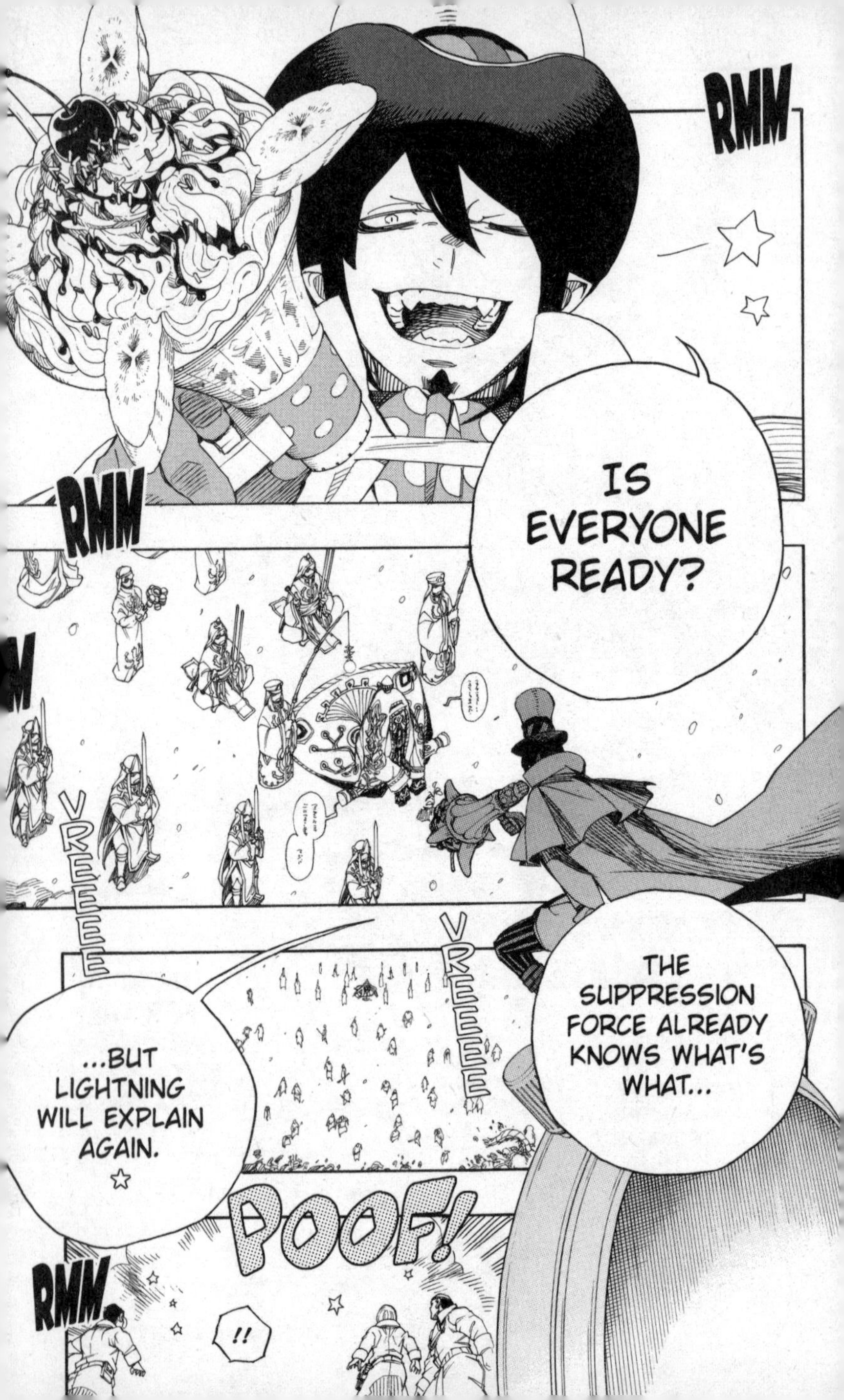
RMM
IS EVERYONE READY?
RMM
VREEEE
VREEEE
THE SUPPRESSION FORCE ALREADY KNOWS WHAT'S WHAT...
...BUT LIGHTNING WILL EXPLAIN AGAIN. ☆
POOF!
RMM
!!

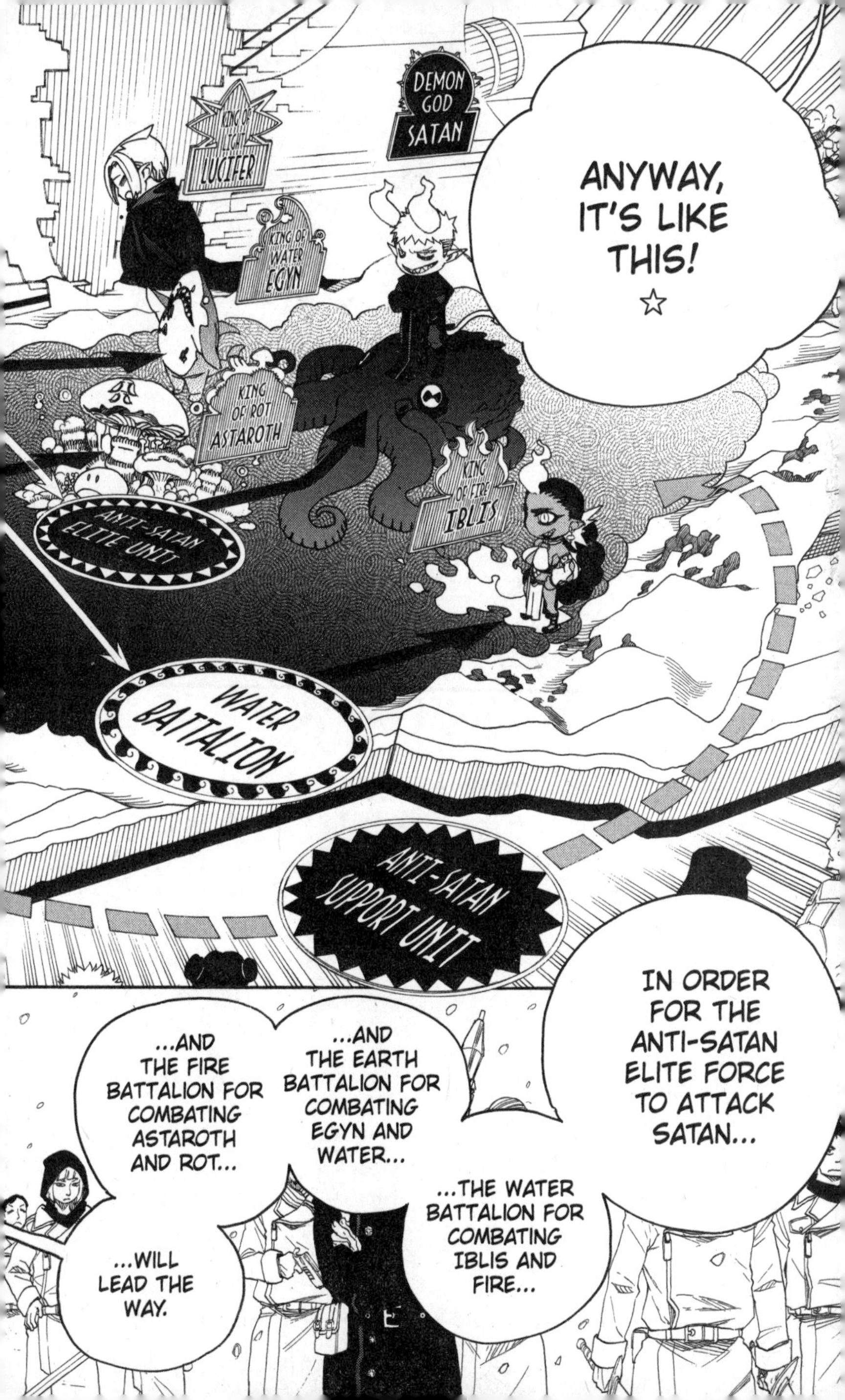
ANYWAY, IT'S LIKE THIS! ☆
DEMON GOD SATAN
KING OF LIGHT LUCIFER
KING OF WATER EGYN
KING OF ROT ASTAROTH
KING OF FIRE IBLIS
ANTI-SATAN ELITE UNIT
WATER BATTALION
ANTI-SATAN SUPPORT UNIT
IN ORDER FOR THE ANTI-SATAN ELITE FORCE TO ATTACK SATAN...
...THE WATER BATTALION FOR COMBATING IBLIS AND FIRE...
...AND THE EARTH BATTALION FOR COMBATING EGYN AND WATER...
...AND THE FIRE BATTALION FOR COMBATING ASTAROTH AND ROT...
...WILL LEAD THE WAY.

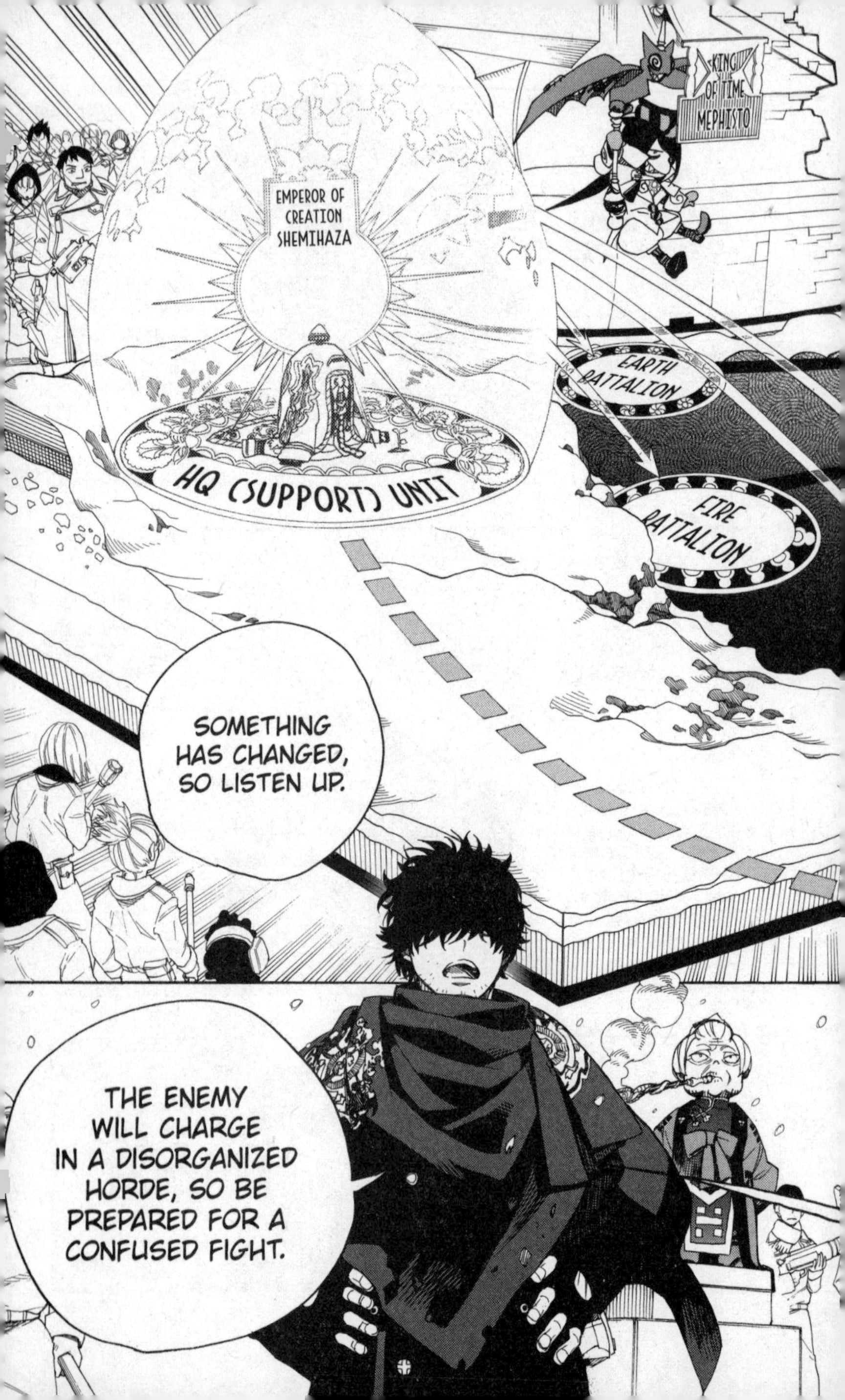
KING OF TIME MEPHISTO
EMPEROR OF CREATION SHEMIHAZA
EARTH BATTALION
FIRE BATTALION
HQ (SUPPORT) UNIT
SOMETHING HAS CHANGED, SO LISTEN UP.
THE ENEMY WILL CHARGE IN A DISORGANIZED HORDE, SO BE PREPARED FOR A CONFUSED FIGHT.

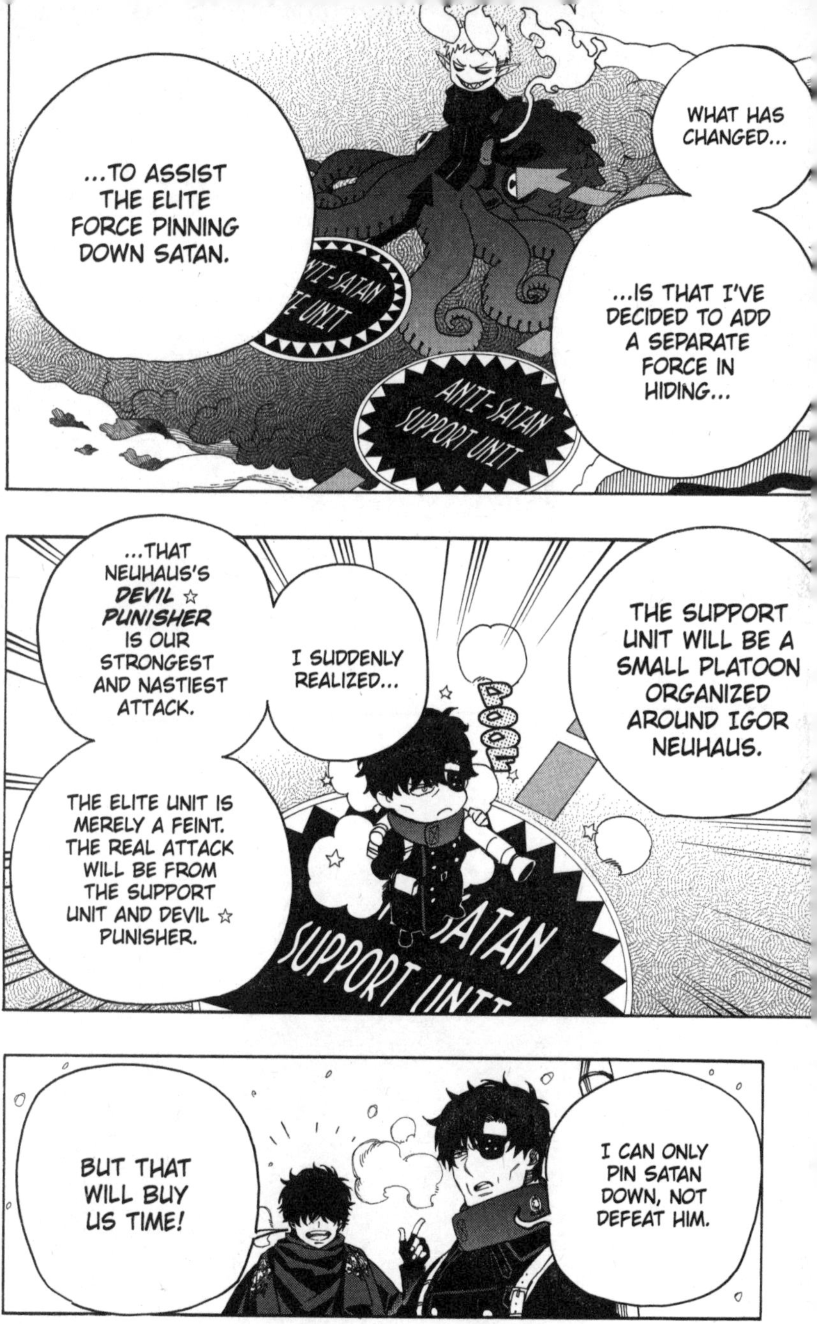
WHAT HAS CHANGED...
...IS THAT I'VE DECIDED TO ADD A SEPARATE FORCE IN HIDING...
ANTI-SATAN SUPPORT UNIT
...TO ASSIST THE ELITE FORCE PINNING DOWN SATAN.
THE SUPPORT UNIT WILL BE A SMALL PLATOON ORGANIZED AROUND IGOR NEUHAUS.
I SUDDENLY REALIZED...
...THAT NEUHAUS'S ***DEVIL ☆ PUNISHER*** IS OUR STRONGEST AND NASTIEST ATTACK.
THE ELITE UNIT IS MERELY A FEINT. THE REAL ATTACK WILL BE FROM THE SUPPORT UNIT AND DEVIL ☆ PUNISHER.
I CAN ONLY PIN SATAN DOWN, NOT DEFEAT HIM.
BUT THAT WILL BUY US TIME!

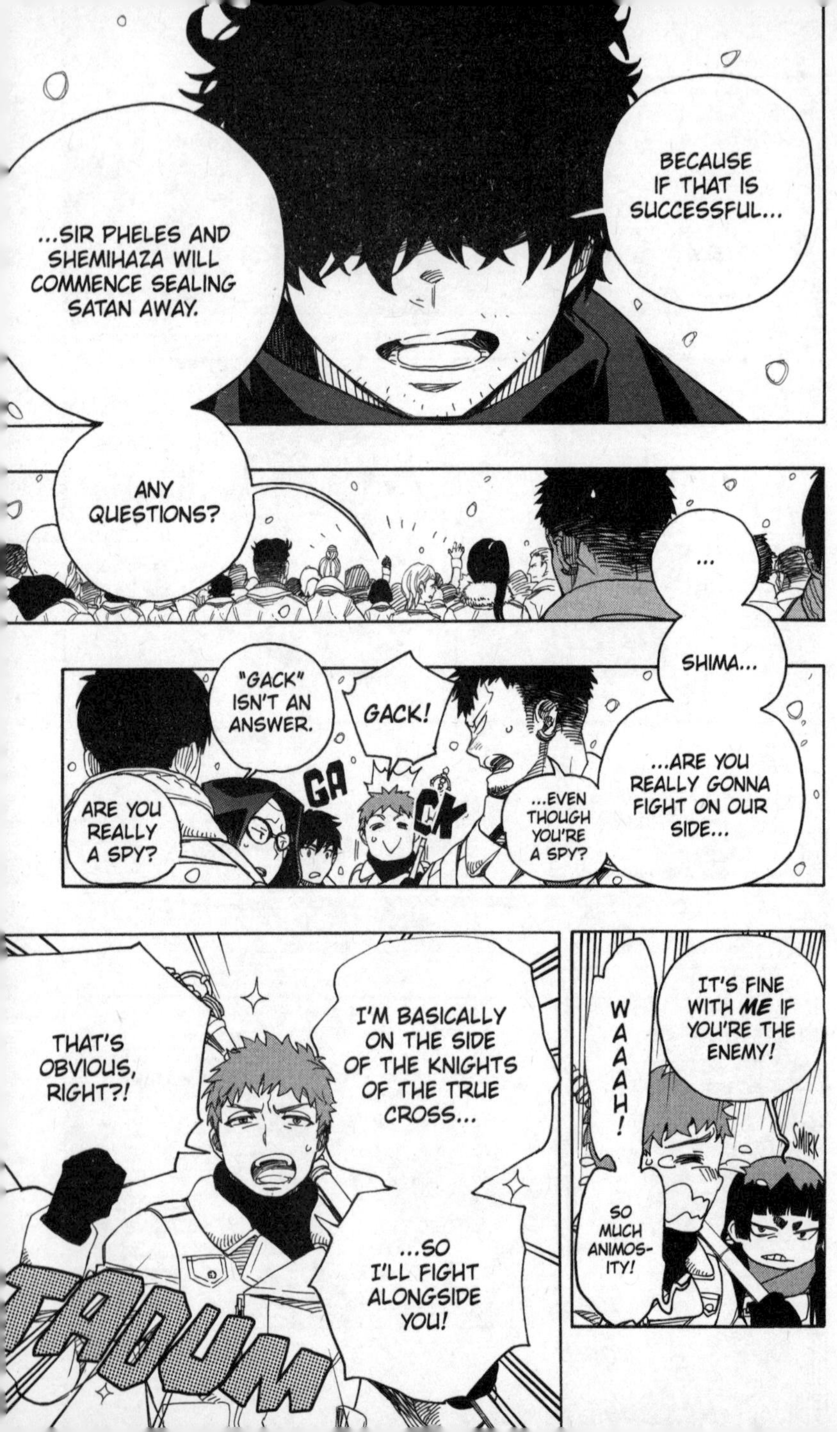
BECAUSE IF THAT IS SUCCESSFUL...
...SIR PHELES AND SHEMIHAZA WILL COMMENCE SEALING SATAN AWAY.
ANY QUESTIONS?
...
SHIMA...
...ARE YOU REALLY GONNA FIGHT ON OUR SIDE...
...EVEN THOUGH YOU'RE A SPY?
GACK!
GACK
"GACK" ISN'T AN ANSWER.
ARE YOU REALLY A SPY?
IT'S FINE WITH ME IF YOU'RE THE ENEMY!
SMIRK
WAAAAH!
SO MUCH ANIMOSITY!
I'M BASICALLY ON THE SIDE OF THE KNIGHTS OF THE TRUE CROSS...
THAT'S OBVIOUS, RIGHT?!
...SO I'LL FIGHT ALONGSIDE YOU!
TADUM

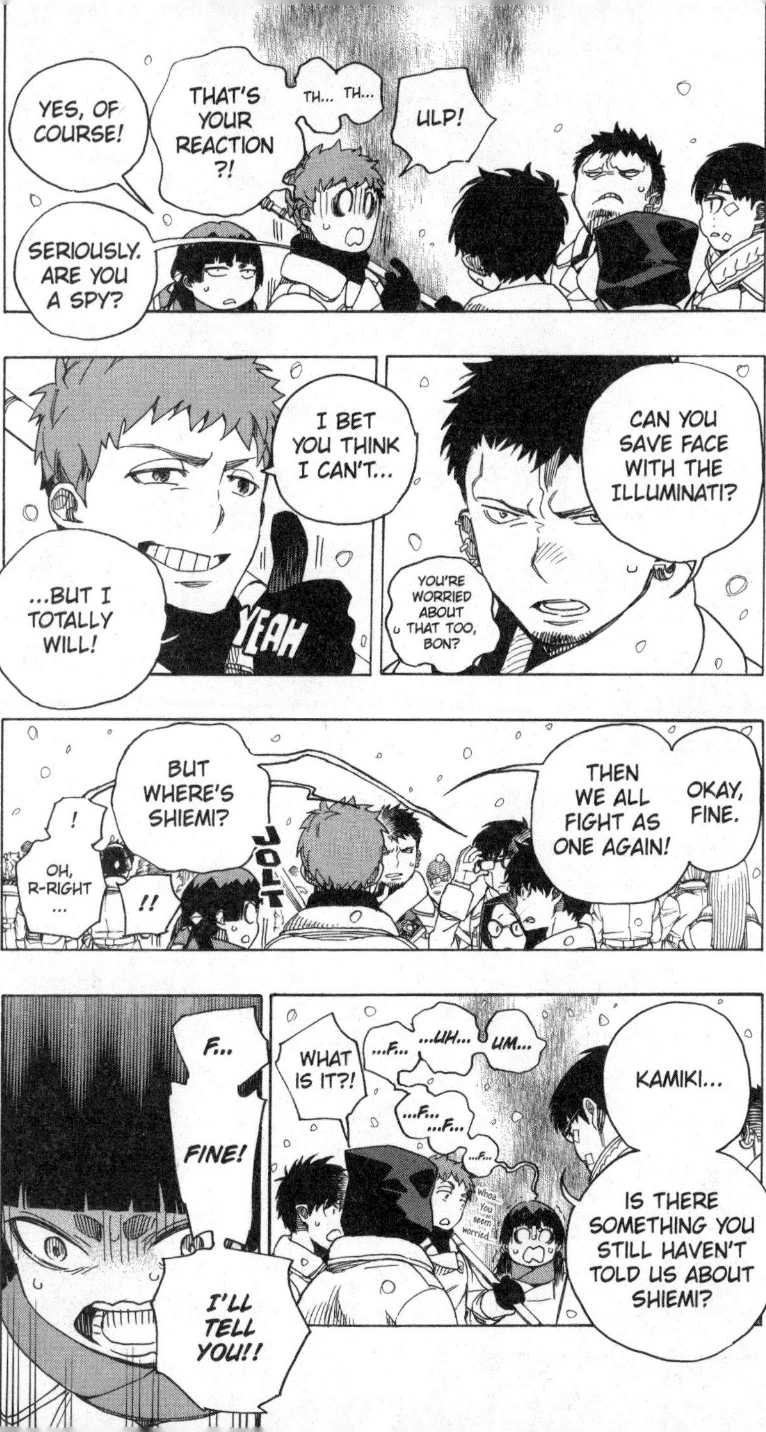
ULP!
TH... TH...
THAT'S YOUR REACTION ?!
YES, OF COURSE!
SERIOUSLY. ARE YOU A SPY?
CAN YOU SAVE FACE WITH THE ILLUMINATI?
YOU'RE WORRIED ABOUT THAT TOO, BON?
I BET YOU THINK I CAN'T...
YEAH
...BUT I TOTALLY WILL!
OKAY, FINE.
THEN WE ALL FIGHT AS ONE AGAIN!
JOLT
BUT WHERE'S SHIEMI?
!!
!
OH, R-RIGHT ...
KAMIKI...
UM...
...UH...
...F...
WHAT IS IT?!
...F... ...F...
...F...
Whoa... You seem worried...
IS THERE SOMETHING YOU STILL HAVEN'T TOLD US ABOUT SHIEMI?
F...
FINE!
I'LL TELL YOU!!

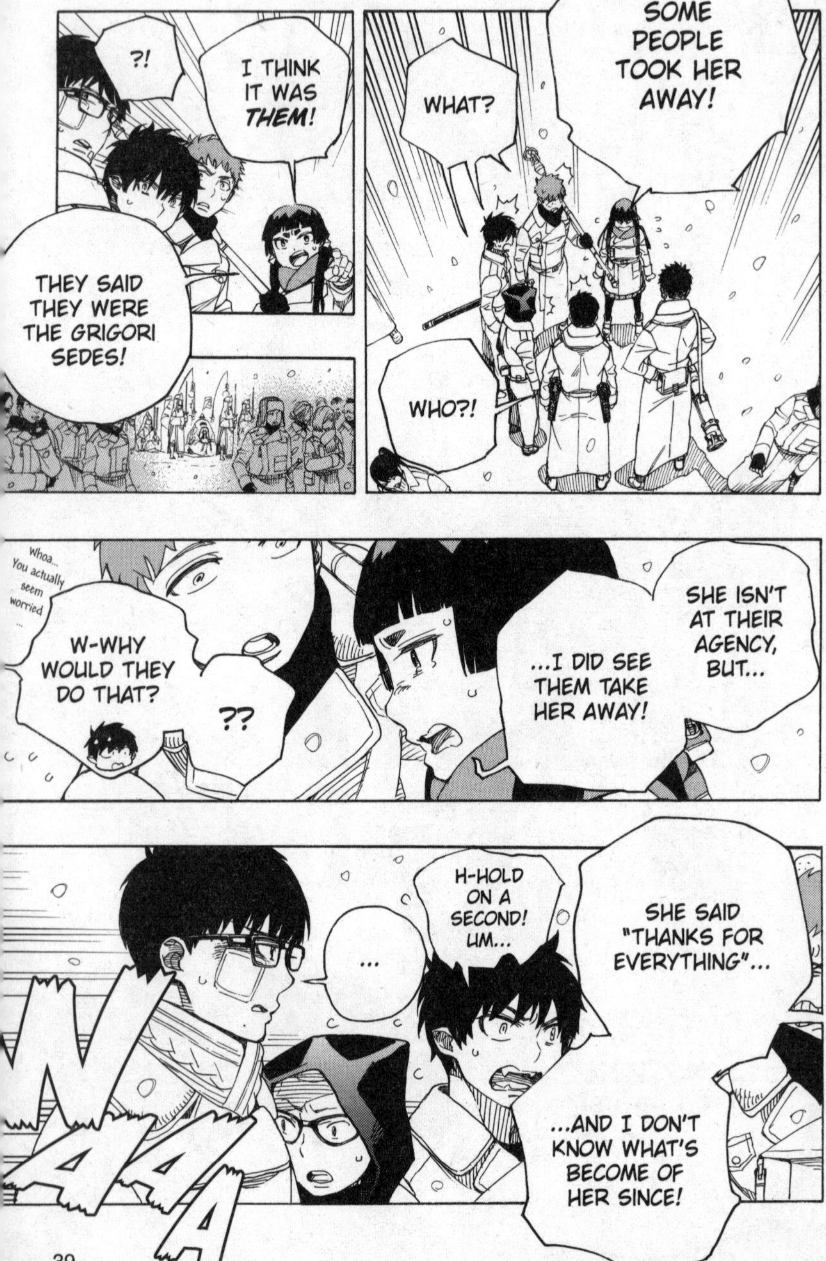
SOME PEOPLE TOOK HER AWAY!
WHAT?
WHO?!
I THINK IT WAS THEM!
?!
THEY SAID THEY WERE THE GRIGORI SEDES!
SHE ISN'T AT THEIR AGENCY, BUT...
...I DID SEE THEM TAKE HER AWAY!
??
W-WHY WOULD THEY DO THAT?
Whoa... You actually seem worried...
SHE SAID "THANKS FOR EVERYTHING"...
...AND I DON'T KNOW WHAT'S BECOME OF HER SINCE!
H-HOLD ON A SECOND! UM...
...
WAAA

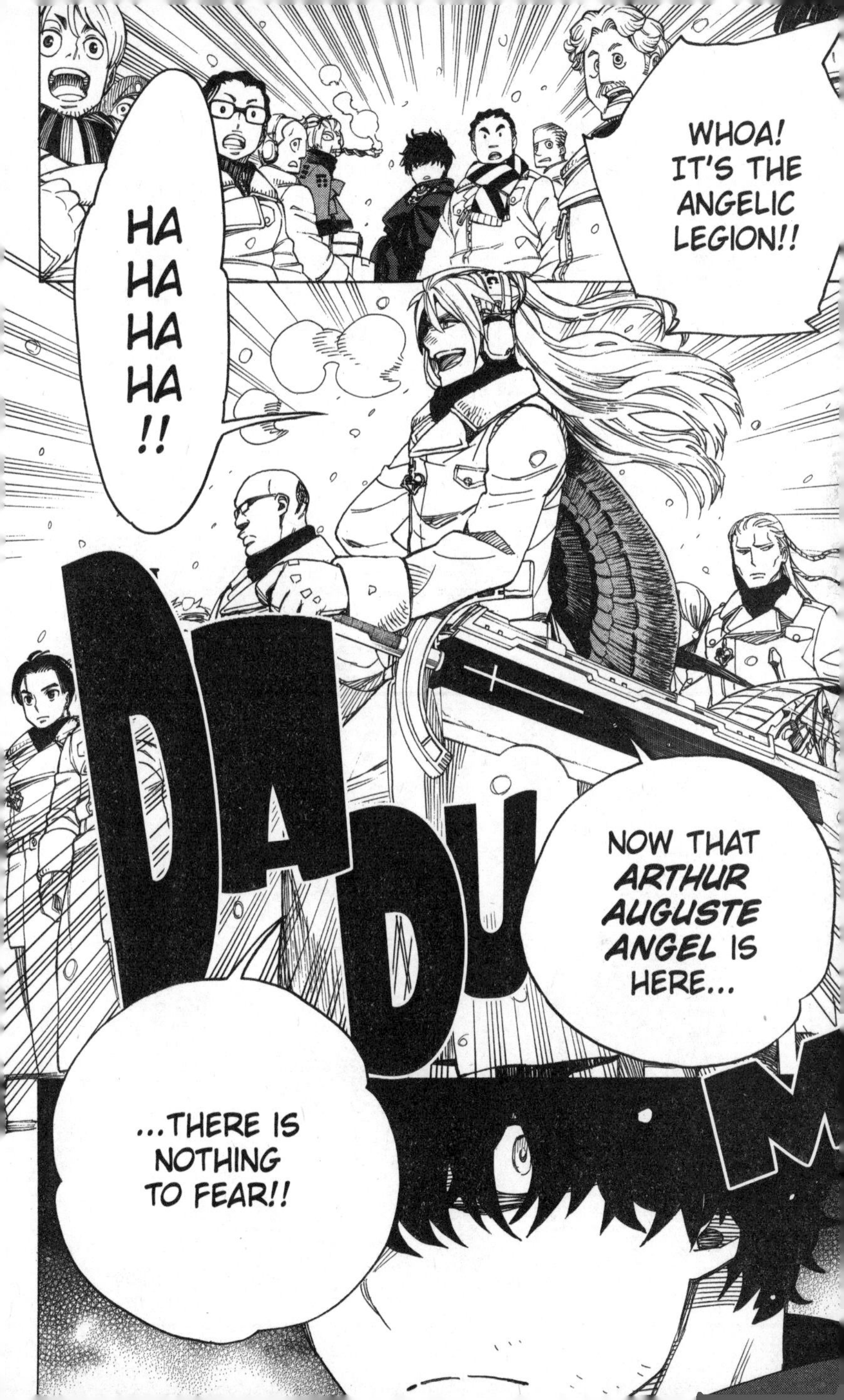
WHOA! IT'S THE ANGELIC LEGION!!
HA HA HA HA!!
DADUM
NOW THAT ARTHUR AUGUSTE ANGEL IS HERE...
...THERE IS NOTHING TO FEAR!!

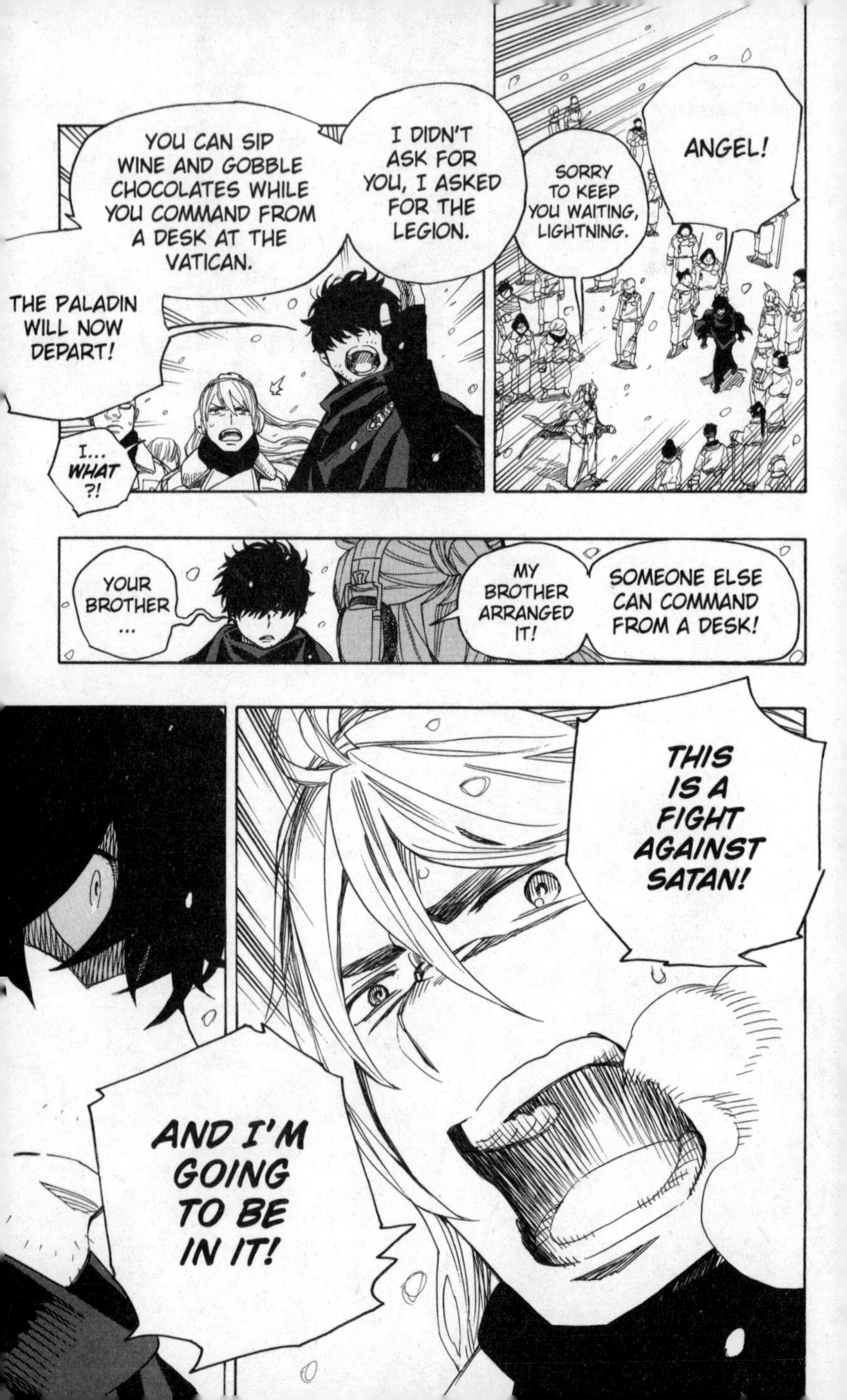
ANGEL!
SORRY TO KEEP YOU WAITING, LIGHTNING.
I DIDN'T ASK FOR YOU, I ASKED FOR THE LEGION.
YOU CAN SIP WINE AND GOBBLE CHOCOLATES WHILE YOU COMMAND FROM A DESK AT THE VATICAN.
THE PALADIN WILL NOW DEPART!
I... WHAT?!
SOMEONE ELSE CAN COMMAND FROM A DESK!
MY BROTHER ARRANGED IT!
YOUR BROTHER...
THIS IS A FIGHT AGAINST SATAN!
AND I'M GOING TO BE IN IT!

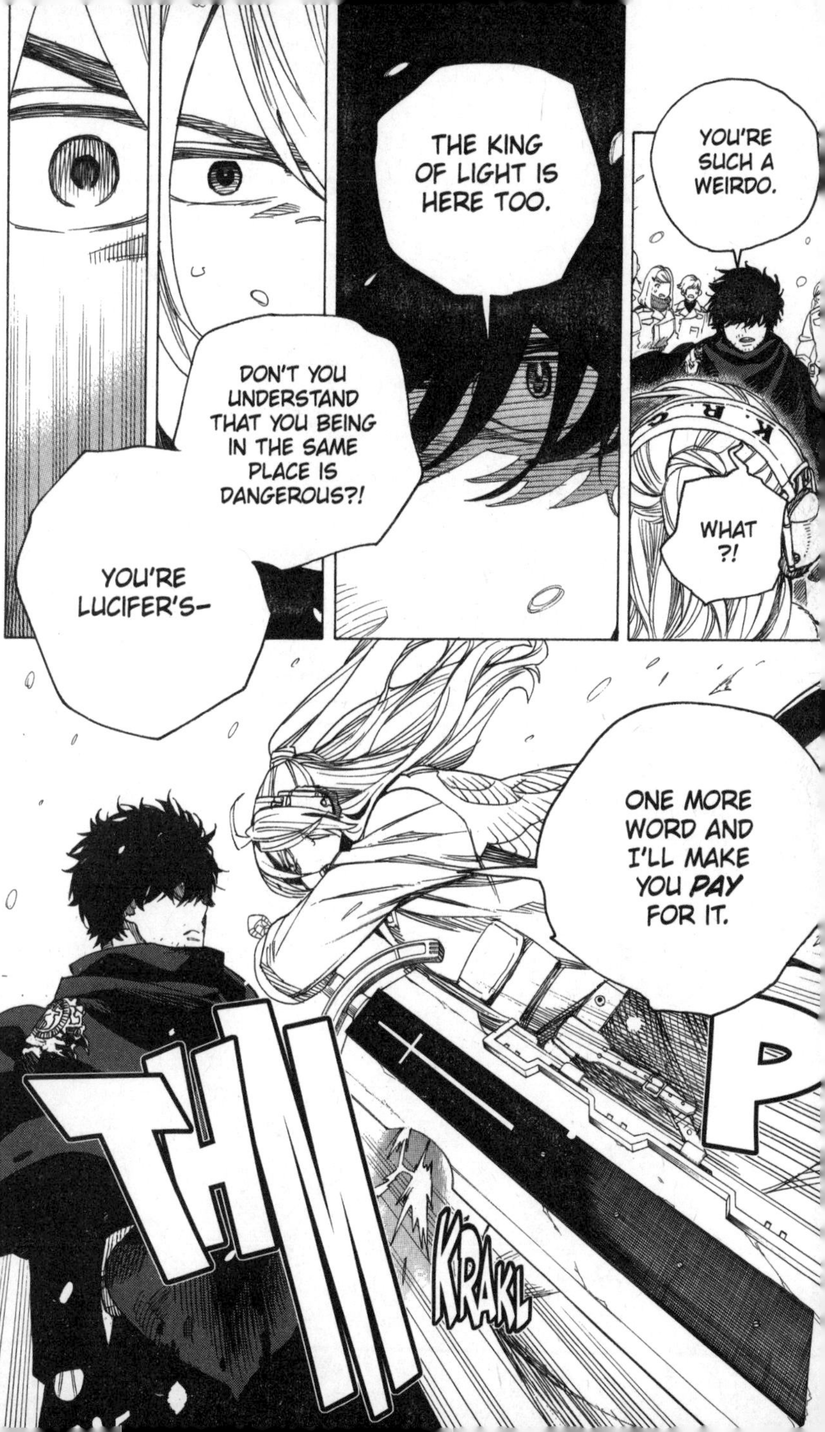
YOU'RE SUCH A WEIRDO.
WHAT?!
THE KING OF LIGHT IS HERE TOO.
DON'T YOU UNDERSTAND THAT YOU BEING IN THE SAME PLACE IS DANGEROUS?!
YOU'RE LUCIFER'S—
ONE MORE WORD AND I'LL MAKE YOU *PAY* FOR IT.
KRAKL

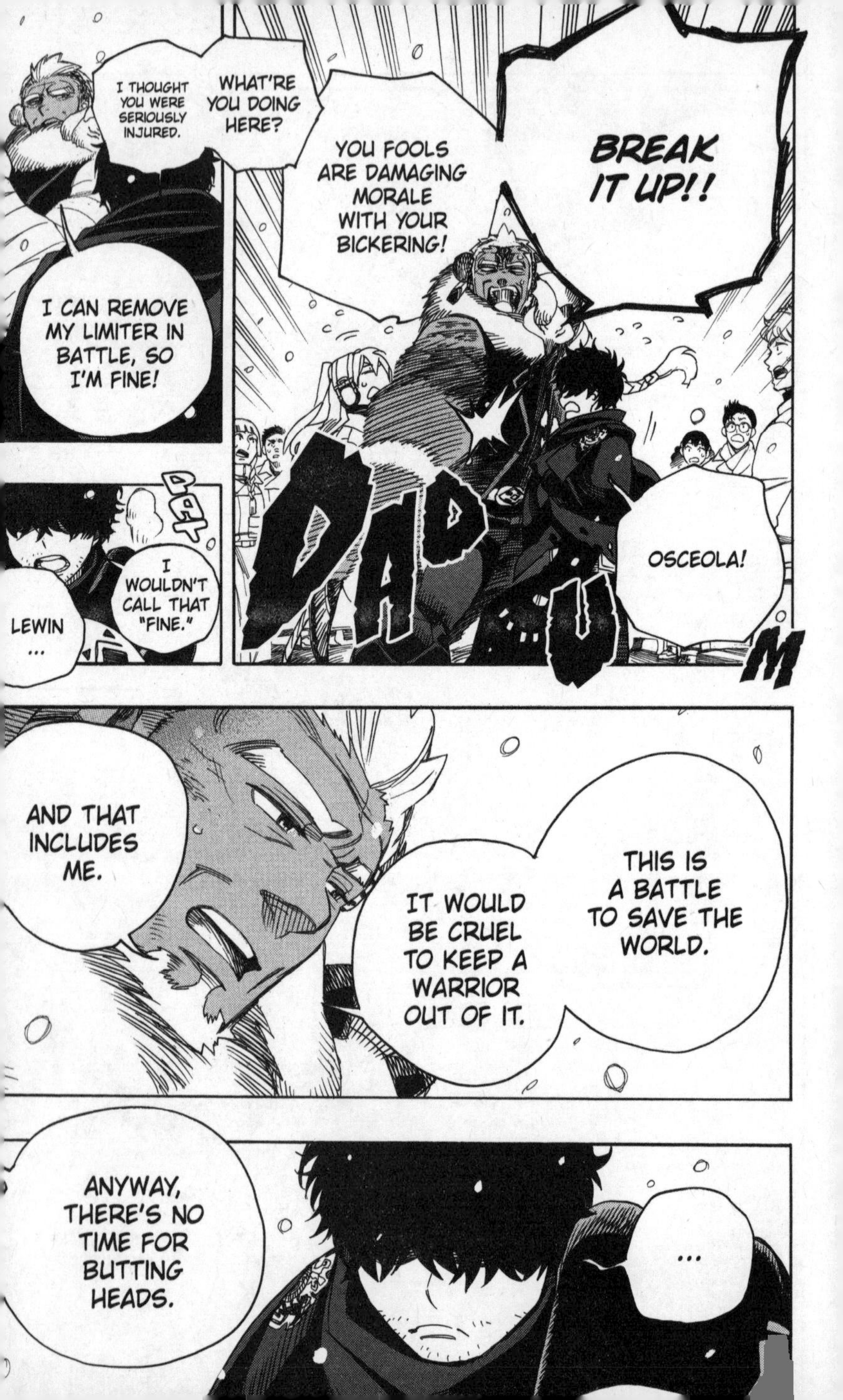
BREAK IT UP!!
YOU FOOLS ARE DAMAGING MORALE WITH YOUR BICKERING!
WHAT'RE YOU DOING HERE?
OSCEOLA!
DADUM
I THOUGHT YOU WERE SERIOUSLY INJURED.
I CAN REMOVE MY LIMITER IN BATTLE, SO I'M FINE!
I WOULDN'T CALL THAT "FINE."
LEWIN ...
THIS IS A BATTLE TO SAVE THE WORLD.
IT WOULD BE CRUEL TO KEEP A WARRIOR OUT OF IT.
AND THAT INCLUDES ME.
...
ANYWAY, THERE'S NO TIME FOR BUTTING HEADS.

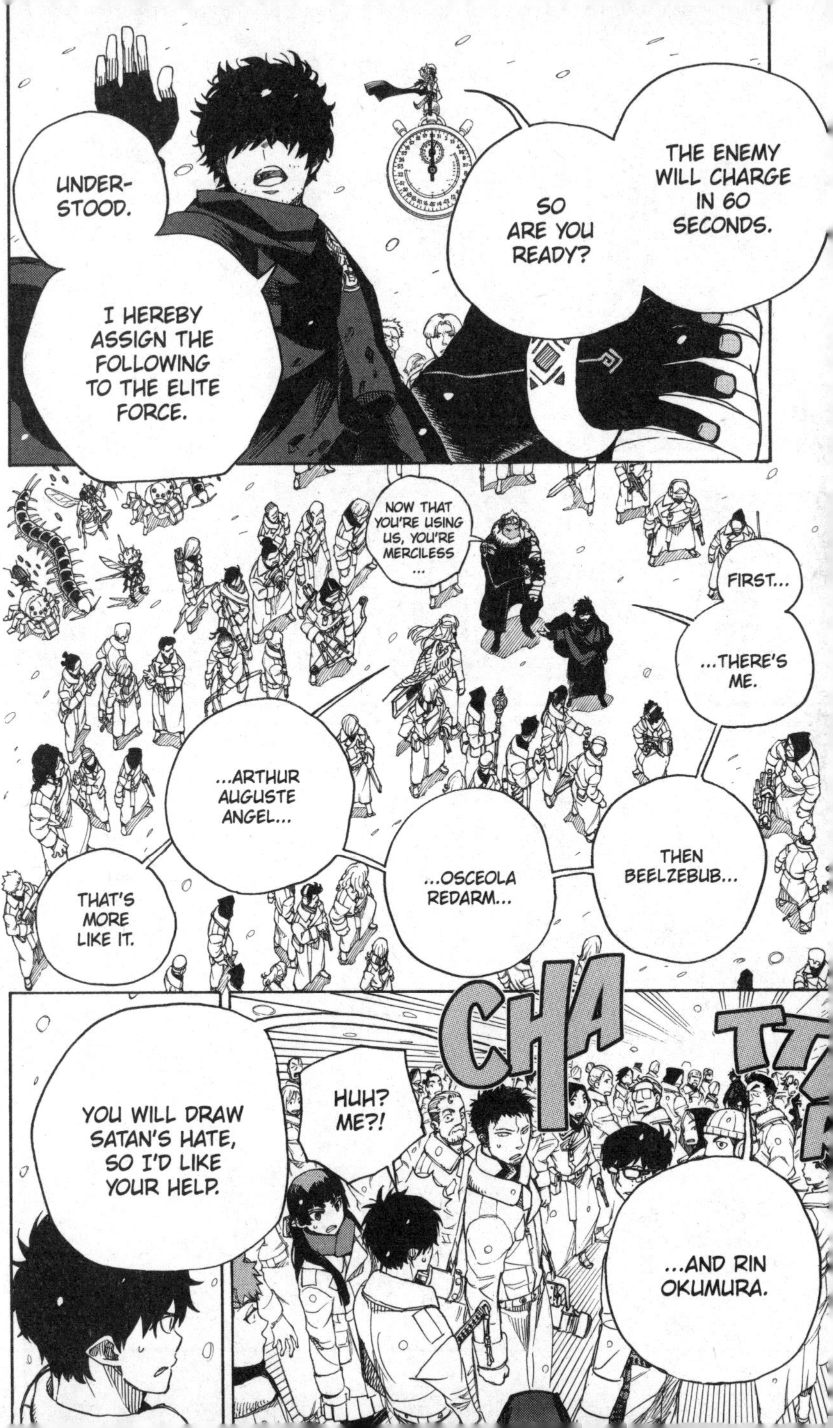
THE ENEMY WILL CHARGE IN 60 SECONDS.
SO ARE YOU READY?
UNDER-STOOD.
I HEREBY ASSIGN THE FOLLOWING TO THE ELITE FORCE.
FIRST...
...THERE'S ME.
NOW THAT YOU'RE USING US, YOU'RE MERCILESS ...
THEN BEELZEBUB...
...OSCEOLA REDARM...
...ARTHUR AUGUSTE ANGEL...
THAT'S MORE LIKE IT.
CHA
...AND RIN OKUMURA.
HUH? ME?!
YOU WILL DRAW SATAN'S HATE, SO I'D LIKE YOUR HELP.

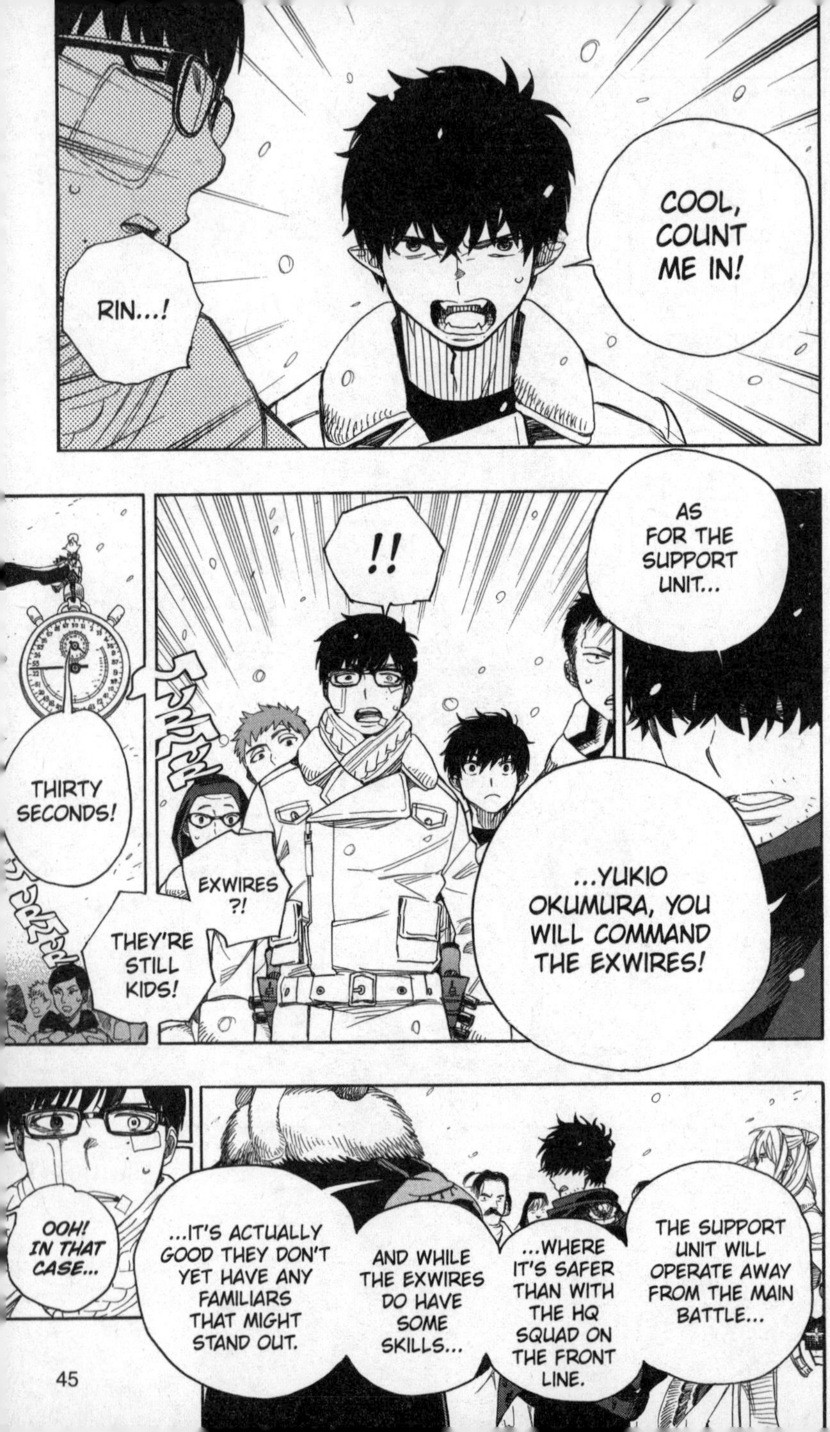
COOL, COUNT ME IN!
RIN...!
AS FOR THE SUPPORT UNIT...
...YUKIO OKUMURA, YOU WILL COMMAND THE EXWIRES!
!!
EXWIRES?!
THEY'RE STILL KIDS!
THIRTY SECONDS!
THE SUPPORT UNIT WILL OPERATE AWAY FROM THE MAIN BATTLE...
...WHERE IT'S SAFER THAN WITH THE HQ SQUAD ON THE FRONT LINE.
AND WHILE THE EXWIRES DO HAVE SOME SKILLS...
...IT'S ACTUALLY GOOD THEY DON'T YET HAVE ANY FAMILIARS THAT MIGHT STAND OUT.
OOH! IN THAT CASE...

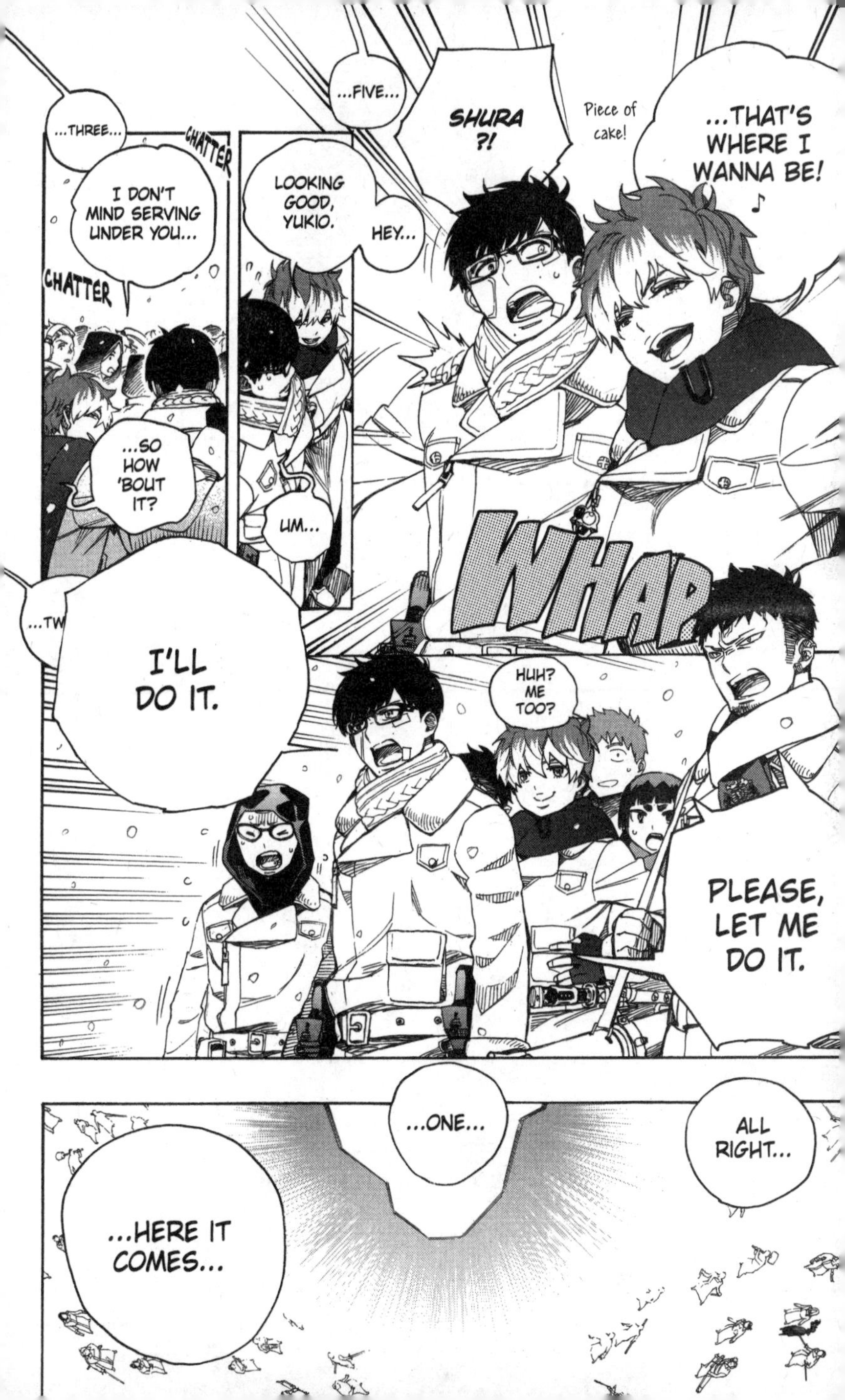
...THAT'S WHERE I WANNA BE! ♪
Piece of cake!
SHURA ?!
WHAP
...FIVE...
HEY...
LOOKING GOOD, YUKIO.
UM...
...THREE...
CHATTER
I DON'T MIND SERVING UNDER YOU...
CHATTER
...SO HOW 'BOUT IT?
PLEASE, LET ME DO IT.
HUH? ME TOO?
I'LL DO IT.
...TW
ALL RIGHT...
...ONE...
...HERE IT COMES...

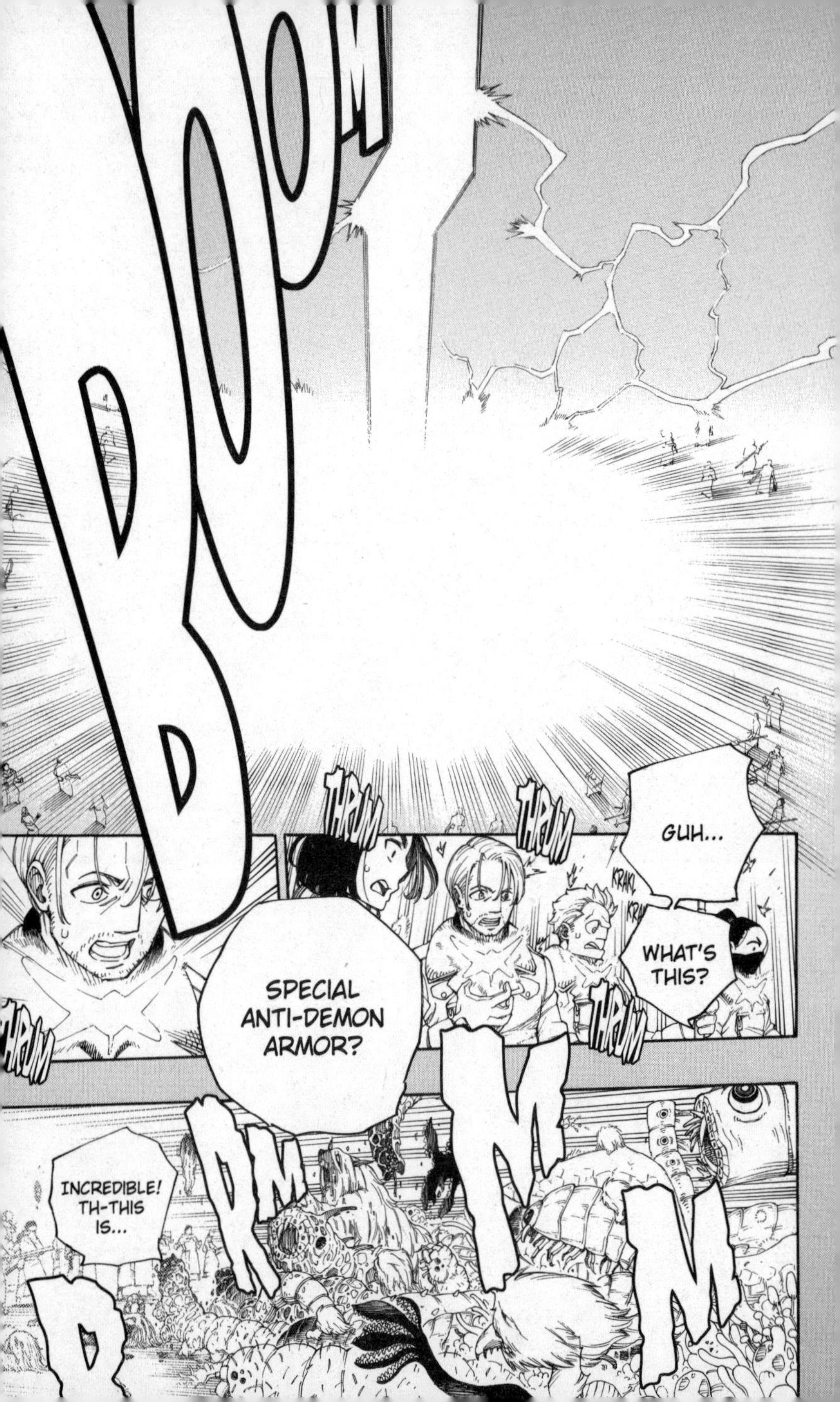
BOOOM
THRUM
THRUM
GUH...
KRAKL
WHAT'S THIS?
THRUM
SPECIAL ANTI-DEMON ARMOR?
THRUM
INCREDIBLE! TH-THIS IS...

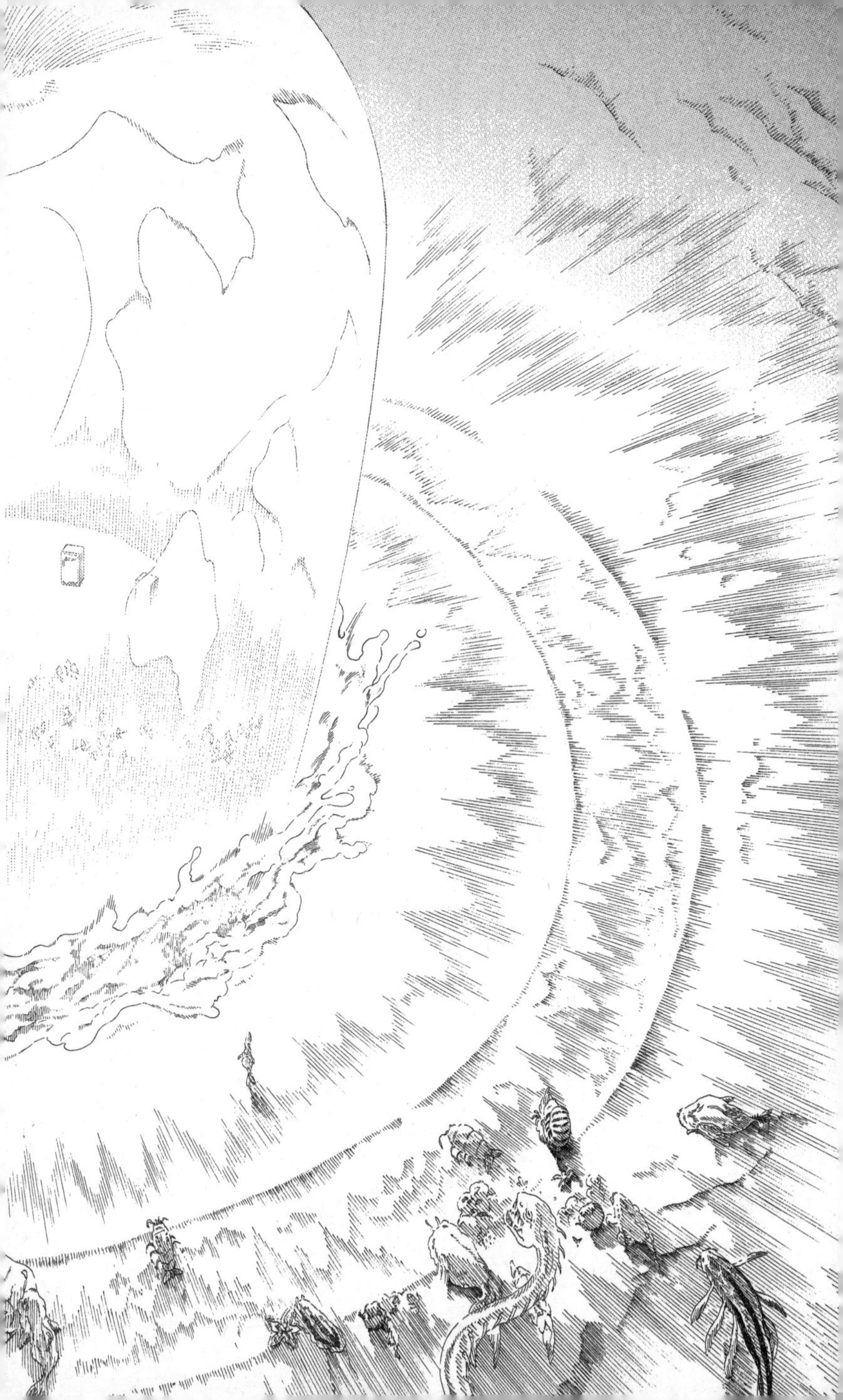

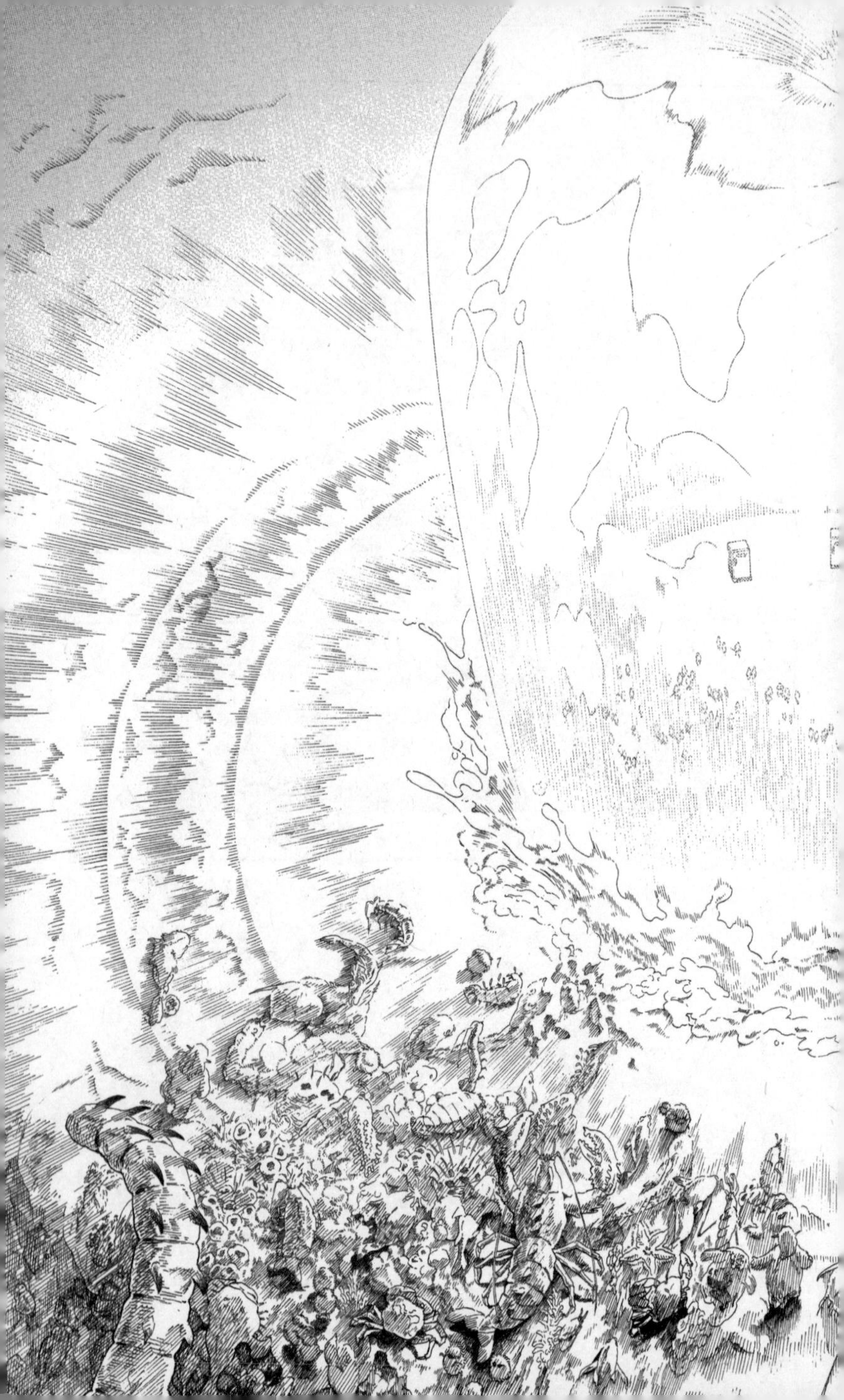

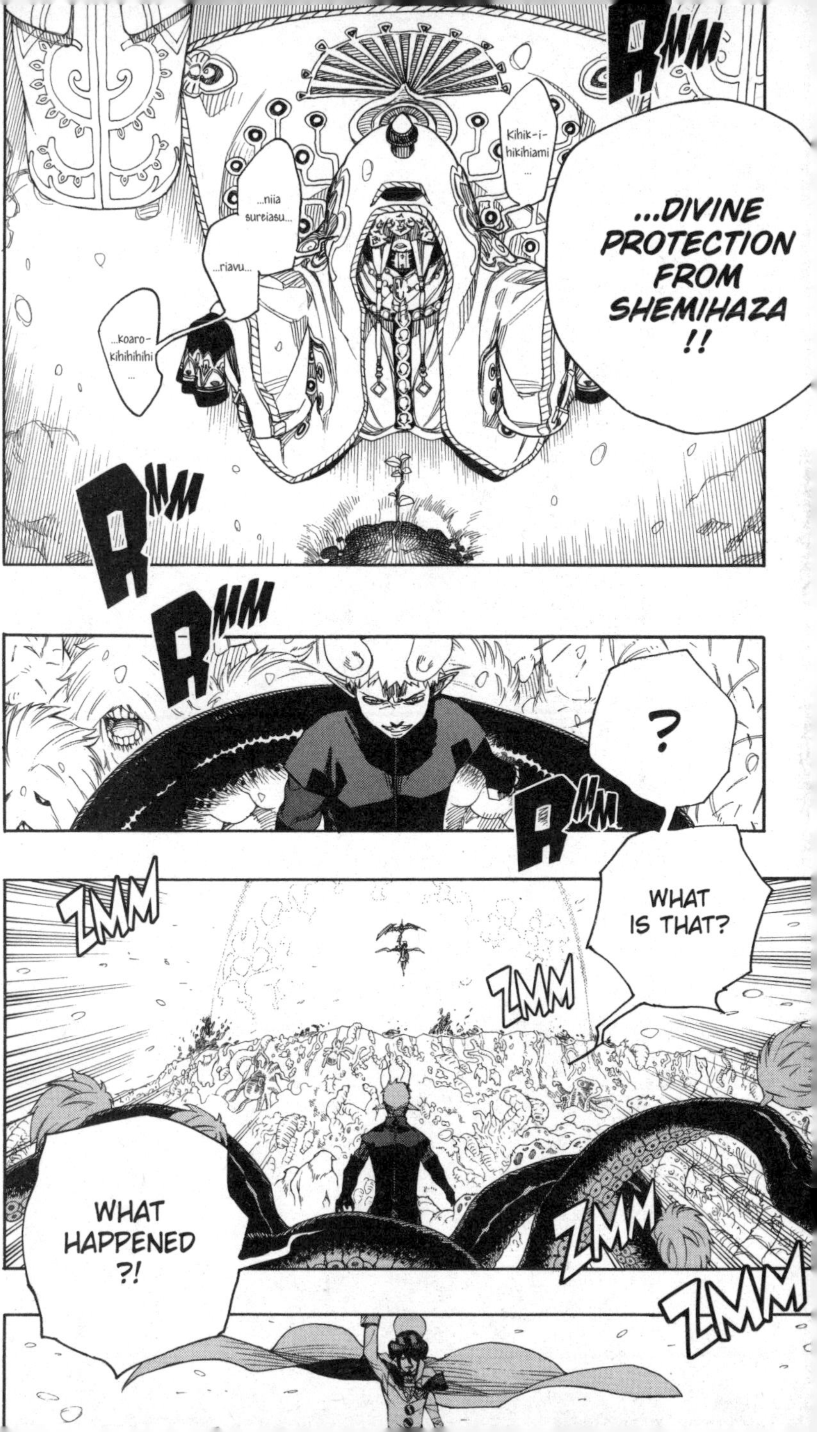
RMM
...DIVINE PROTECTION FROM SHEMIHAZA !!
Kihik-i-hikihiami ...
...niia sureiasu...
...riavu...
...koaro-kihihihihi ...
RMM
RMM
?
RMM
WHAT IS THAT?
ZMM
ZMM
WHAT HAPPENED ?!
ZMM
ZMM

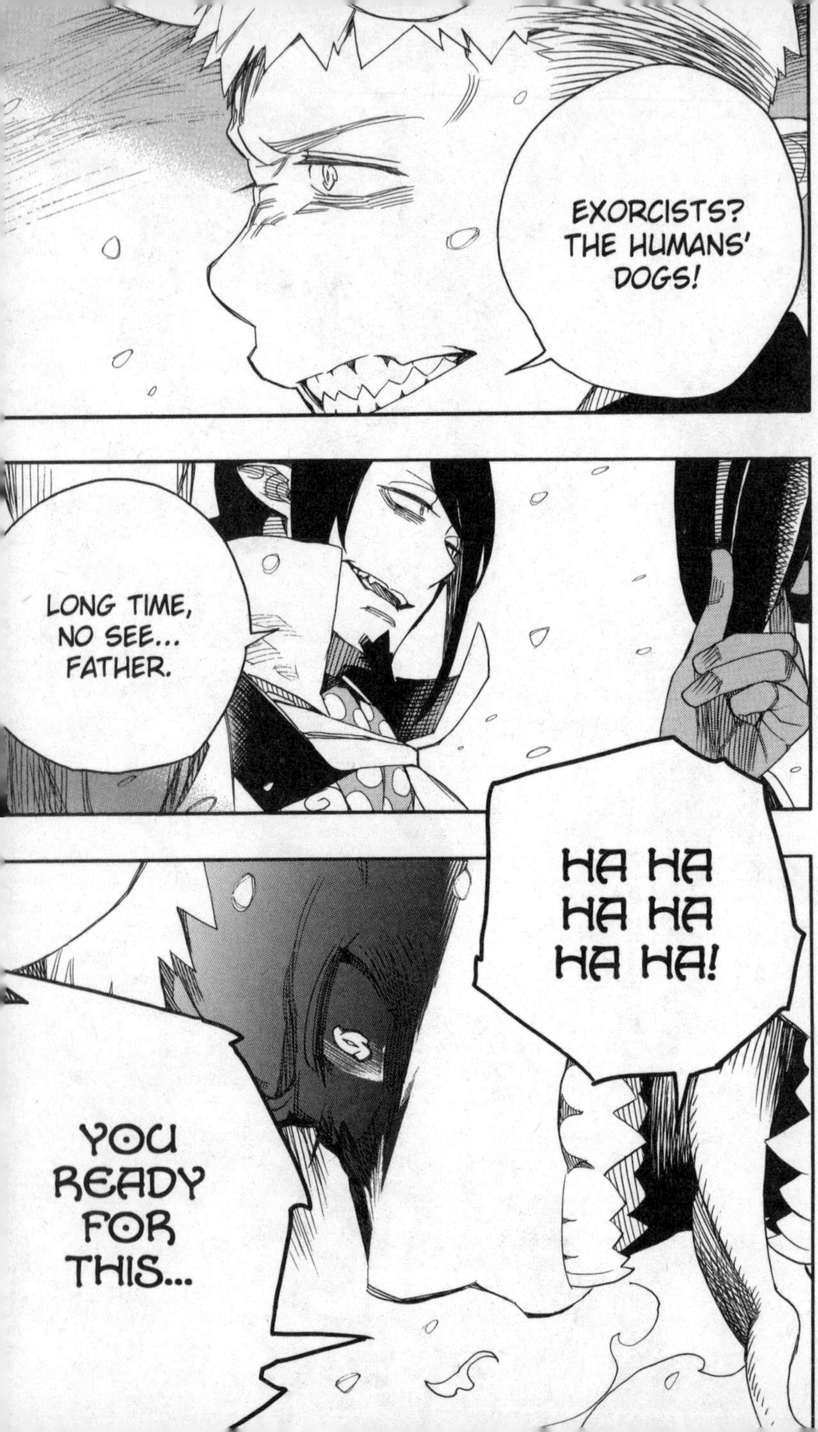

EXORCISTS? THE HUMANS' DOGS!
LONG TIME, NO SEE... FATHER.
HA HA HA HA HA HA!
YOU READY FOR THIS...

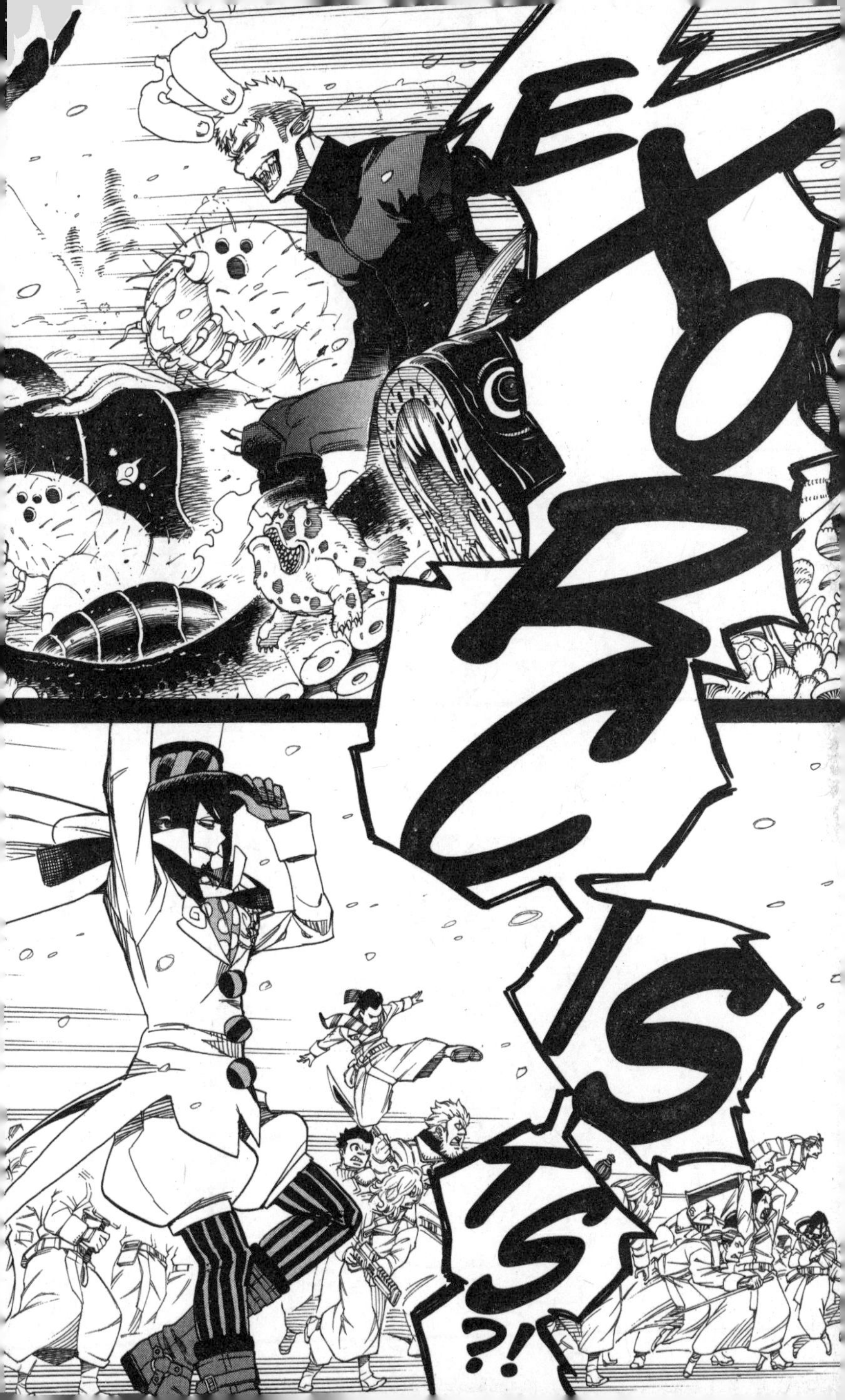
EXORCISTS?!

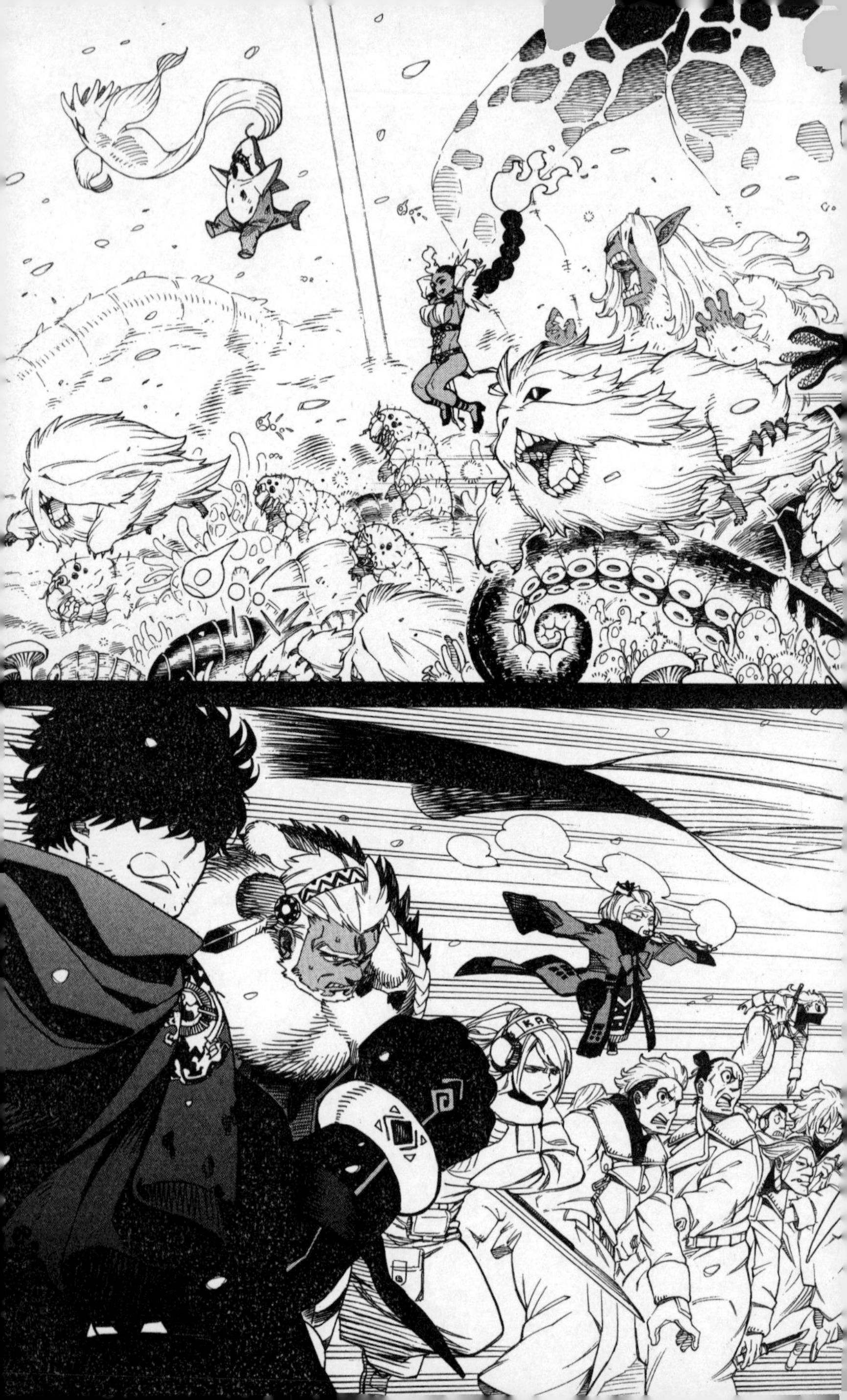

Blue Exorcist Chapter 131: Of One Cloth—Clarification

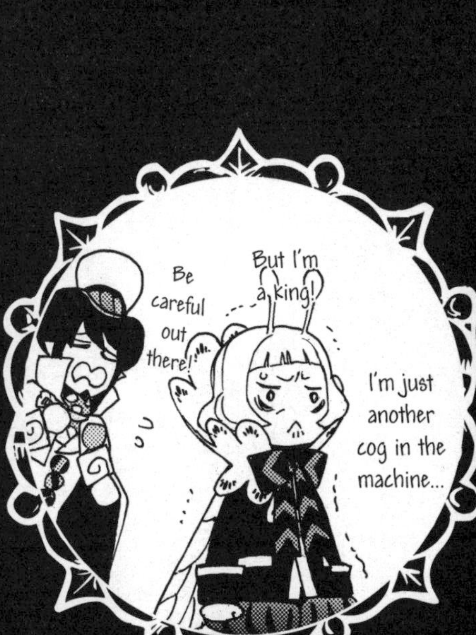
I'm just another cog in the machine...
But I'm a king!
Be careful out there!

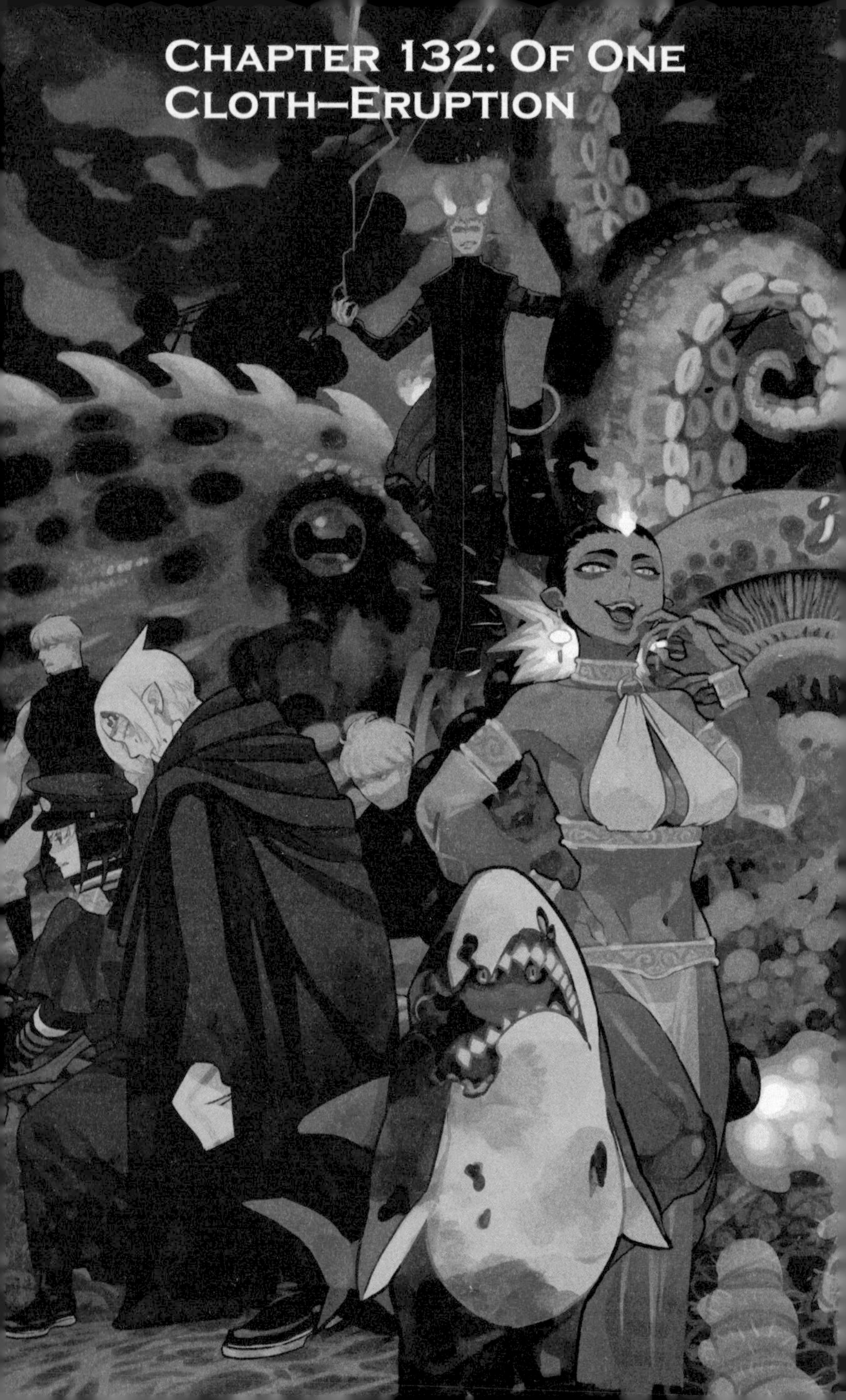
Chapter 132: Of One Cloth—Eruption

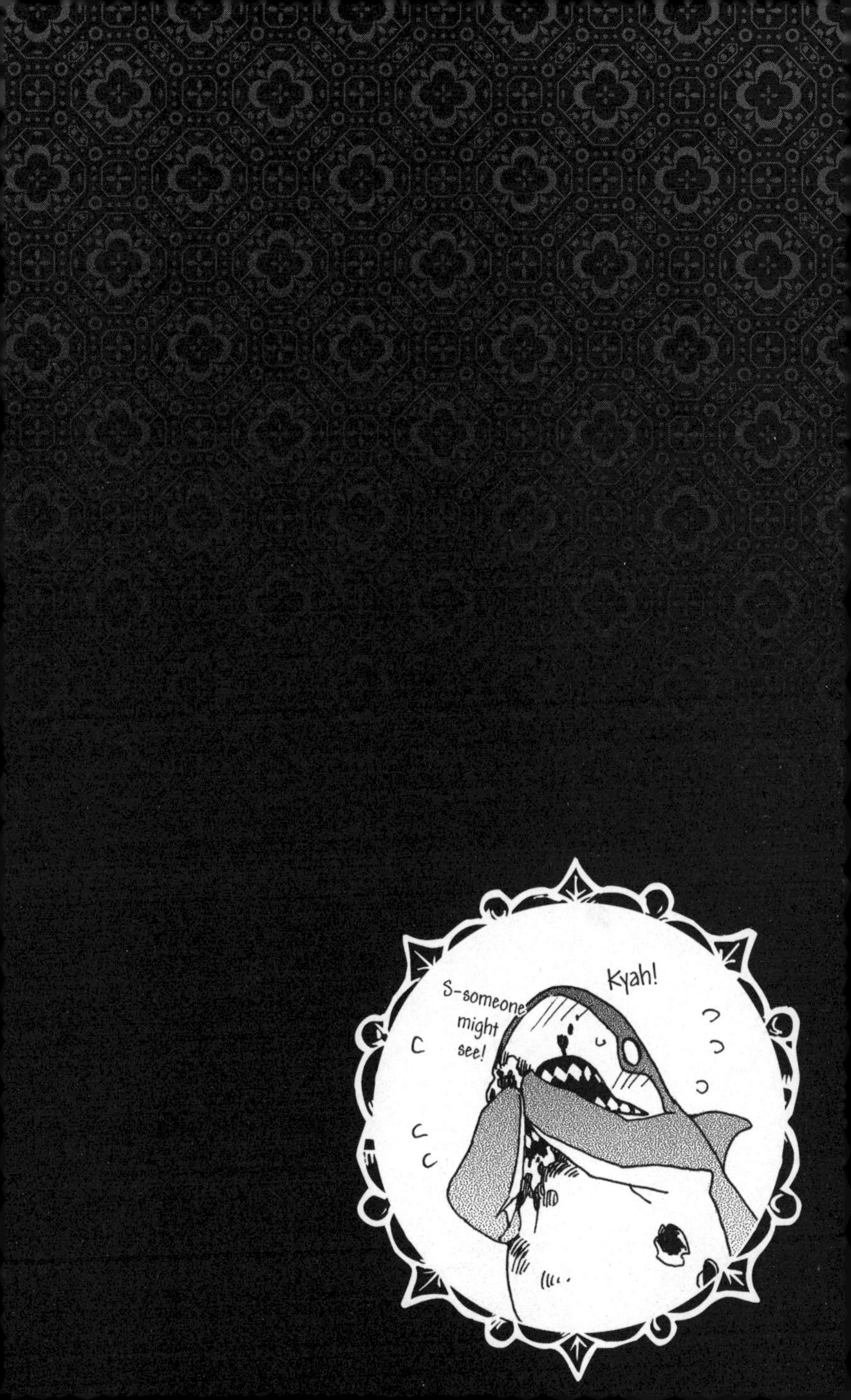
Kyah!
S-someone might see!

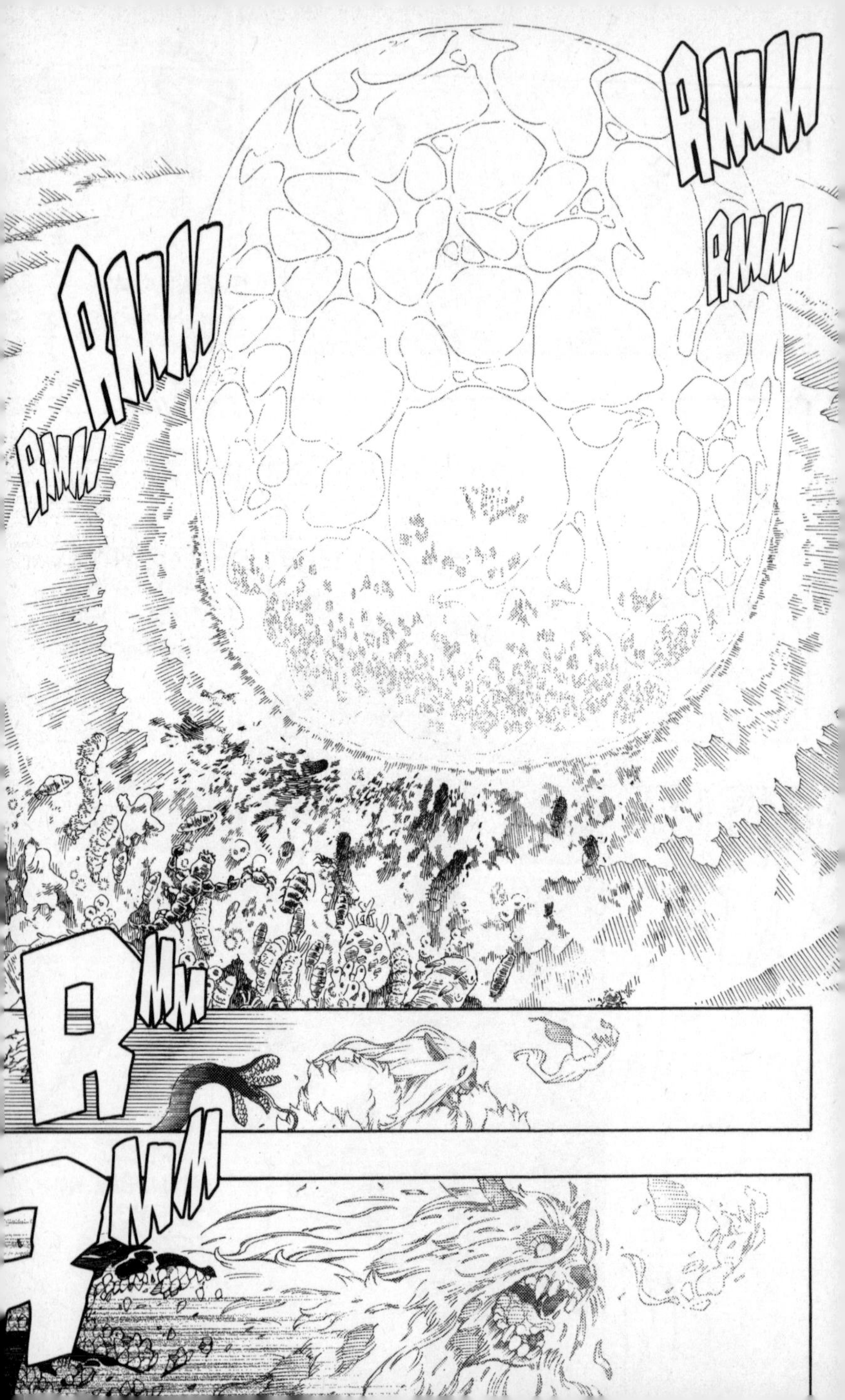

RMM
RMM
RMM
RMM

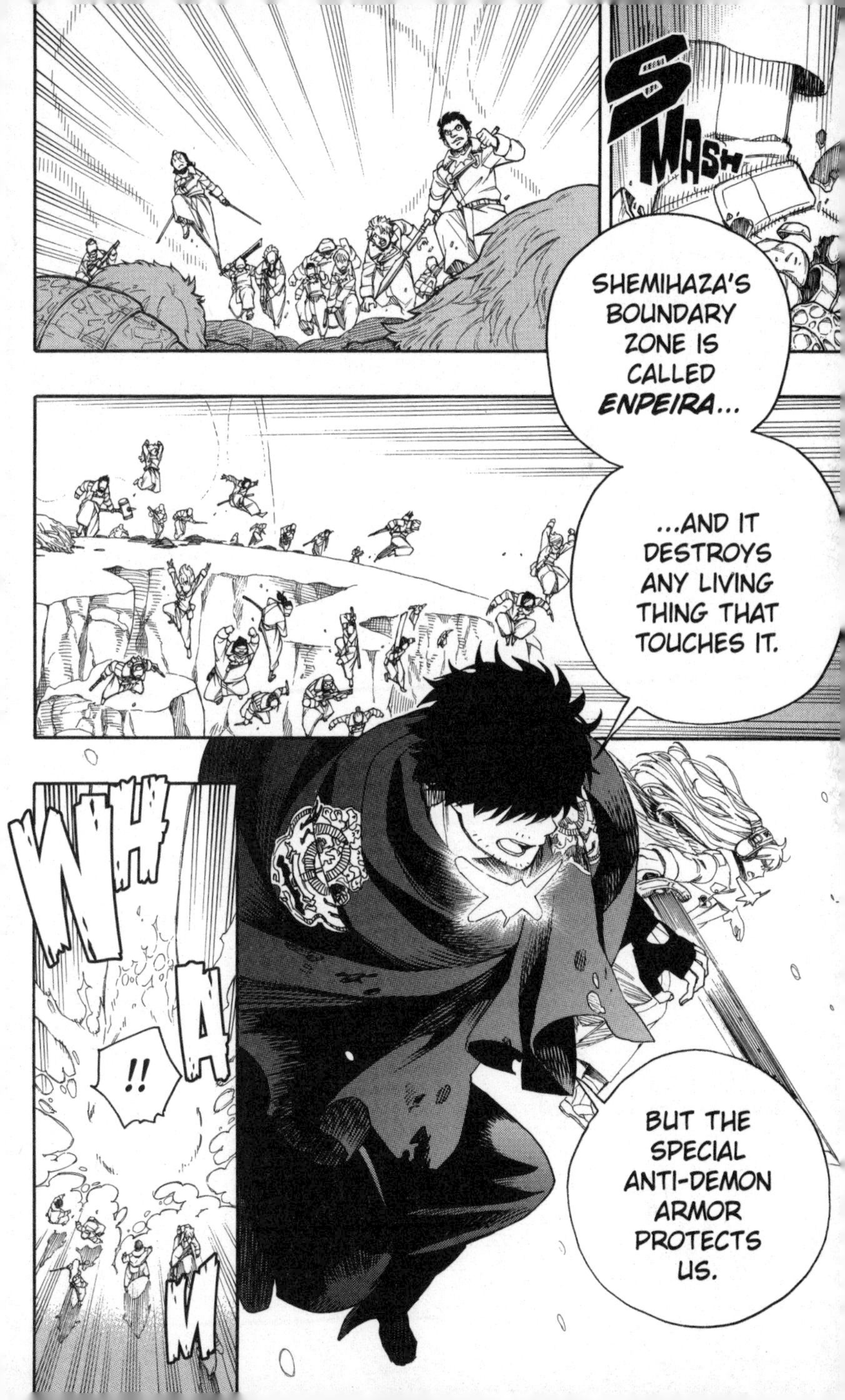
SMASH
SHEMIHAZA'S BOUNDARY ZONE IS CALLED *ENPEIRA*...
...AND IT DESTROYS ANY LIVING THING THAT TOUCHES IT.
BUT THE SPECIAL ANTI-DEMON ARMOR PROTECTS US.
WHAM
!!

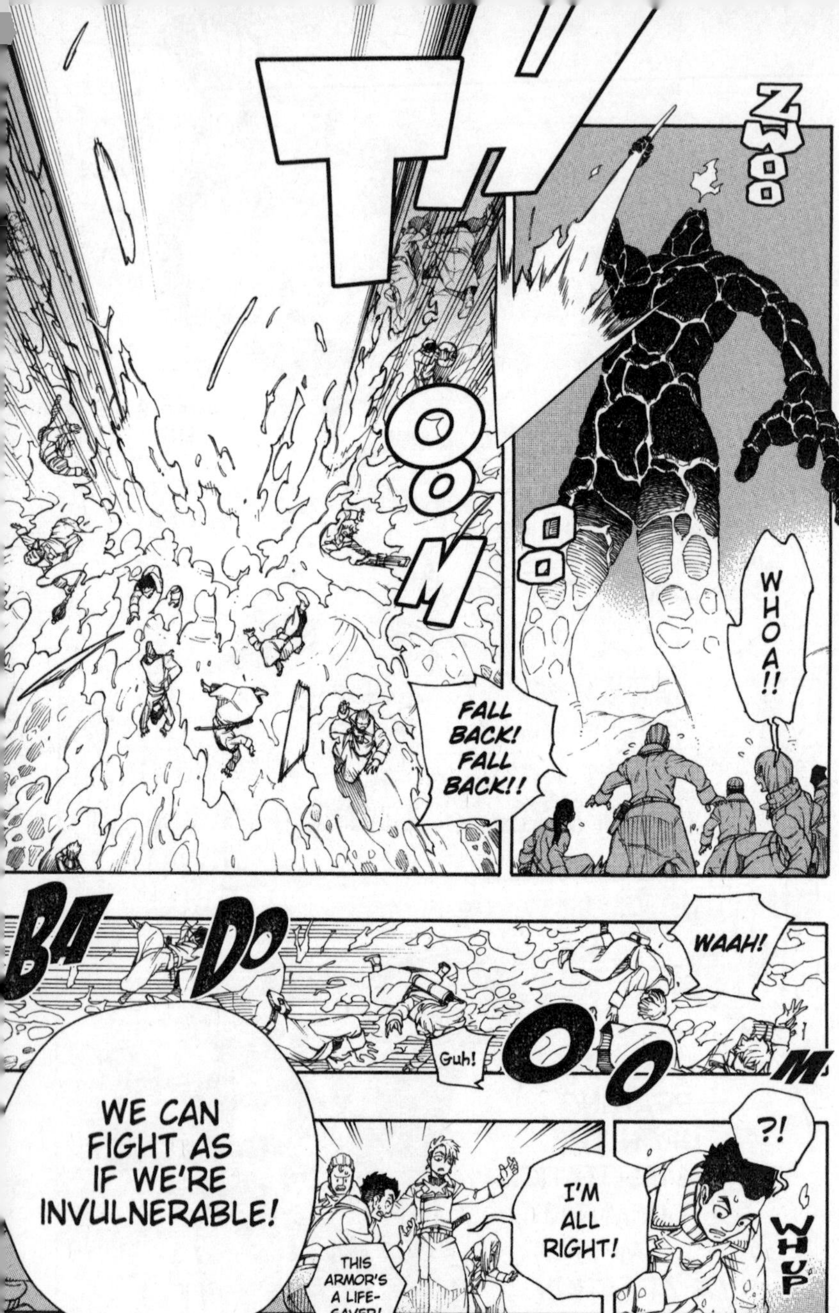
ZWOOOO
WHOA!!
THOOM
FALL BACK! FALL BACK!!
BADOOOM
WAAH!
Guh!
?!
WHUP
I'M ALL RIGHT!
THIS ARMOR'S A LIFE-SAVER!
WE CAN FIGHT AS IF WE'RE INVULNERABLE!

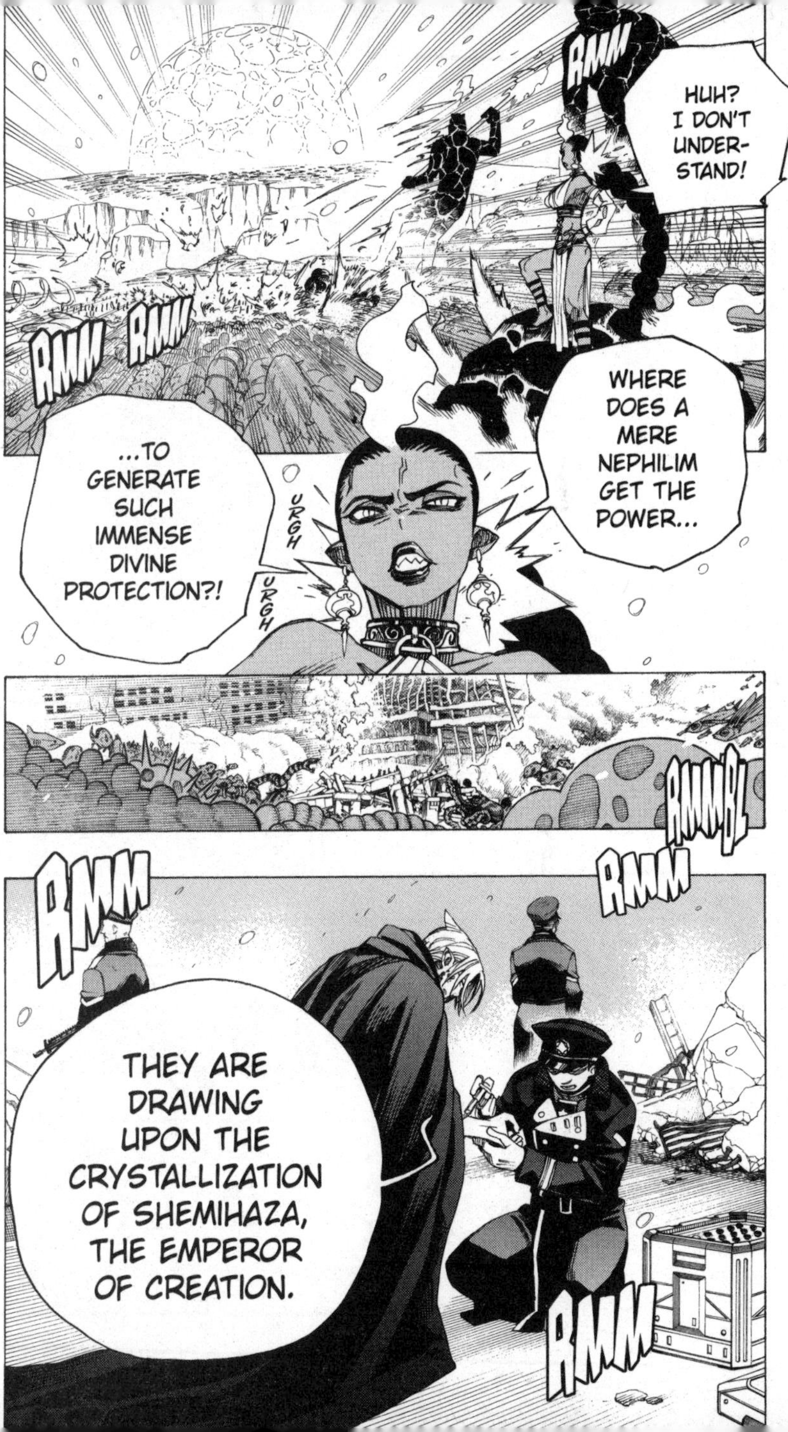
RMM
HUH? I DON'T UNDER-STAND!
RMM RMM
WHERE DOES A MERE NEPHILIM GET THE POWER...
URGH URGH
...TO GENERATE SUCH IMMENSE DIVINE PROTECTION?!
RMMBL
RMM
RMM
THEY ARE DRAWING UPON THE CRYSTALLIZATION OF SHEMIHAZA, THE EMPEROR OF CREATION.
RMM

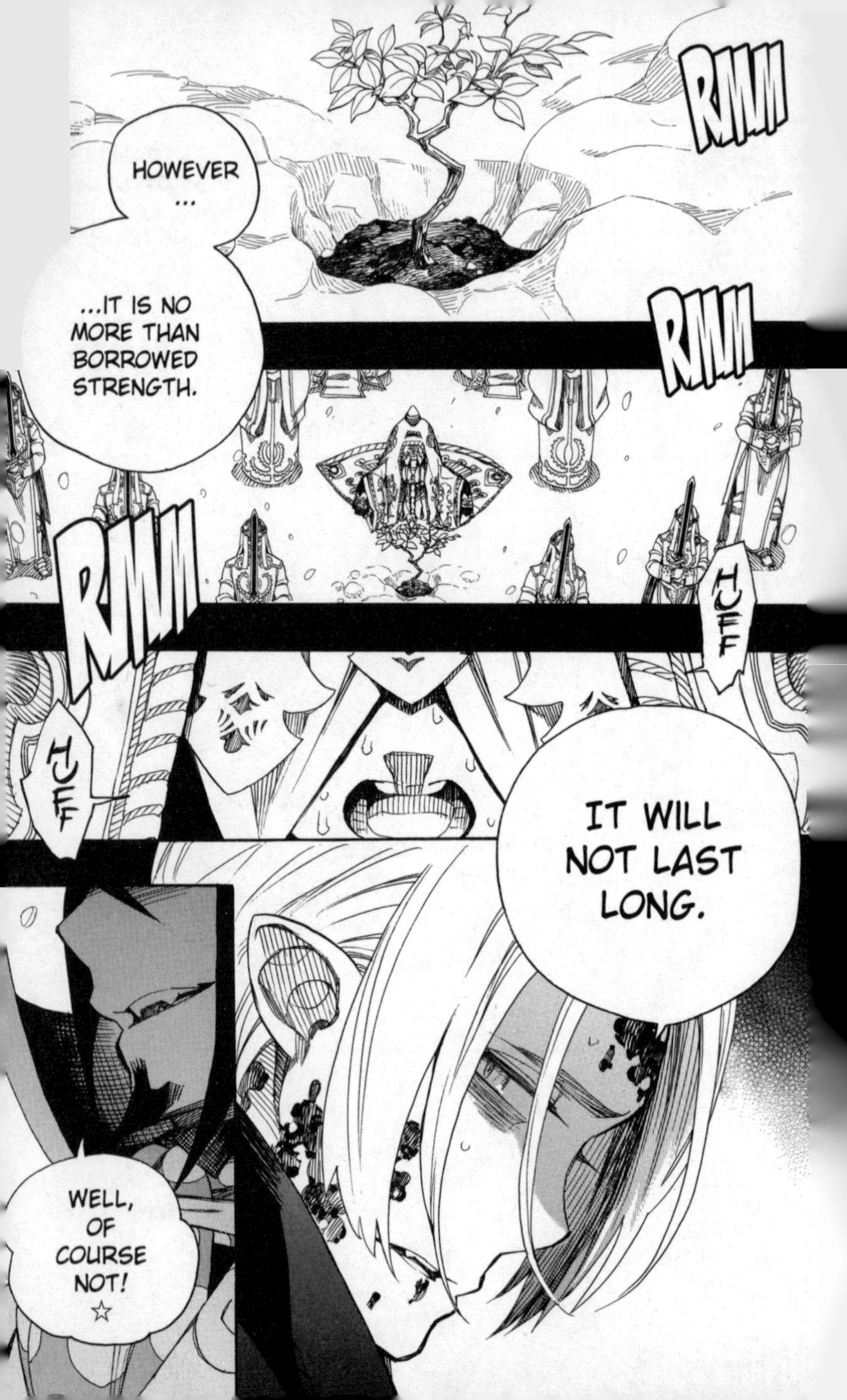
RMMM
HOWEVER ...
...IT IS NO MORE THAN BORROWED STRENGTH.
RMMM
HUFF
RMMM
HUFF
IT WILL NOT LAST LONG.
WELL, OF COURSE NOT! ☆

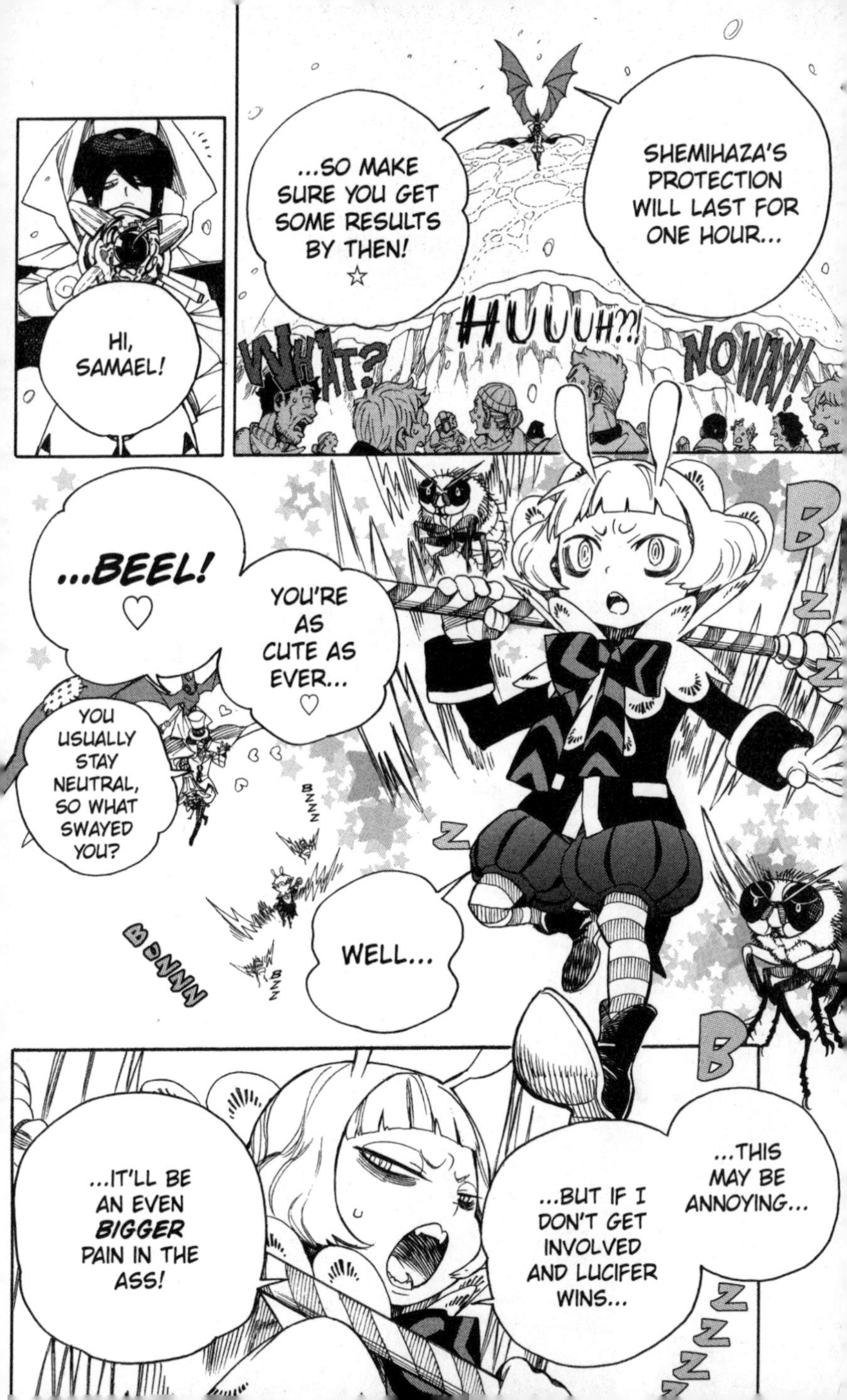
SHEMIHAZA'S PROTECTION WILL LAST FOR ONE HOUR...
...SO MAKE SURE YOU GET SOME RESULTS BY THEN! ☆
NOWAY!
HUUUH??!
WHAT?
HI, SAMAEL!
BZZZ
...BEEL! ♡
YOU'RE AS CUTE AS EVER... ♡
YOU USUALLY STAY NEUTRAL, SO WHAT SWAYED YOU?
WELL...
BZZZ
BUNNN
B
...THIS MAY BE ANNOYING...
...BUT IF I DON'T GET INVOLVED AND LUCIFER WINS...
...IT'LL BE AN EVEN BIGGER PAIN IN THE ASS!
ZZZZ

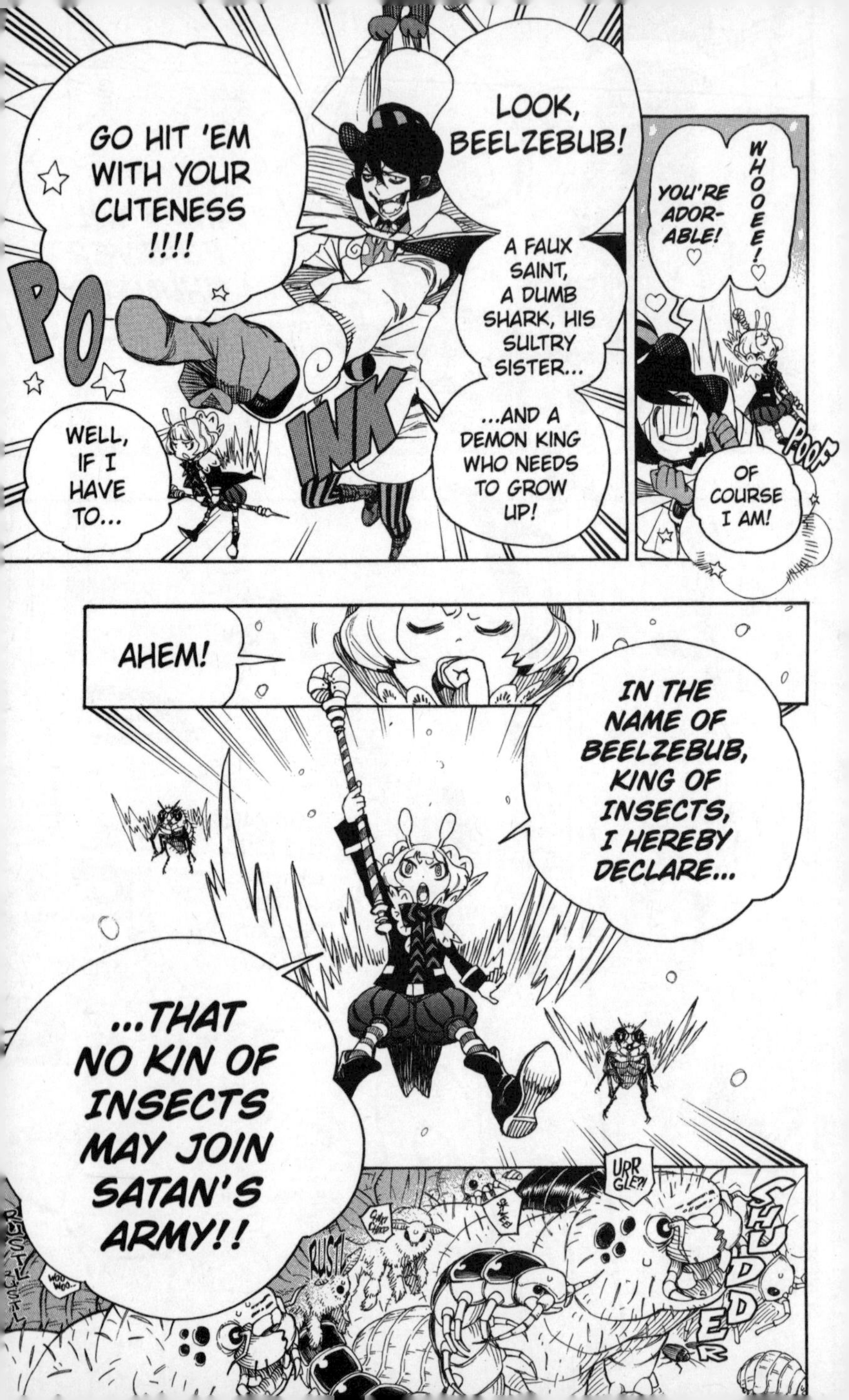
LOOK, BEELZEBUB!
A FAUX SAINT, A DUMB SHARK, HIS SULTRY SISTER...
...AND A DEMON KING WHO NEEDS TO GROW UP!
GO HIT 'EM WITH YOUR CUTENESS !!!!
POINK
WELL, IF I HAVE TO...
WHOOOEE!
YOU'RE ADORABLE!
POOF
OF COURSE I AM!
AHEM!
IN THE NAME OF BEELZEBUB, KING OF INSECTS, I HEREBY DECLARE...
...THAT NO KIN OF INSECTS MAY JOIN SATAN'S ARMY!!
URR GLE?!
SHUDDER
RUSTLE
RUST!
WOO WOO...

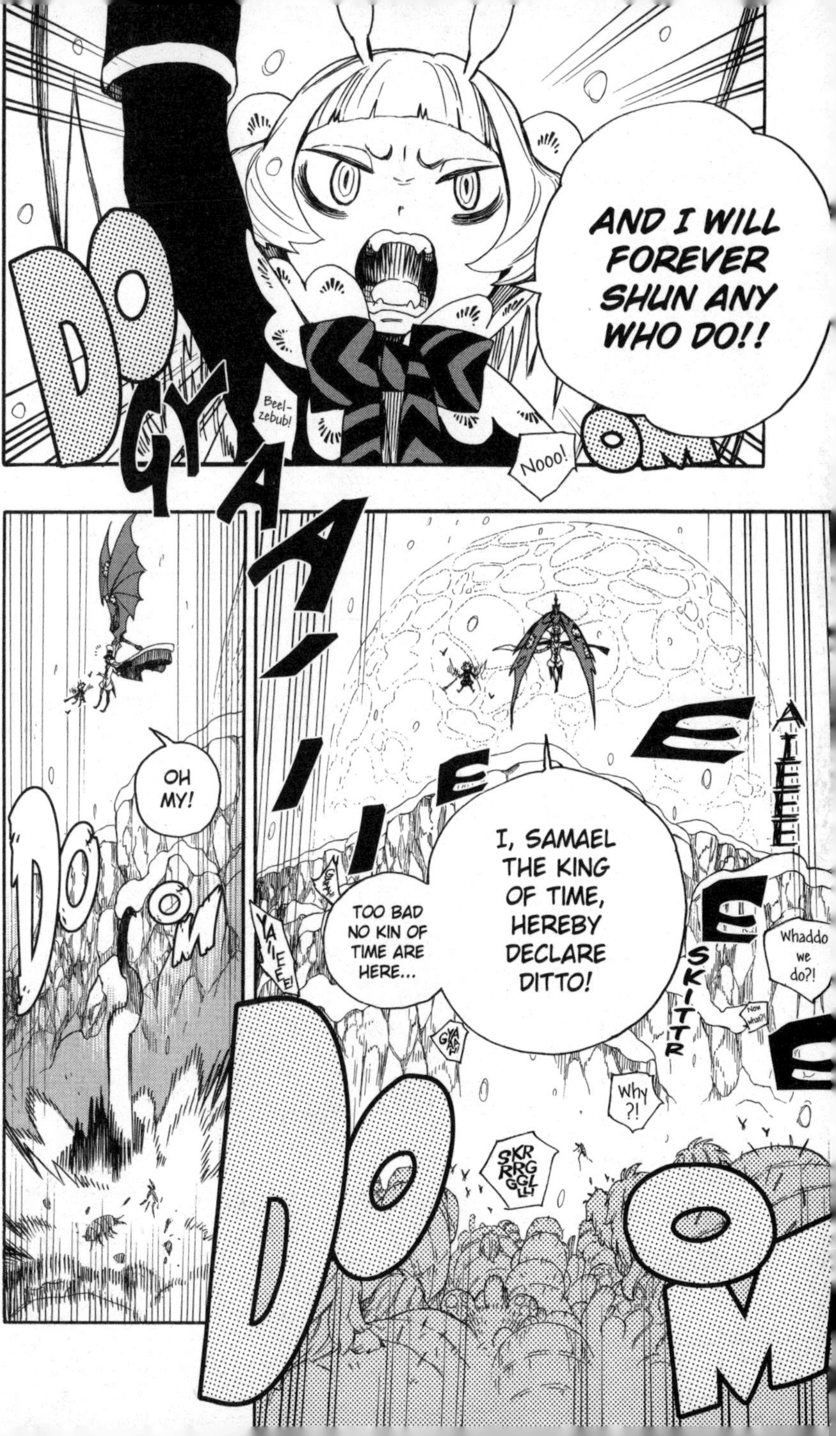
AND I WILL FOREVER SHUN ANY WHO DO!!
DOOM
Nooo!
Beel-zebub!
GYAAAIIEEE
I, SAMAEL THE KING OF TIME, HEREBY DECLARE DITTO!
TOO BAD NO KIN OF TIME ARE HERE...
AIEEEE
Whaddo we do?!
Now what?!
SKITTR
Why?!
SKRRGGL
DOOM
OH MY!
DOOM

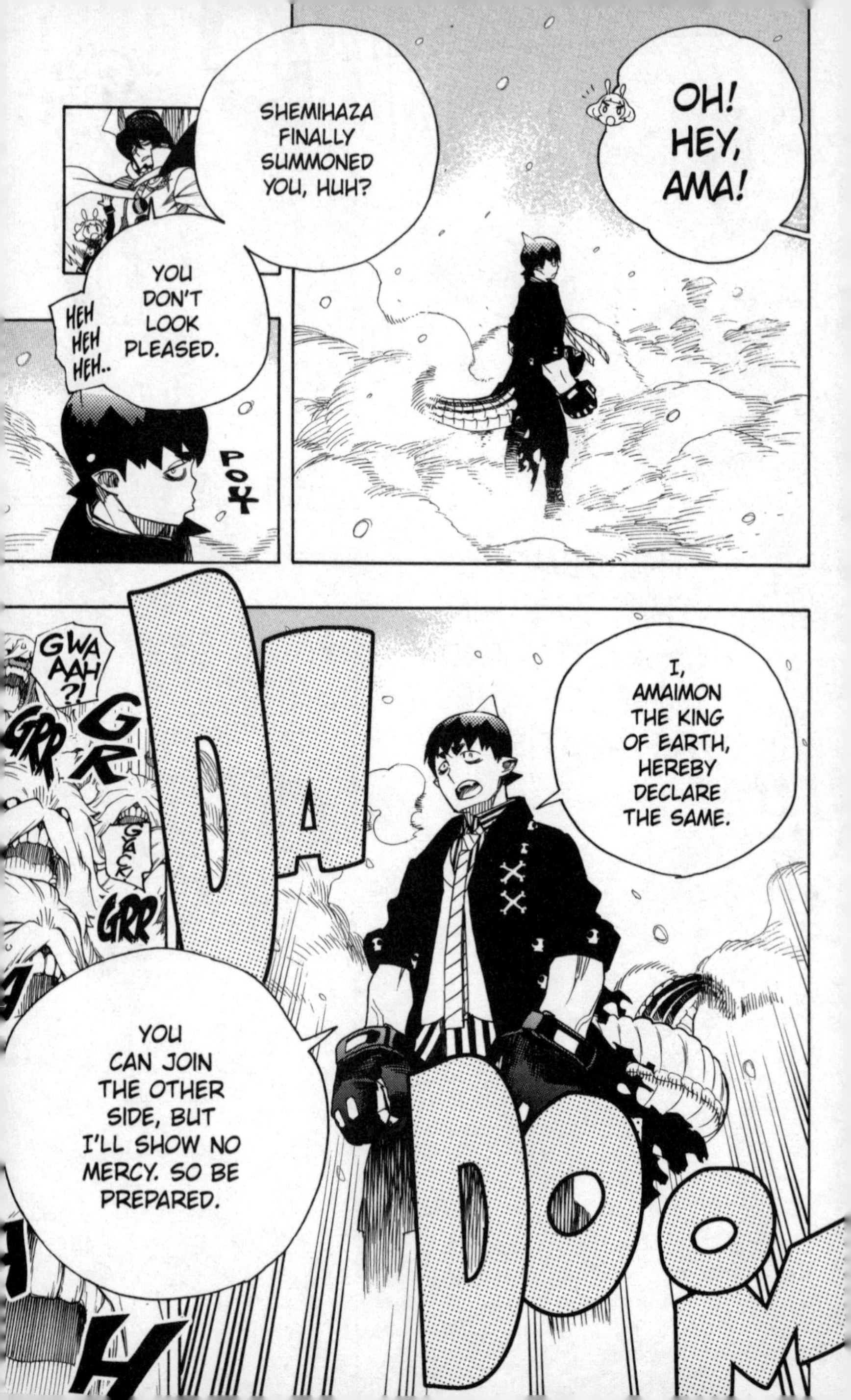
OH! HEY, AMA!
SHEMIHAZA FINALLY SUMMONED YOU, HUH?
HEH HEH HEH..
YOU DON'T LOOK PLEASED.
POUT
I, AMAIMON THE KING OF EARTH, HEREBY DECLARE THE SAME.
GWAAAH?!
GRR
GR
GYACK
GRR
DA
YOU CAN JOIN THE OTHER SIDE, BUT I'LL SHOW NO MERCY. SO BE PREPARED.
DOOOM

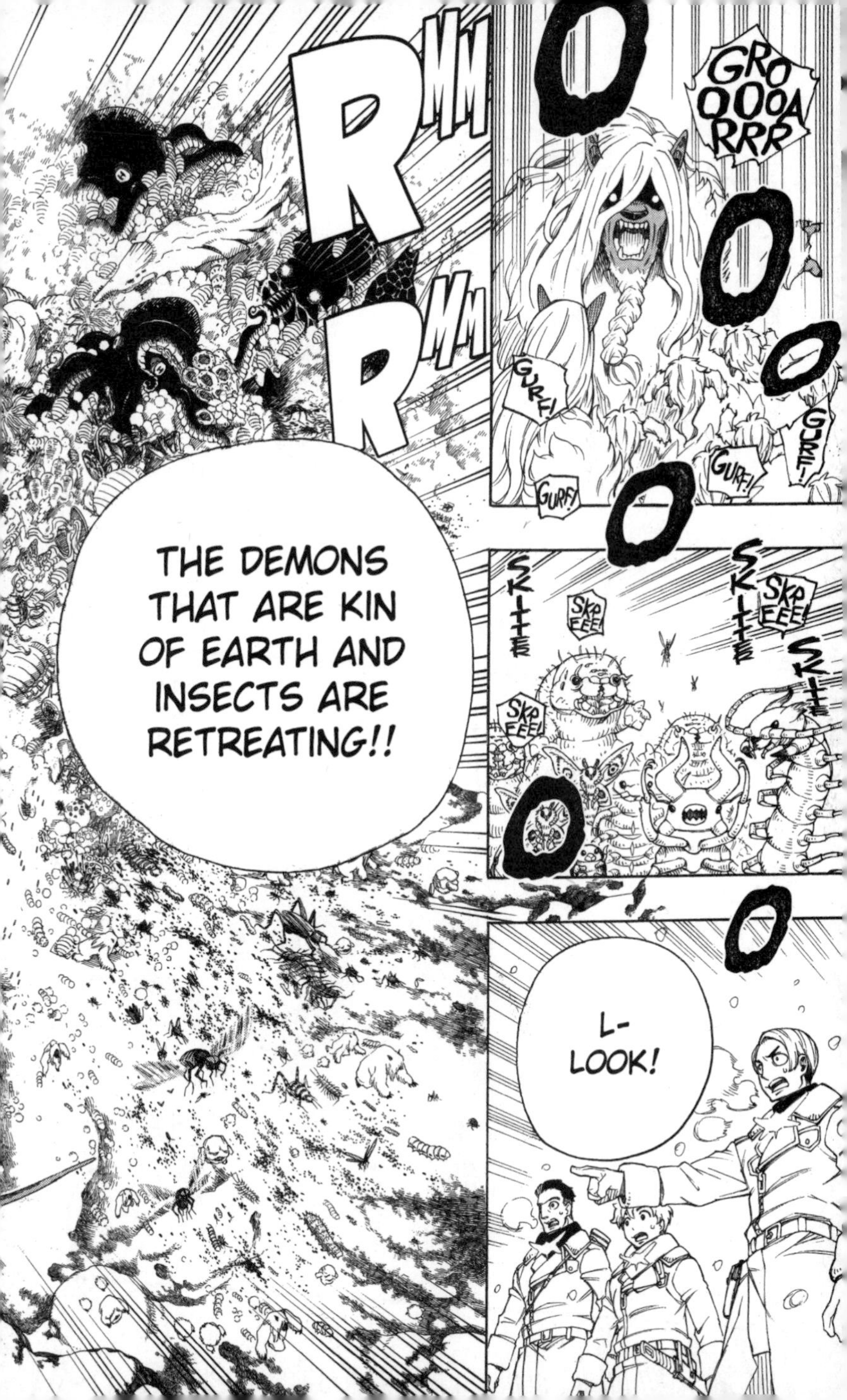
GROOOOARRR
GURF!
GURF!
GURF!
GURF!
SKITTER
SKREEE!
SKITTER
SKREEE!
SKREEE!
SKITT
RMMM
RMMM
OOOOOO
THE DEMONS THAT ARE KIN OF EARTH AND INSECTS ARE RETREATING!!
L-LOOK!

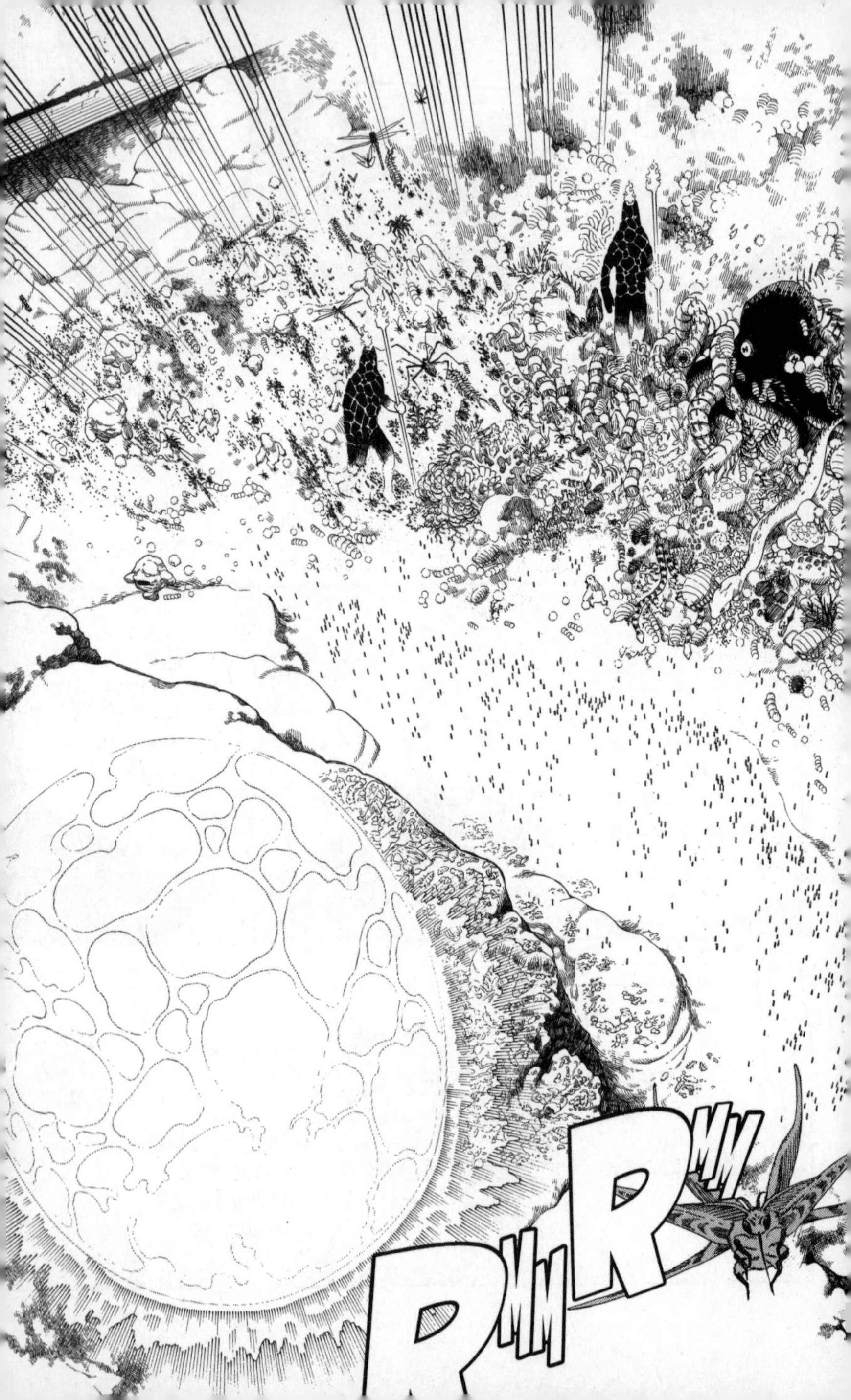
DMMMRMMM

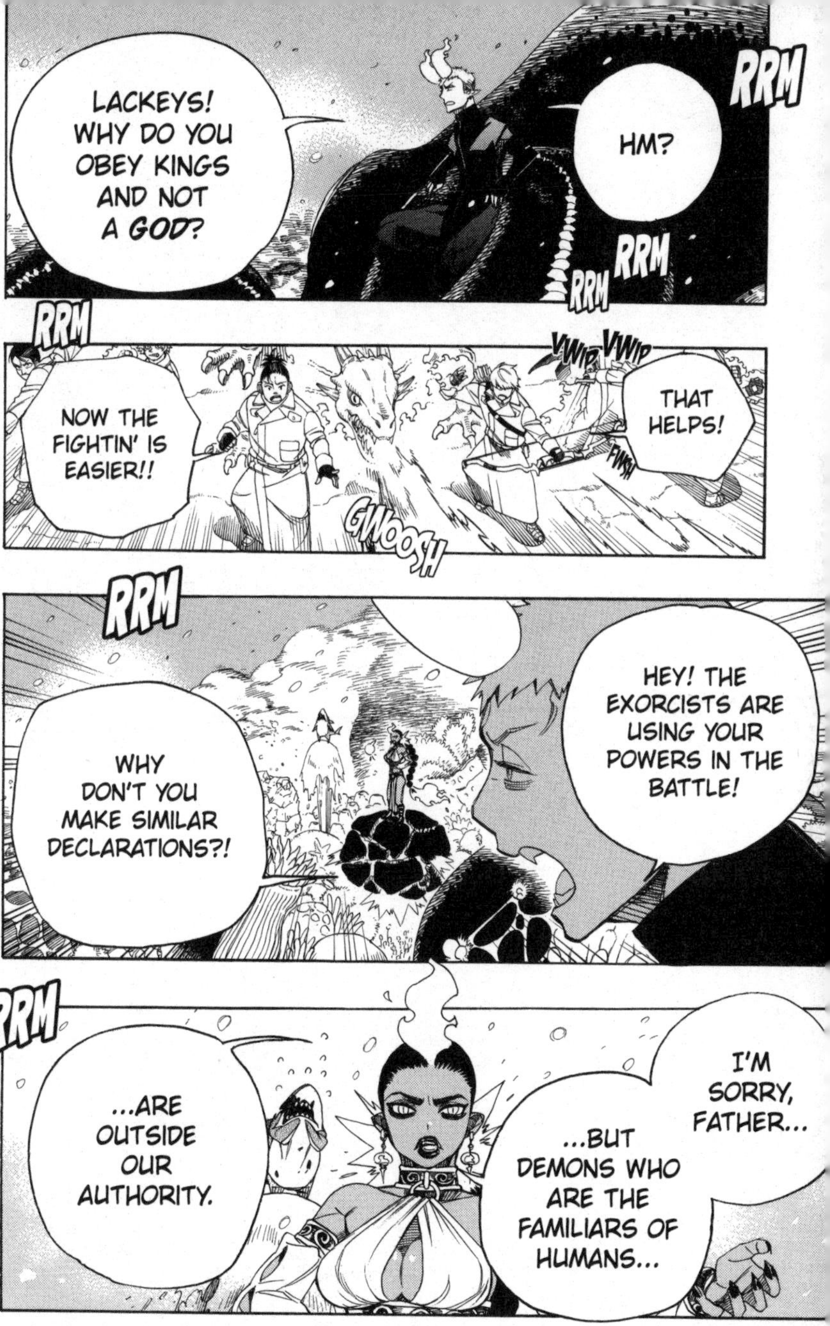
RRM
HM?
LACKEYS! WHY DO YOU OBEY KINGS AND NOT A *GOD?*
RRM
RRM
RRM
VWIP VWIP
THAT HELPS!
FWSH
NOW THE FIGHTIN' IS EASIER!!
GWOOSH
RRM
HEY! THE EXORCISTS ARE USING YOUR POWERS IN THE BATTLE!
WHY DON'T YOU MAKE SIMILAR DECLARATIONS?!
RRM
I'M SORRY, FATHER...
...BUT DEMONS WHO ARE THE FAMILIARS OF HUMANS...
...ARE OUTSIDE OUR AUTHORITY.

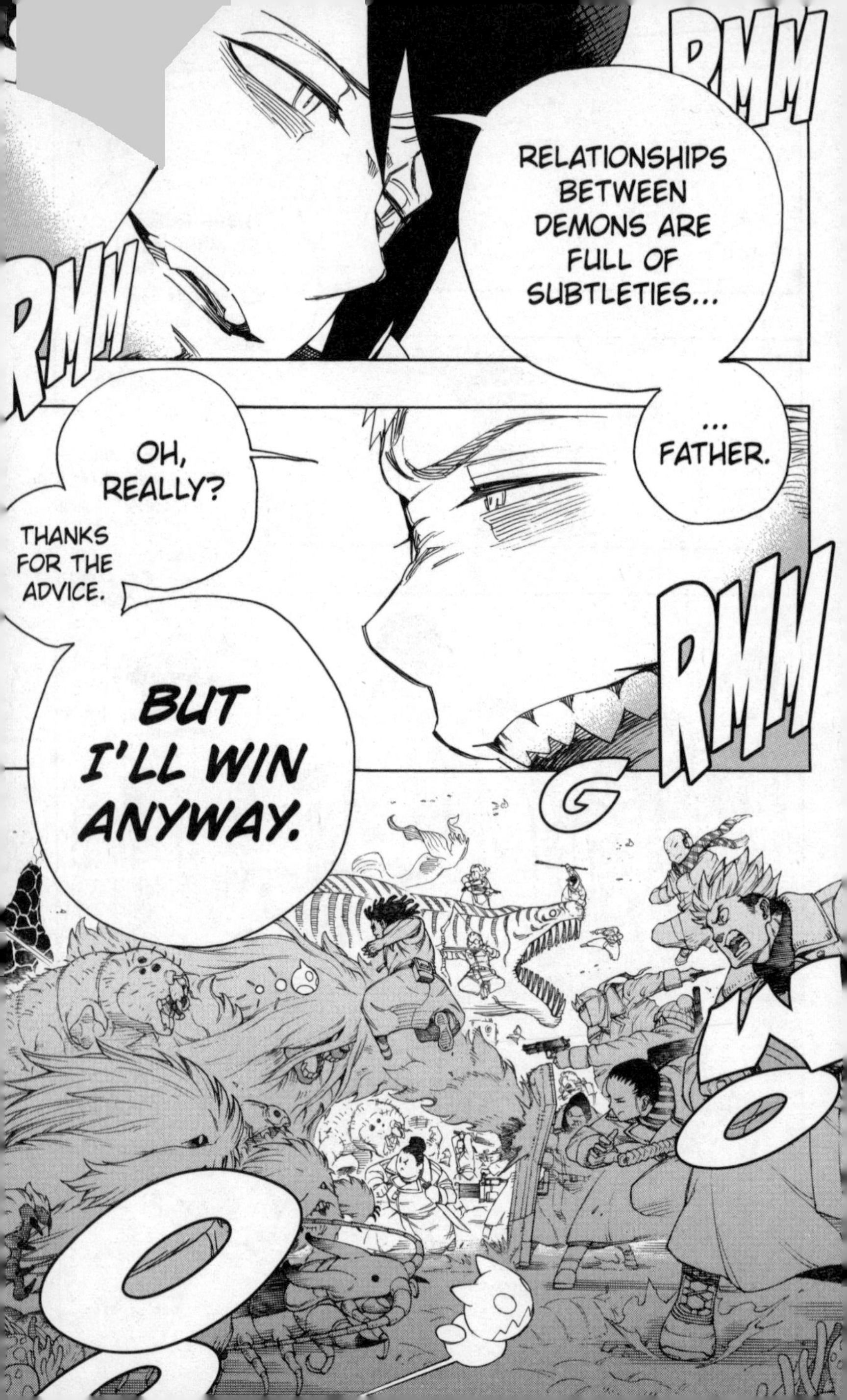
RMM
RELATIONSHIPS BETWEEN DEMONS ARE FULL OF SUBTLETIES...
RMM
... FATHER.
OH, REALLY?
THANKS FOR THE ADVICE.
BUT I'LL WIN ANYWAY.
RMM
G
WO
O

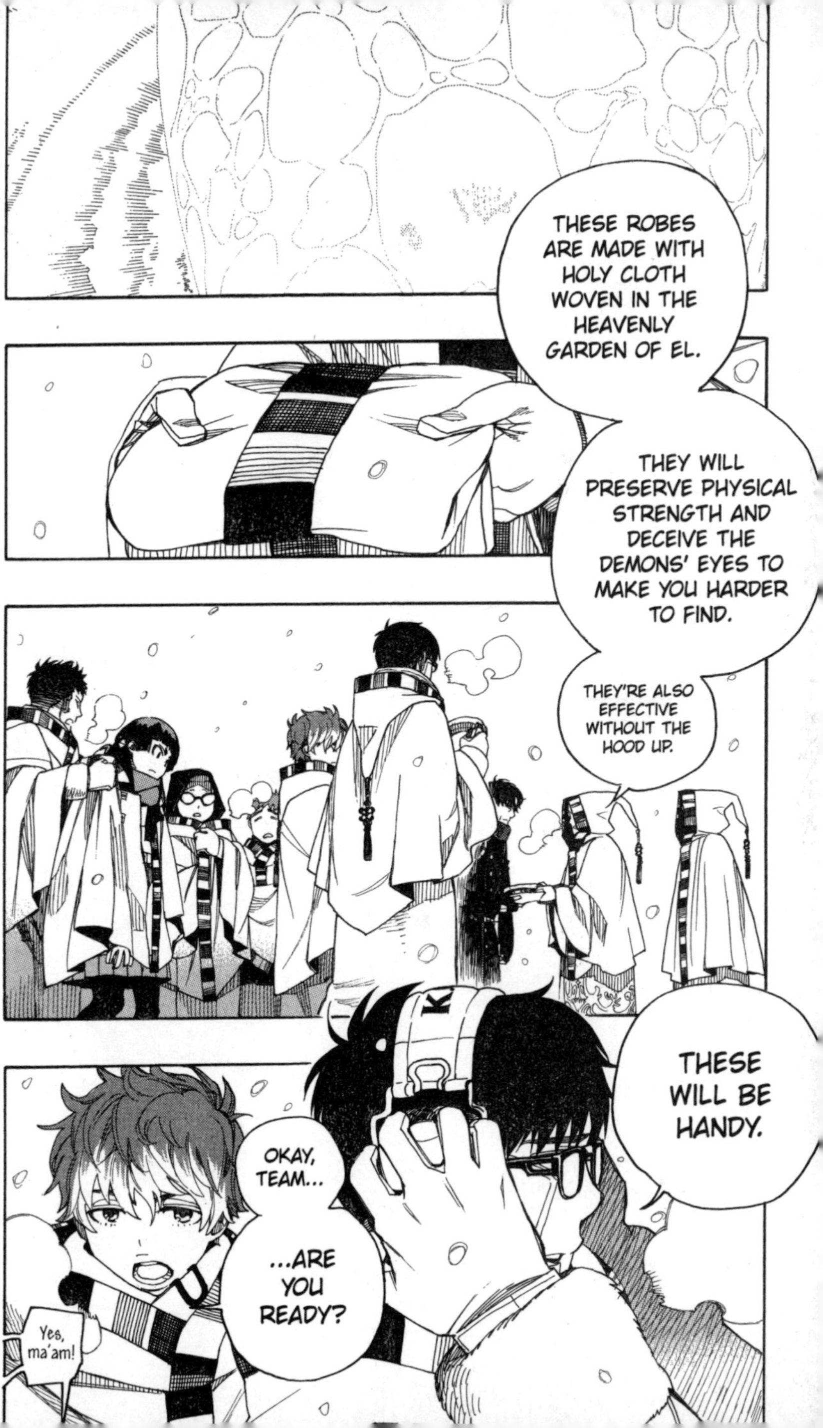

THESE ROBES ARE MADE WITH HOLY CLOTH WOVEN IN THE HEAVENLY GARDEN OF EL.
THEY WILL PRESERVE PHYSICAL STRENGTH AND DECEIVE THE DEMONS' EYES TO MAKE YOU HARDER TO FIND.
THEY'RE ALSO EFFECTIVE WITHOUT THE HOOD UP.
THESE WILL BE HANDY.
OKAY, TEAM...
...ARE YOU READY?
Yes, ma'am!

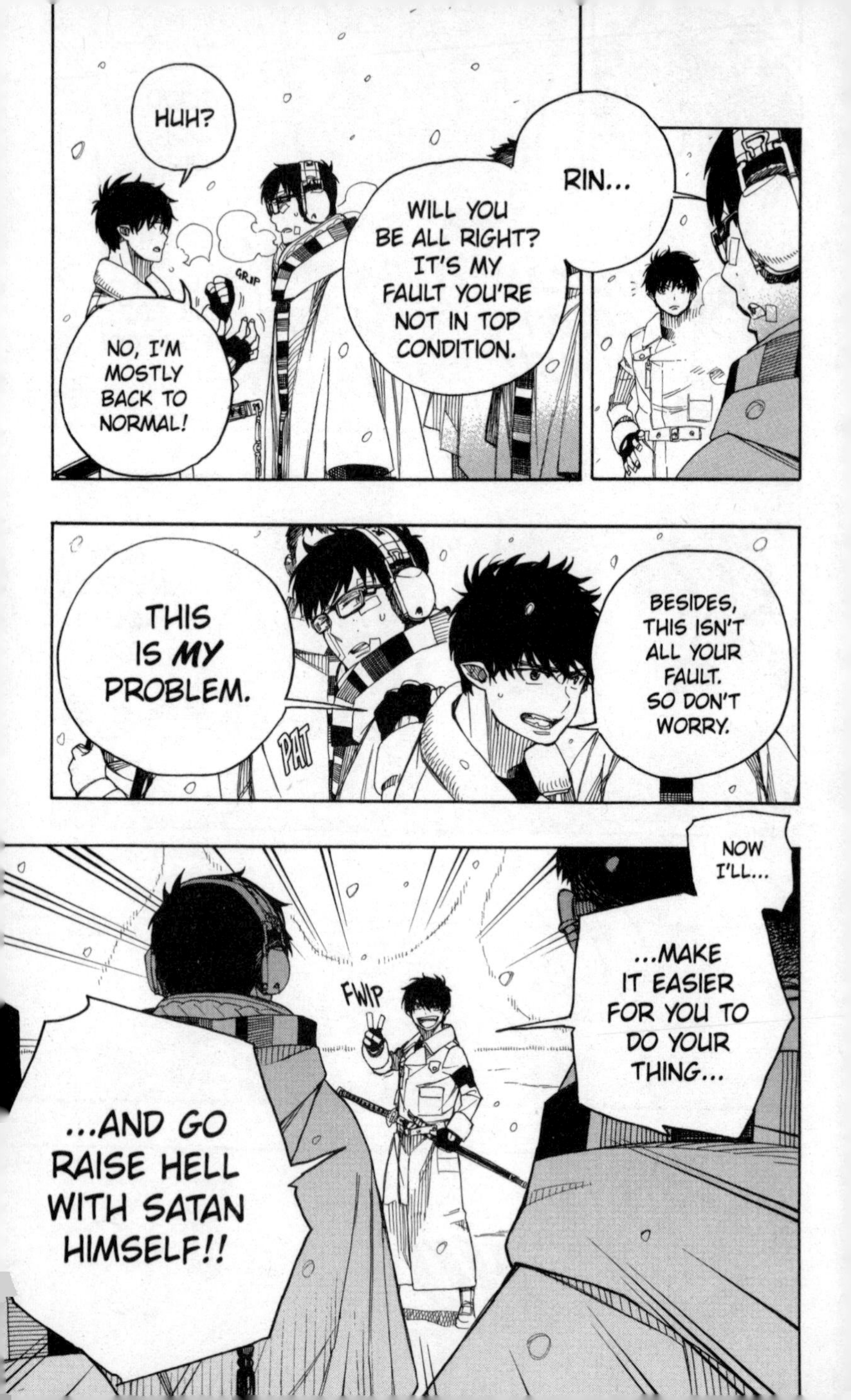
RIN...
WILL YOU BE ALL RIGHT? IT'S MY FAULT YOU'RE NOT IN TOP CONDITION.
HUH?
GRIP
NO, I'M MOSTLY BACK TO NORMAL!
BESIDES, THIS ISN'T ALL YOUR FAULT. SO DON'T WORRY.
PAT
THIS IS *MY* PROBLEM.
NOW I'LL...
...MAKE IT EASIER FOR YOU TO DO YOUR THING...
FWIP
...AND GO RAISE HELL WITH SATAN HIMSELF!!

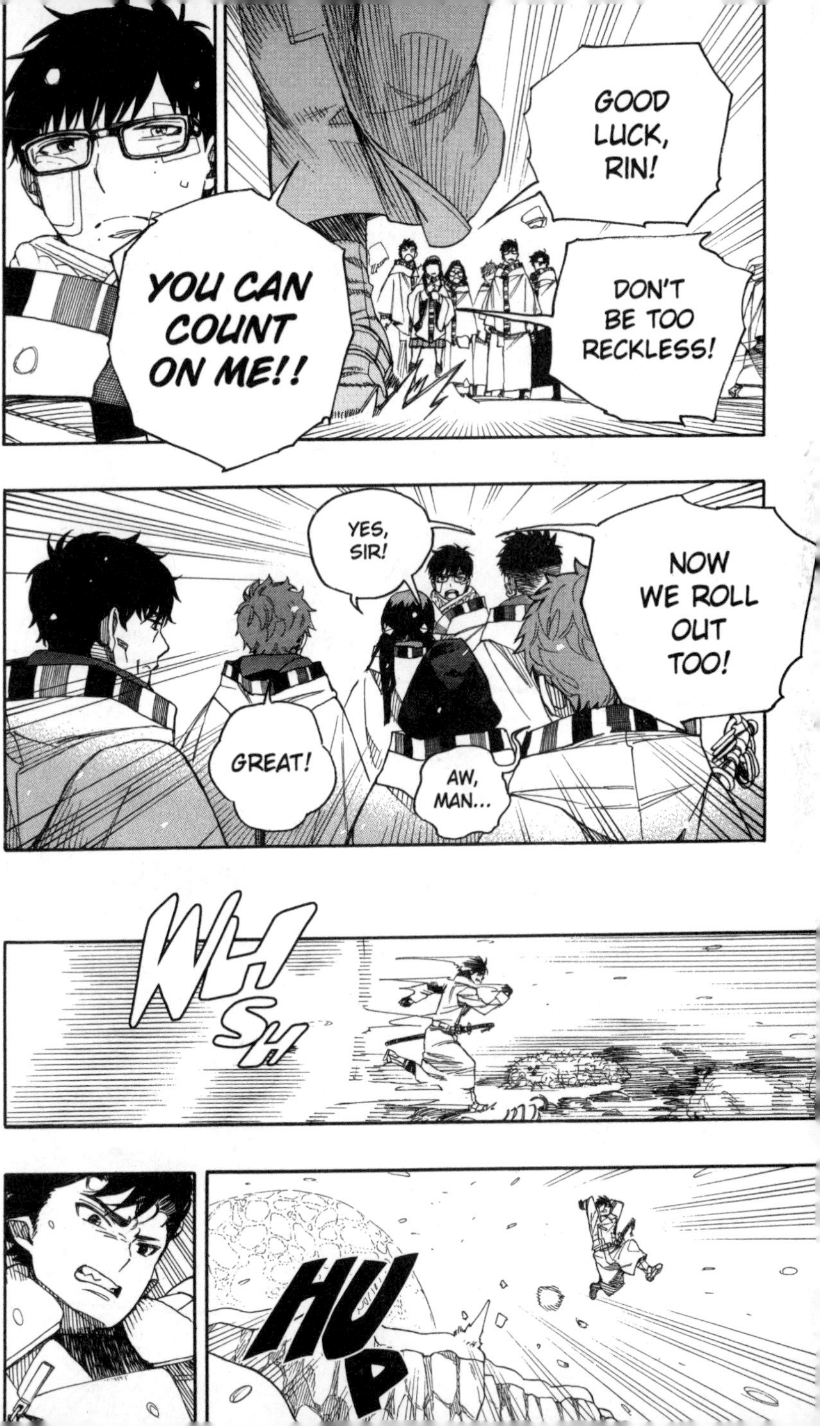
GOOD LUCK, RIN!
DON'T BE TOO RECKLESS!
YOU CAN COUNT ON ME!!
NOW WE ROLL OUT TOO!
YES, SIR!
AW, MAN...
GREAT!
WHSH
HUP

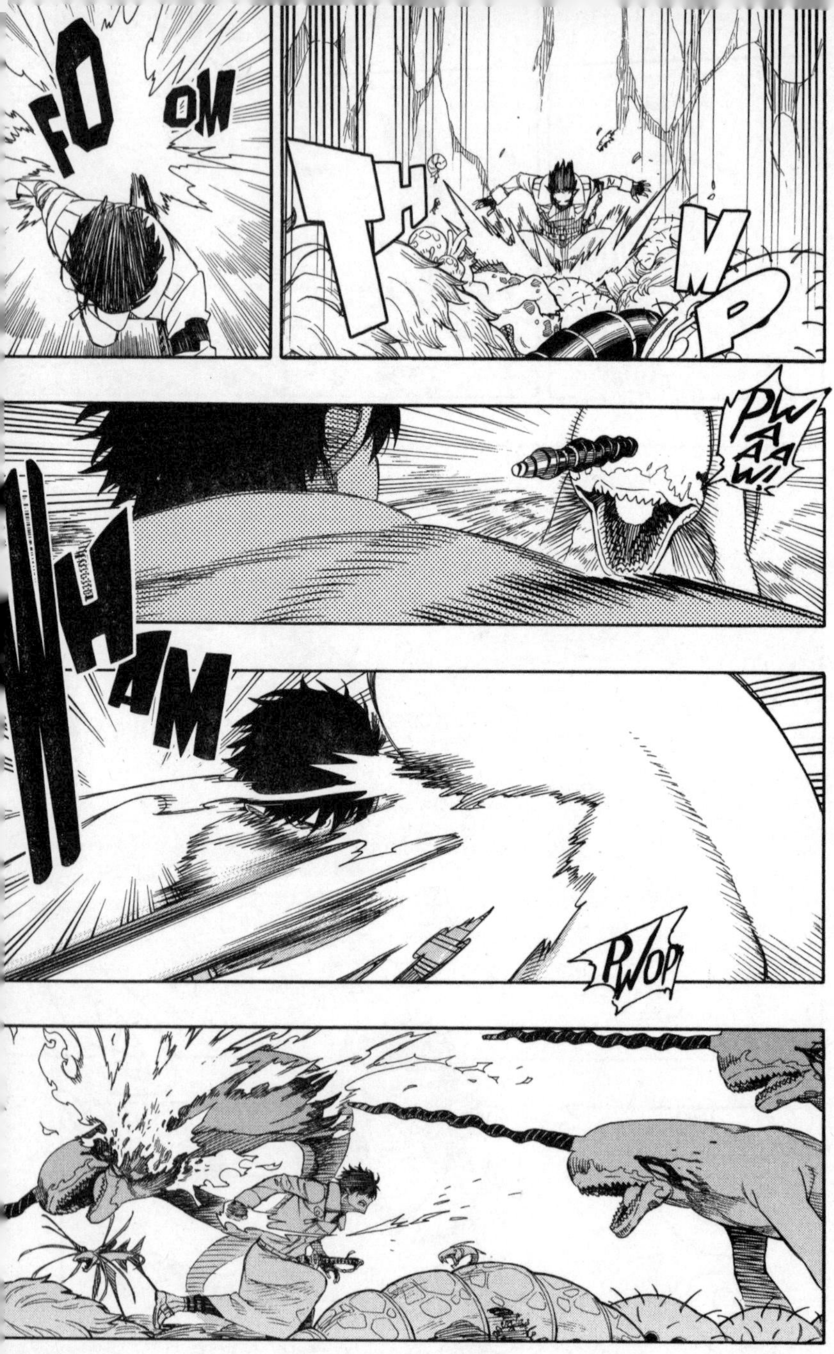
THMP
FOOM
PWAAAW!
WHAM
PWOP!

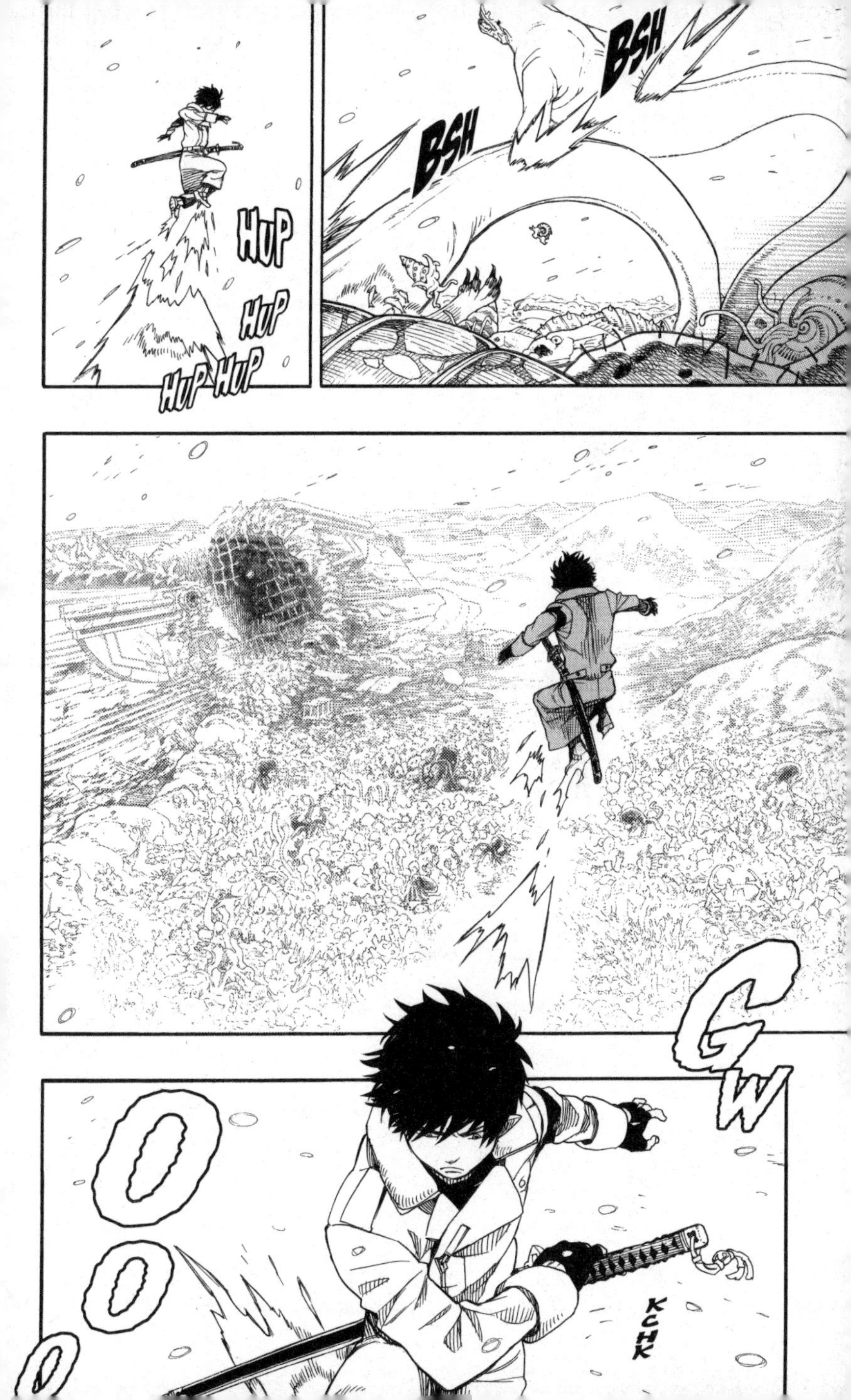

BSH
BSH
HUP
HUP
HUP HUP
GW
OOO
KCHK

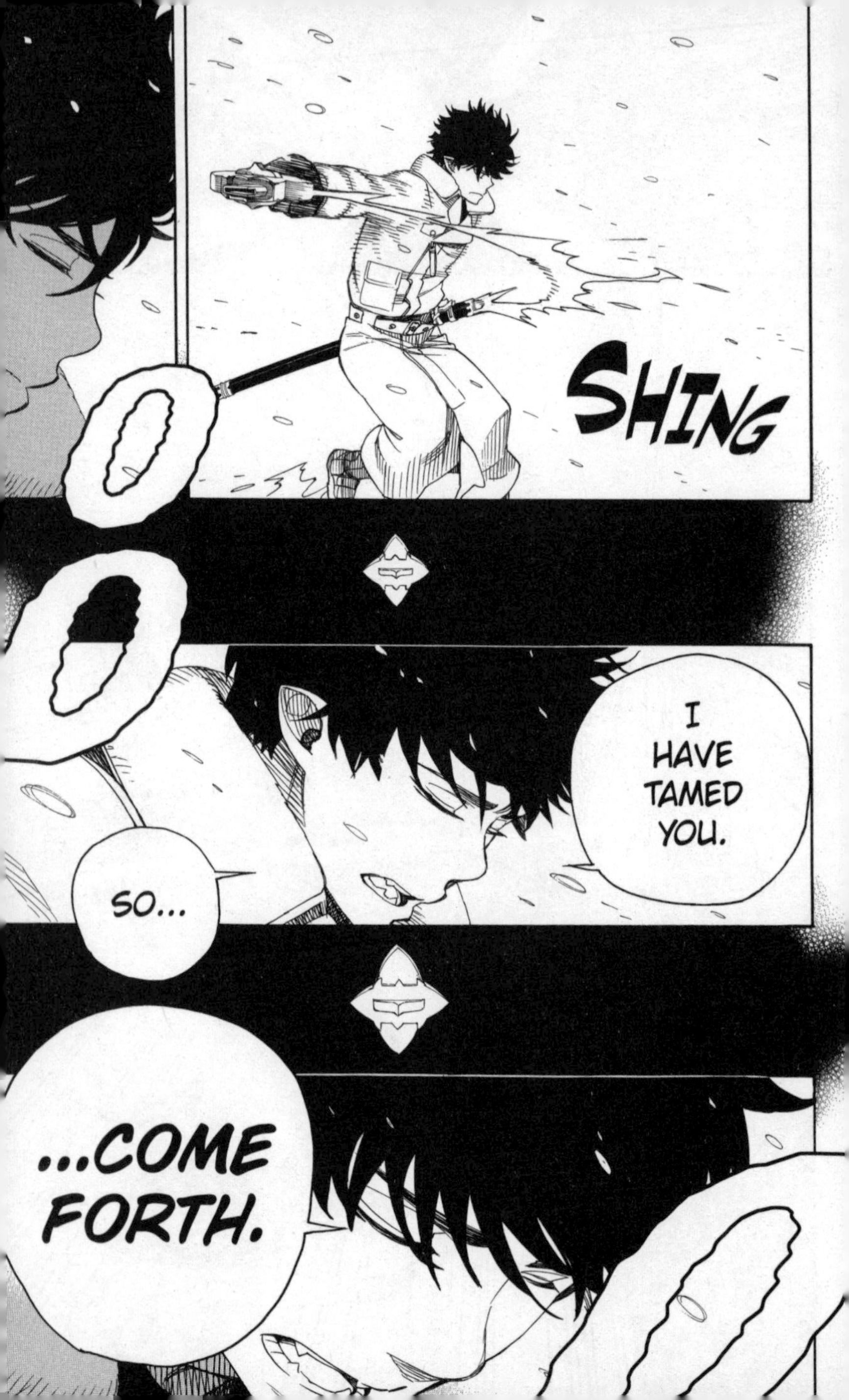
SHING
I HAVE TAMED YOU.
SO...
...COME FORTH.

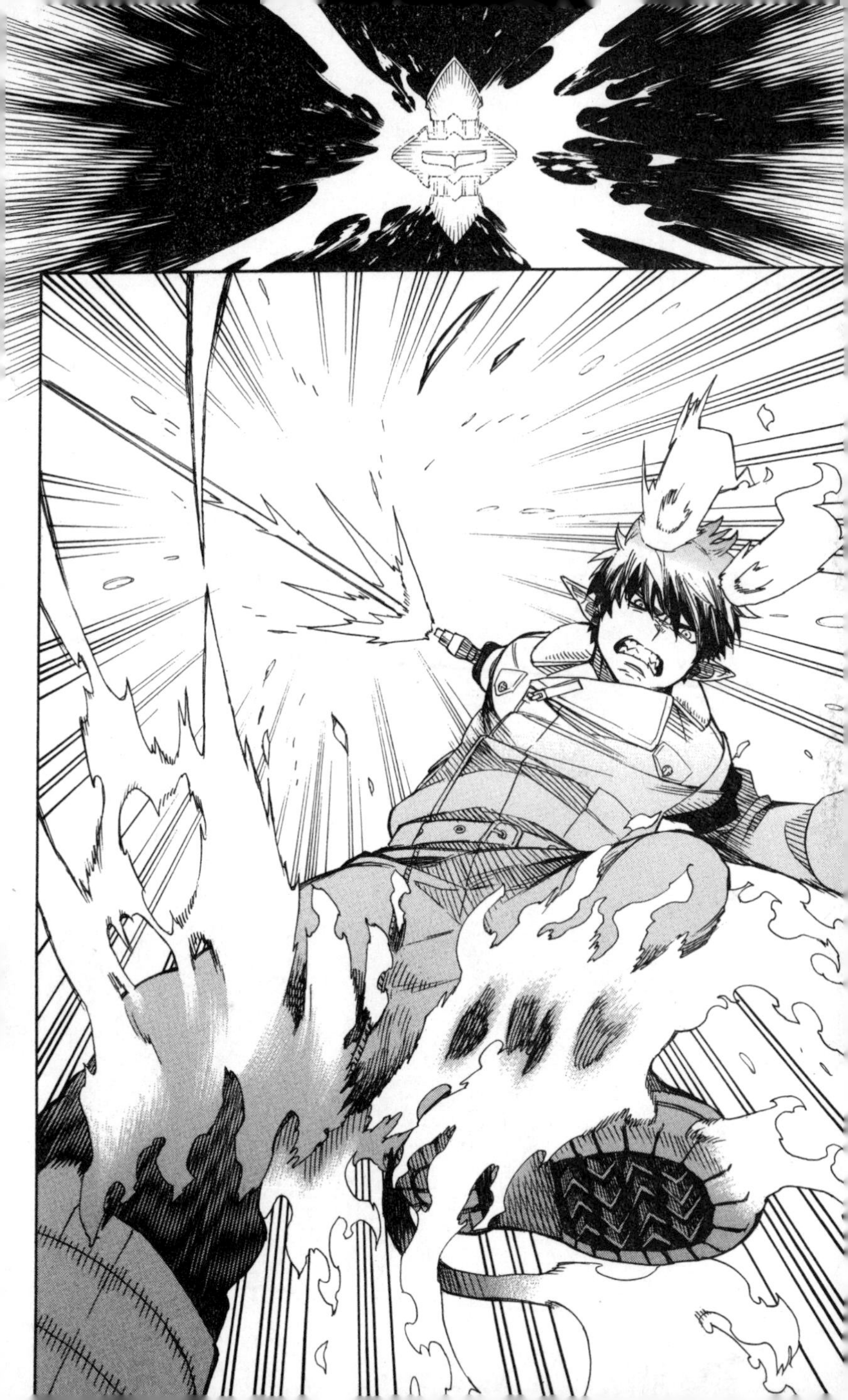

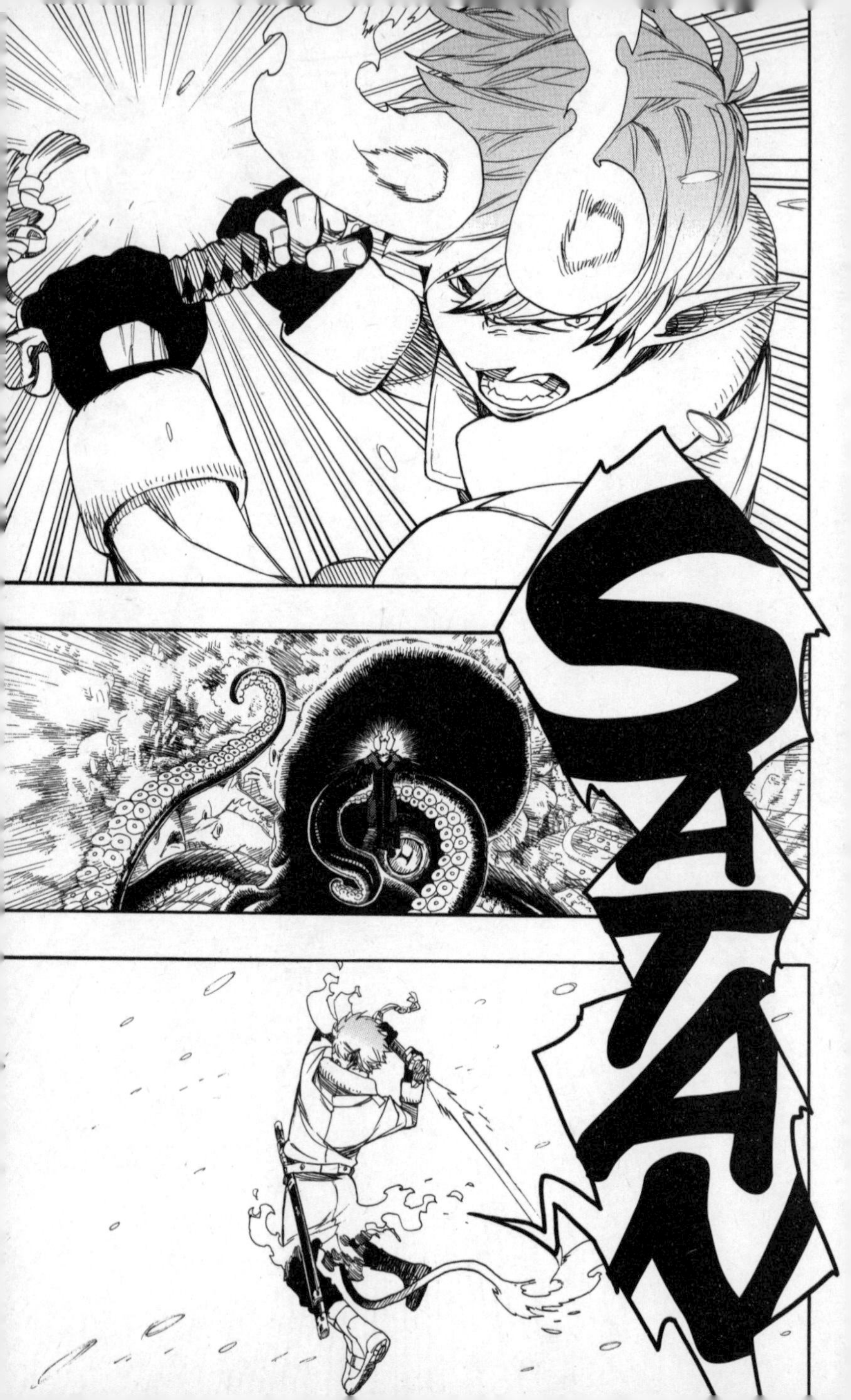

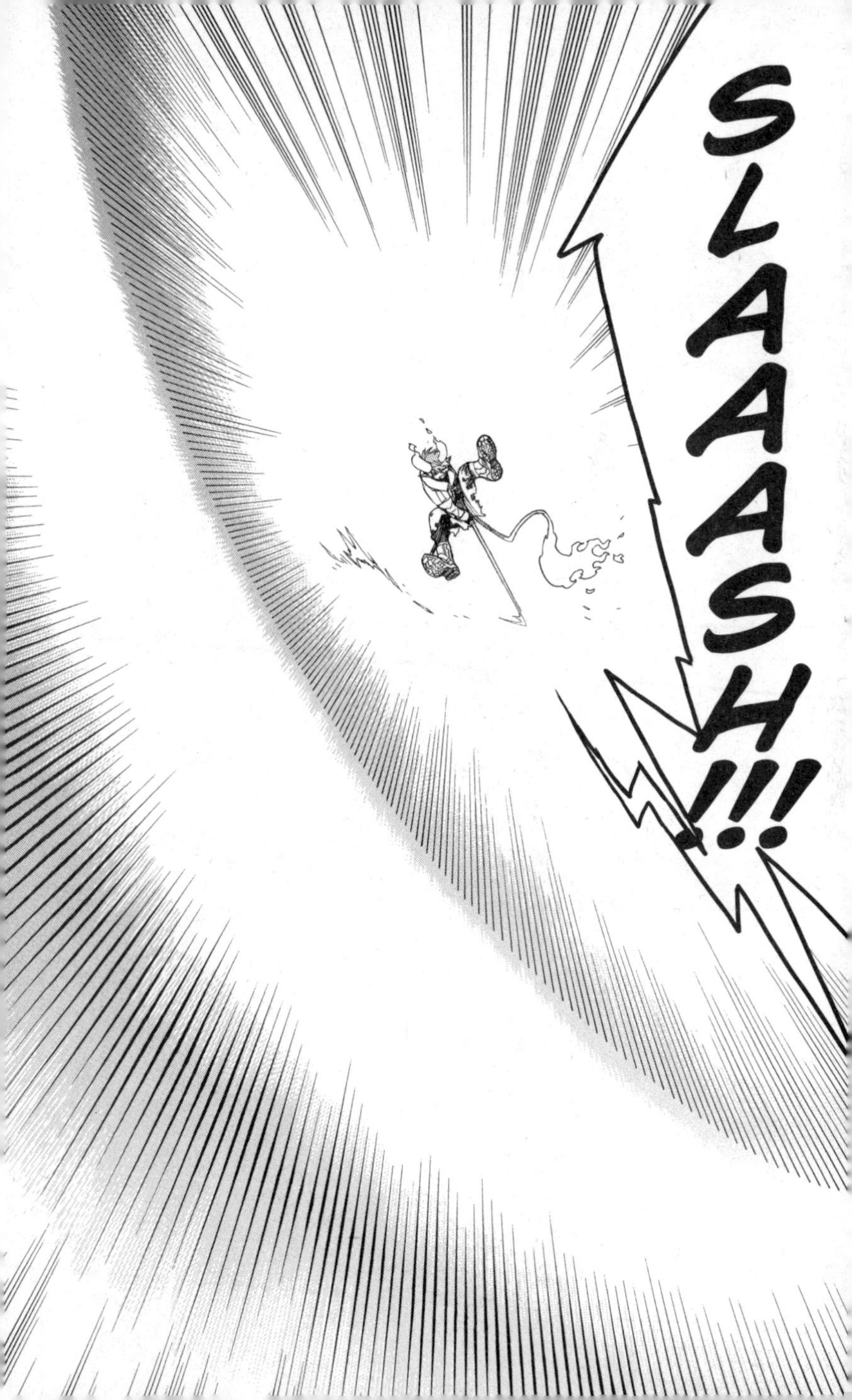
SLAAASH!!!

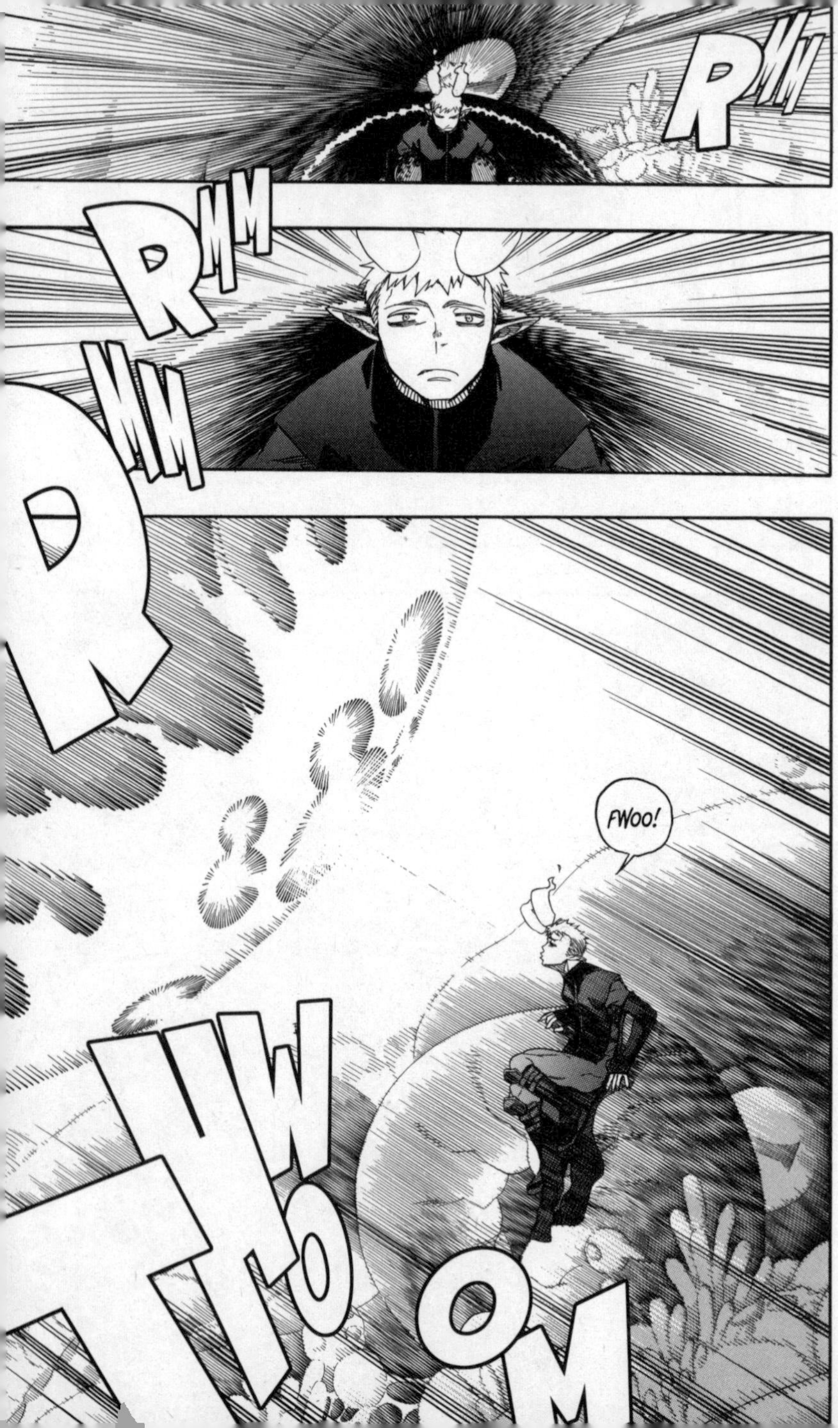
RMM
RMMM
RMMM
FWOO!
WHOOM

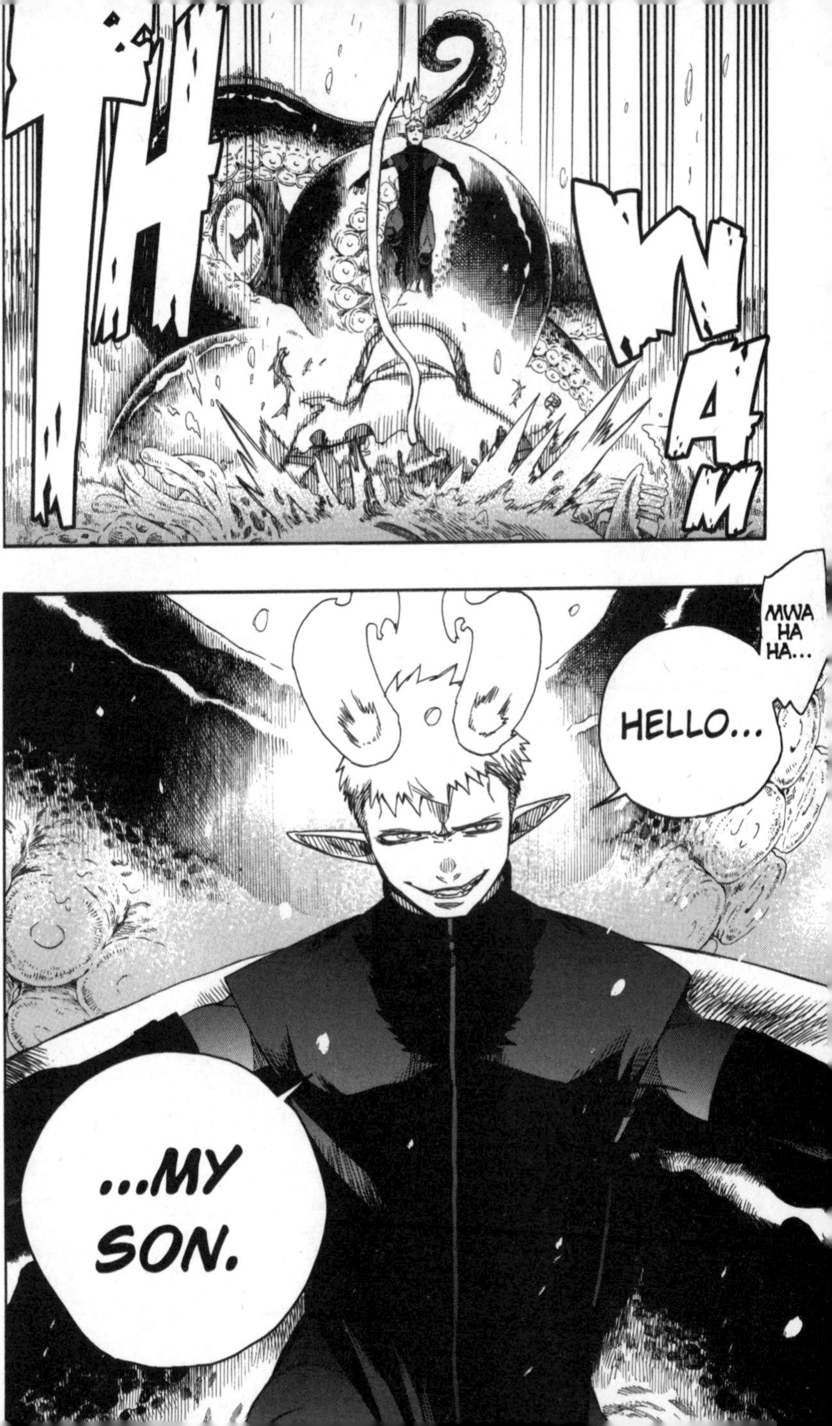
THWAM
MWA HA HA...
HELLO...
...MY SON.

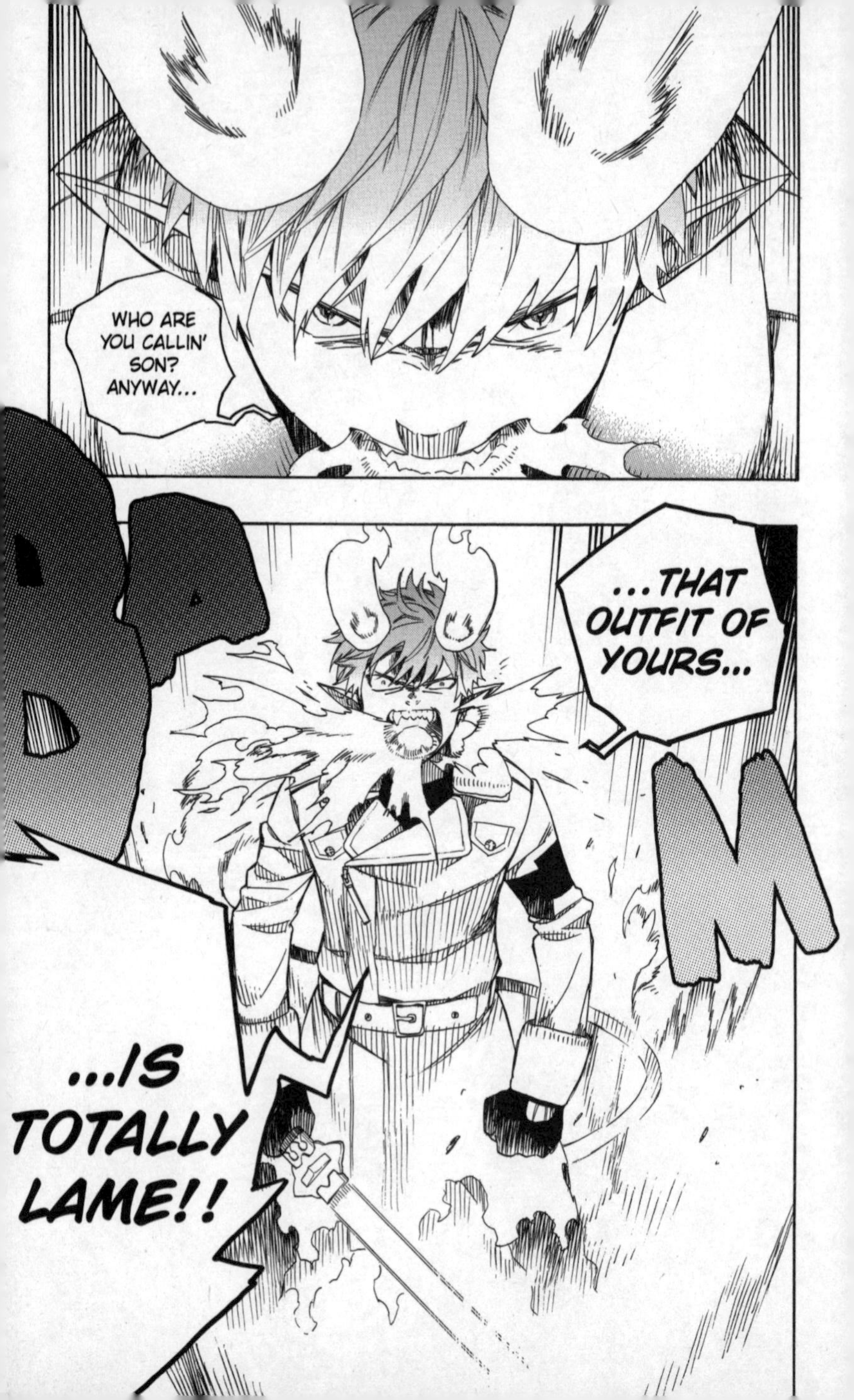
WHO ARE YOU CALLIN' SON? ANYWAY...
...THAT OUTFIT OF YOURS...
BAM
...IS TOTALLY LAME!!

Blue Exorcist Chapter 132: Of One Cloth—Eruption

Huh?

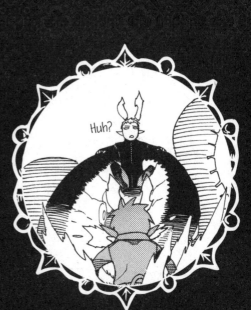

Chapter 133: Of One Cloth—Flutter

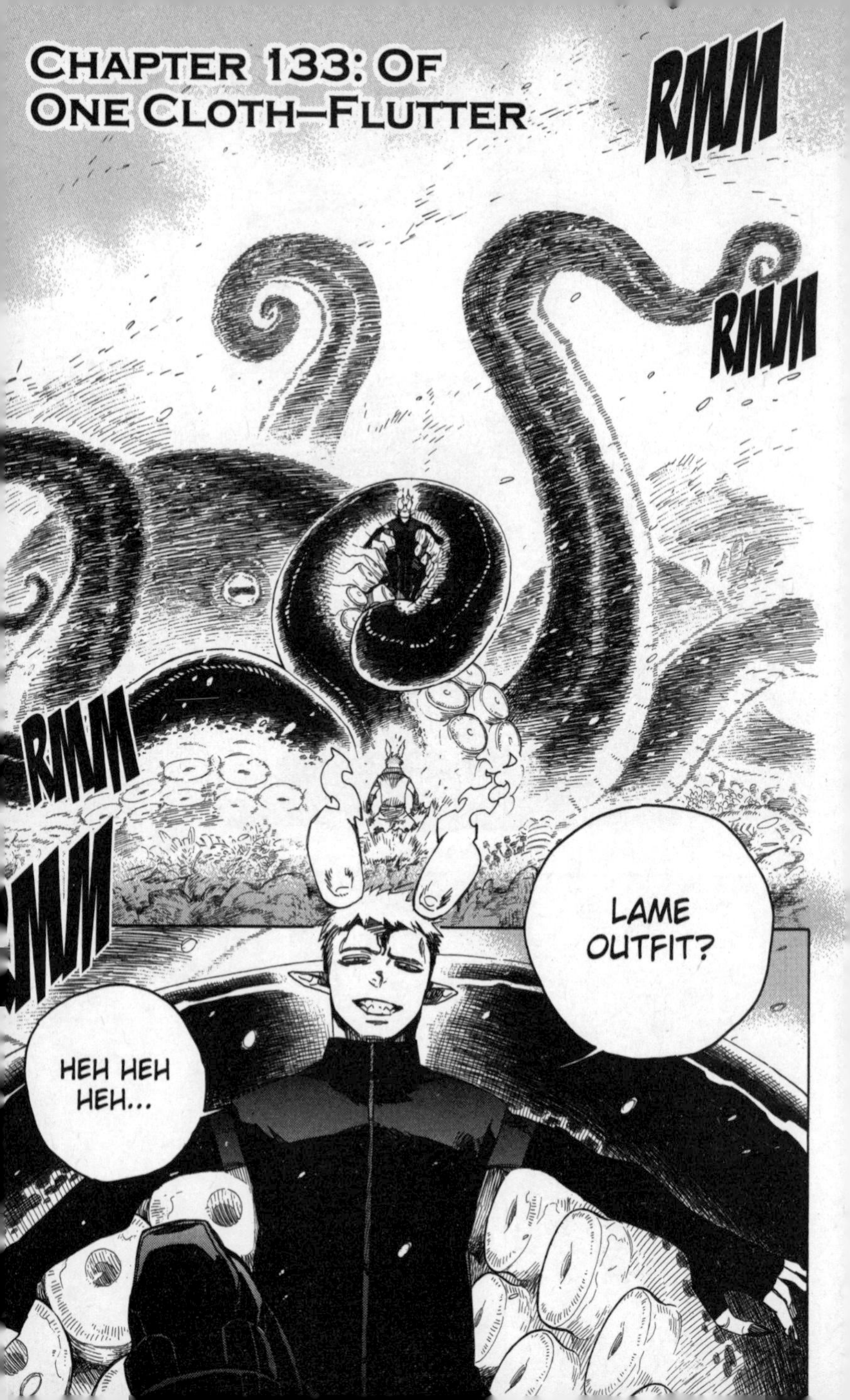
RMM
RMM
RMMM
LAME OUTFIT?
HEH HEH HEH...

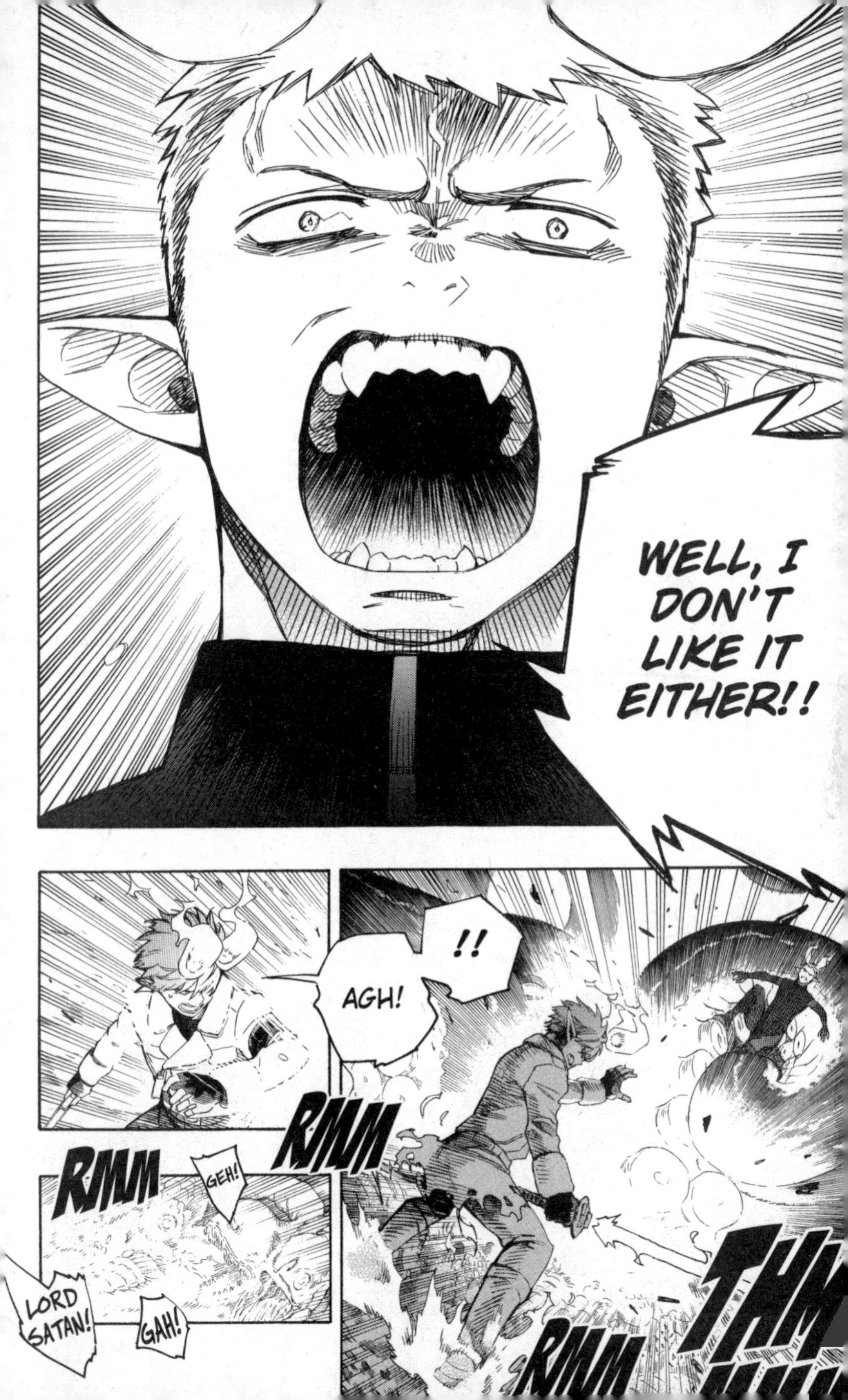
WELL, I DON'T LIKE IT EITHER!!
!!
RMM
RMM
THM
AGH!
RMM
GEH!
LORD SATAN!
GAH!

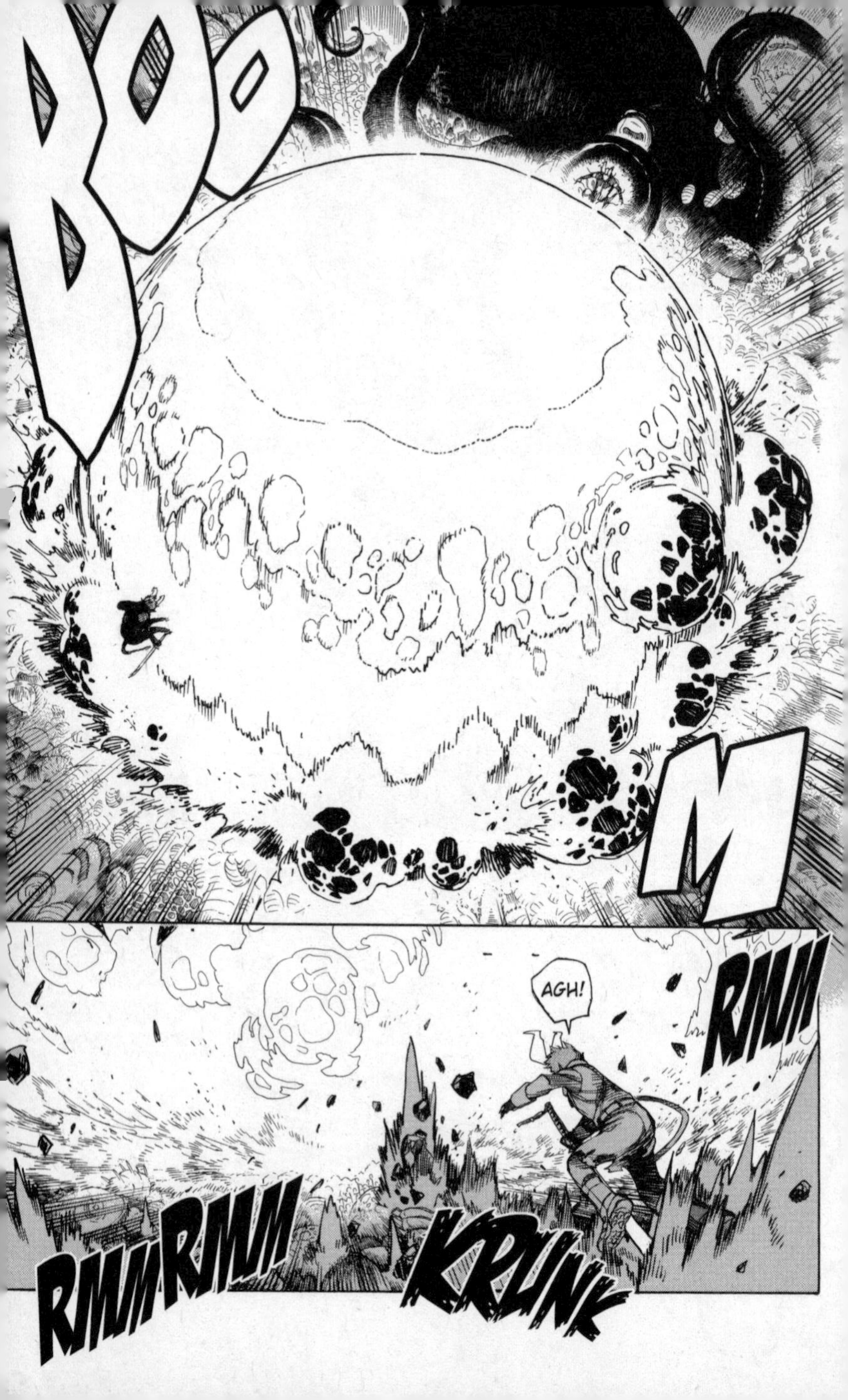
BOOM
RMM
AGH!
KRUNK
RMMRMM

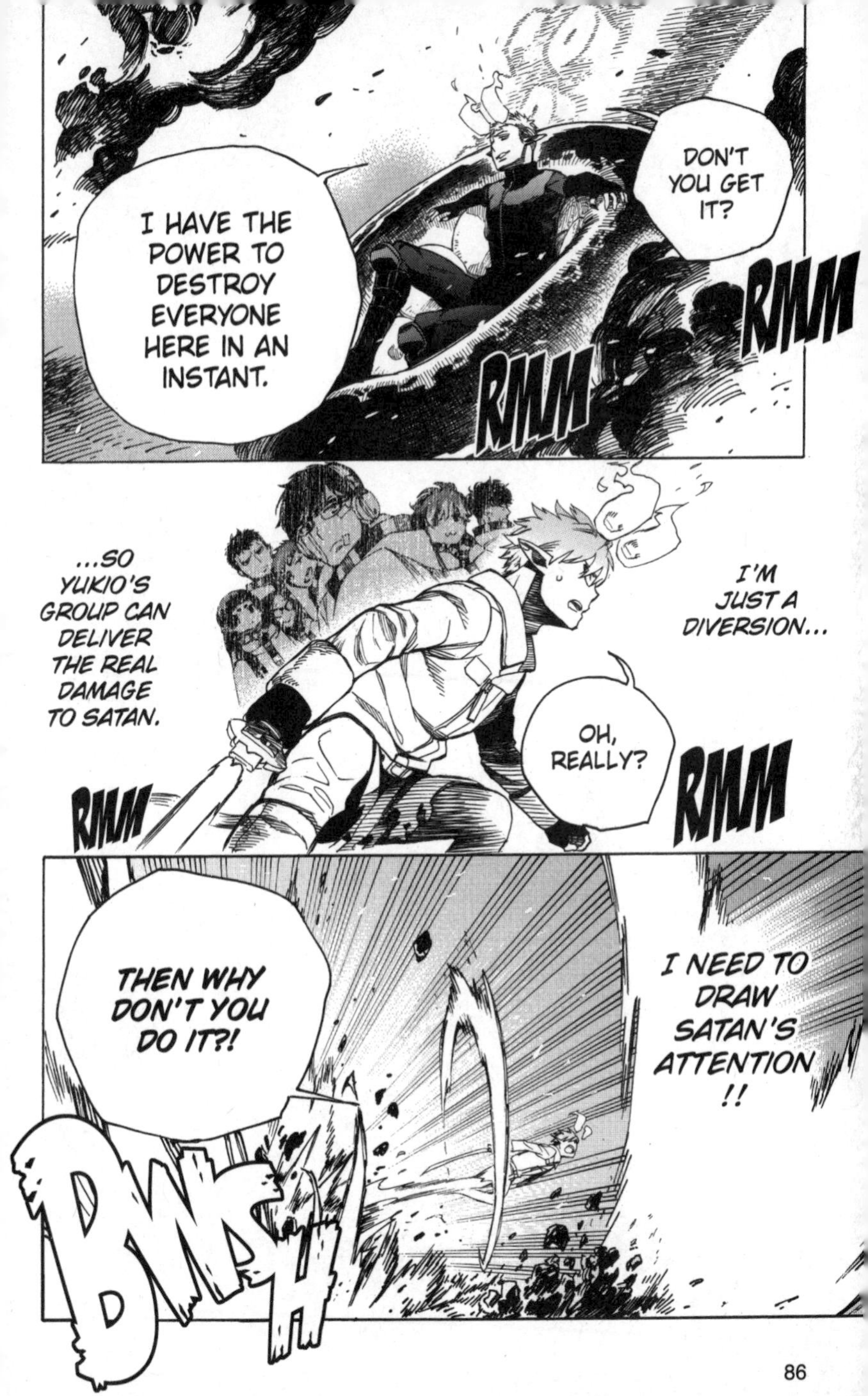
DON'T YOU GET IT?
I HAVE THE POWER TO DESTROY EVERYONE HERE IN AN INSTANT.
RMM
RMM
I'M JUST A DIVERSION...
...SO YUKIO'S GROUP CAN DELIVER THE REAL DAMAGE TO SATAN.
OH, REALLY?
RMM
RMM
I NEED TO DRAW SATAN'S ATTENTION !!
THEN WHY DON'T YOU DO IT?!
BWSH

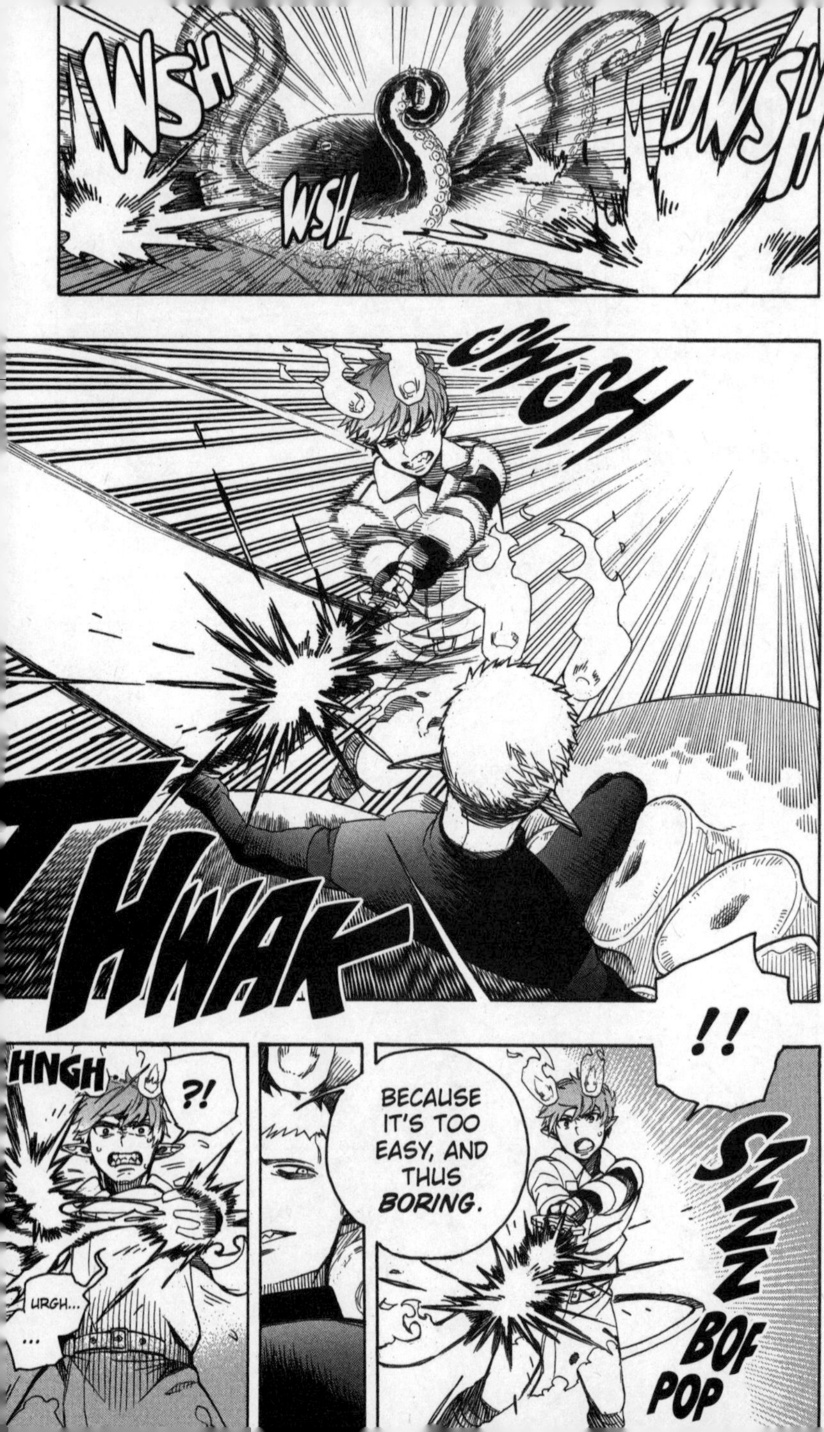
BWSH
WSH
WSH
SWSH
THWAK
!!
SWZZ
BOF
POP
BECAUSE IT'S TOO EASY, AND THUS *BORING*.
HNGH
?!
URGH...
...

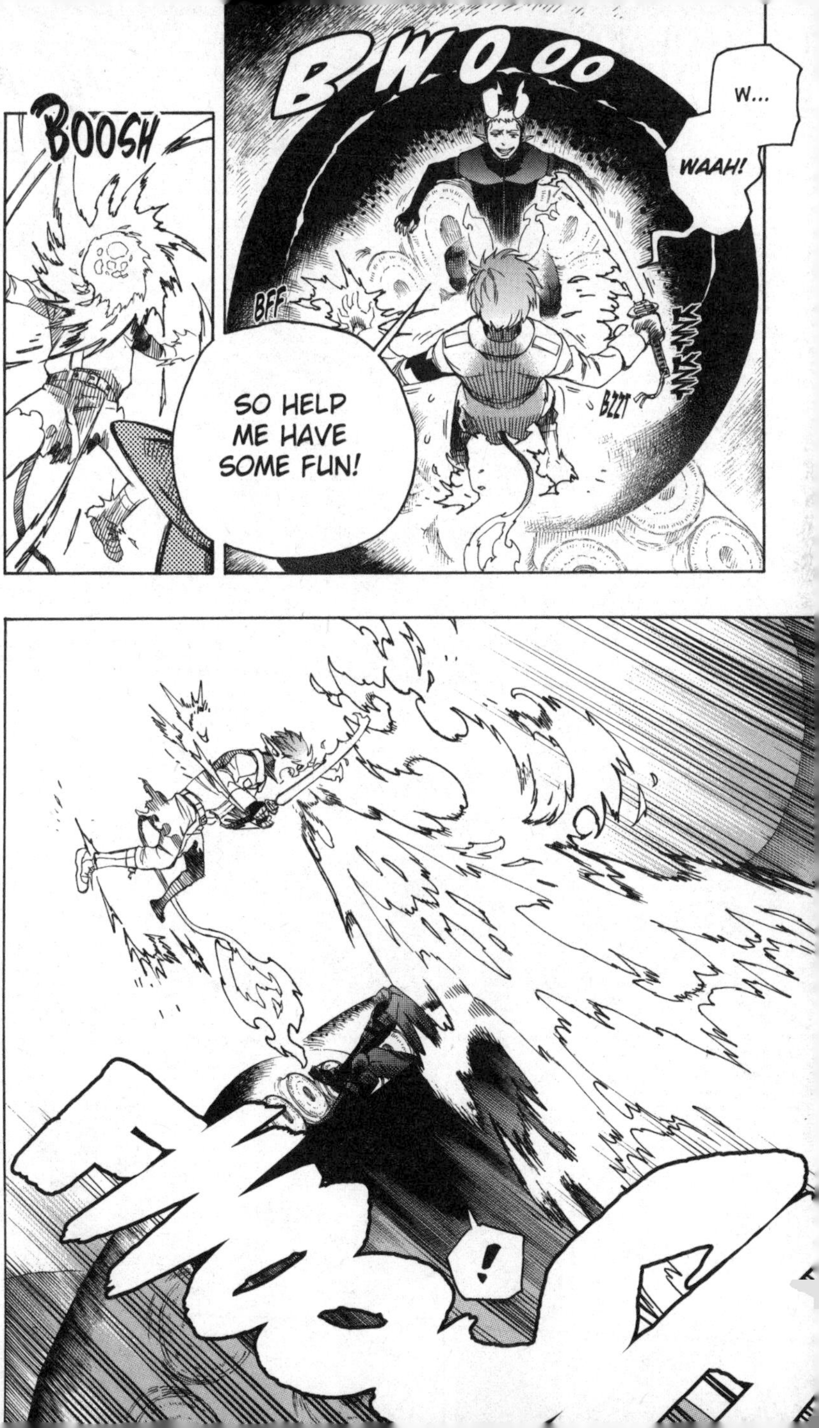

BWOOO
W...
WAAH!
BFF
BZZT
SO HELP ME HAVE SOME FUN!
BOOSH
!

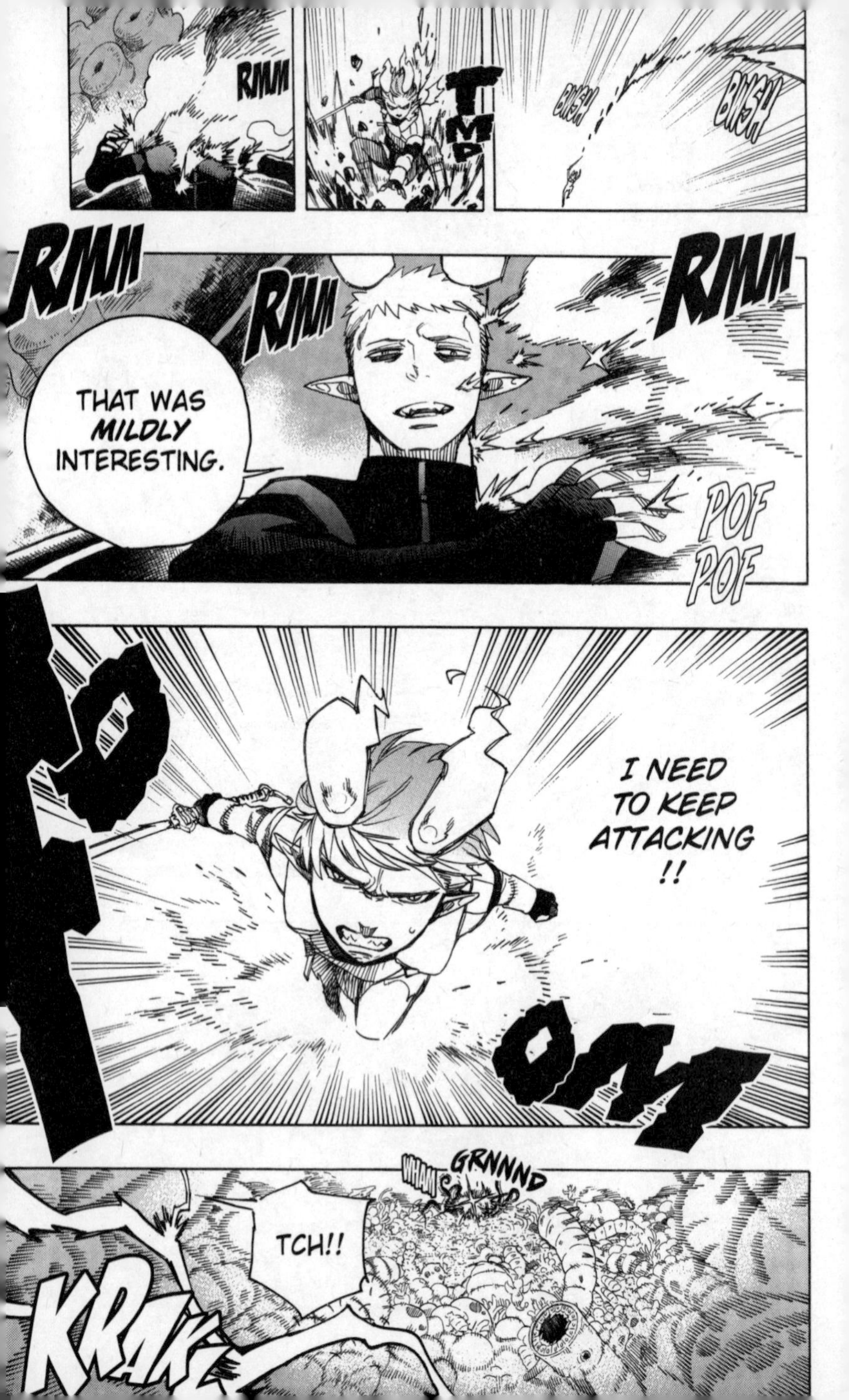
BWSH
BWSH
TMP
RMM
RMM
RMM
RMM
THAT WAS MILDLY INTERESTING.
POF POF
I NEED TO KEEP ATTACKING !!
GRNNND
WHAM
TCH!!
KRAK

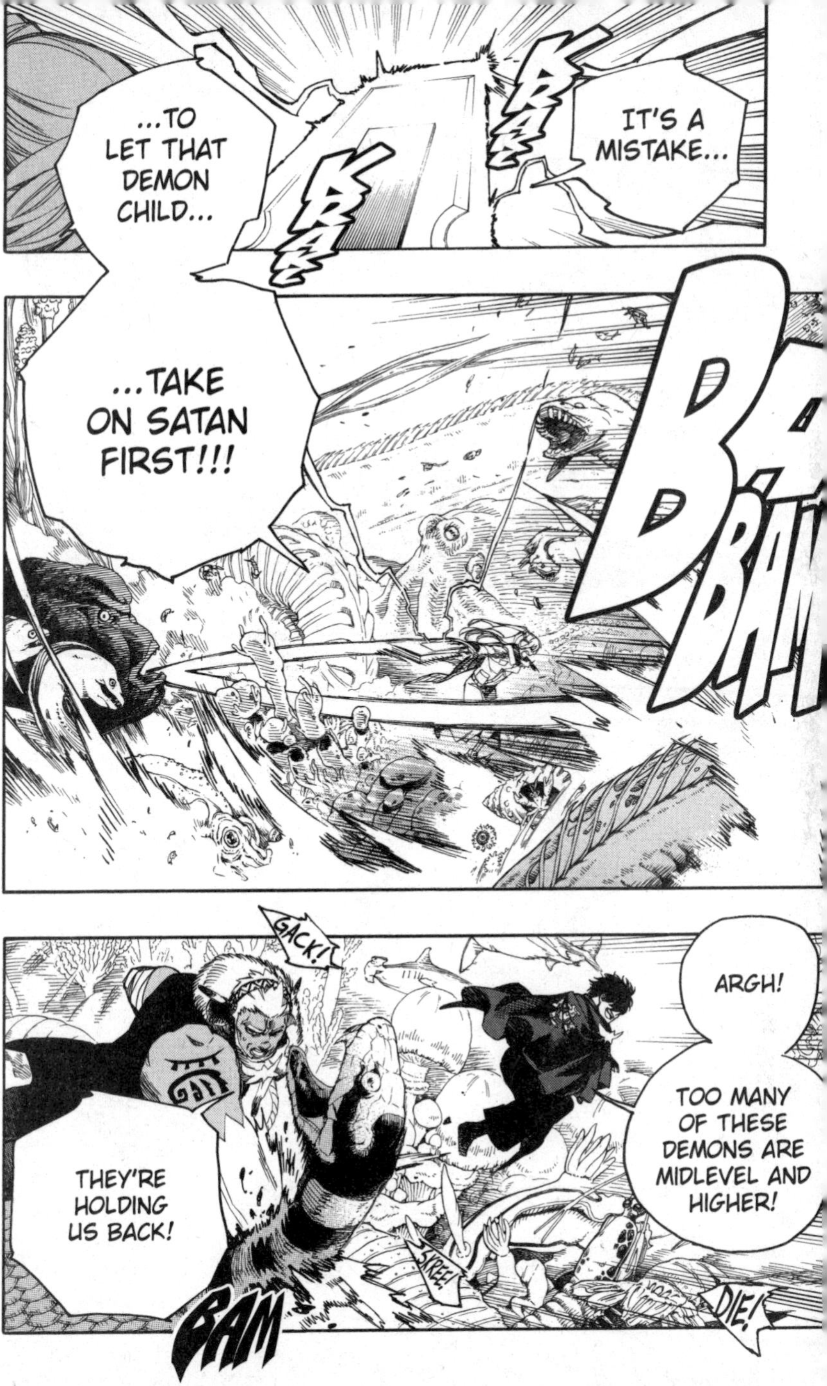
IT'S A MISTAKE...
...TO LET THAT DEMON CHILD...
...TAKE ON SATAN FIRST!!!
ARGH!
TOO MANY OF THESE DEMONS ARE MIDLEVEL AND HIGHER!
GACK!
THEY'RE HOLDING US BACK!
SKREE!
DIE!
BAM

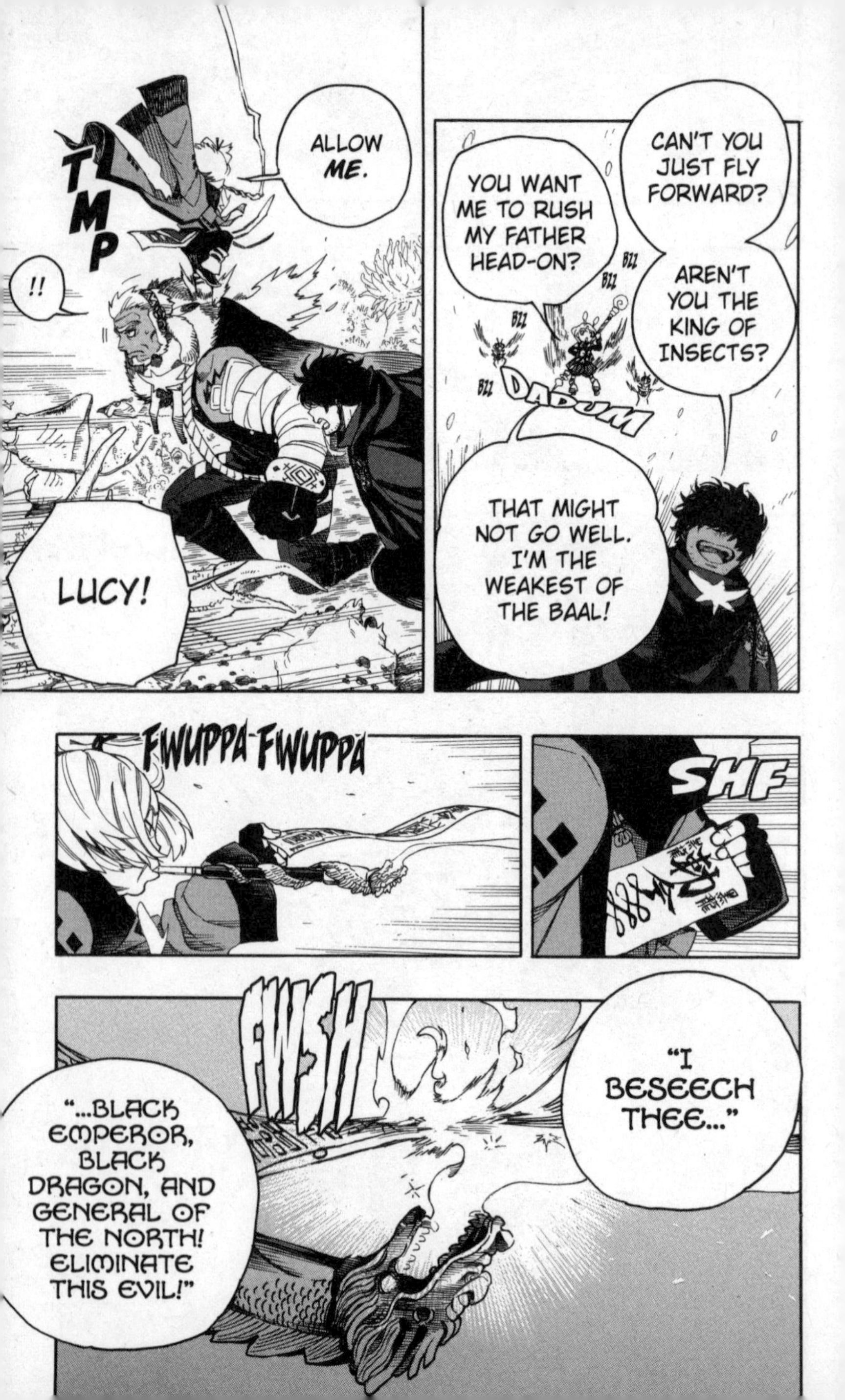

CAN'T YOU JUST FLY FORWARD?
AREN'T YOU THE KING OF INSECTS?
YOU WANT ME TO RUSH MY FATHER HEAD-ON?
BZZ
BZZ
BZZ
BZZ
DADUM
THAT MIGHT NOT GO WELL. I'M THE WEAKEST OF THE BAAL!
ALLOW ME.
TMP
!!
LUCY!
SHF
FWUPPA FWUPPA
"I BESEECH THEE..."
FWSH
"...BLACK EMPEROR, BLACK DRAGON, AND GENERAL OF THE NORTH! ELIMINATE THIS EVIL!"

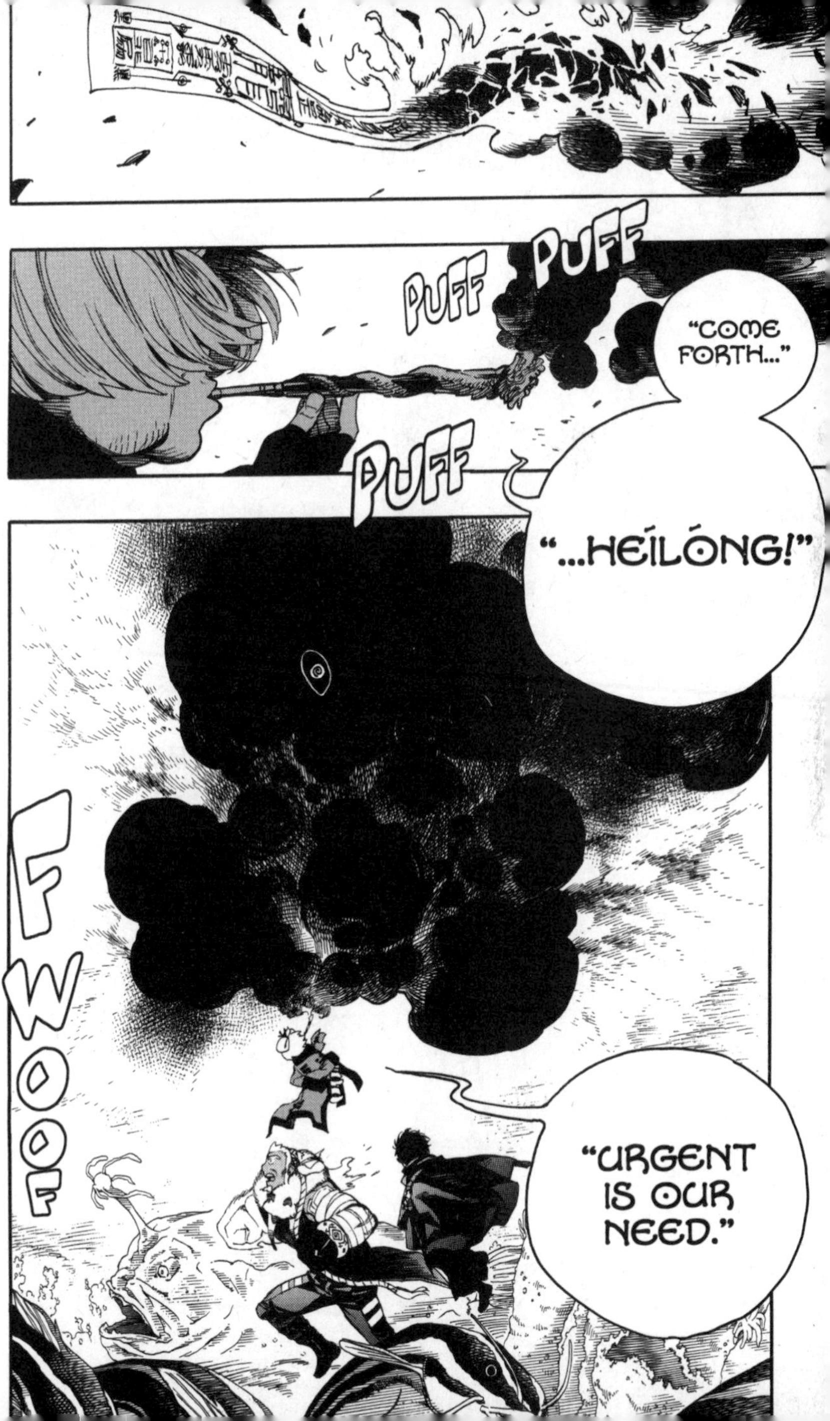
PUFF
PUFF
"COME FORTH..."
PUFF
"...HEÍLÓNG!"
"URGENT IS OUR NEED."
FWOOF

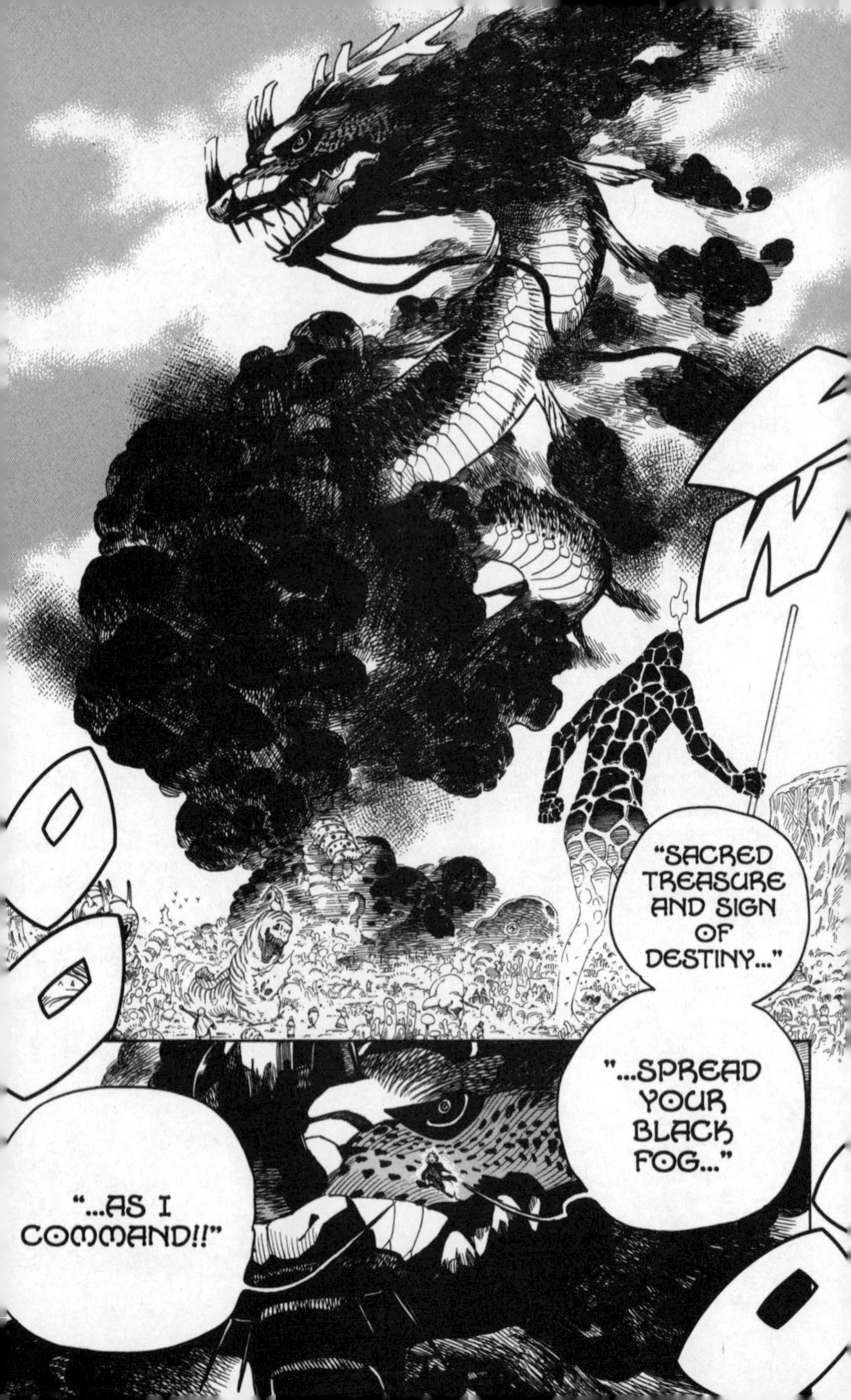
"SACRED TREASURE AND SIGN OF DESTINY..."
"...SPREAD YOUR BLACK FOG..."
"...AS I COMMAND!!"

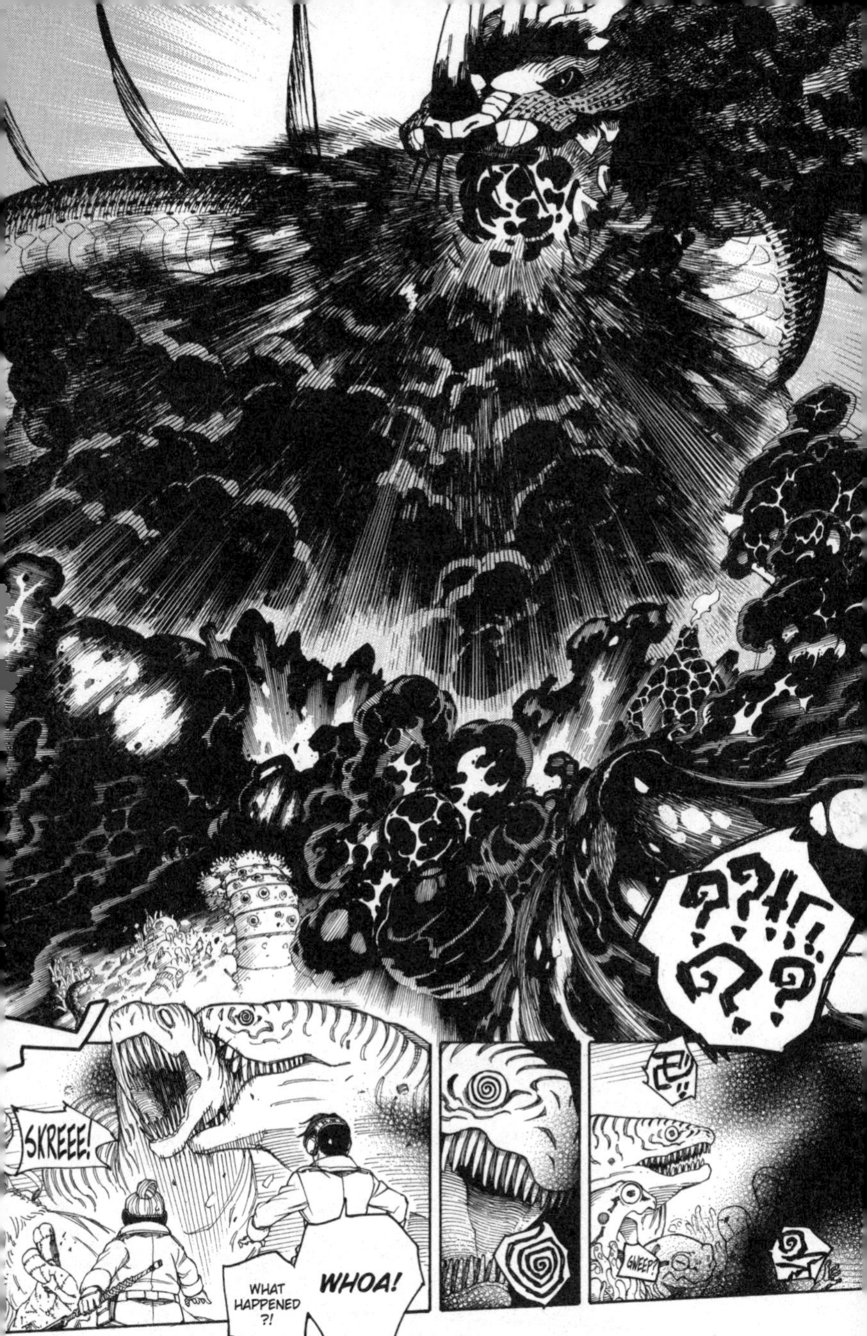
??!!
??
GWEEP?
SKREEE!
WHOA!
WHAT HAPPENED ?!

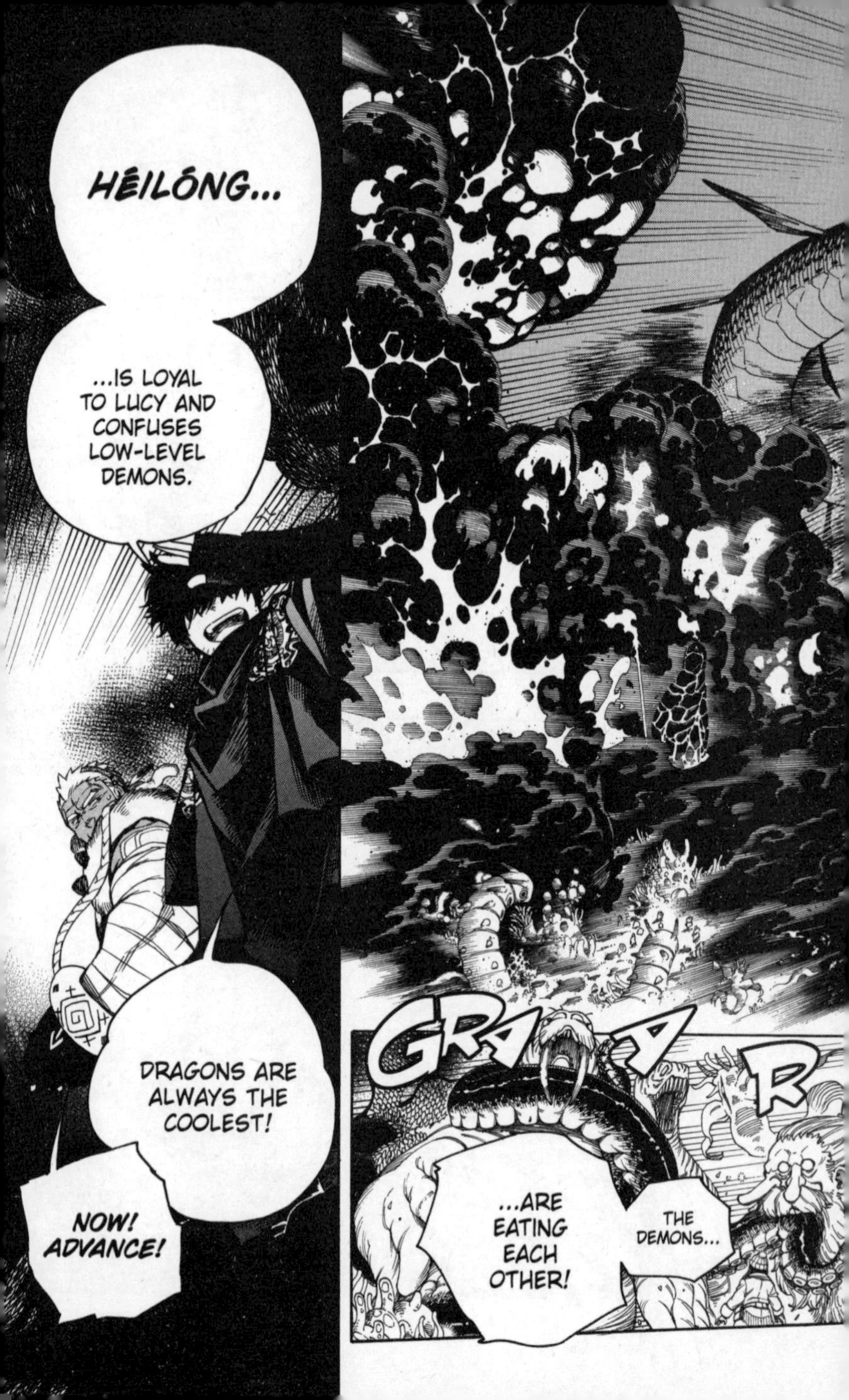
GRAAR
THE DEMONS...
...ARE EATING EACH OTHER!
HÊILÓNG...
...IS LOYAL TO LUCY AND CONFUSES LOW-LEVEL DEMONS.
DRAGONS ARE ALWAYS THE COOLEST!
NOW! ADVANCE!

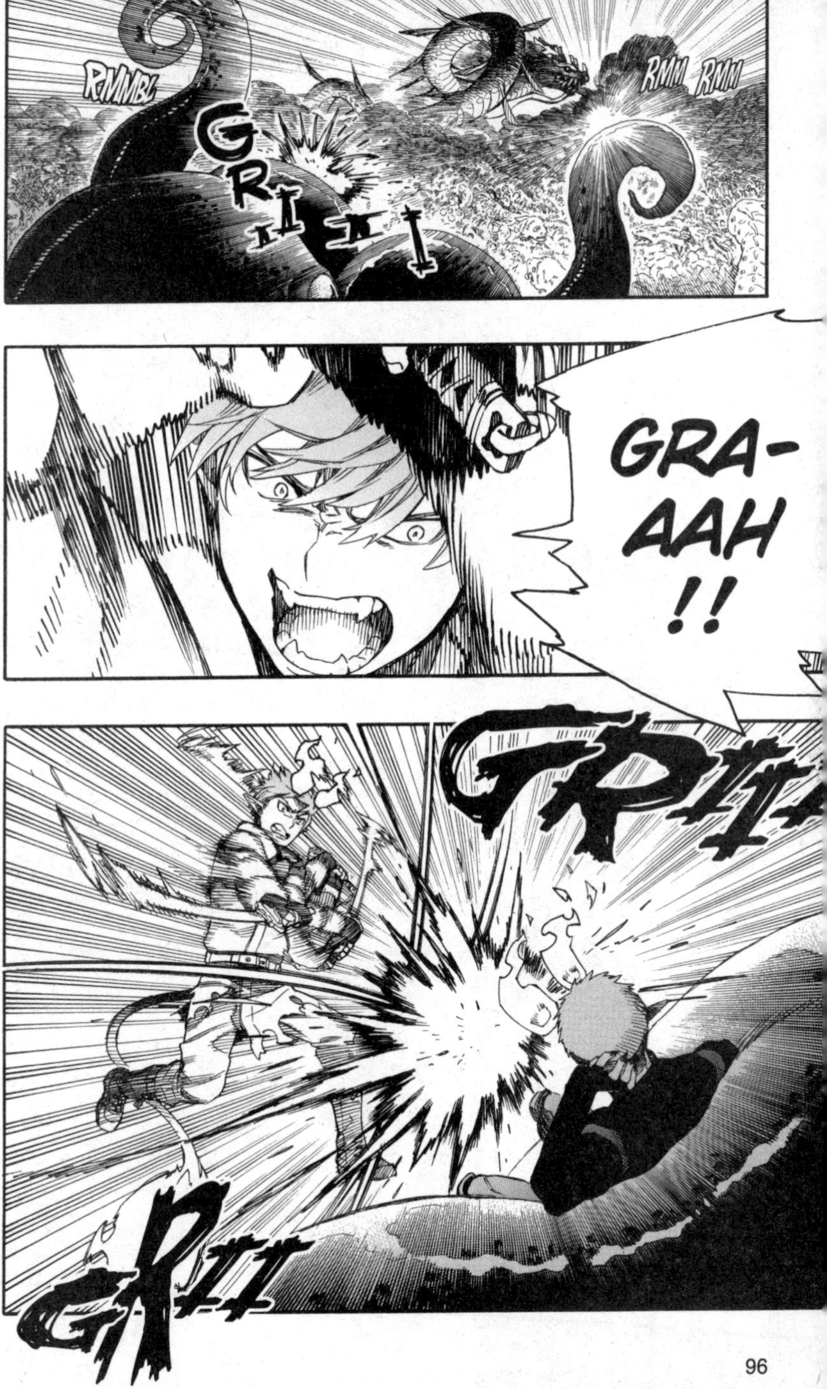
RMM RMM
RMMBL
GRIII
GRA-AAH!!
GRII
GRII

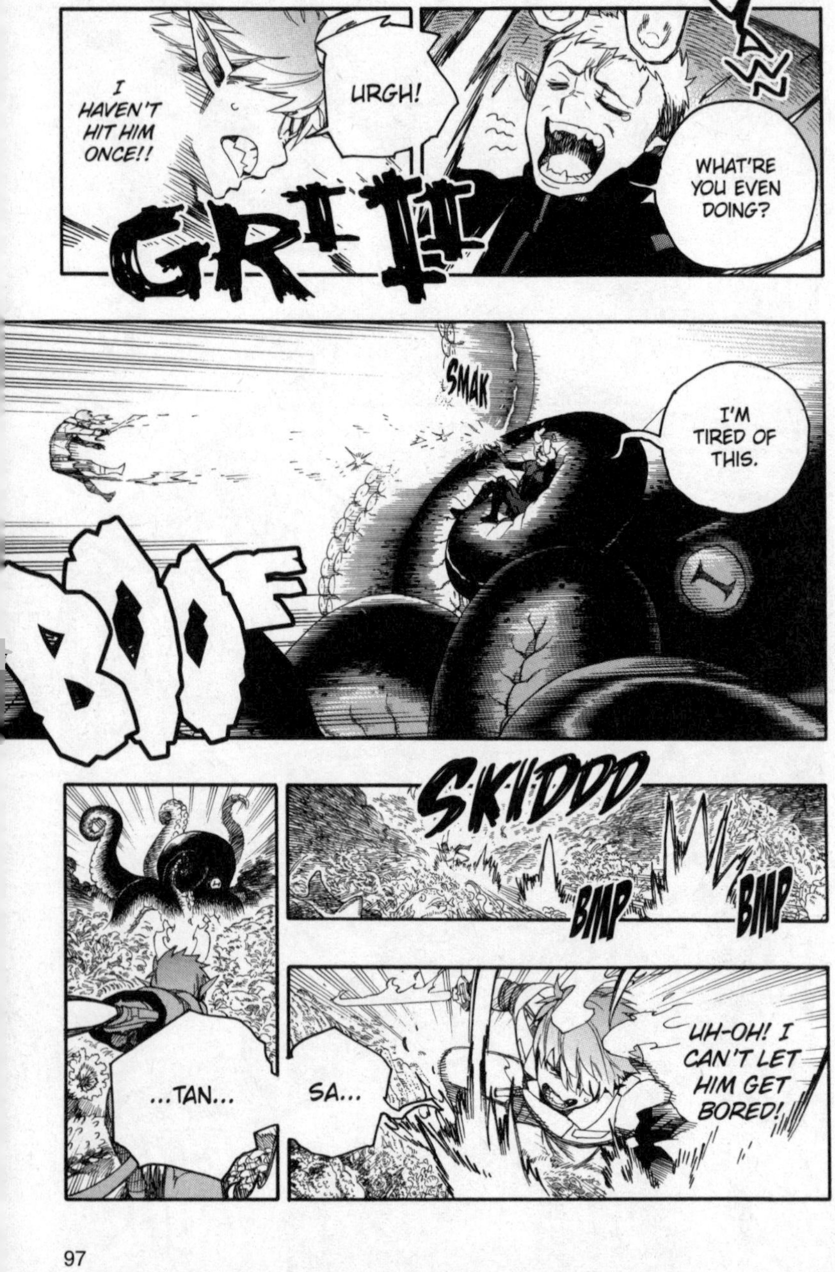
YAWN
WHAT'RE YOU EVEN DOING?
URGH!
I HAVEN'T HIT HIM ONCE!!
GRIII
I'M TIRED OF THIS.
SMAK
BOOF
SKIDDD
BMP
BMP
UH-OH! I CAN'T LET HIM GET BORED!
SA...
...TAN...

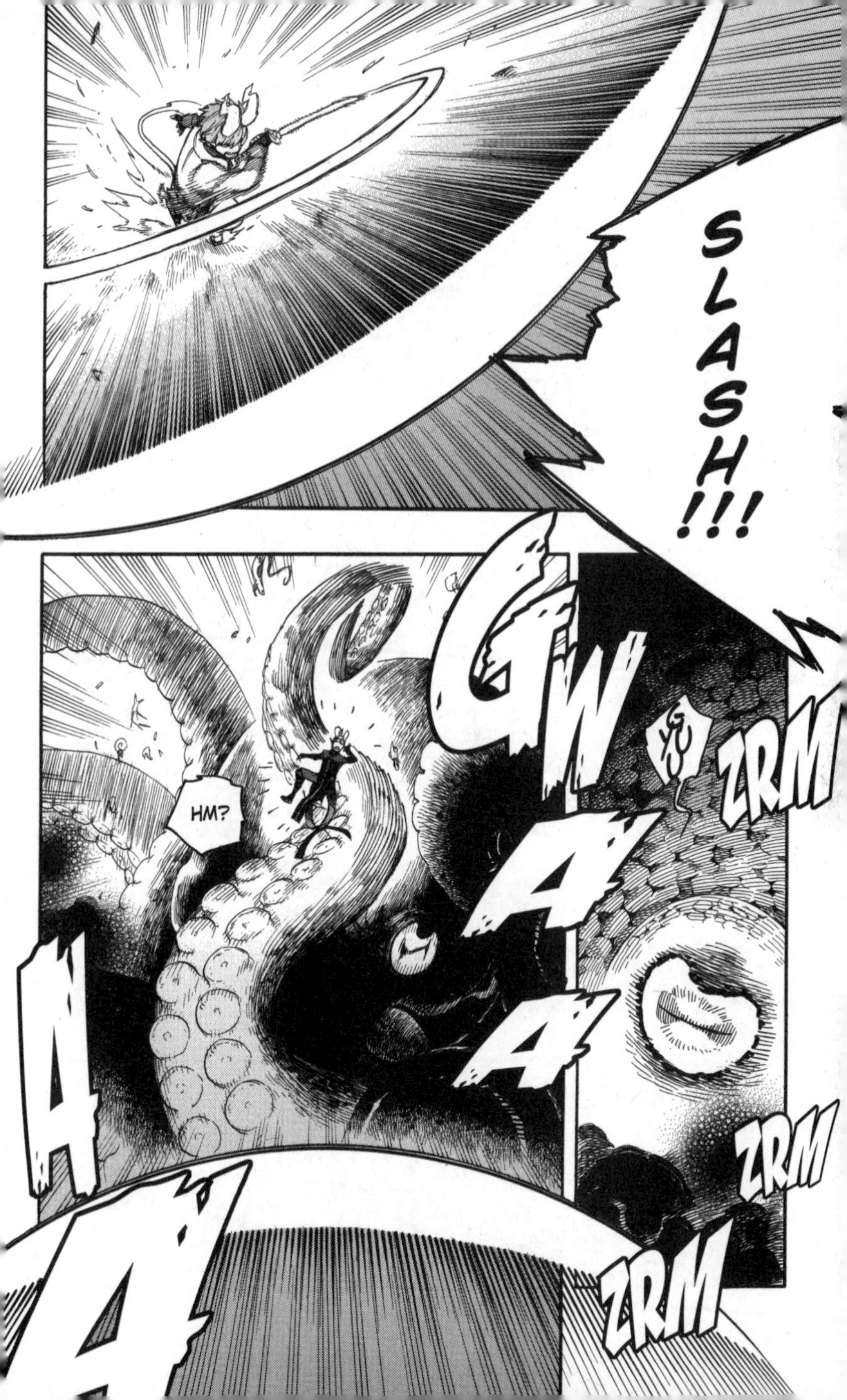
SLASH!!!
GWAAAAA
ZRM
ZRM
ZRM
HM?

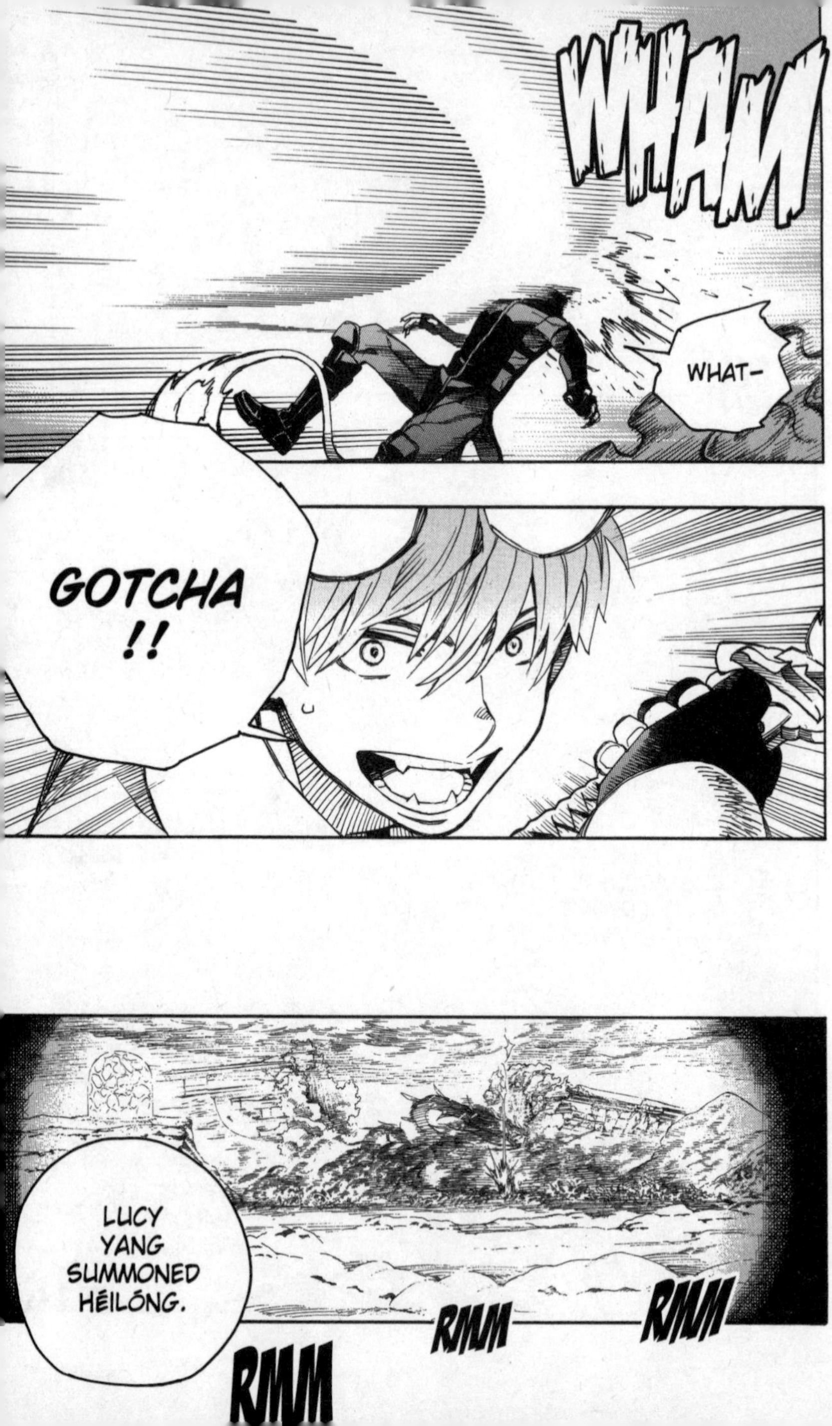
WHAM
WHAT-
GOTCHA !!
LUCY YANG SUMMONED HÉILÓNG.
RMM
RMM
RMM

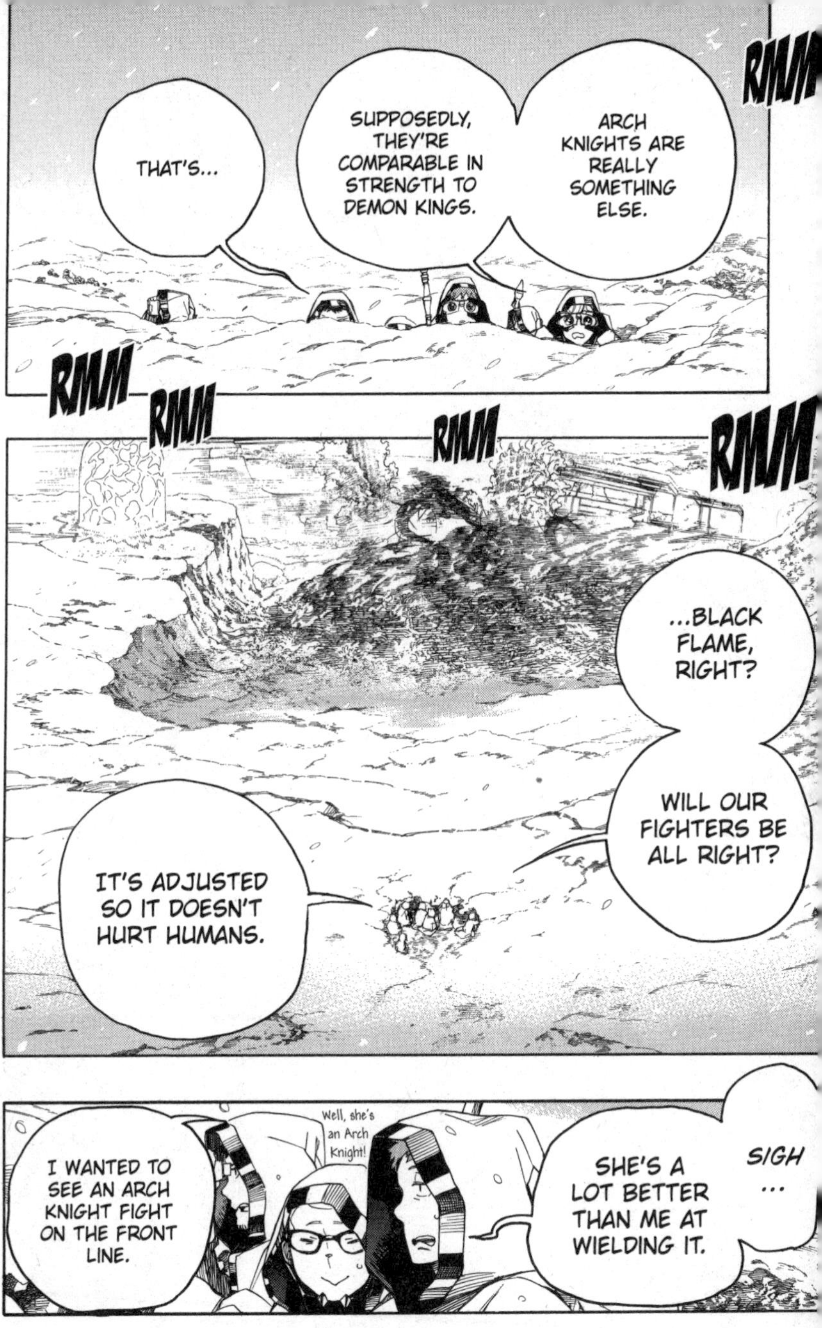
RMM
ARCH KNIGHTS ARE REALLY SOMETHING ELSE.
SUPPOSEDLY, THEY'RE COMPARABLE IN STRENGTH TO DEMON KINGS.
THAT'S...
RMM
RMM
RMM
RMM
RMM
...BLACK FLAME, RIGHT?
WILL OUR FIGHTERS BE ALL RIGHT?
IT'S ADJUSTED SO IT DOESN'T HURT HUMANS.
SIGH ...
SHE'S A LOT BETTER THAN ME AT WIELDING IT.
Well, she's an Arch Knight!
I WANTED TO SEE AN ARCH KNIGHT FIGHT ON THE FRONT LINE.

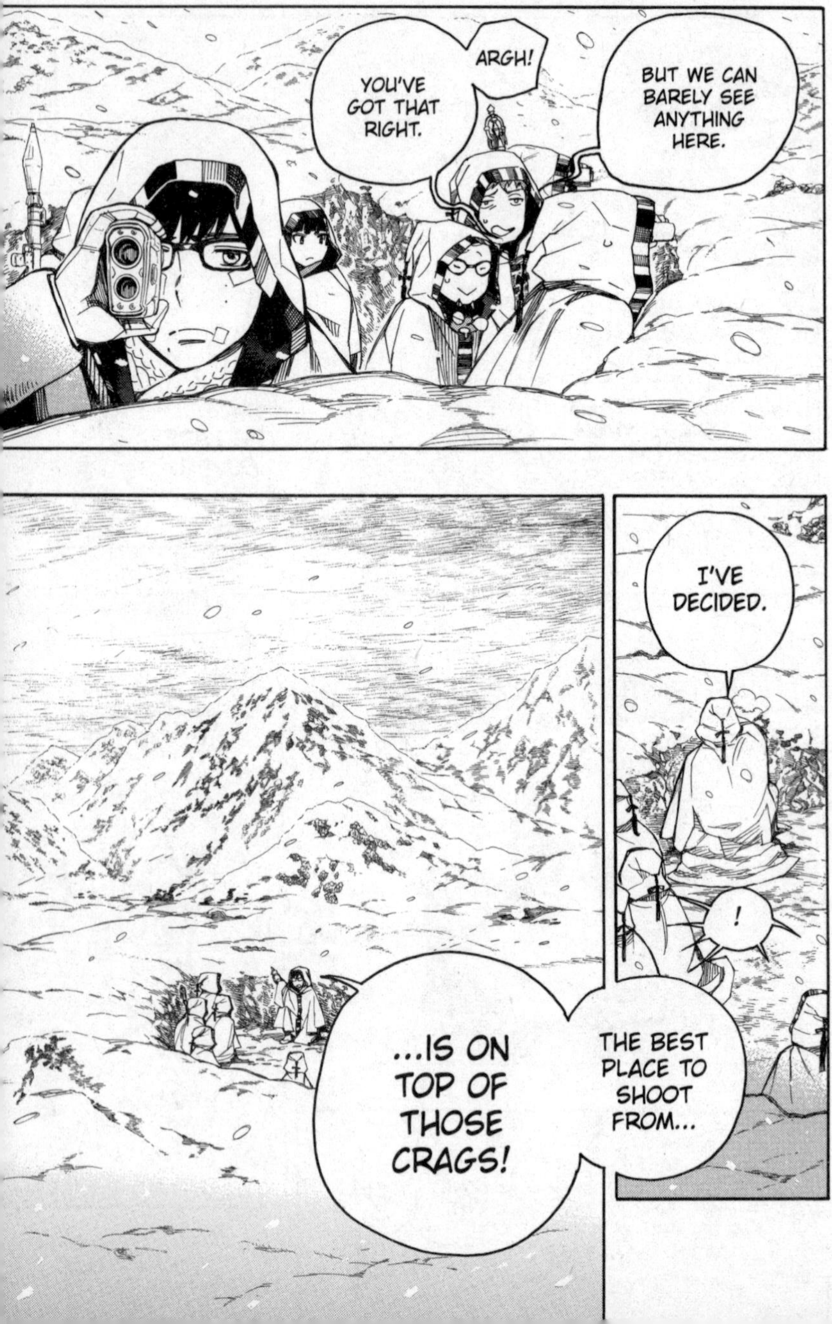
BUT WE CAN BARELY SEE ANYTHING HERE.
ARGH!
YOU'VE GOT THAT RIGHT.
I'VE DECIDED.
!
THE BEST PLACE TO SHOOT FROM...
...IS ON TOP OF THOSE CRAGS!

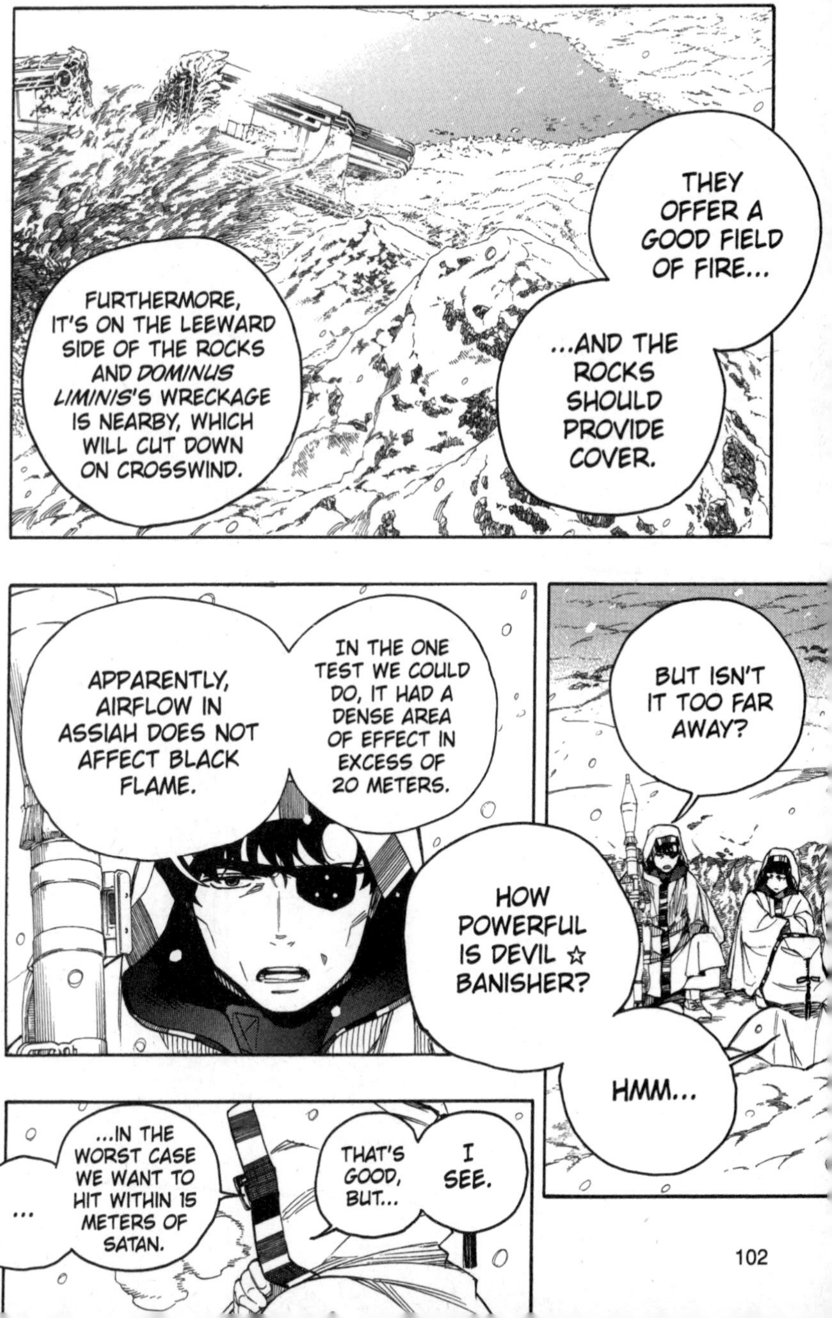
THEY OFFER A GOOD FIELD OF FIRE...
...AND THE ROCKS SHOULD PROVIDE COVER.
FURTHERMORE, IT'S ON THE LEEWARD SIDE OF THE ROCKS AND *DOMINUS LIMINIS*'S WRECKAGE IS NEARBY, WHICH WILL CUT DOWN ON CROSSWIND.
BUT ISN'T IT TOO FAR AWAY?
HOW POWERFUL IS DEVIL ☆ BANISHER?
HMM...
APPARENTLY, AIRFLOW IN ASSIAH DOES NOT AFFECT BLACK FLAME.
IN THE ONE TEST WE COULD DO, IT HAD A DENSE AREA OF EFFECT IN EXCESS OF 20 METERS.
I SEE.
THAT'S GOOD, BUT...
...IN THE WORST CASE WE WANT TO HIT WITHIN 15 METERS OF SATAN.
...

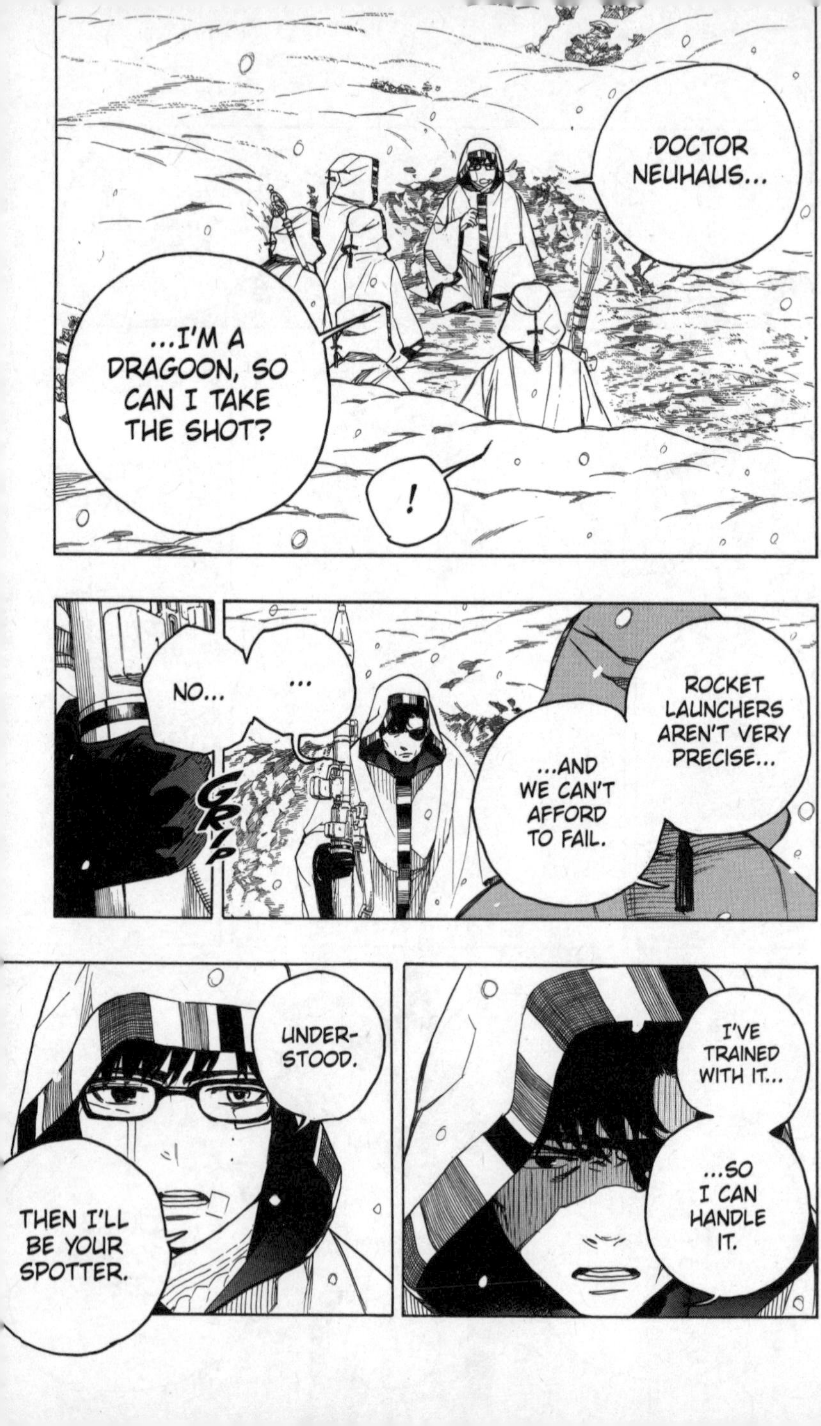

DOCTOR NEUHAUS...
...I'M A DRAGOON, SO CAN I TAKE THE SHOT?
!
ROCKET LAUNCHERS AREN'T VERY PRECISE...
...AND WE CAN'T AFFORD TO FAIL.
...
NO...
GRIP
I'VE TRAINED WITH IT...
...SO I CAN HANDLE IT.
UNDER-STOOD.
THEN I'LL BE YOUR SPOTTER.

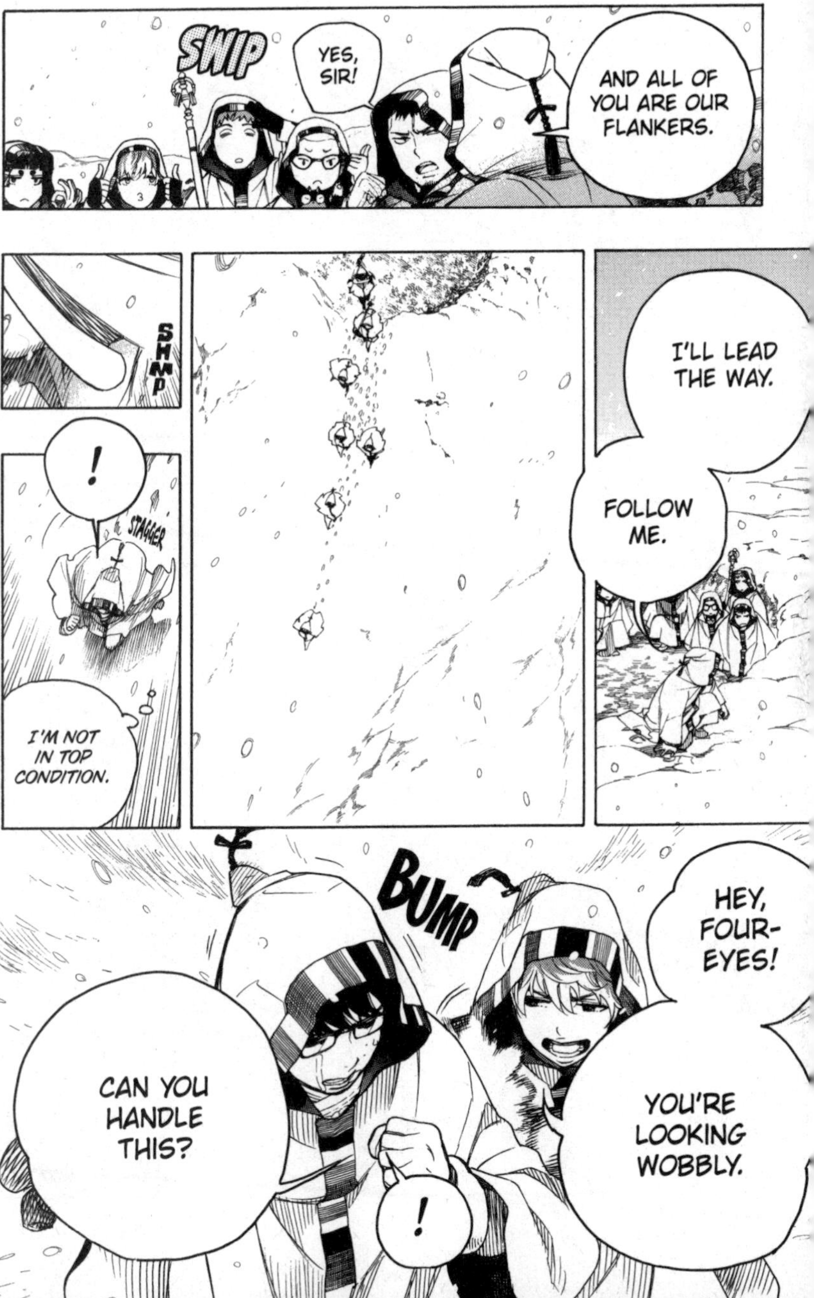
AND ALL OF YOU ARE OUR FLANKERS.
YES, SIR!
SWIP
I'LL LEAD THE WAY.
FOLLOW ME.
SHMP
!
STAGGER
I'M NOT IN TOP CONDITION.
HEY, FOUR-EYES!
YOU'RE LOOKING WOBBLY.
BUMP
!
CAN YOU HANDLE THIS?

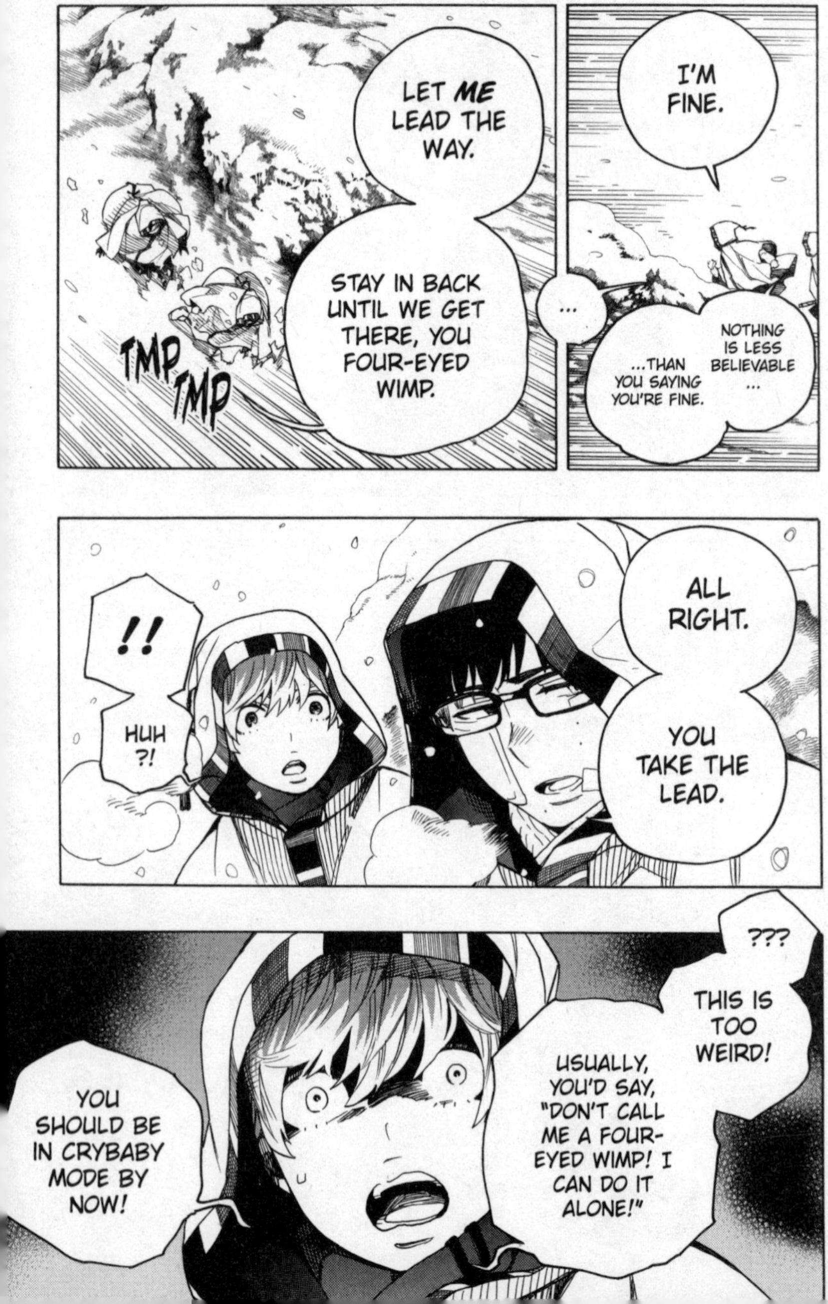
I'M FINE.
...
NOTHING IS LESS BELIEVABLE...
...THAN YOU SAYING YOU'RE FINE.
LET ME LEAD THE WAY.
STAY IN BACK UNTIL WE GET THERE, YOU FOUR-EYED WIMP.
TMP TMP
ALL RIGHT.
YOU TAKE THE LEAD.
!!
HUH ?!
???
THIS IS TOO WEIRD!
USUALLY, YOU'D SAY, "DON'T CALL ME A FOUR-EYED WIMP! I CAN DO IT ALONE!"
YOU SHOULD BE IN CRYBABY MODE BY NOW!

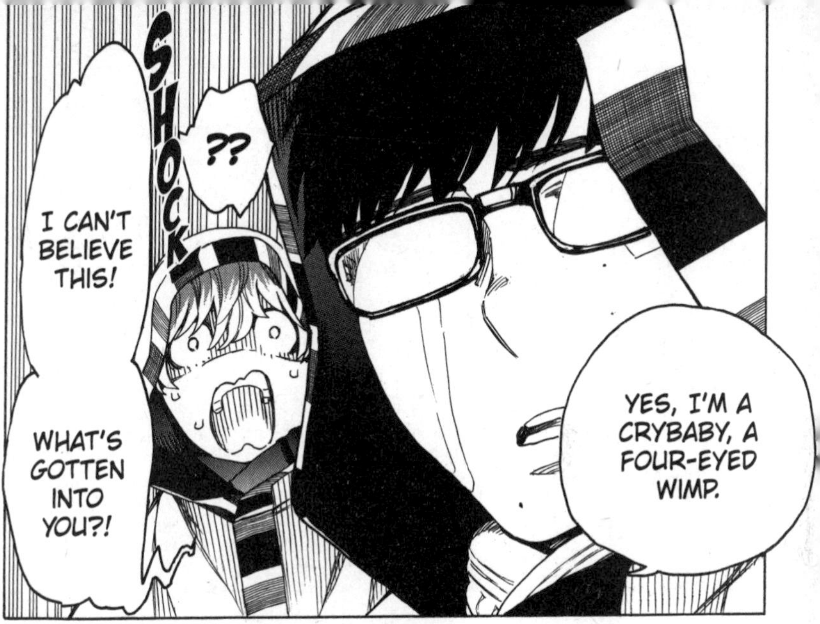
YES, I'M A CRYBABY, A FOUR-EYED WIMP.
??
SHOCK
I CAN'T BELIEVE THIS!
WHAT'S GOTTEN INTO YOU?!
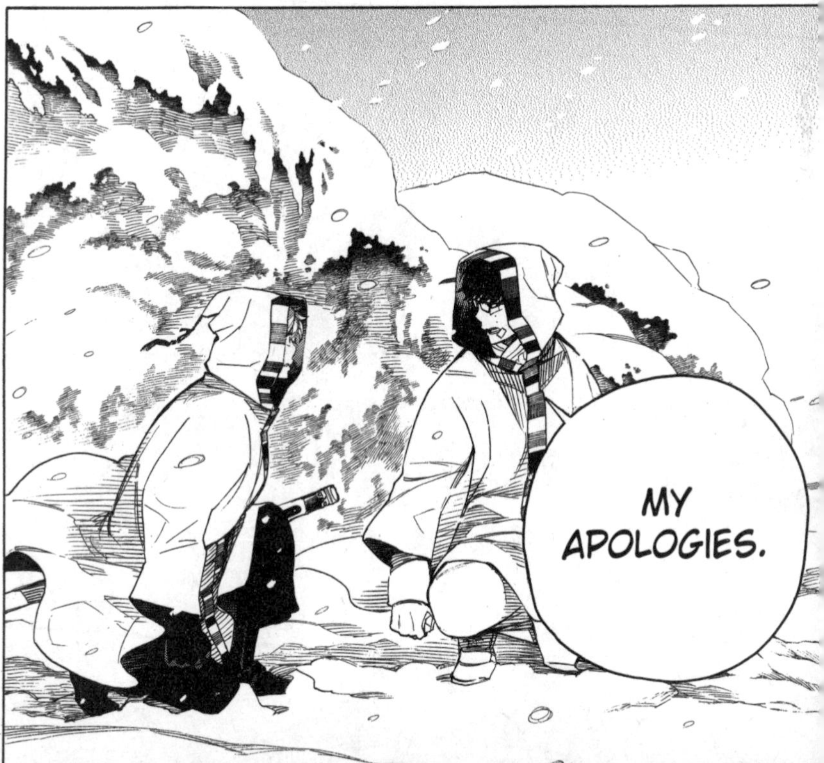
MY APOLOGIES.

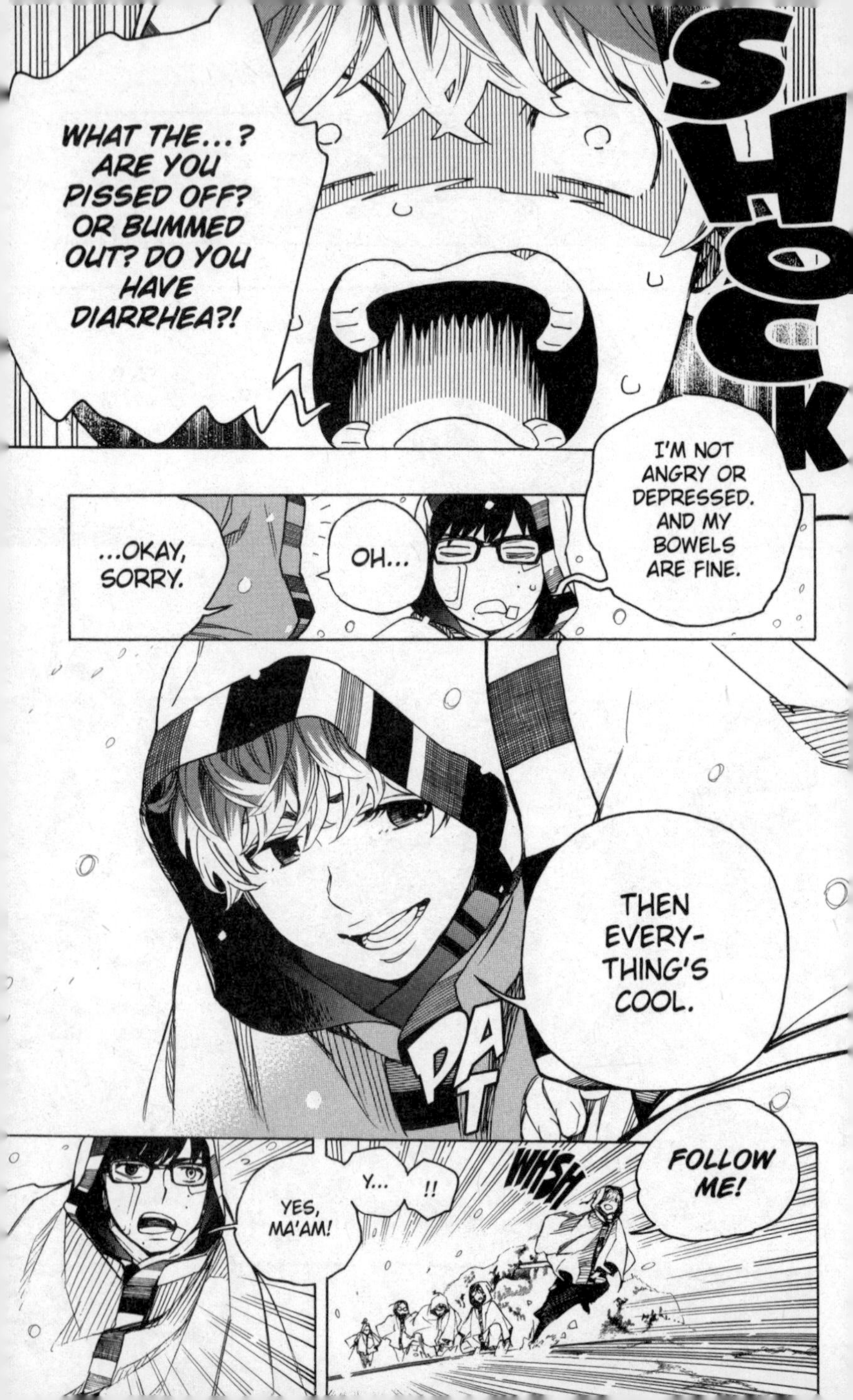
SHOCK
WHAT THE...? ARE YOU PISSED OFF? OR BUMMED OUT? DO YOU HAVE DIARRHEA?!
I'M NOT ANGRY OR DEPRESSED. AND MY BOWELS ARE FINE.
OH...
...OKAY, SORRY.
THEN EVERY-THING'S COOL.
DAT
FOLLOW ME!
WHSH
!!
Y...
YES, MA'AM!

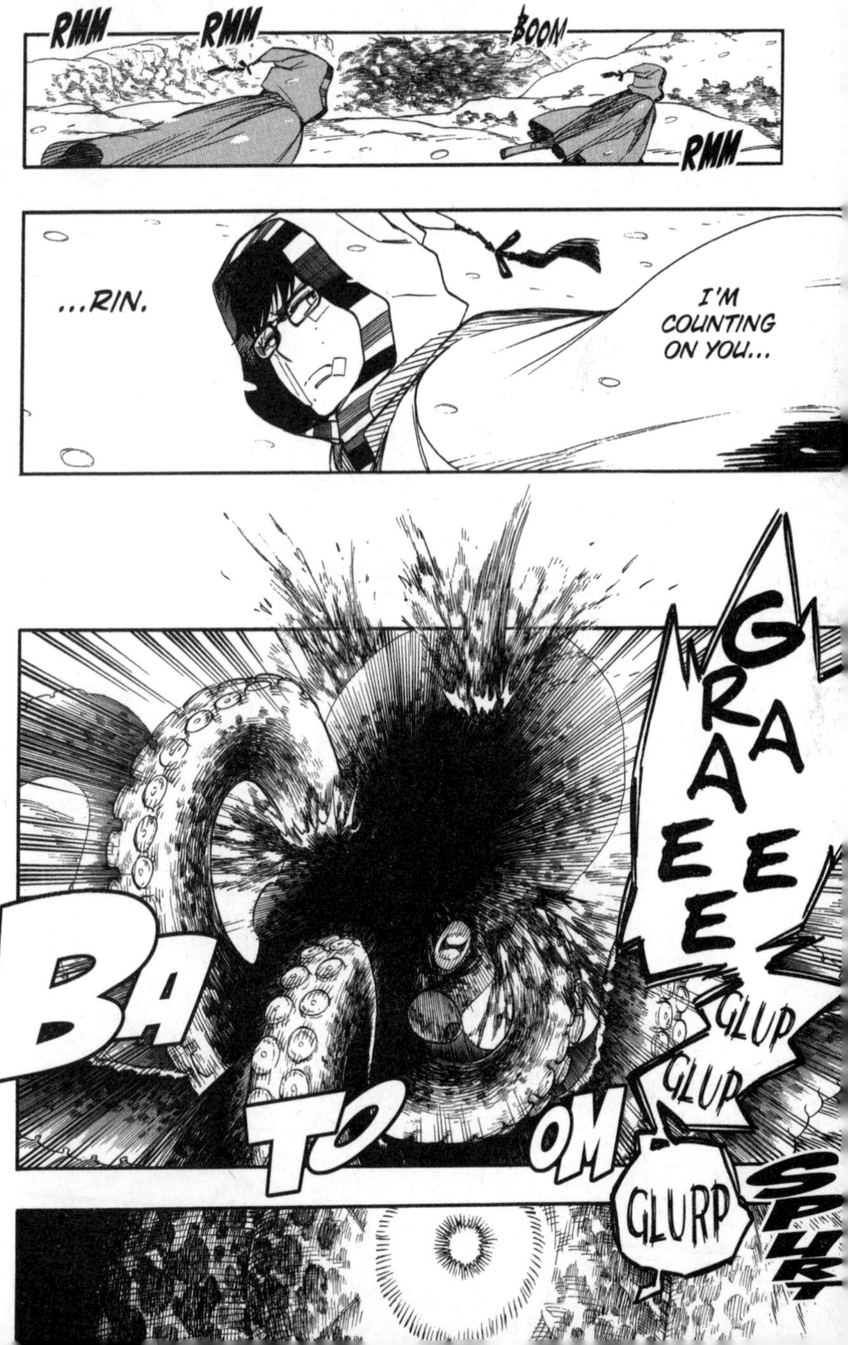
RMM
BOOM
RMM
RMM
I'M COUNTING ON YOU...
...RIN.
GRAAEEEE
GLUP
GLUP
BA
TO
OM
GLURP
SPURT

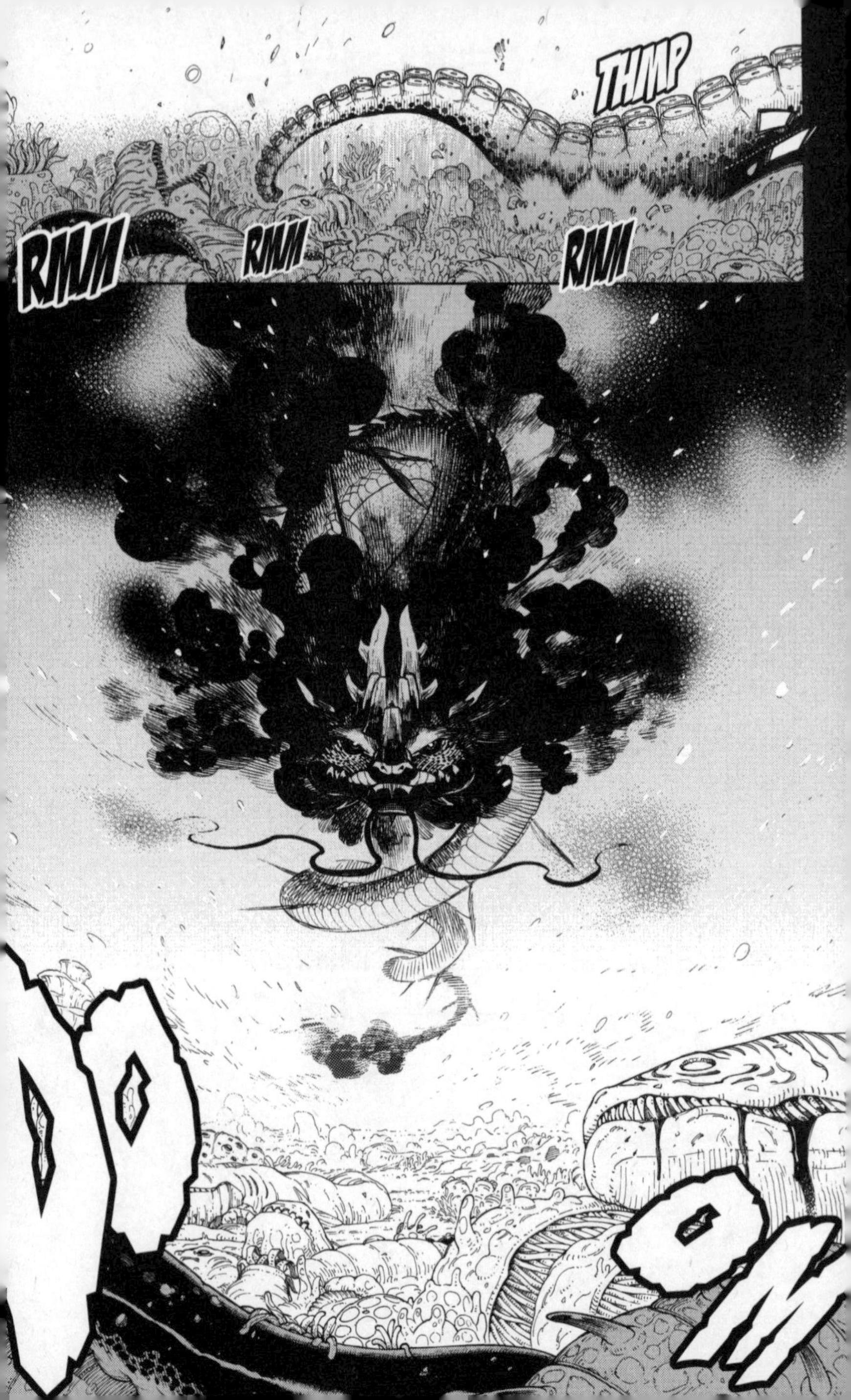
THMP
RMM
RMM
RMM
DOOM

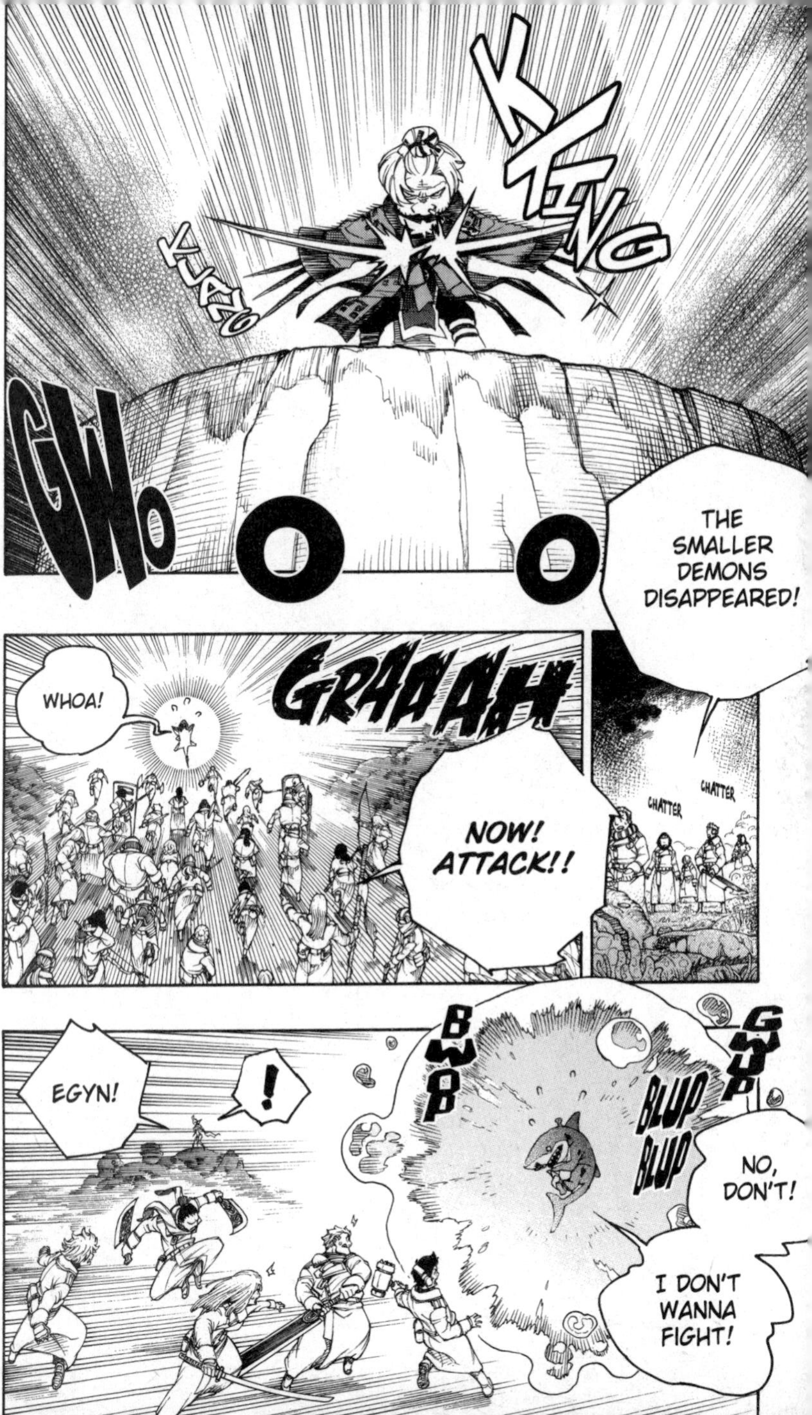
KYING
KUANG
GWOOO
THE SMALLER DEMONS DISAPPEARED!
CHATTER
CHATTER
NOW! ATTACK!!
GRAAAH
WHOA!
NO, DON'T!
I DON'T WANNA FIGHT!
GWUP
BLUP BLUP
BWOP
!
EGYN!

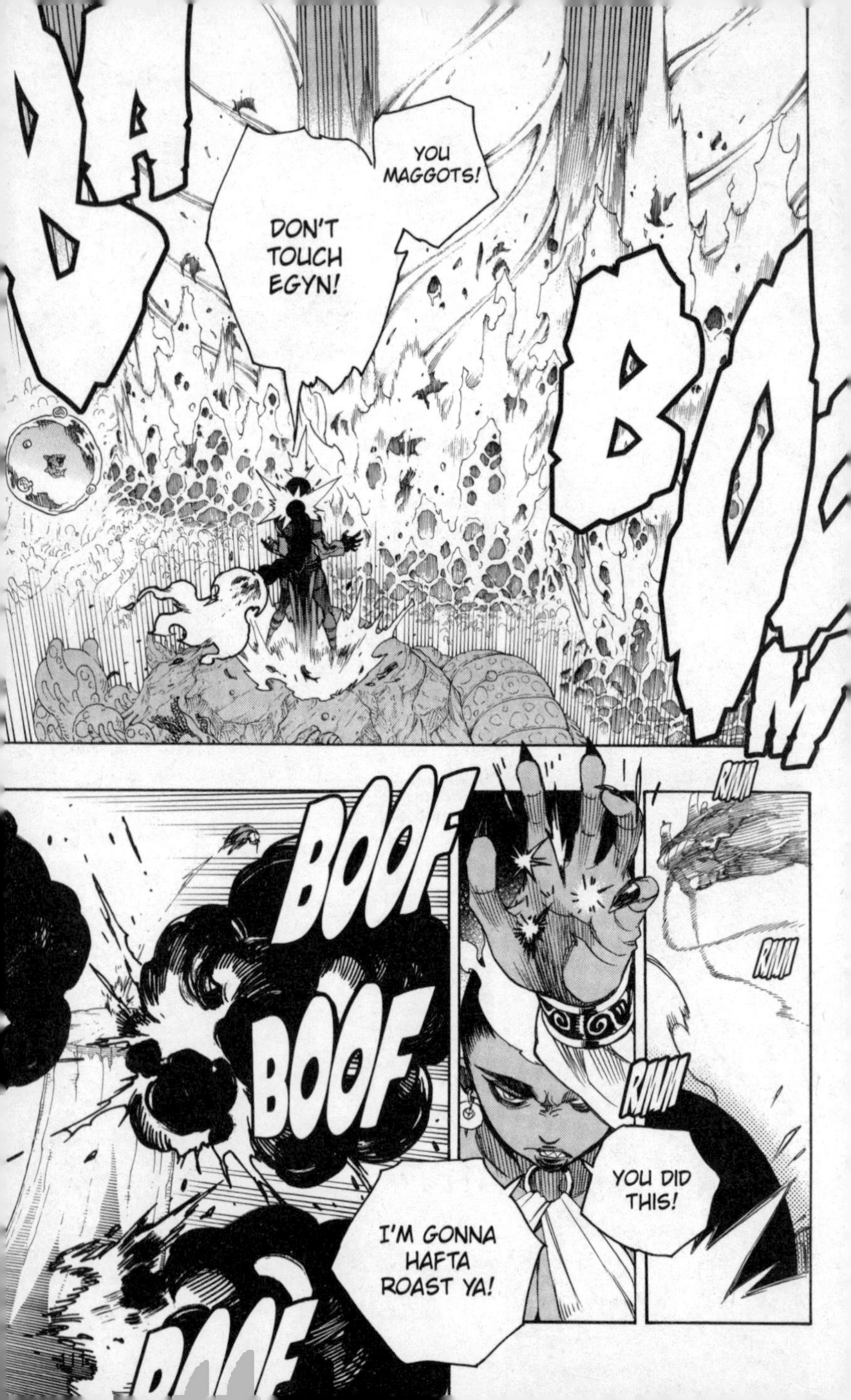
YOU MAGGOTS!
DON'T TOUCH EGYN!
RMM
RMM
RMM
YOU DID THIS!
I'M GONNA HAFTA ROAST YA!
BOOF
BOOF

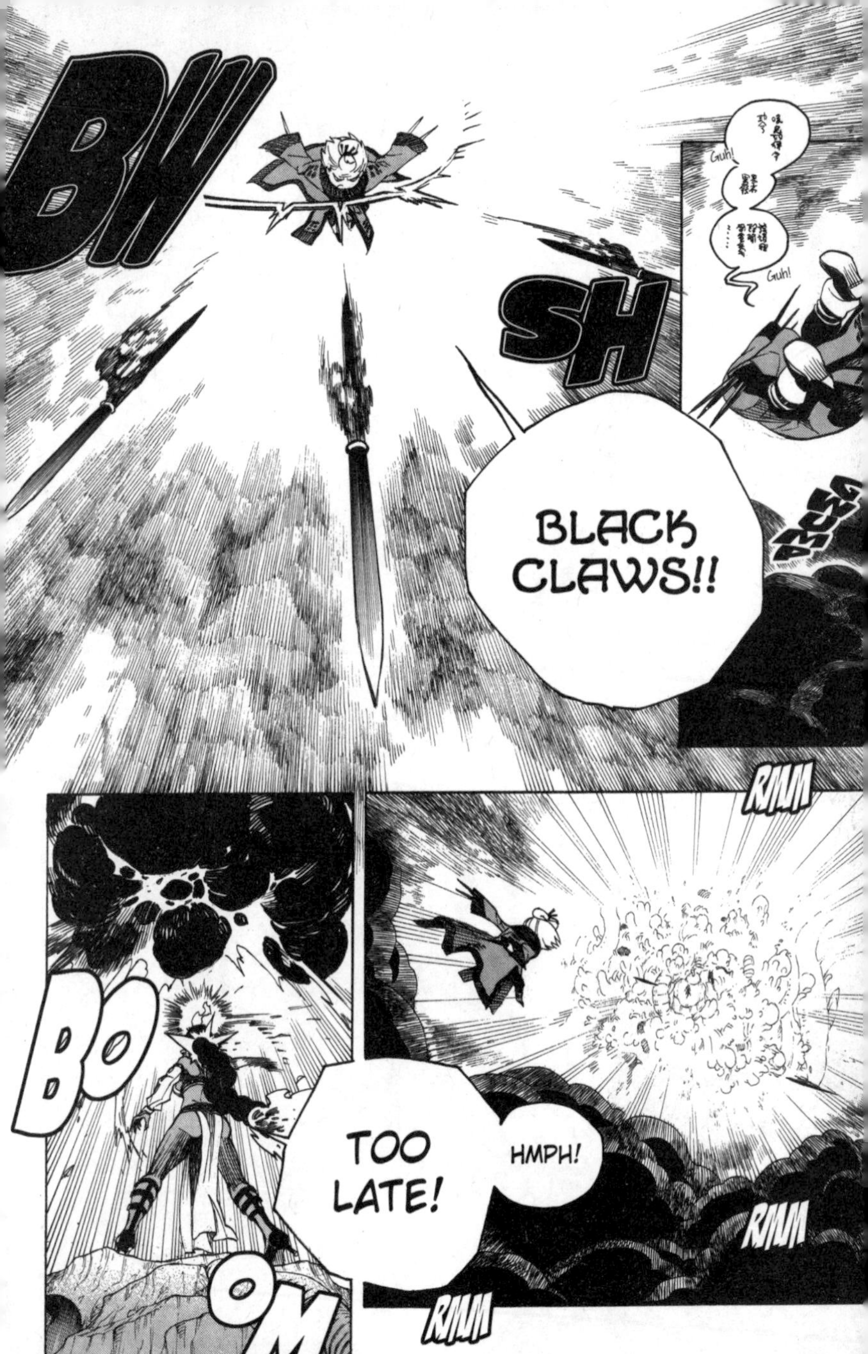
Guh!
Guh!
GWUMP
BW
SH
BLACK CLAWS!!
RMM
HMPH!
RMM
RMM
BOOM
TOO LATE!

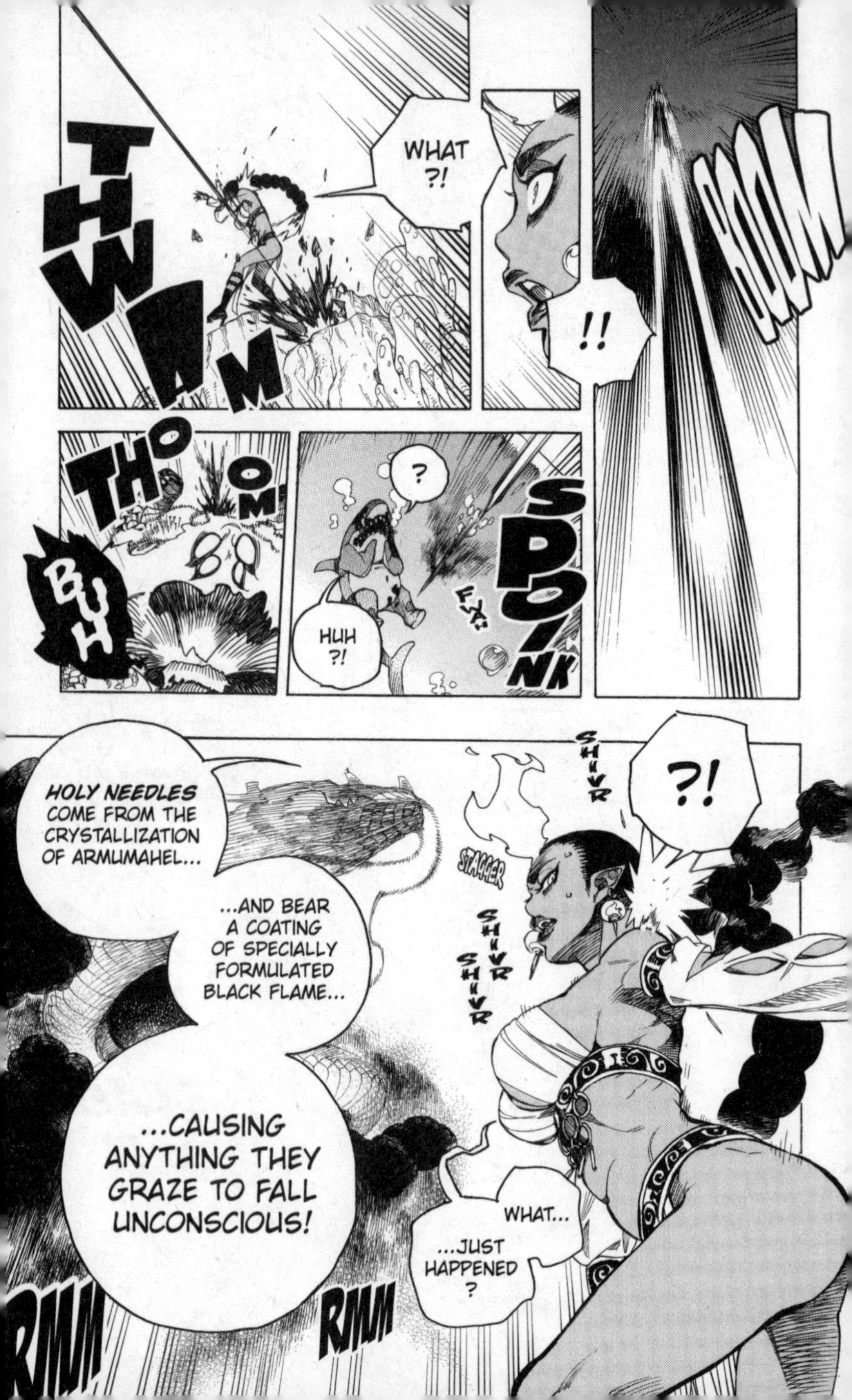
!!
WHAT ?!
THWAM
?
HUH ?!
FWAH
SPOINK
THOOM
BUH
?!
SHIVR
STAGGER
SHIVR
SHIVR
WHAT...
...JUST HAPPENED ?
HOLY NEEDLES COME FROM THE CRYSTALLIZATION OF ARMUMAHEL...
...AND BEAR A COATING OF SPECIALLY FORMULATED BLACK FLAME...
...CAUSING ANYTHING THEY GRAZE TO FALL UNCONSCIOUS!
RMM
RMM

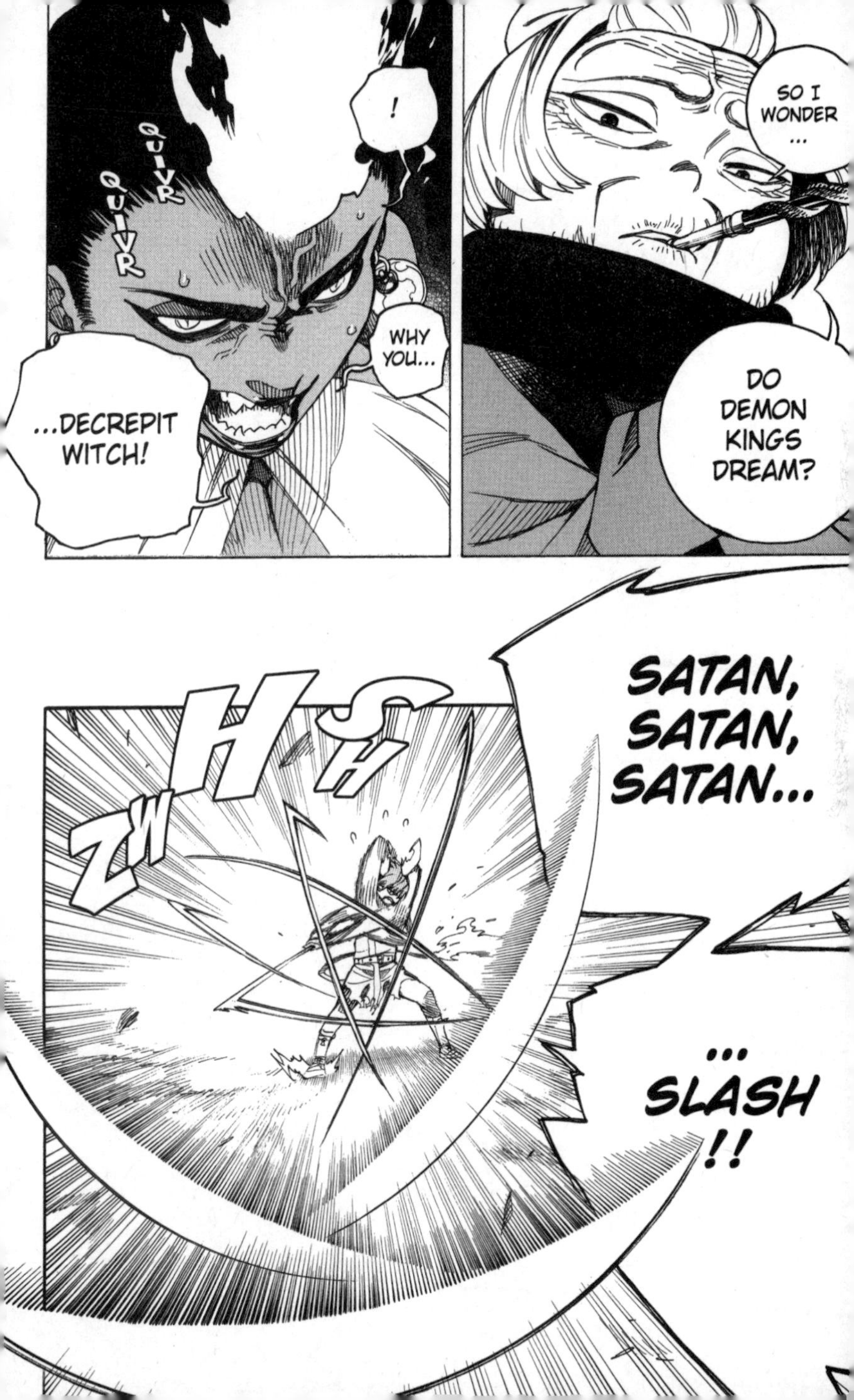
SO I WONDER ...
DO DEMON KINGS DREAM?
!
QUIVR
QUIVR
WHY YOU...
...DECREPIT WITCH!
SATAN, SATAN, SATAN...
ZWHSH
... SLASH !!

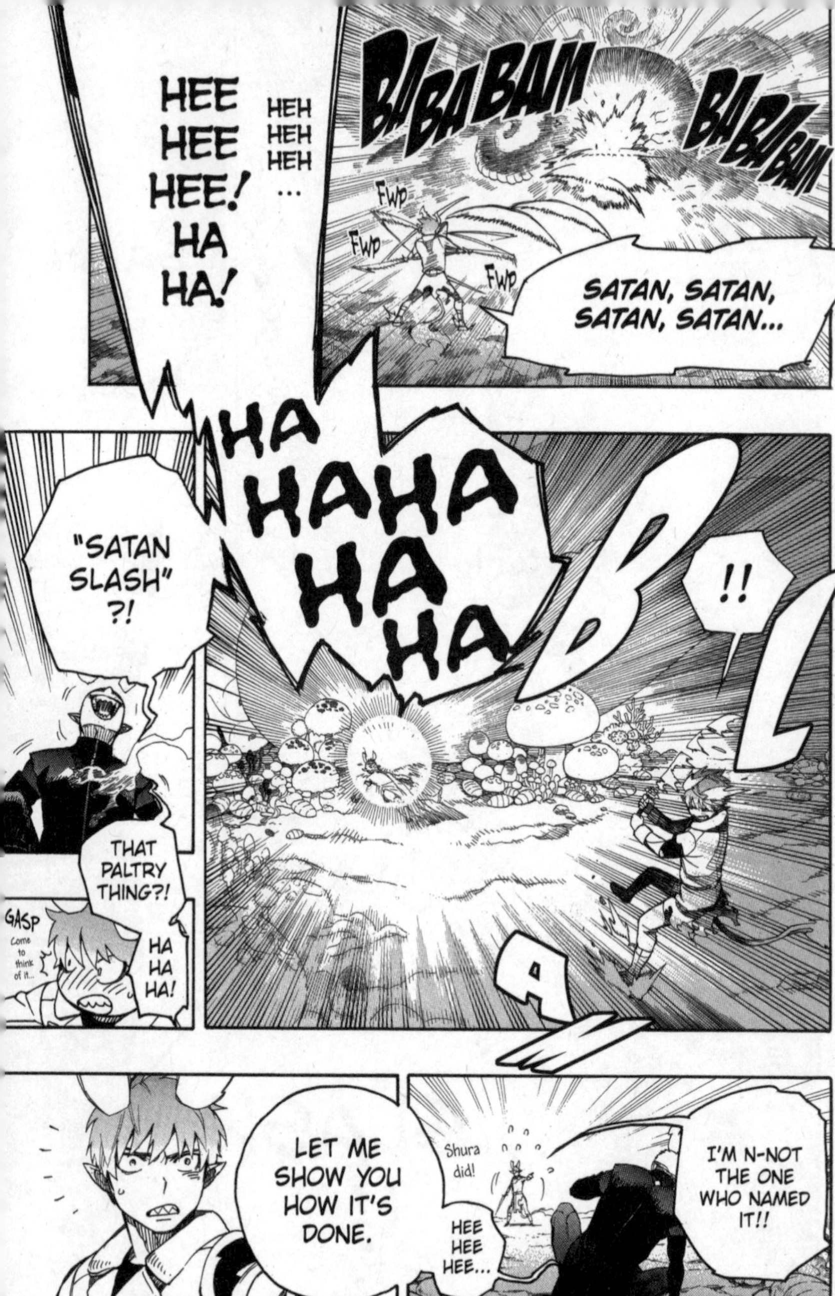
BABABAM
BABABAM
Fwp
Fwp
Fwp
SATAN, SATAN, SATAN, SATAN...
HEH HEH HEH...
HEE HEE HEE! HA HA!
HA HAHA HA HA
!!
B
L
A
"SATAN SLASH"?!
THAT PALTRY THING?!
HA HA HA!
GASP
Come to think of it...
I'M N-NOT THE ONE WHO NAMED IT!!
Shura did!
HEE HEE HEE...
LET ME SHOW YOU HOW IT'S DONE.

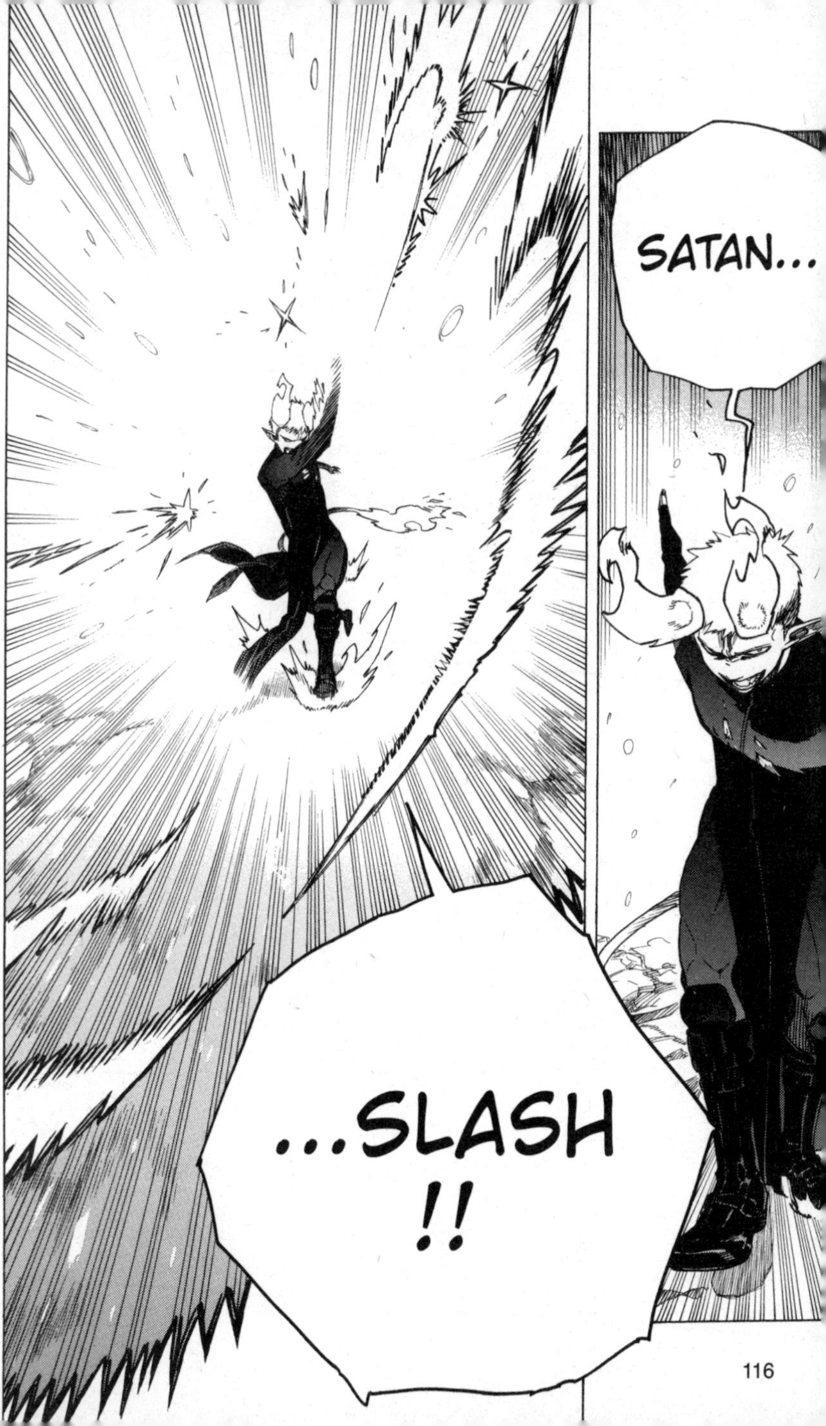
SATAN...
...SLASH !!

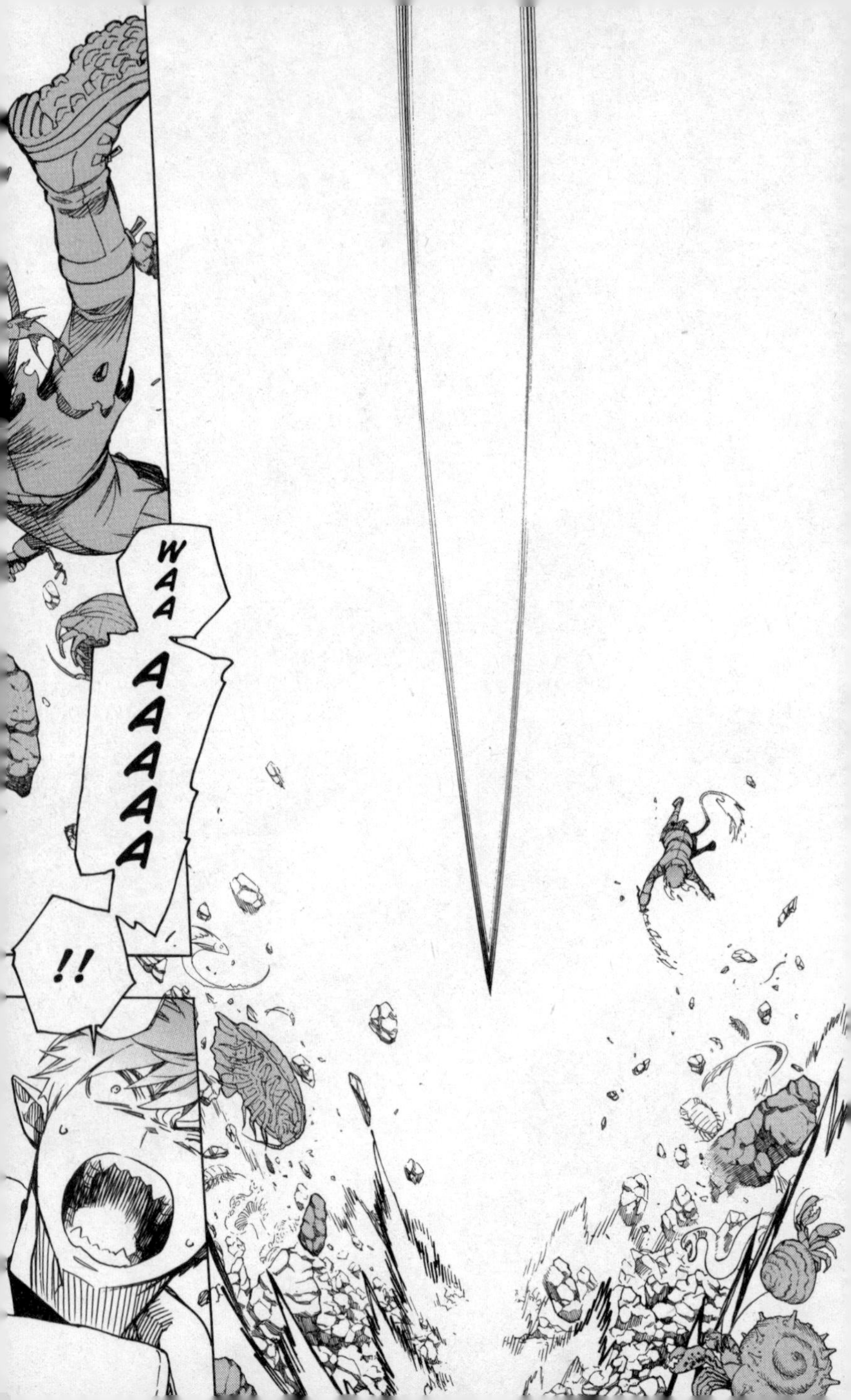
WAAAAAAAAA
!!

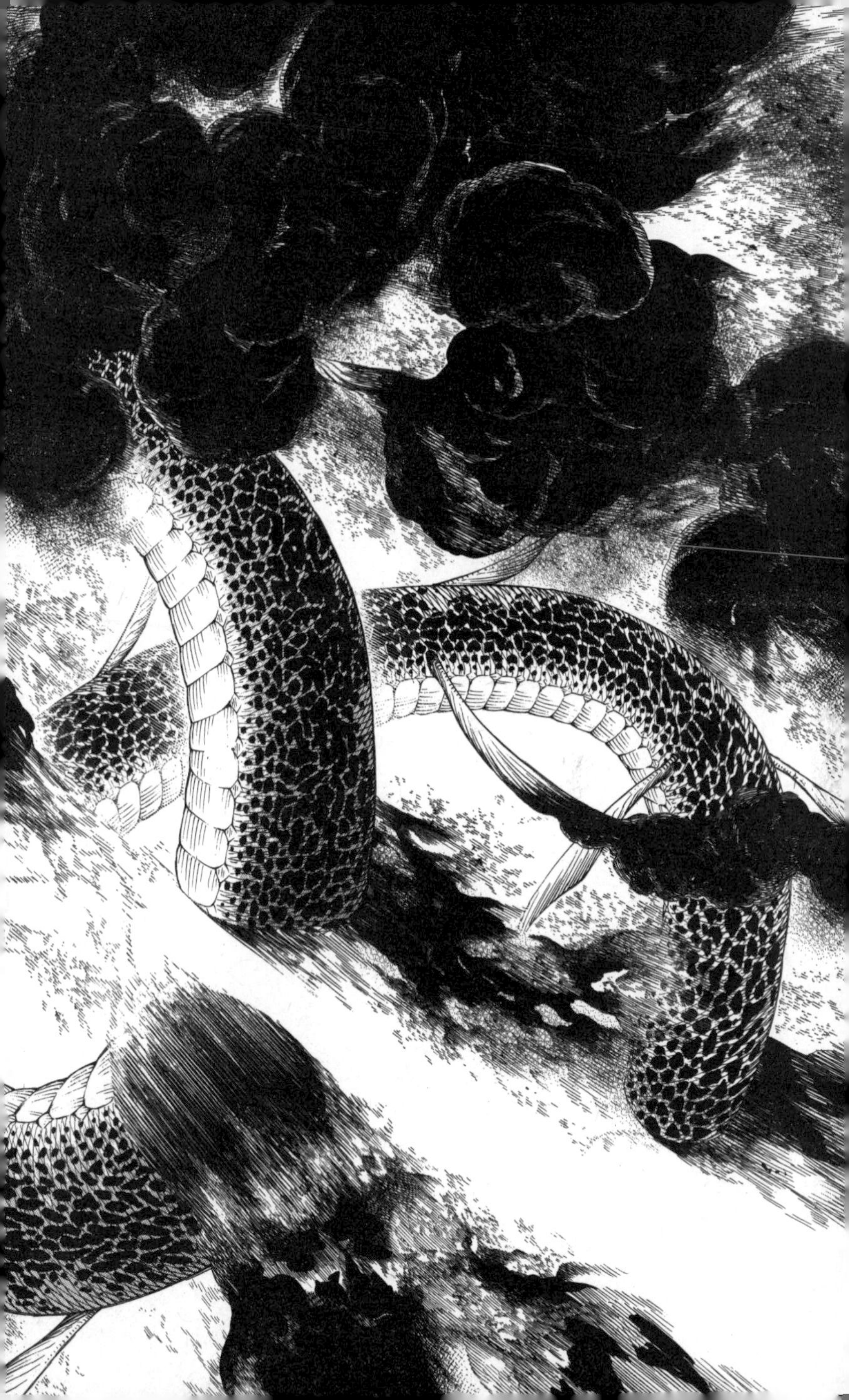

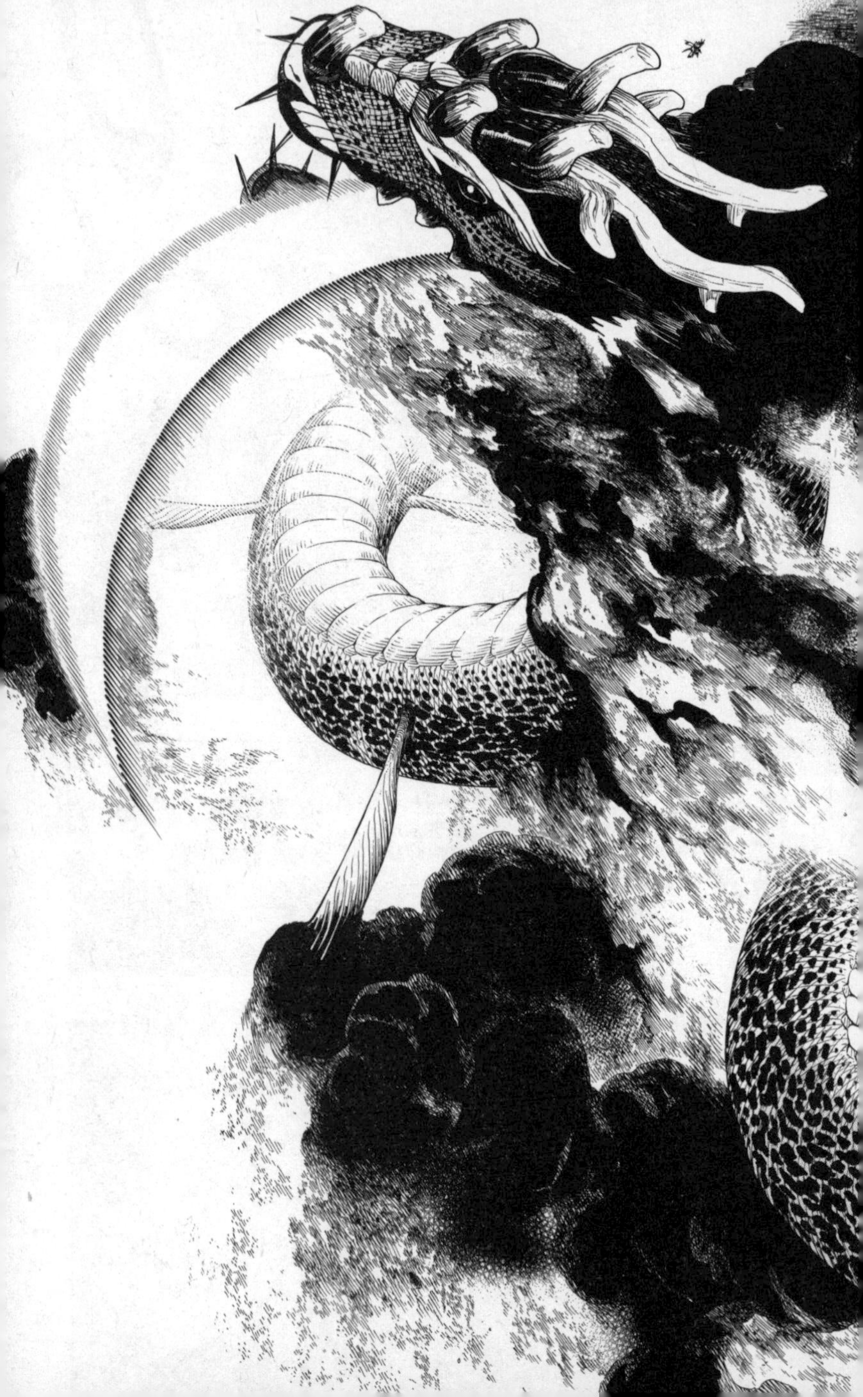

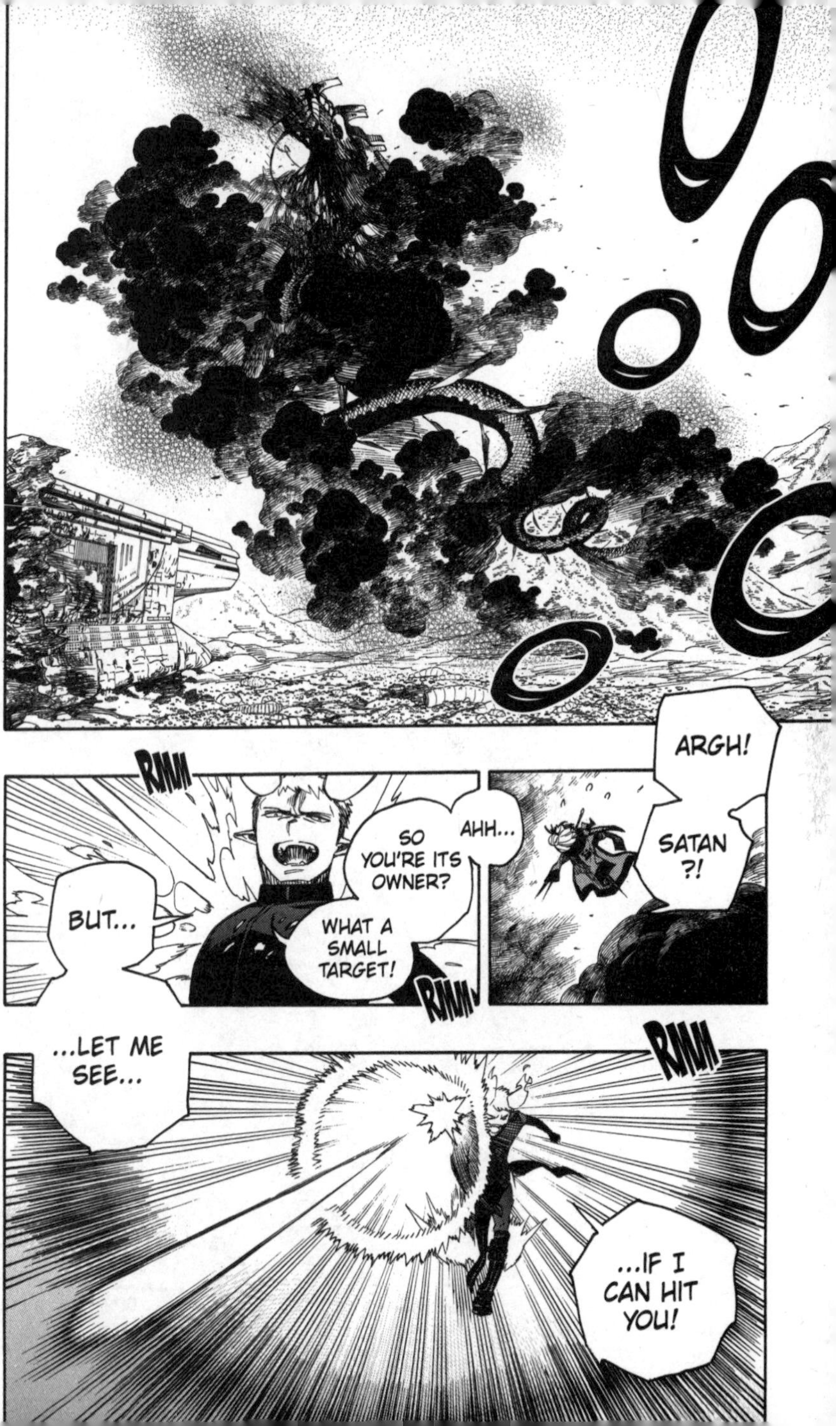
ARGH!
SATAN ?!
AHH...
SO YOU'RE ITS OWNER?
RMM
WHAT A SMALL TARGET!
RMM
BUT...
RMM
...LET ME SEE...
...IF I CAN HIT YOU!

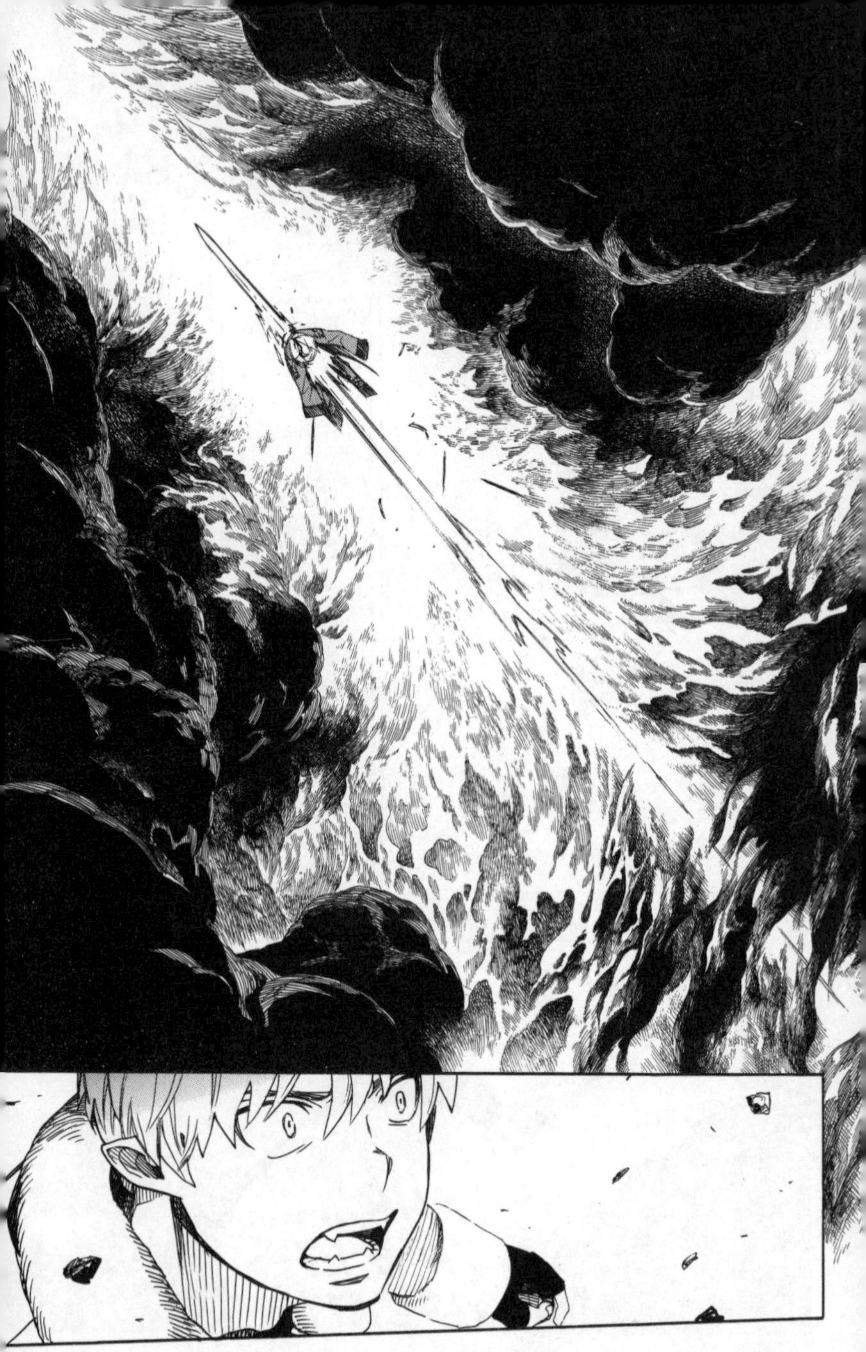

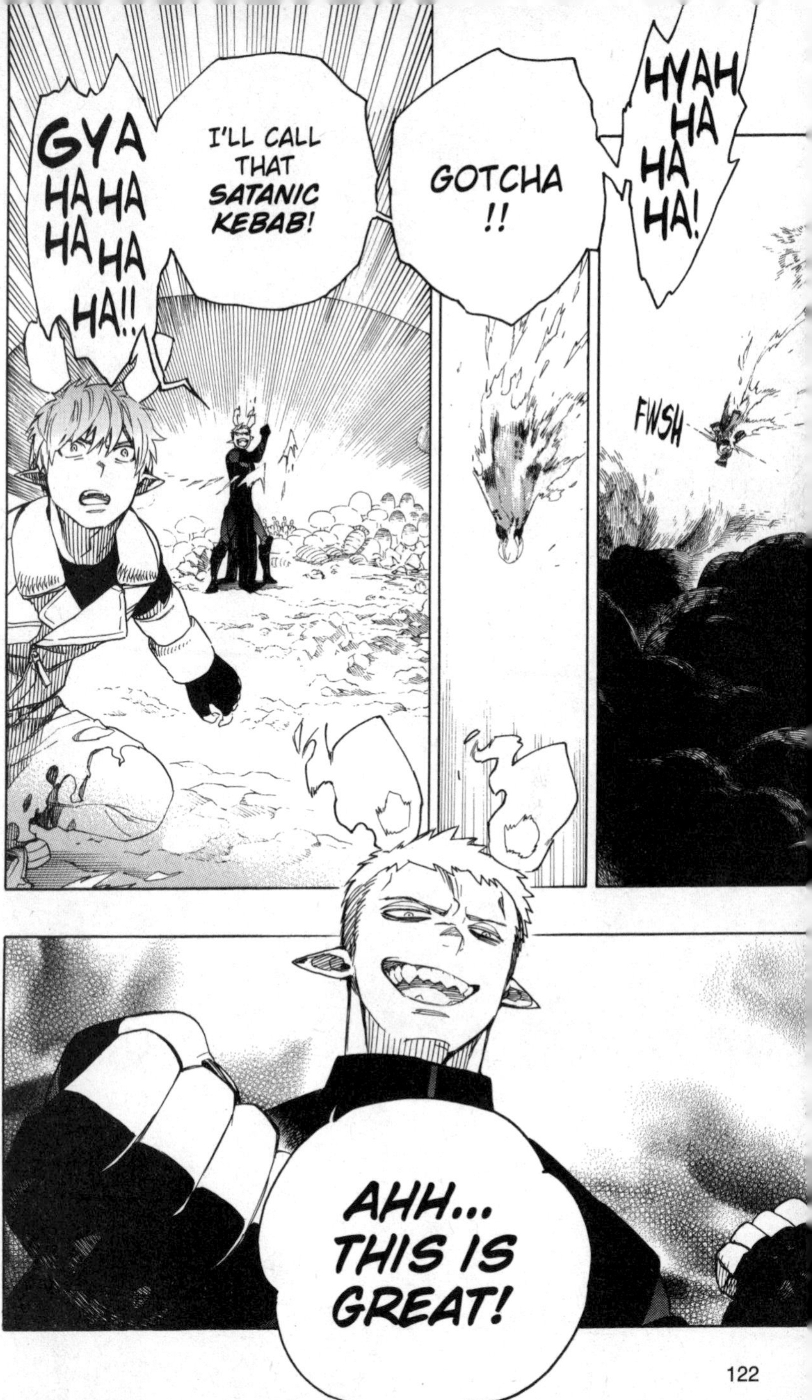
HYAH HA HA HA!
FWSH
GOTCHA !!
I'LL CALL THAT SATANIC KEBAB!
GYA HA HA HA HA HA HA!!
AHH... THIS IS GREAT!

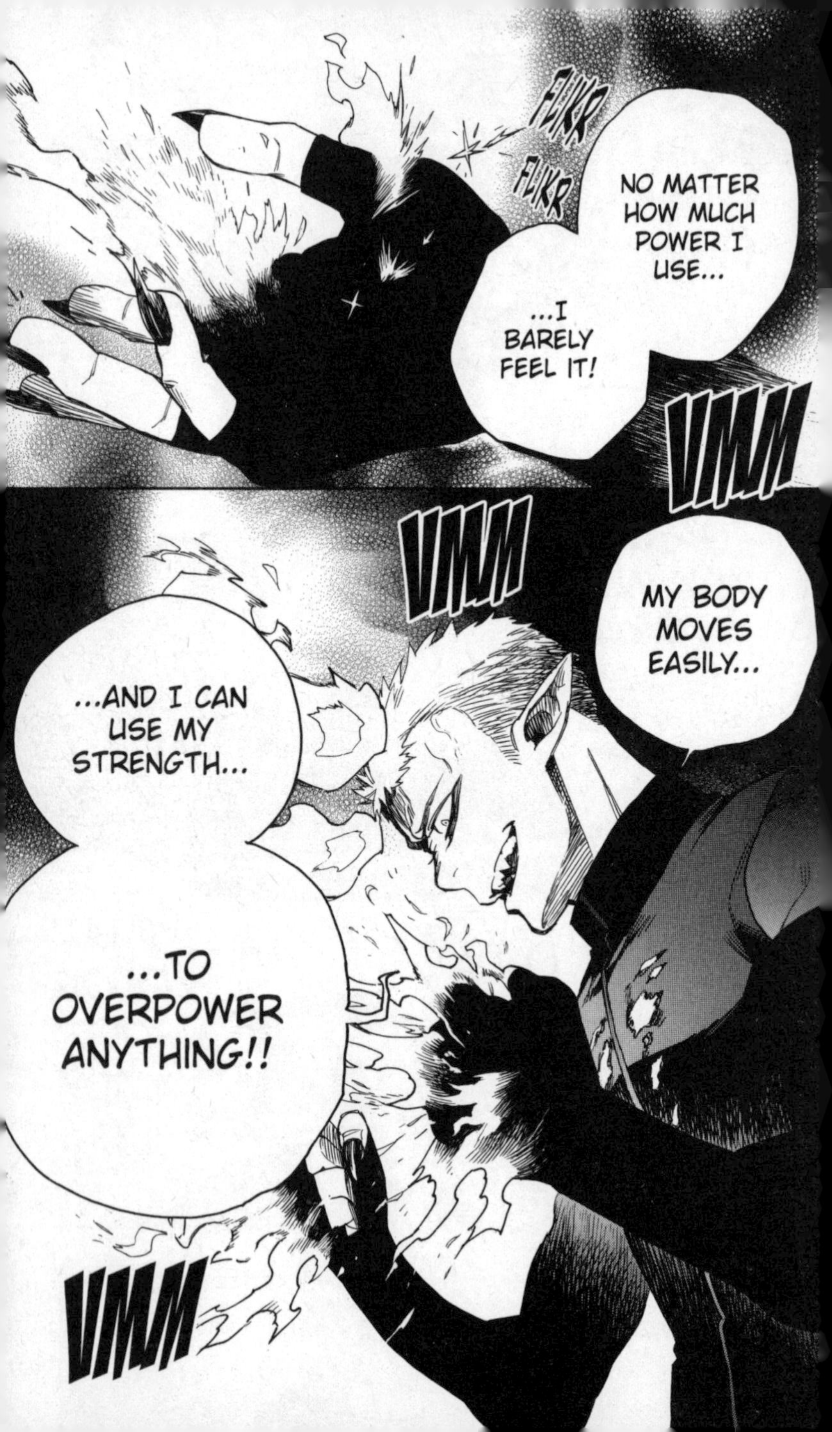
FLIKR
FLIKR
NO MATTER HOW MUCH POWER I USE...
...I BARELY FEEL IT!
VMMM
VMMM
MY BODY MOVES EASILY...
...AND I CAN USE MY STRENGTH...
...TO OVERPOWER ANYTHING!!
VMMM

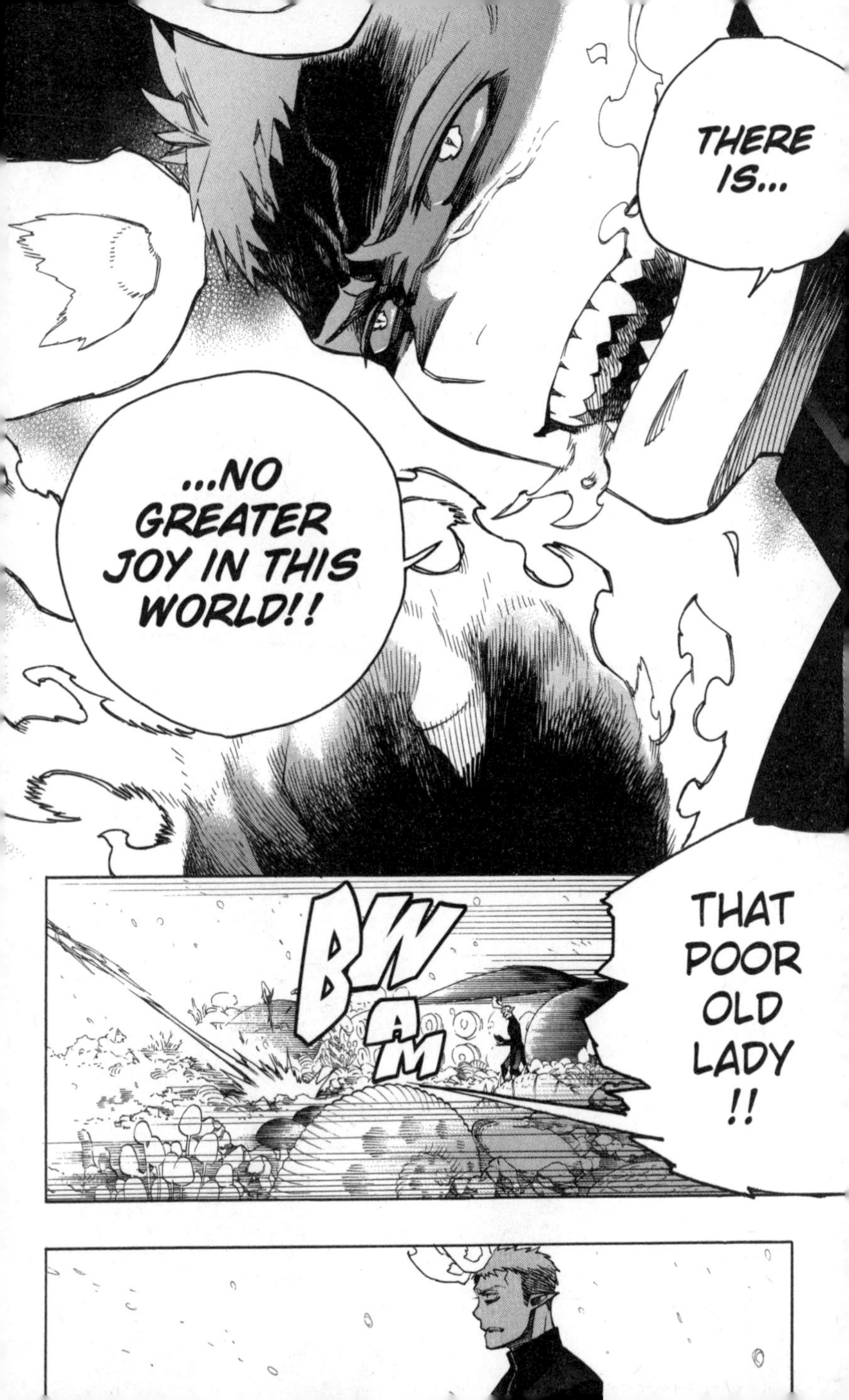
THERE IS...
...NO GREATER JOY IN THIS WORLD!!
THAT POOR OLD LADY !!
BWAM

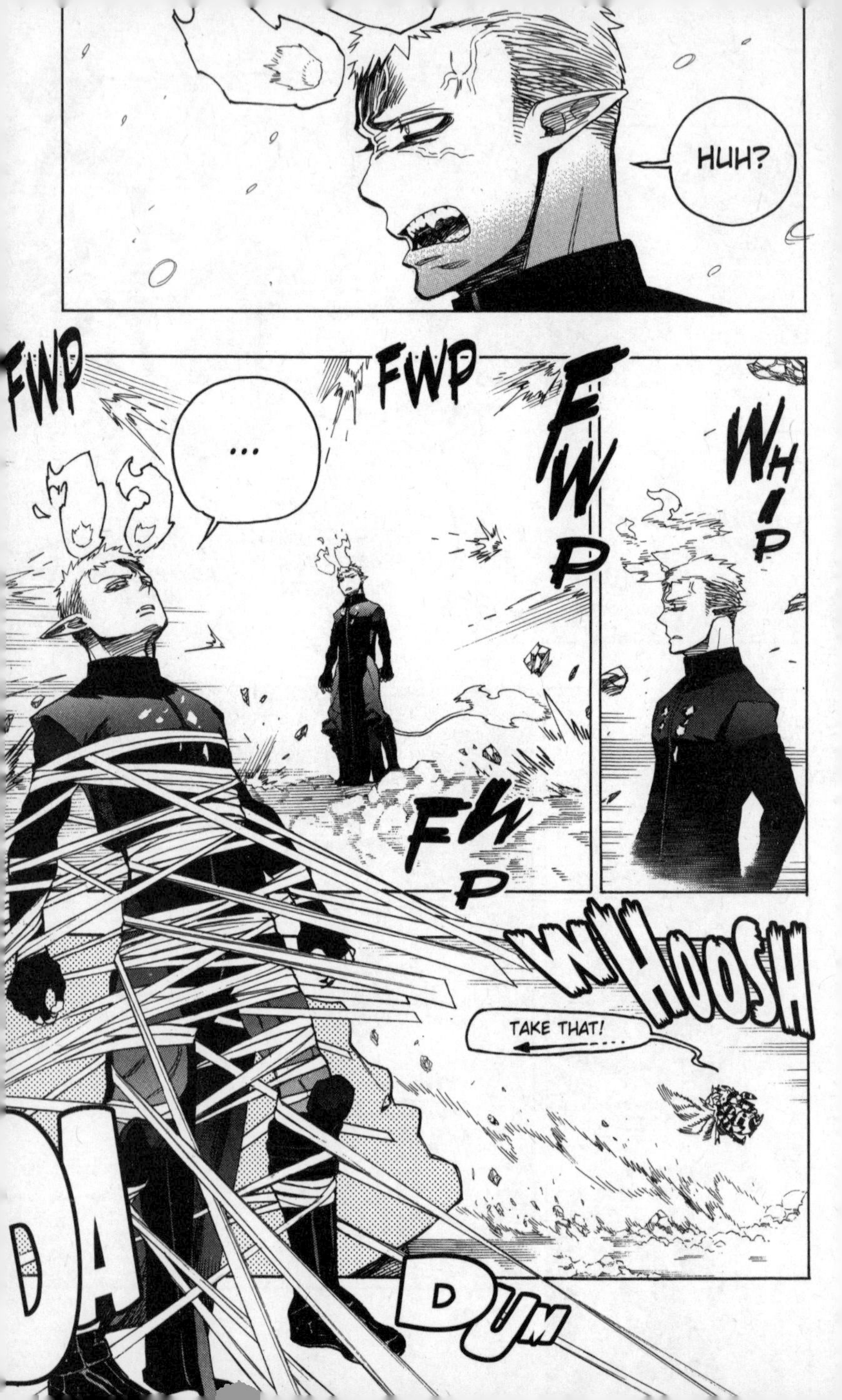
HUH?
WHIP
FWP
FWP
FWP
FWP
...
WHOOSH
TAKE THAT!
DA
DUM

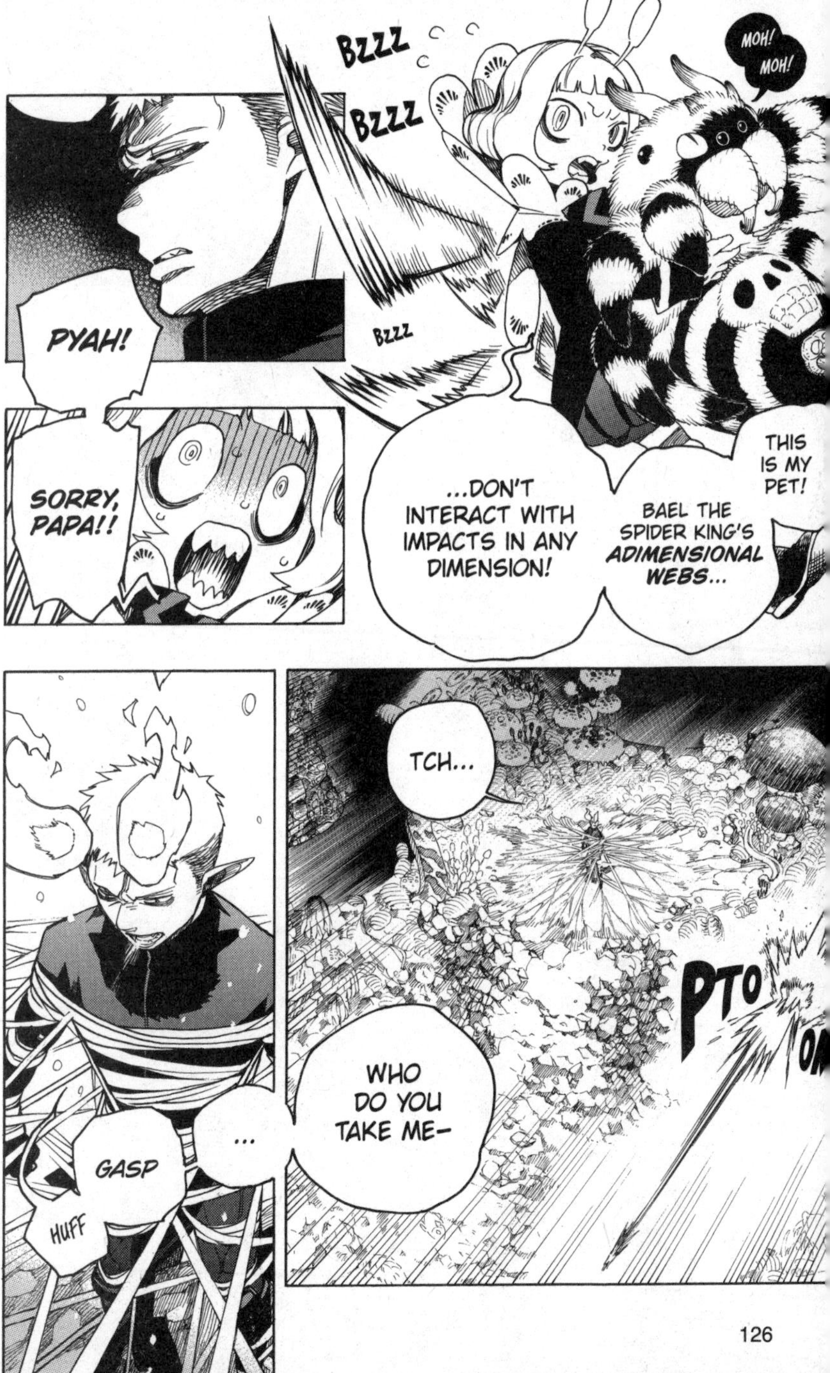
MOH! MOH!
BZZZ
BZZZ
THIS IS MY PET!
BAEL THE SPIDER KING'S ADIMENSIONAL WEBS...
...DON'T INTERACT WITH IMPACTS IN ANY DIMENSION!
BZZZ
PYAH!
SORRY, PAPA!!
TCH...
PTO
WHO DO YOU TAKE ME-
...
GASP
HUFF

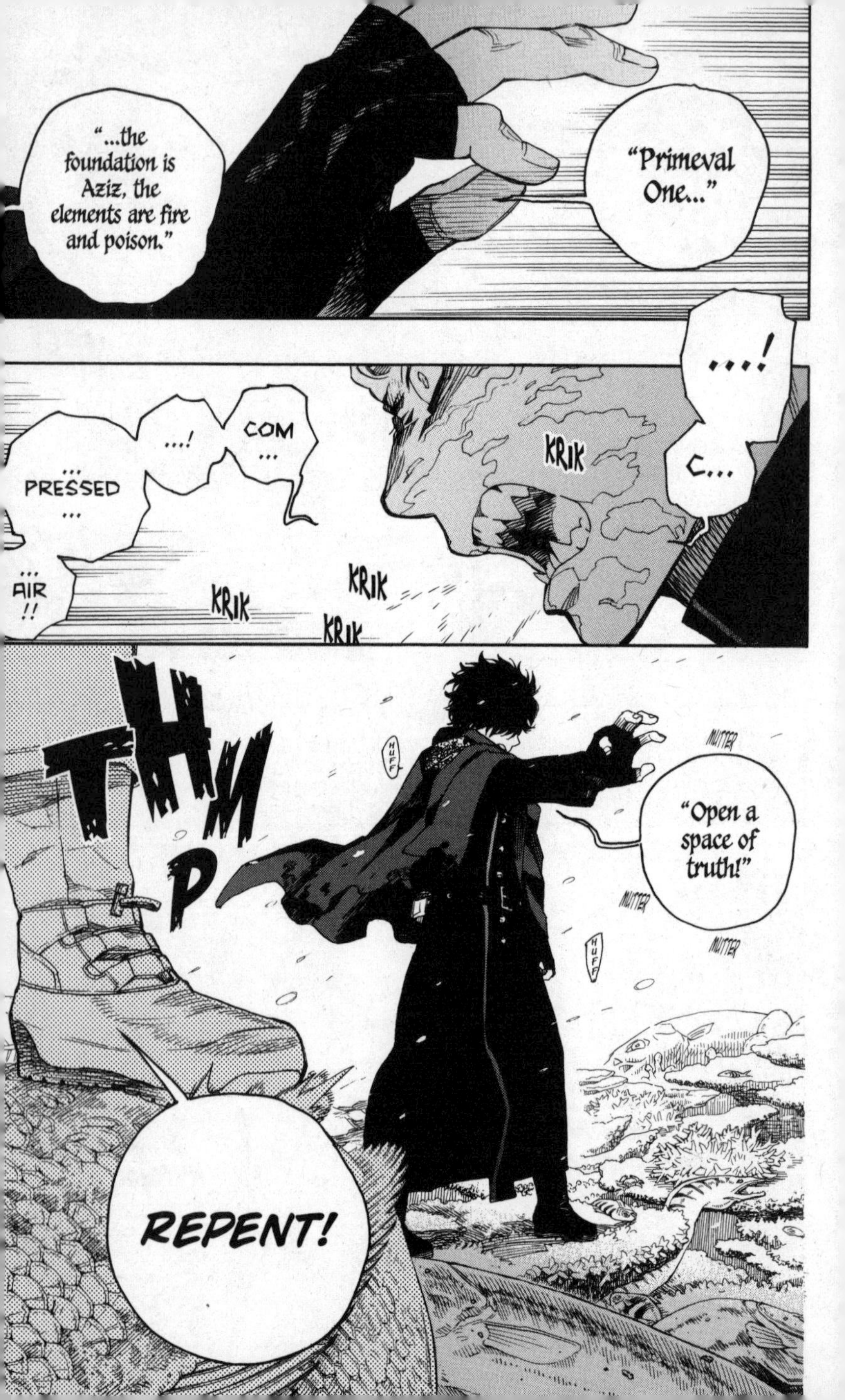
"Primeval One..."
"...the foundation is Aziz, the elements are fire and poison."
...!
C...
KRIK
COM ...
...!
... PRESSED ...
... AIR !!
KRIK
KRIK
KRIK
MUTTER
HUFF
"Open a space of truth!"
MUTTER
MUTTER
HUFF
THMP
REPENT!

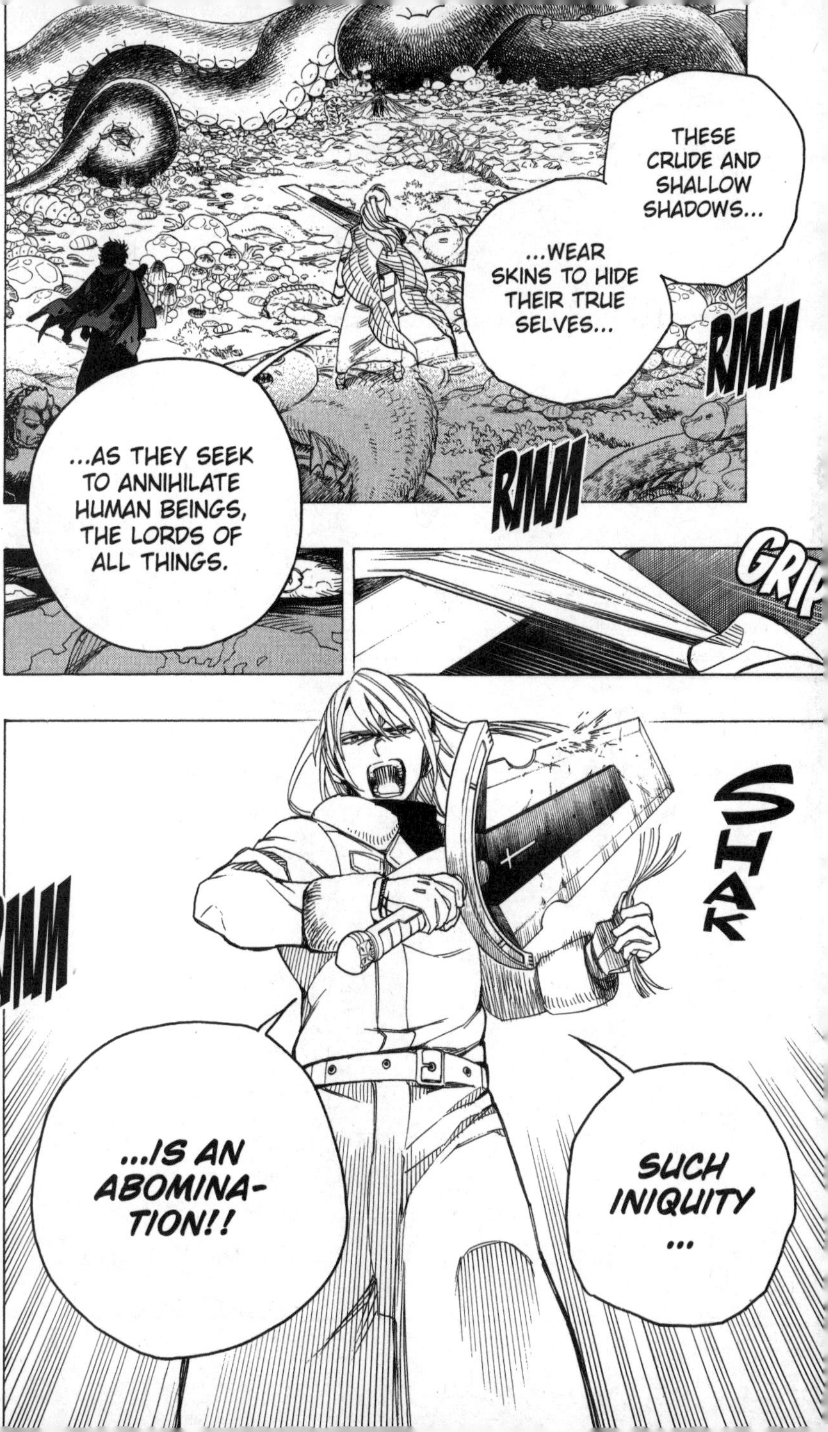
THESE CRUDE AND SHALLOW SHADOWS...
...WEAR SKINS TO HIDE THEIR TRUE SELVES...
RMM
RMM
...AS THEY SEEK TO ANNIHILATE HUMAN BEINGS, THE LORDS OF ALL THINGS.
GRIP
SHAK
RMM
SUCH INIQUITY ...
...IS AN ABOMINA-TION!!

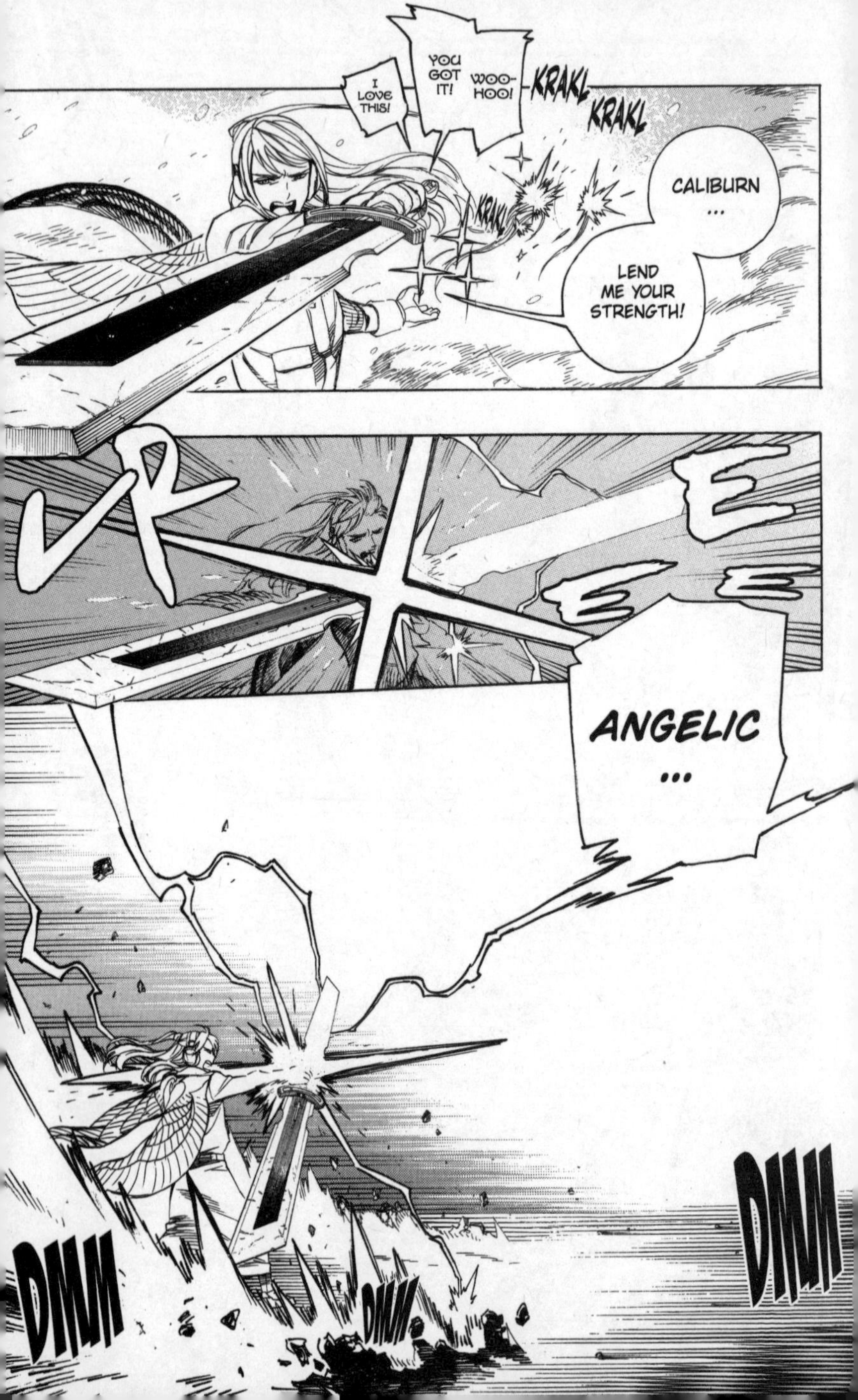

KRAKL
KRAKL
WOO-HOO!
YOU GOT IT!
I LOVE THIS!
CALIBURN ...
KRAKL
LEND ME YOUR STRENGTH!
EEE
VR
ANGELIC ...
DMM
DMM
DMM

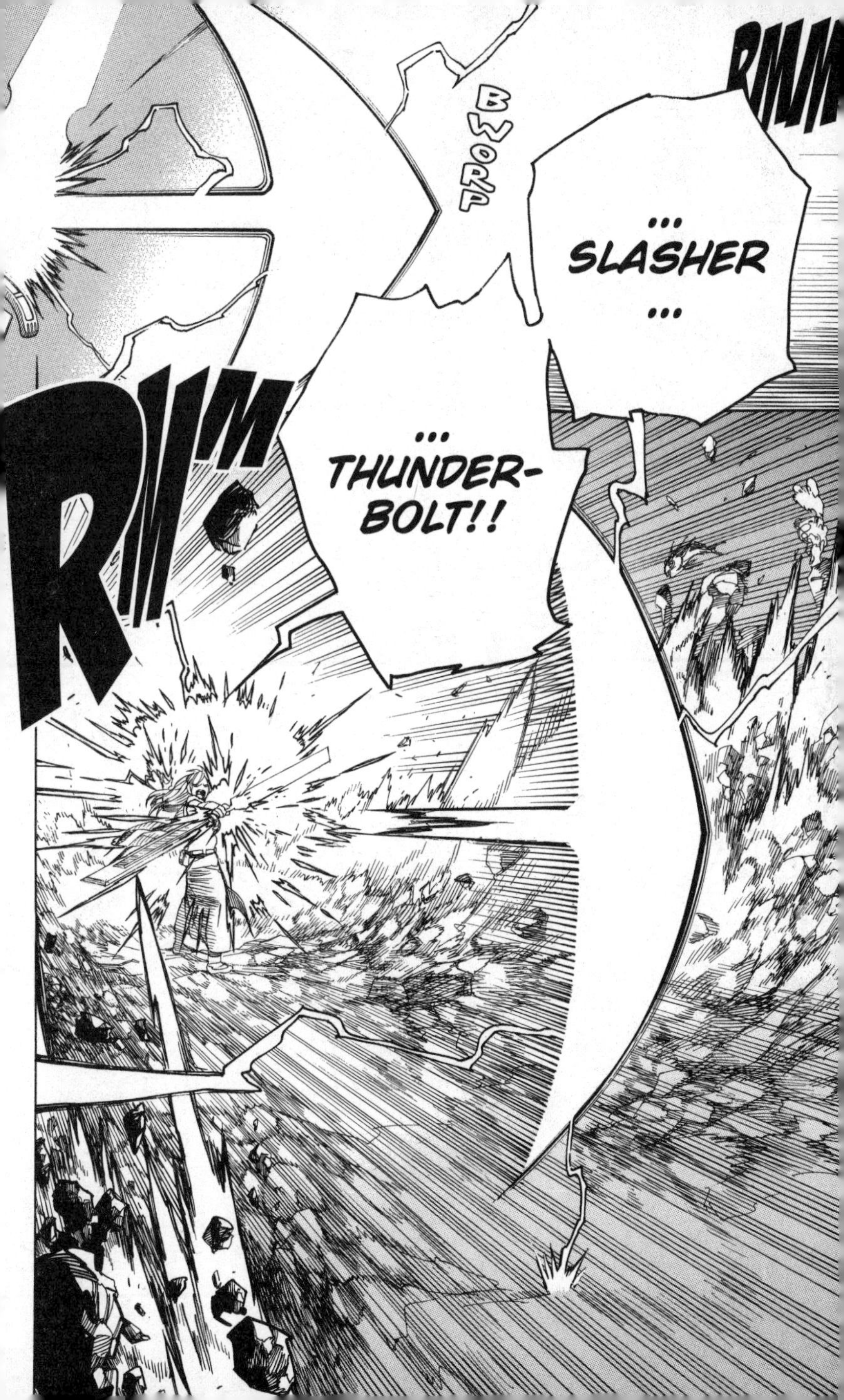
RMM
BWORP
... SLASHER ...
... THUNDER-BOLT!!
RMM

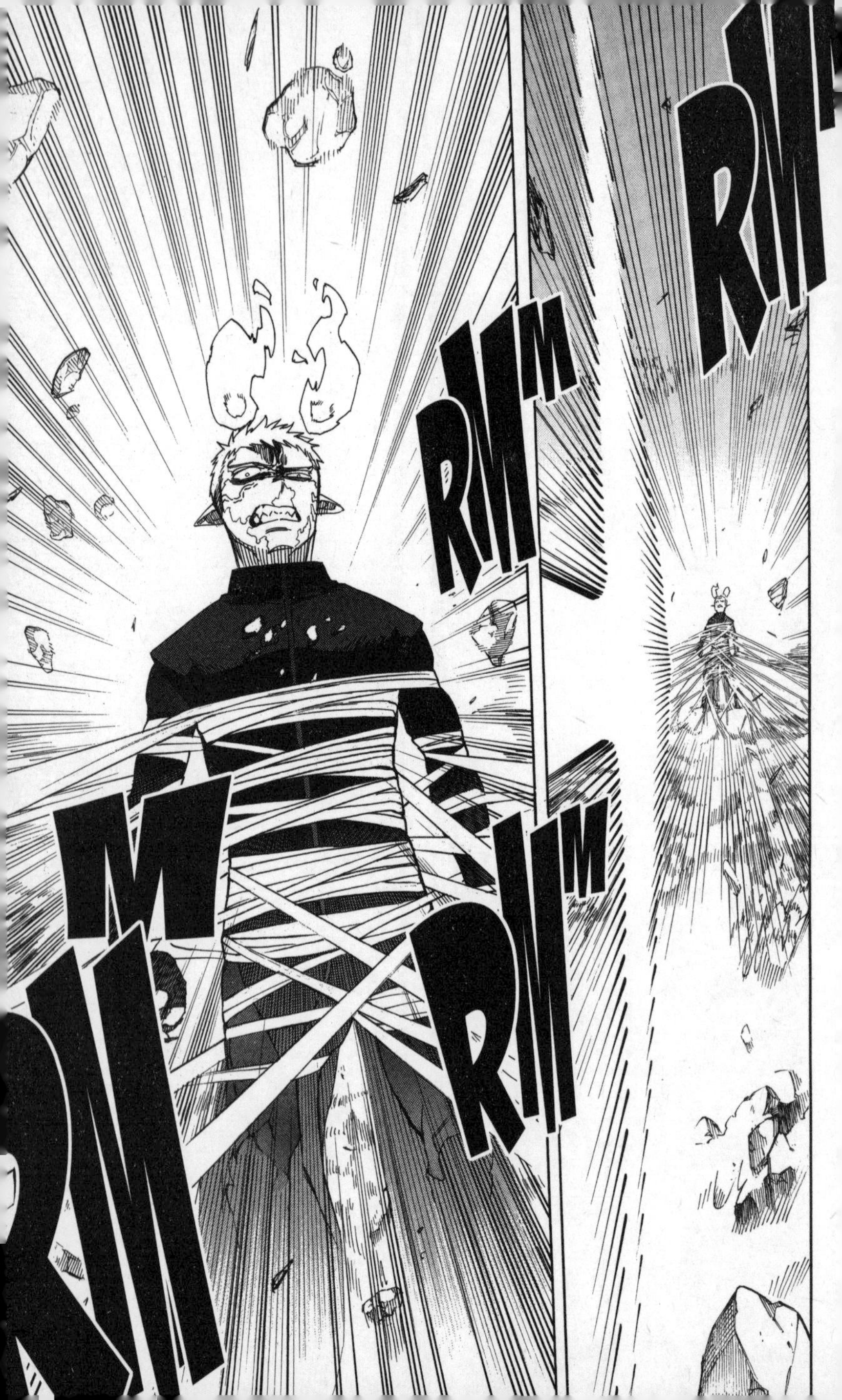

RM
RMMM
RMMM
RMMM

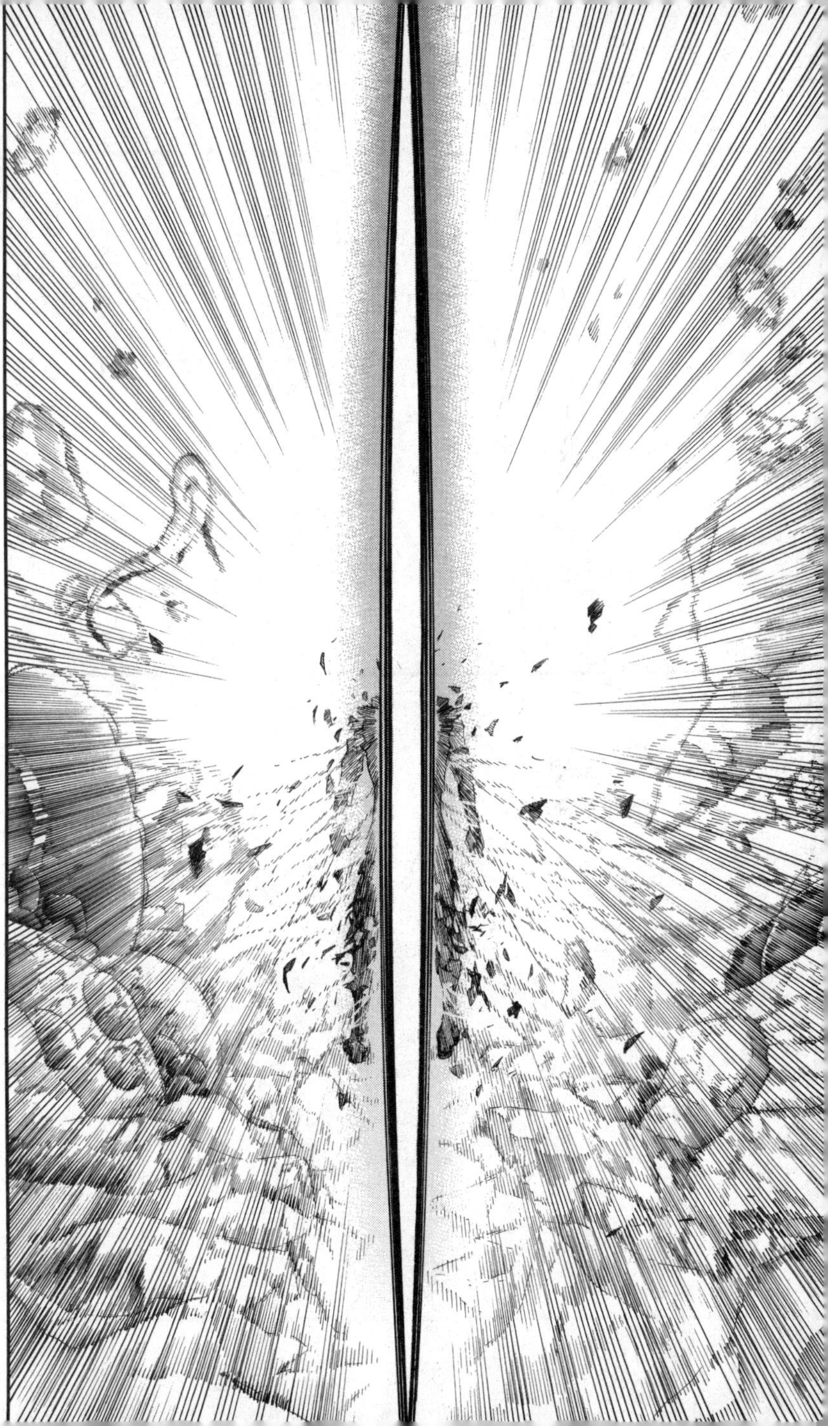

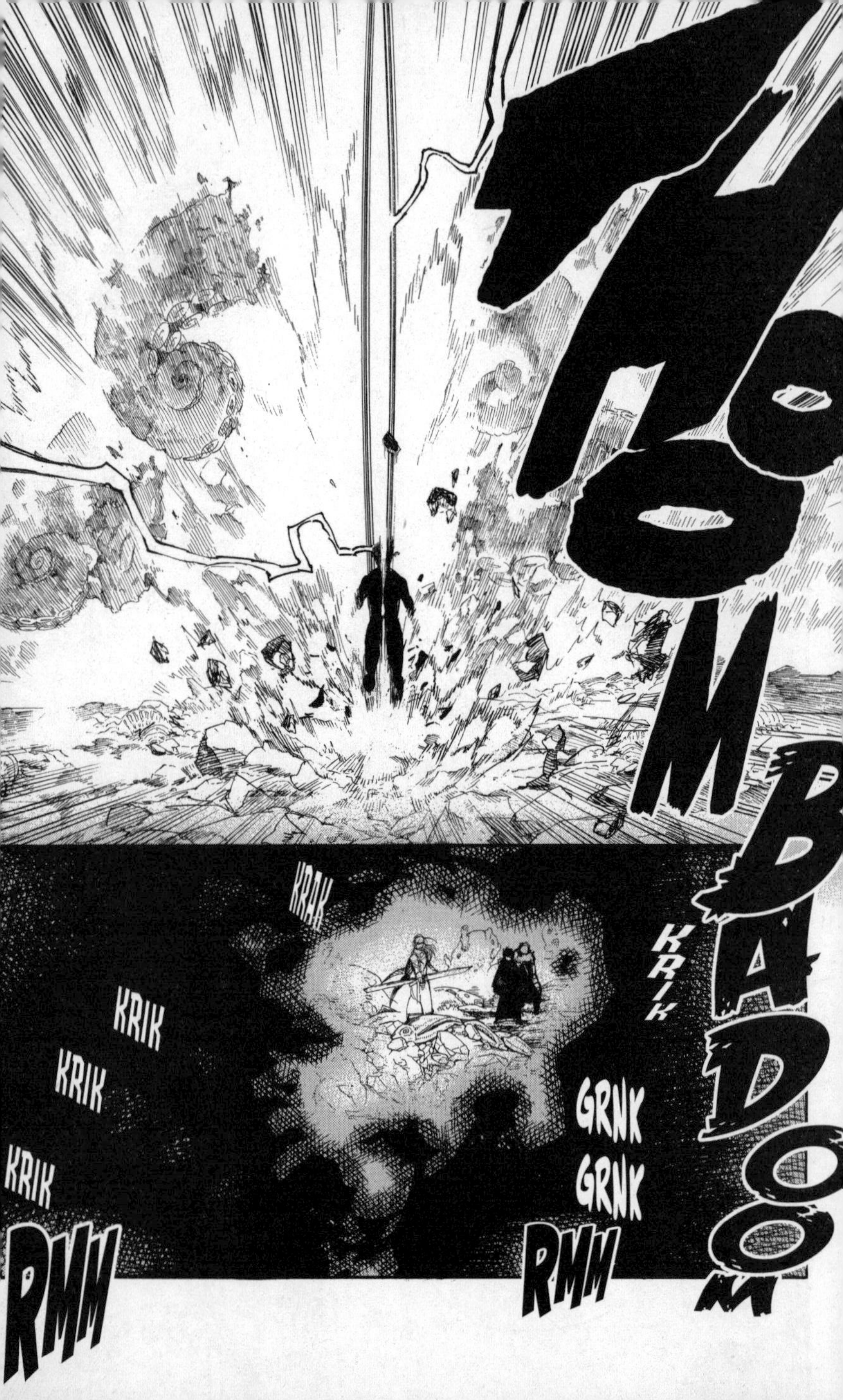
BADOOM
KRIK
GRNK
GRNK
RMM
KRAK
KRIK
KRIK
KRIK
RMM

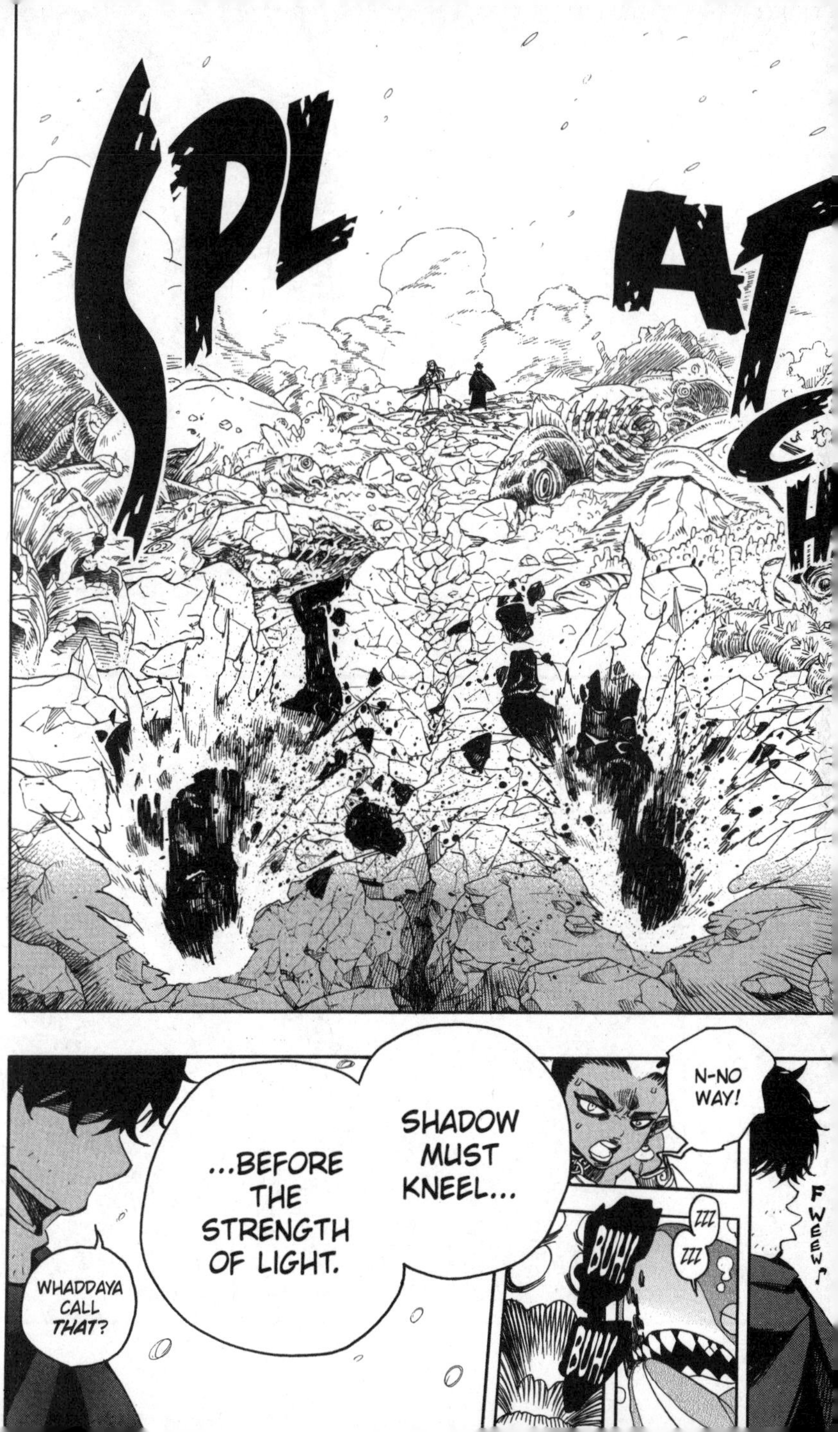
SPLATCH
N-NO WAY!
ZZZ
ZZZ
BUH!
BUH!
FWEEW
SHADOW MUST KNEEL...
...BEFORE THE STRENGTH OF LIGHT.
WHADDAYA CALL THAT?

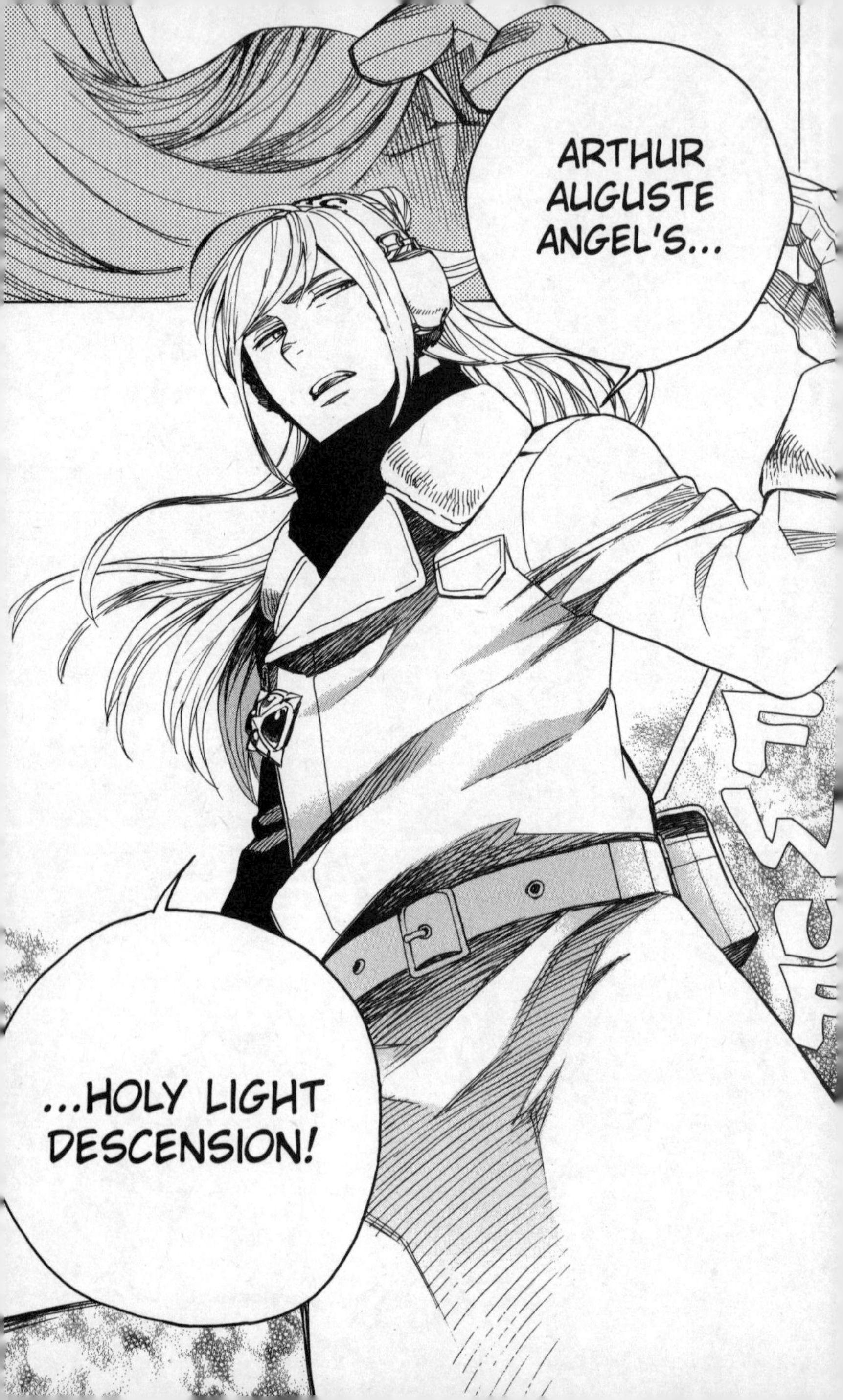
ARTHUR AUGUSTE ANGEL'S...
...HOLY LIGHT DESCENSION!

Blue Exorcist Chapter 133: Of One Cloth—Flutter

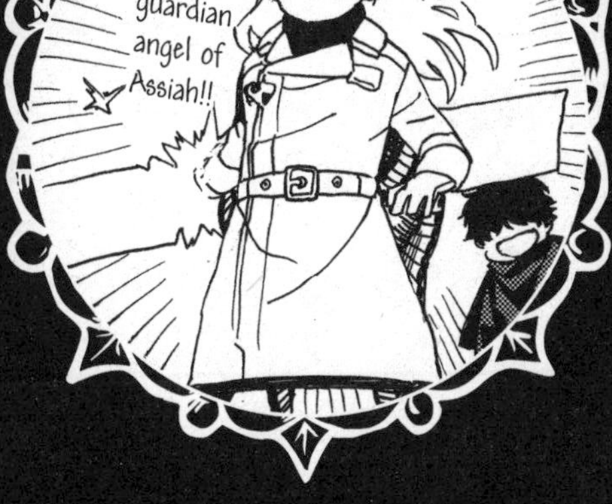

I-am...
...the guardian angel of Assiah!!

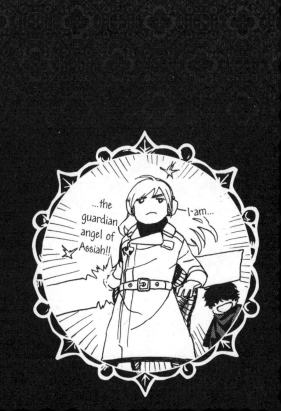

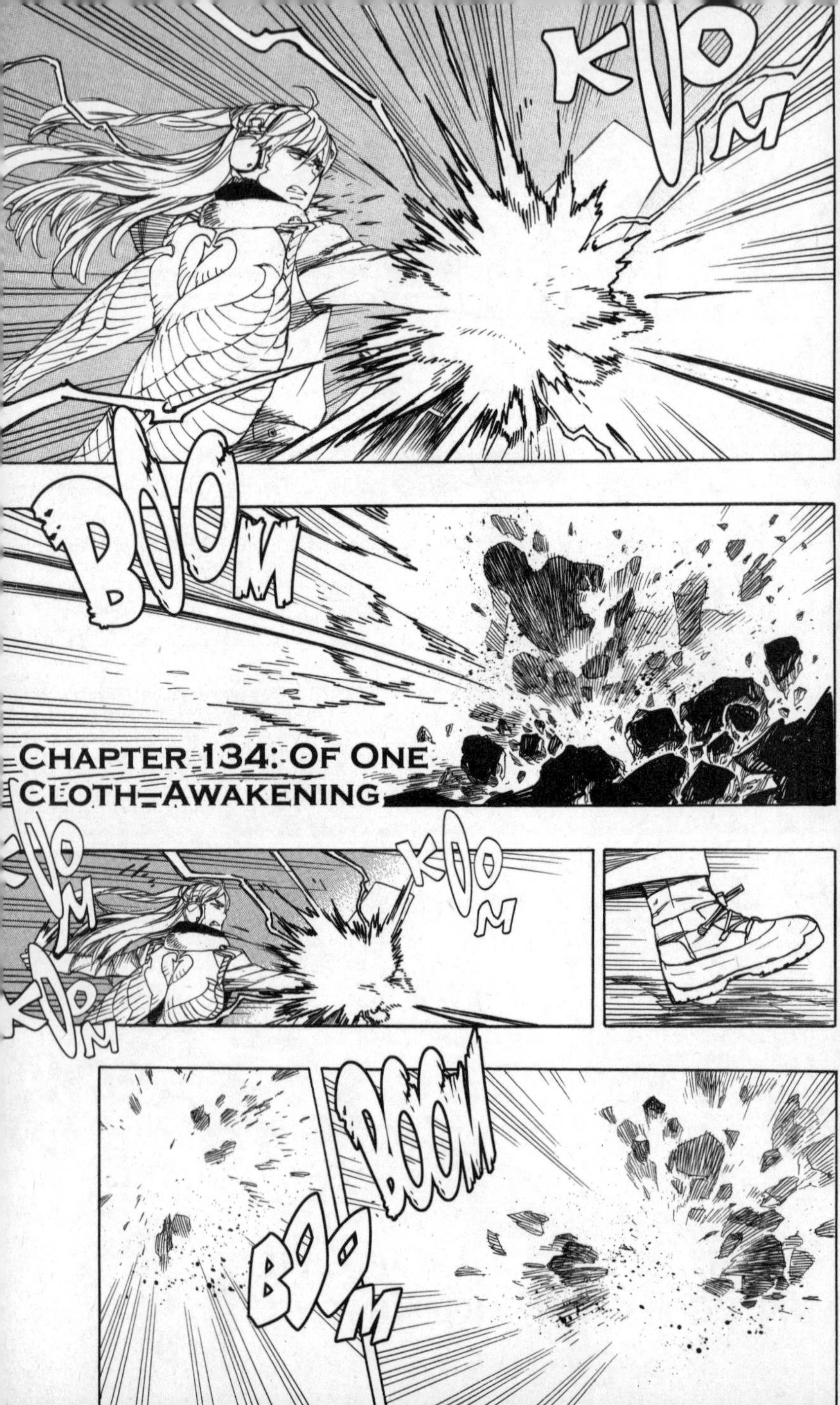
KOOM
BOOM
CHAPTER 134: OF ONE CLOTH—AWAKENING
KOOM
OOM
KOOM
BOOM
BOOM

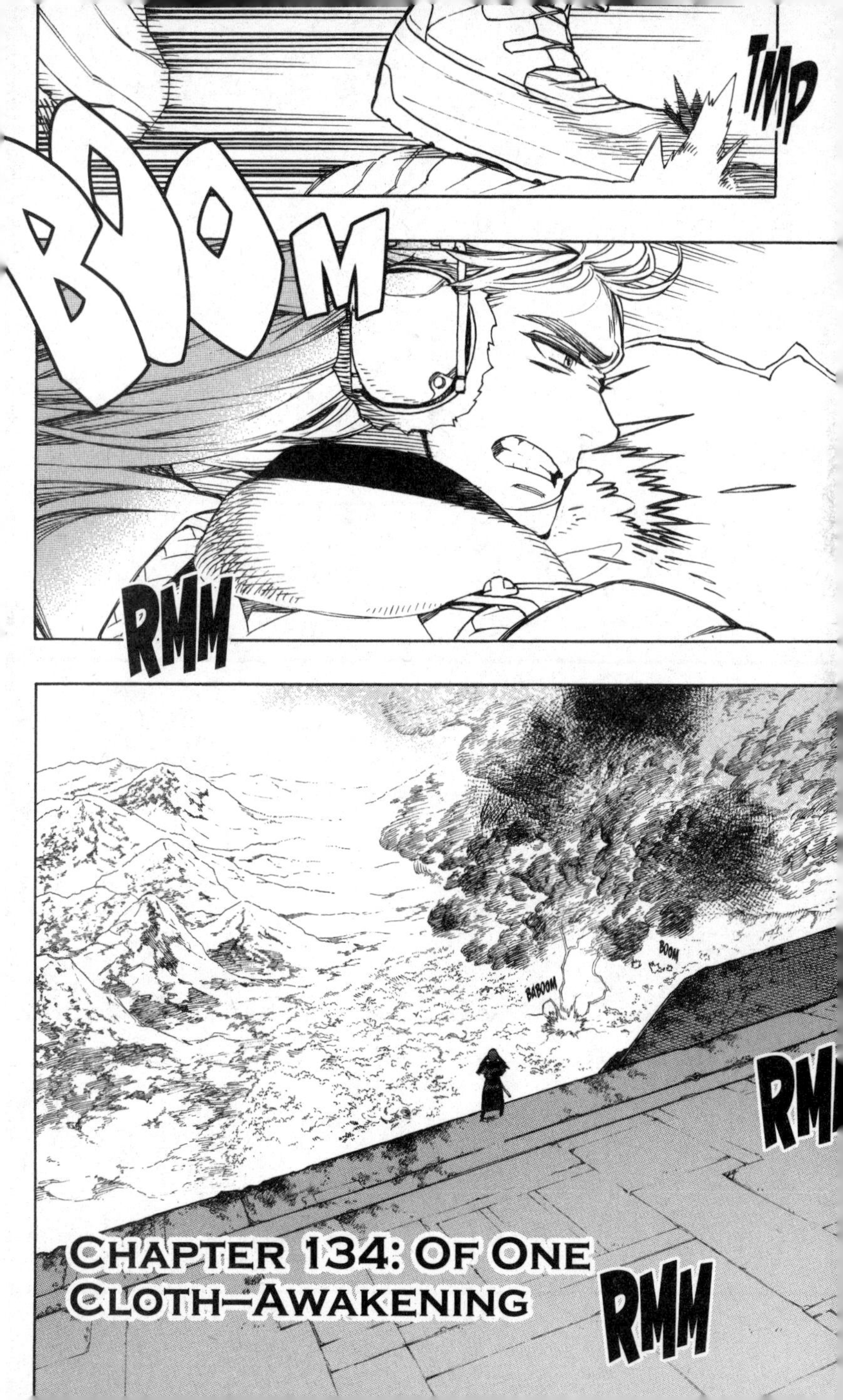
TMP
BOOM
RMM
RM
BOOM
BABOOM
RMM

Chapter 134: Of One Cloth—Awakening

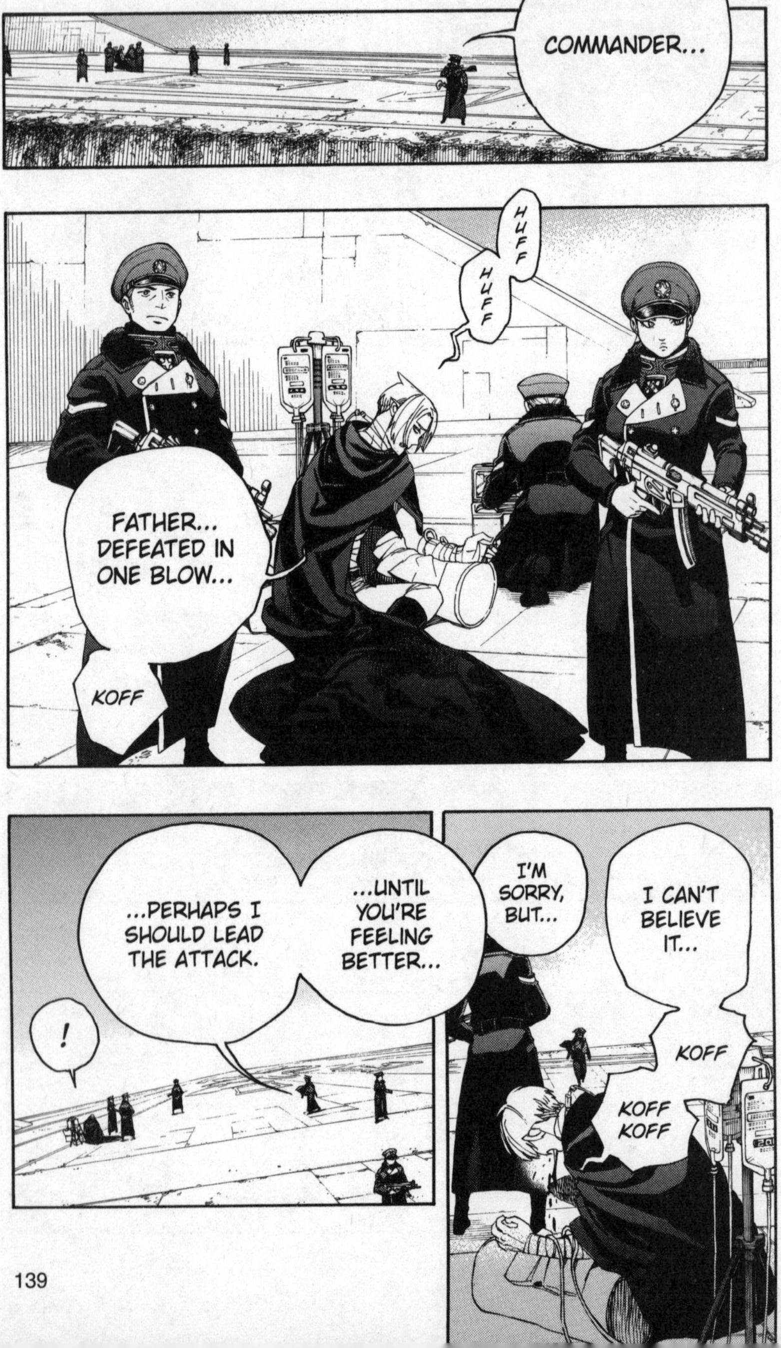
COMMANDER...
HUFF HUFF
FATHER... DEFEATED IN ONE BLOW...
KOFF
I CAN'T BELIEVE IT...
KOFF
KOFF KOFF
I'M SORRY, BUT...
...UNTIL YOU'RE FEELING BETTER...
...PERHAPS I SHOULD LEAD THE ATTACK.
!

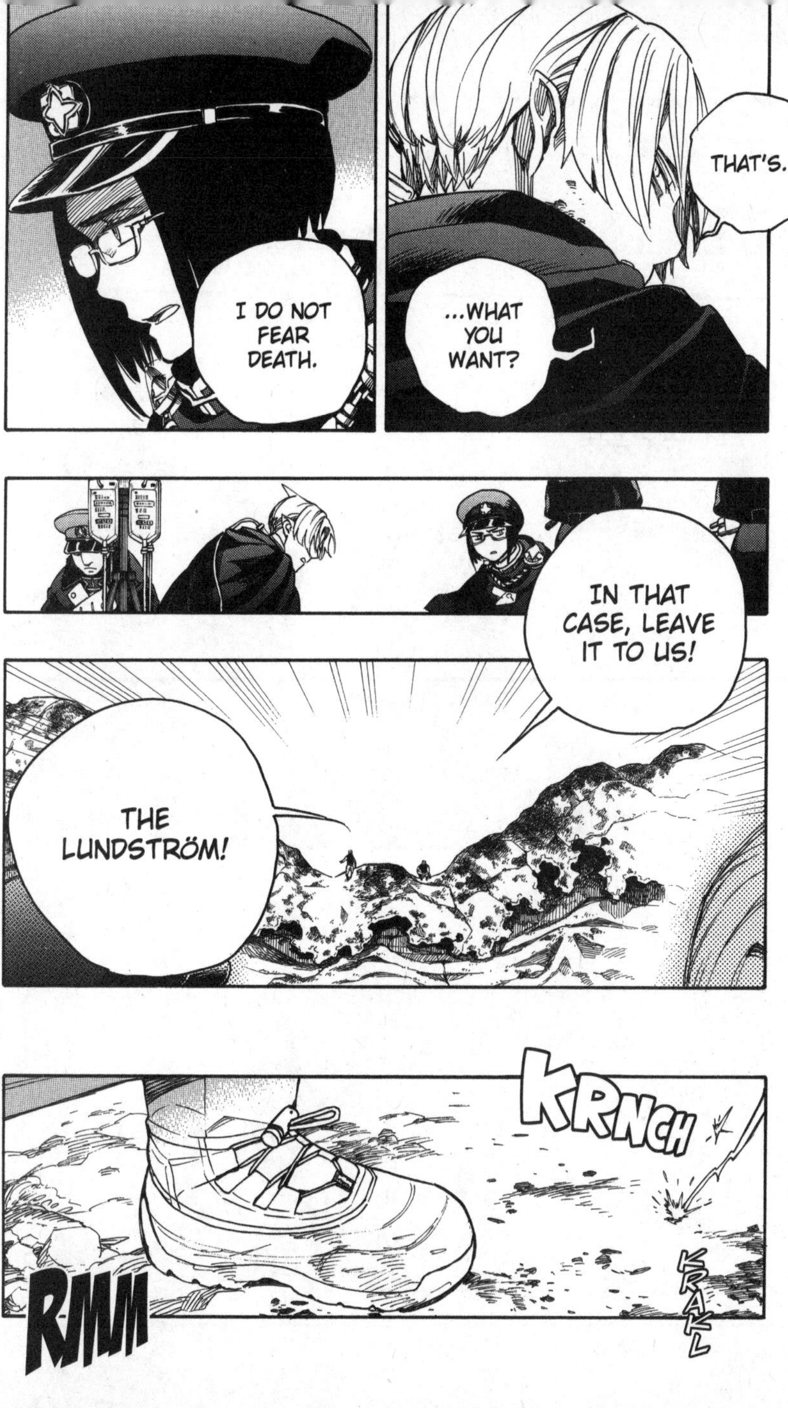
THAT'S...
...WHAT YOU WANT?
I DO NOT FEAR DEATH.
IN THAT CASE, LEAVE IT TO US!
THE LUNDSTRÖM!
KRNCH
KRAKL
RMM

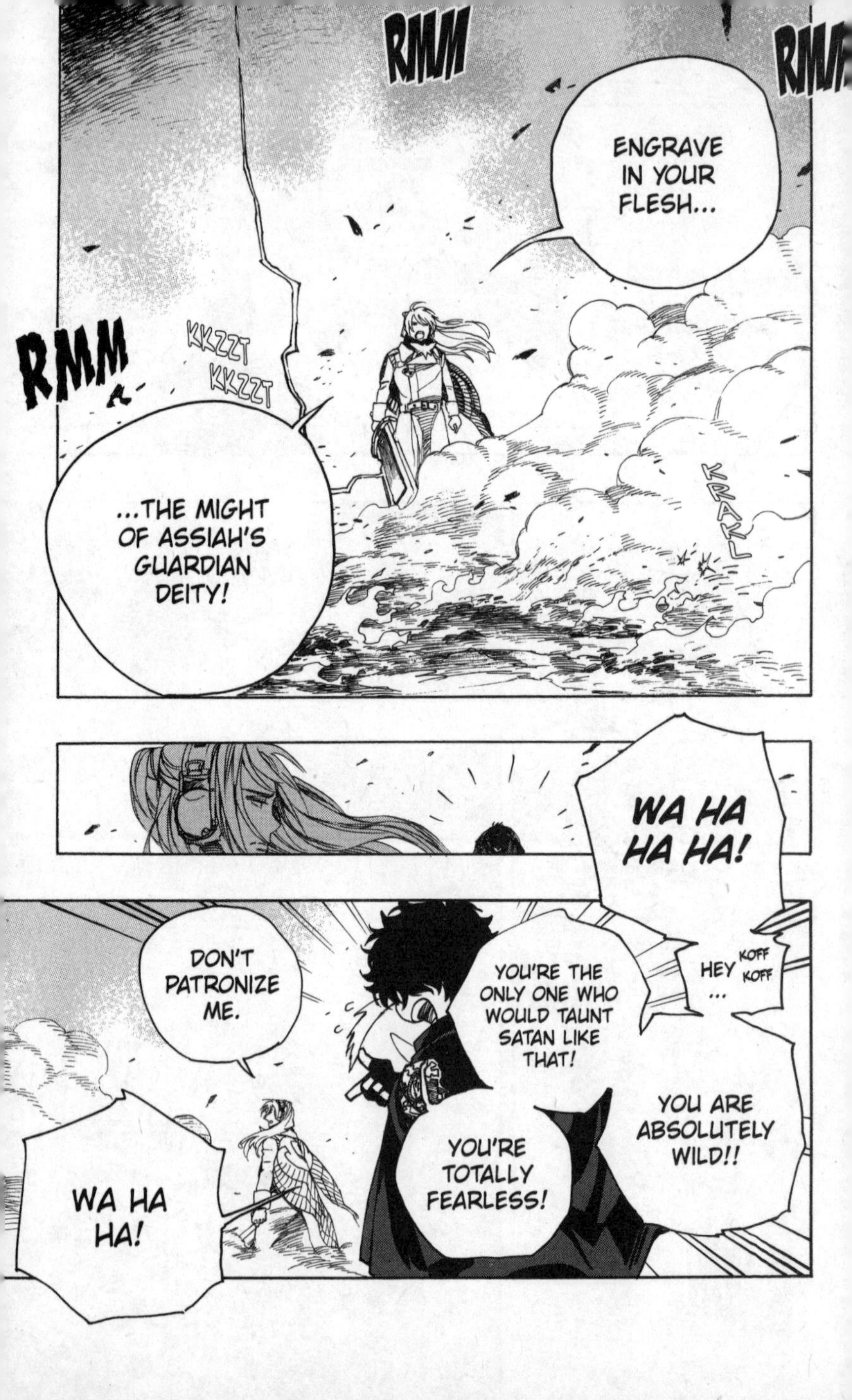
RMM
RMM
ENGRAVE IN YOUR FLESH...
KKZZT KKZZT
RMM
KRAKL
...THE MIGHT OF ASSIAH'S GUARDIAN DEITY!
WA HA HA HA!
HEY ... KOFF KOFF
YOU'RE THE ONLY ONE WHO WOULD TAUNT SATAN LIKE THAT!
DON'T PATRONIZE ME.
YOU ARE ABSOLUTELY WILD!!
YOU'RE TOTALLY FEARLESS!
WA HA HA!

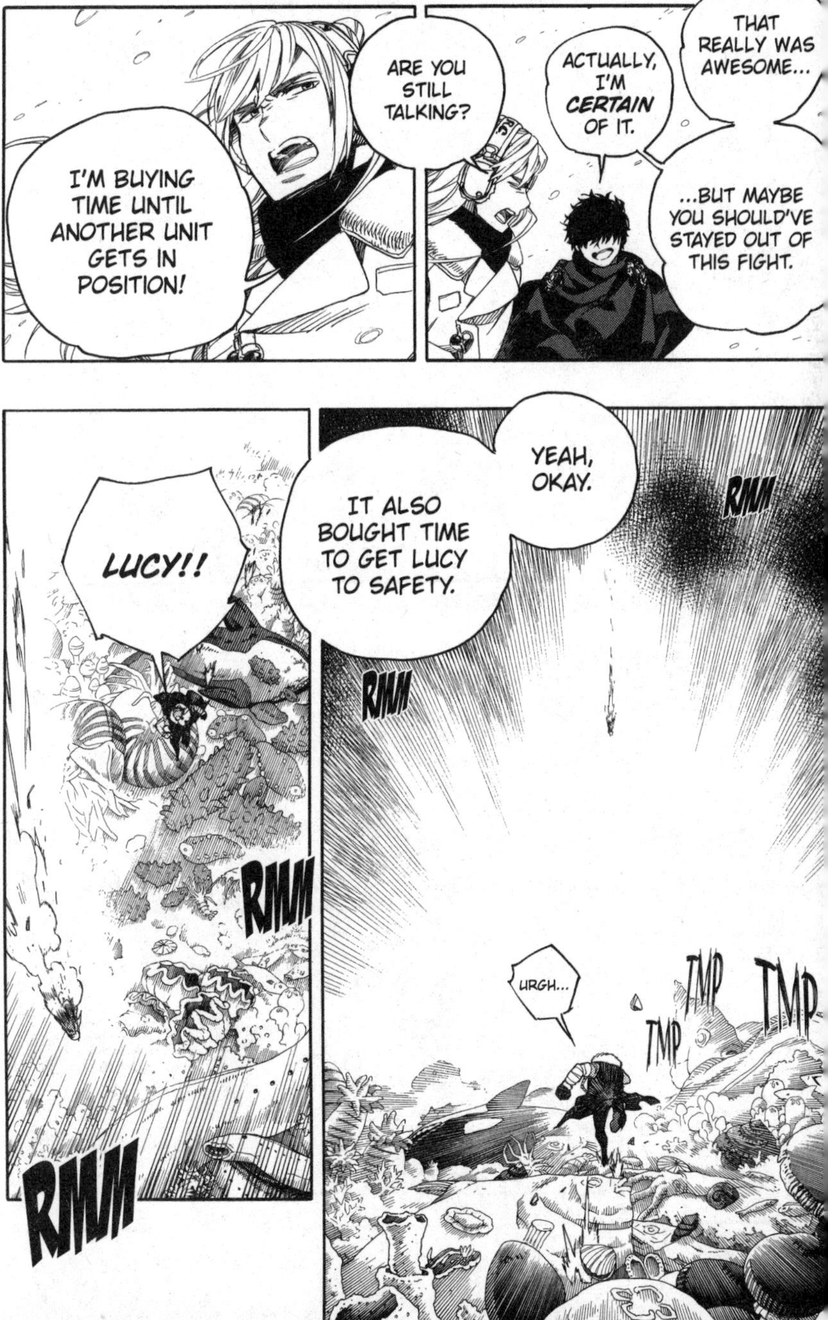
THAT REALLY WAS AWESOME...
...BUT MAYBE YOU SHOULD'VE STAYED OUT OF THIS FIGHT.
ACTUALLY, I'M CERTAIN OF IT.
ARE YOU STILL TALKING?
I'M BUYING TIME UNTIL ANOTHER UNIT GETS IN POSITION!
YEAH, OKAY.
IT ALSO BOUGHT TIME TO GET LUCY TO SAFETY.
RMM
RMM
URGH...
TMP
TMP
TMP
LUCY!!
RMM
RMM

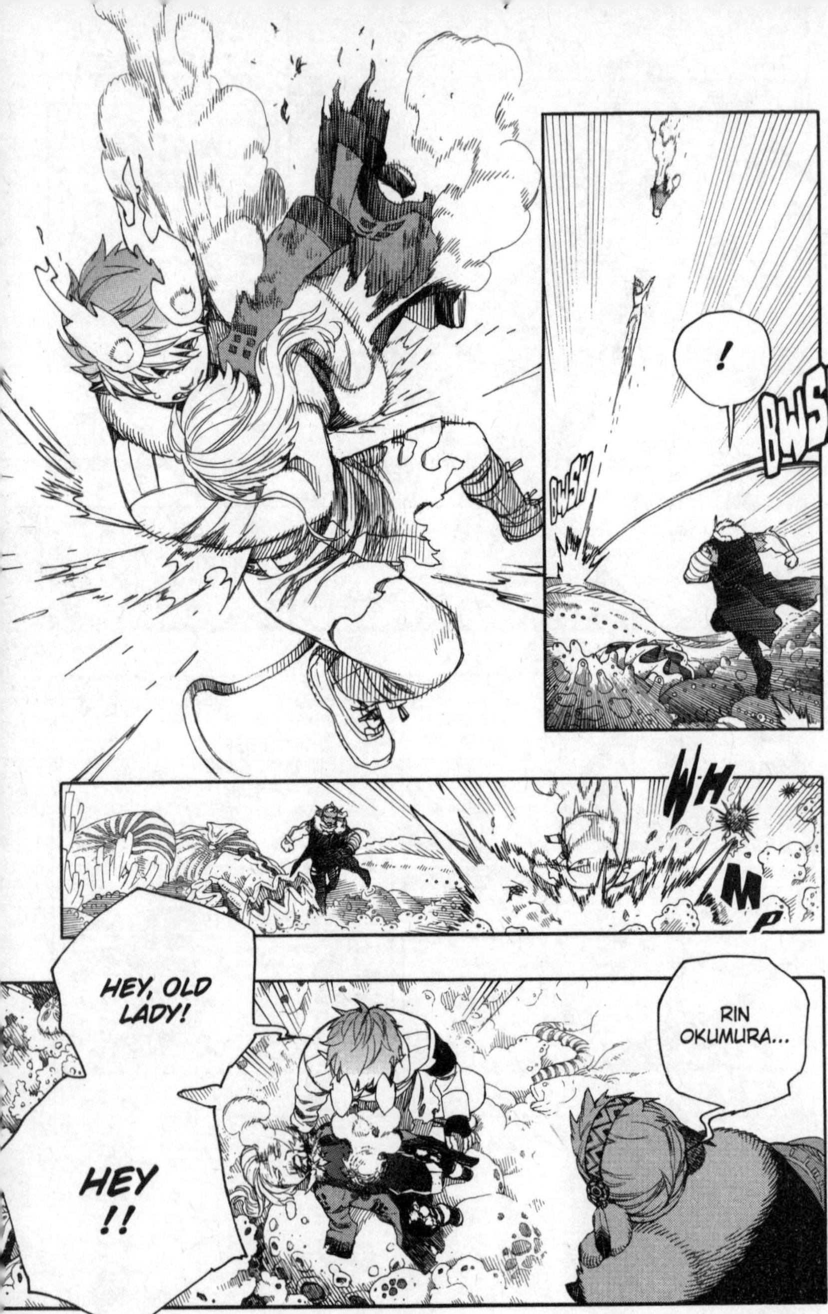
!
BWSH
BWSH
W-H-M-P
RIN OKUMURA...
HEY, OLD LADY!
HEY !!

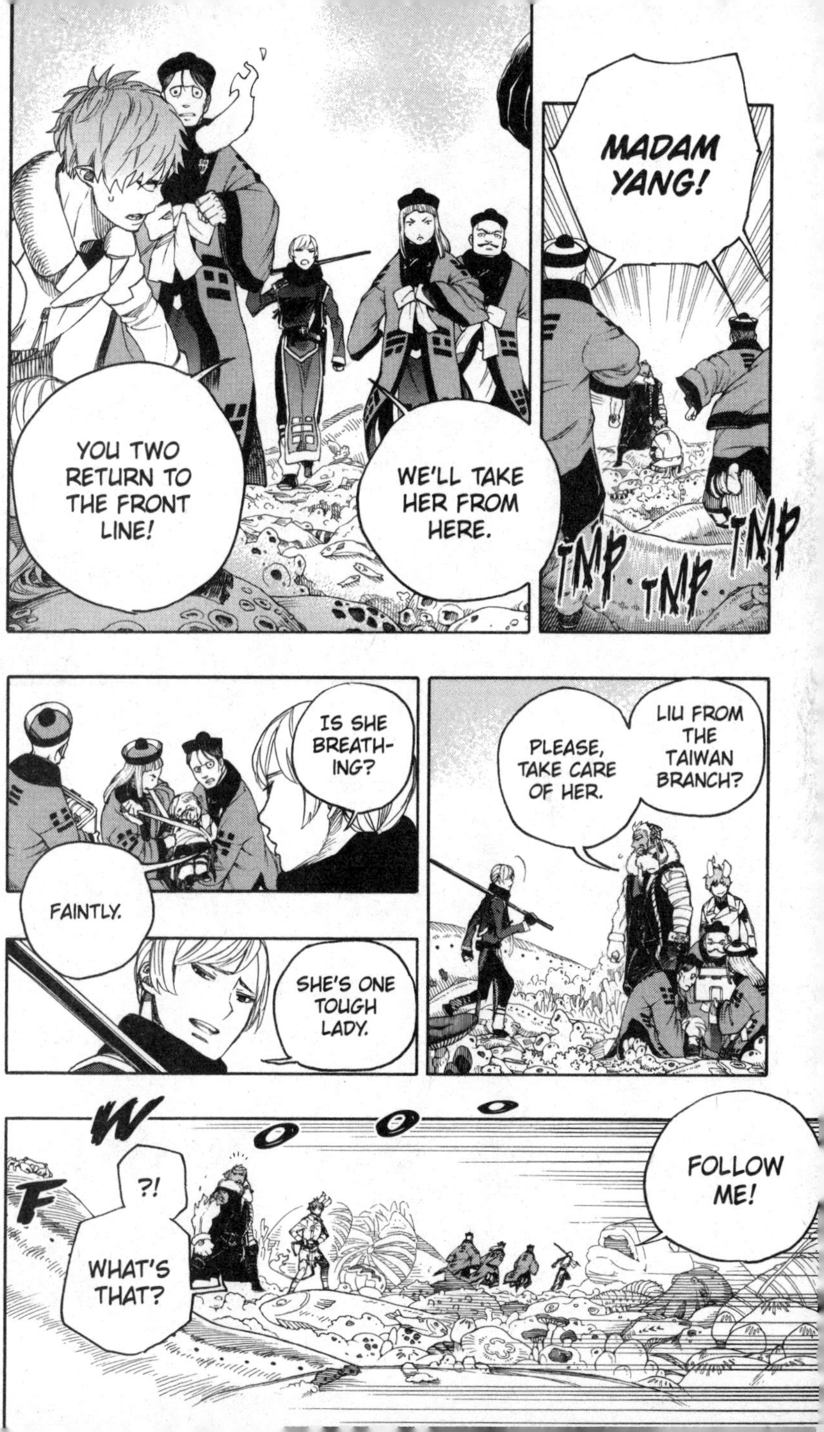
MADAM YANG!
TMP TMP TMP
WE'LL TAKE HER FROM HERE.
YOU TWO RETURN TO THE FRONT LINE!
LIU FROM THE TAIWAN BRANCH?
PLEASE, TAKE CARE OF HER.
IS SHE BREATHING?
FAINTLY.
SHE'S ONE TOUGH LADY.
FOLLOW ME!
WOOOF
?!
WHAT'S THAT?

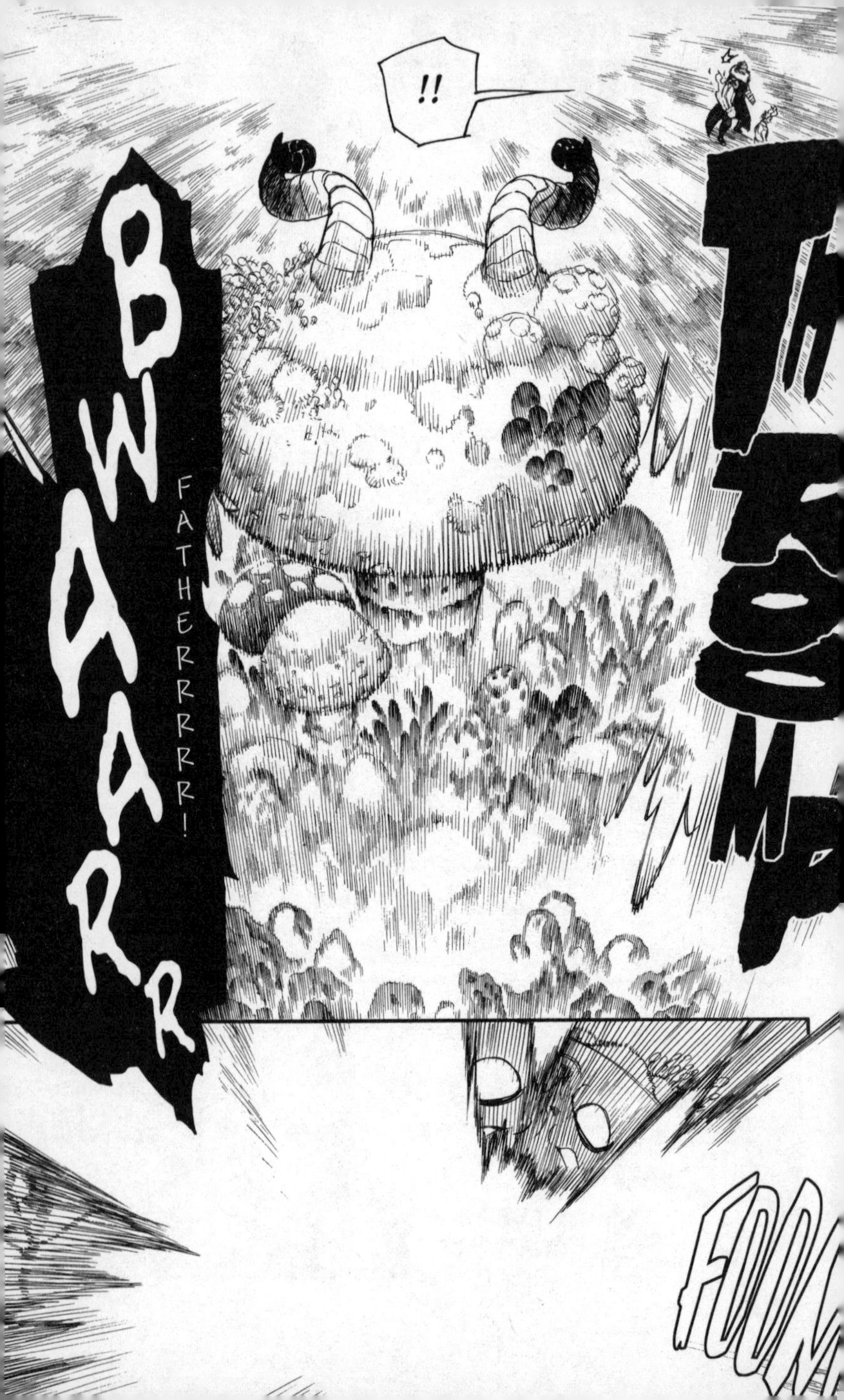
!!
THROOMP
BWAARR
FATHERRRRR!
FOOM

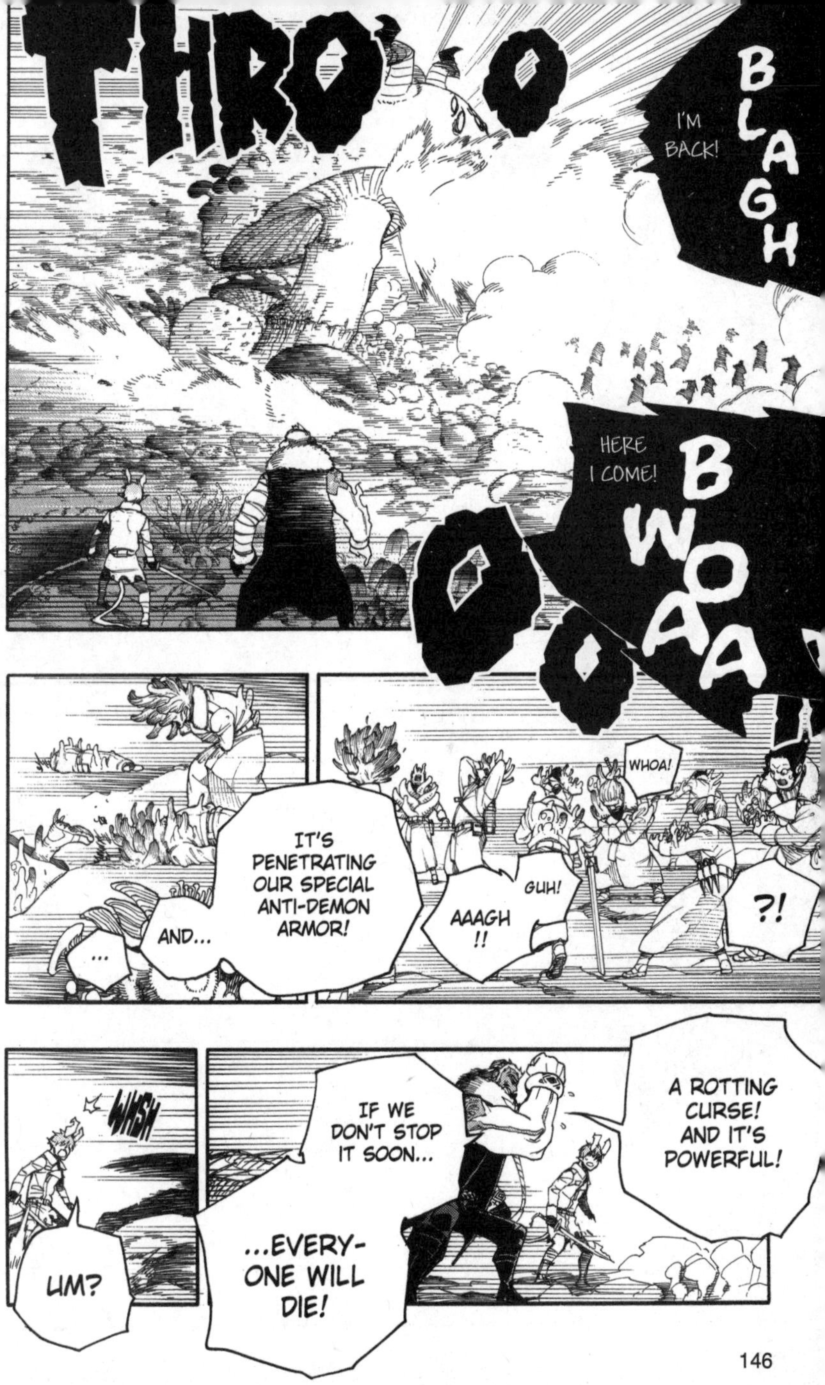
BLAGH
I'M BACK!
THRO O
HERE I COME!
BWOAAA
OOO
?!
WHOA!
GUH!
AAAGH !!
IT'S PENETRATING OUR SPECIAL ANTI-DEMON ARMOR!
AND...
...
A ROTTING CURSE! AND IT'S POWERFUL!
IF WE DON'T STOP IT SOON...
...EVERY-ONE WILL DIE!
WHSH
UM?

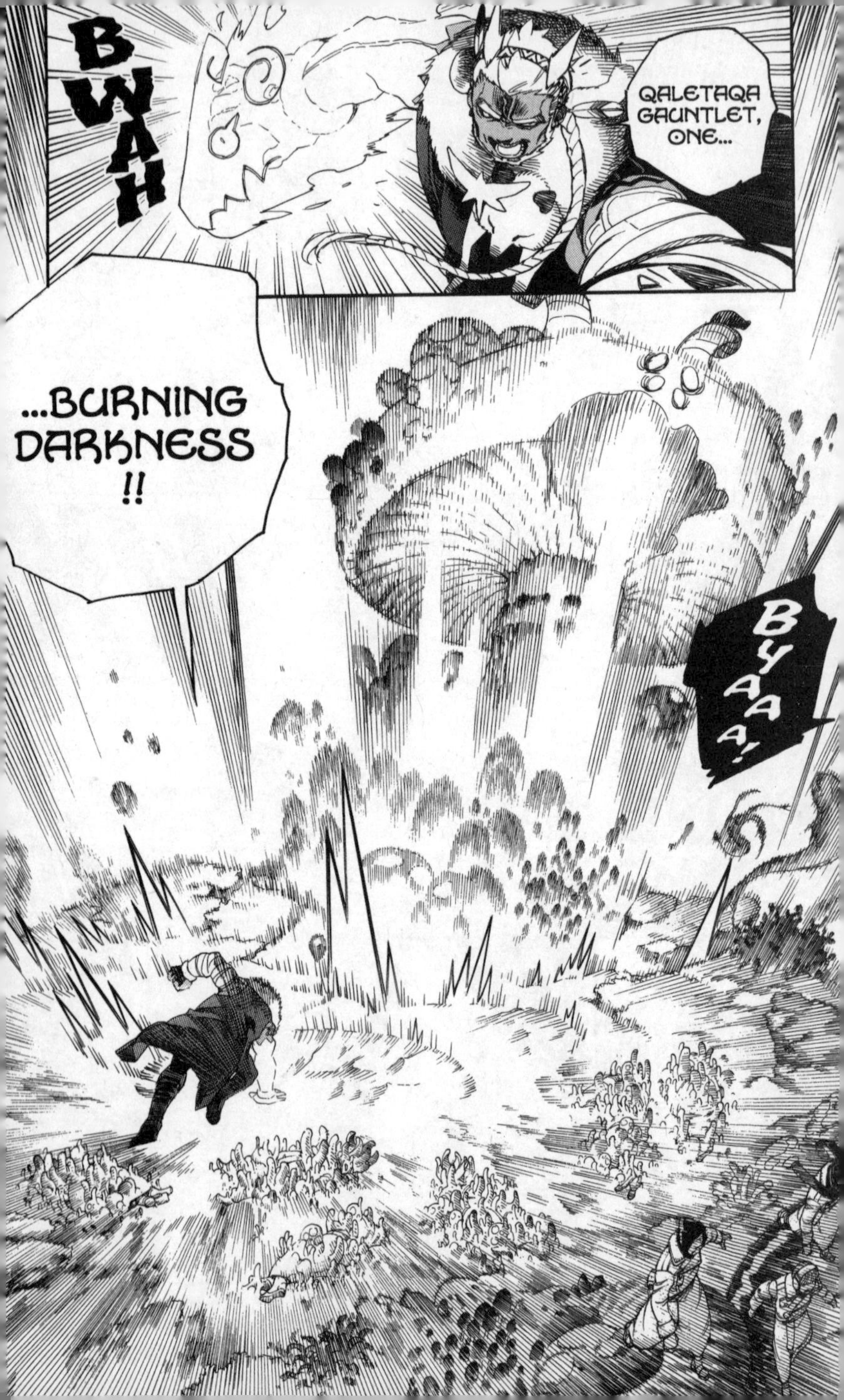
QALETAQA GAUNTLET, ONE...
BWAH
...BURNING DARKNESS!!
BYAAAA!

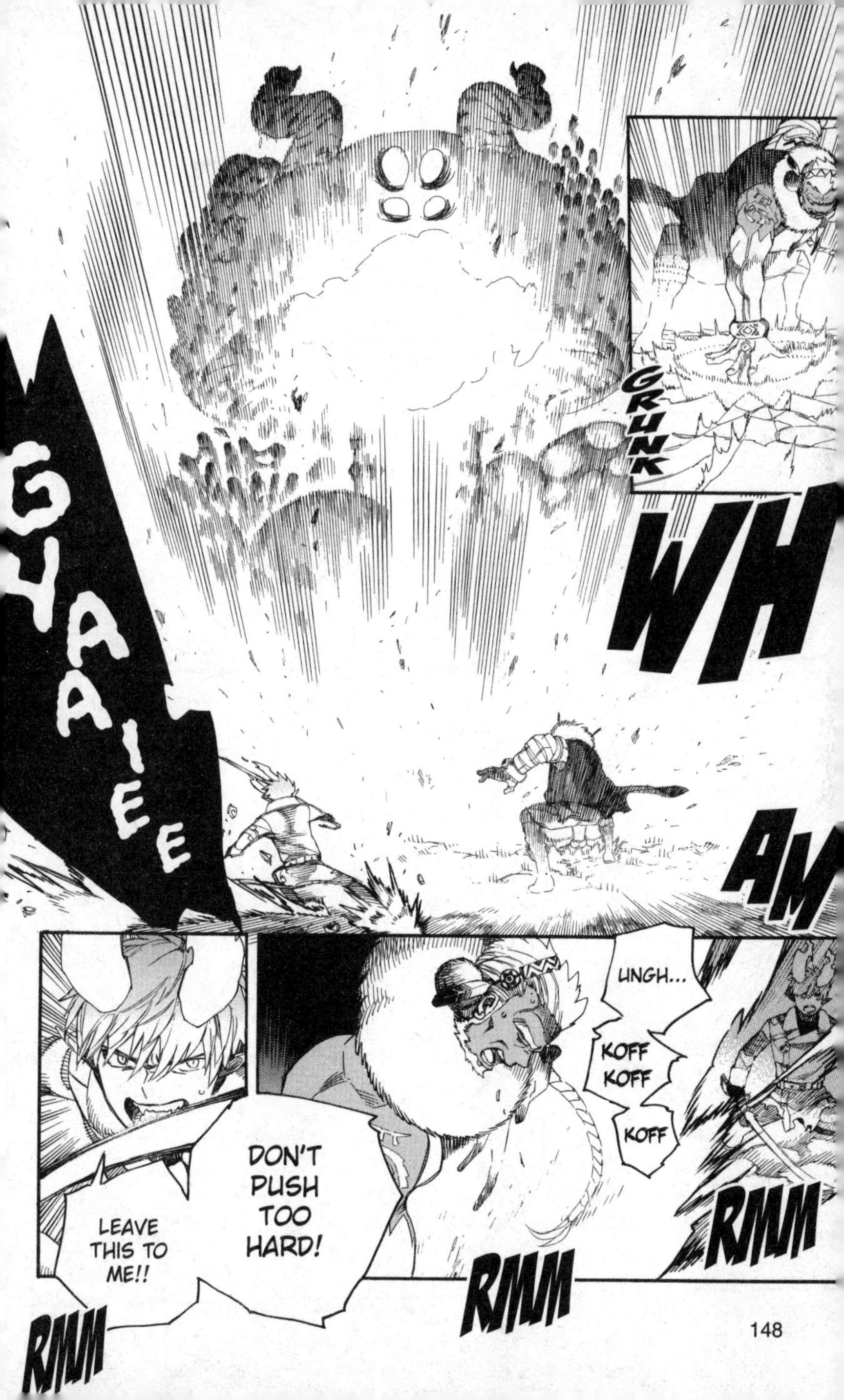
GRUNK
WHAM
GYAAIEE
RMM
UNGH...
KOFF KOFF
KOFF
DON'T PUSH TOO HARD!
RMM
LEAVE THIS TO ME!!
RMM

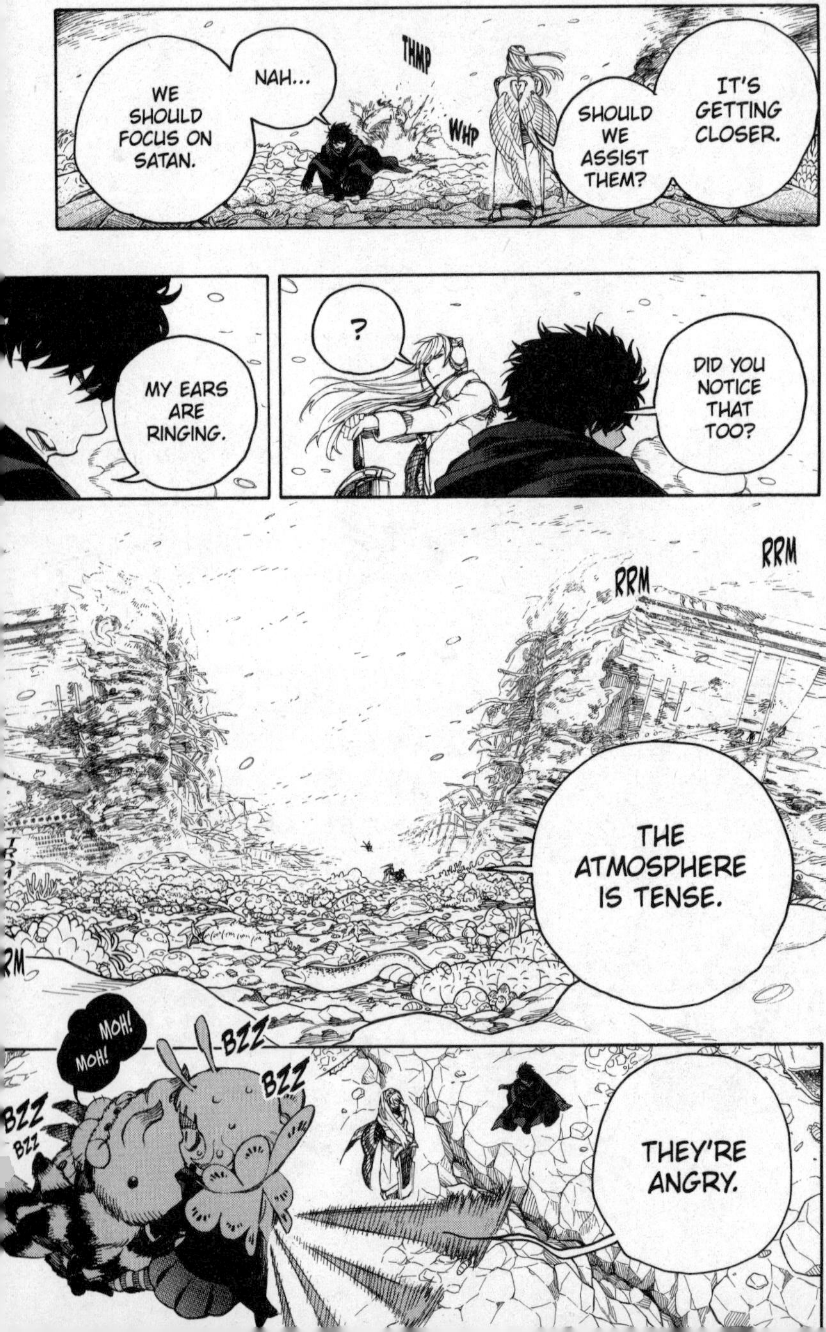
IT'S GETTING CLOSER.
SHOULD WE ASSIST THEM?
WHP
THMP
NAH...
WE SHOULD FOCUS ON SATAN.
DID YOU NOTICE THAT TOO?
?
MY EARS ARE RINGING.
RRM
RRM
THE ATMOSPHERE IS TENSE.
RM
THEY'RE ANGRY.
BZZ
BZZ
MOH!
MOH!
BZZ
BZZ

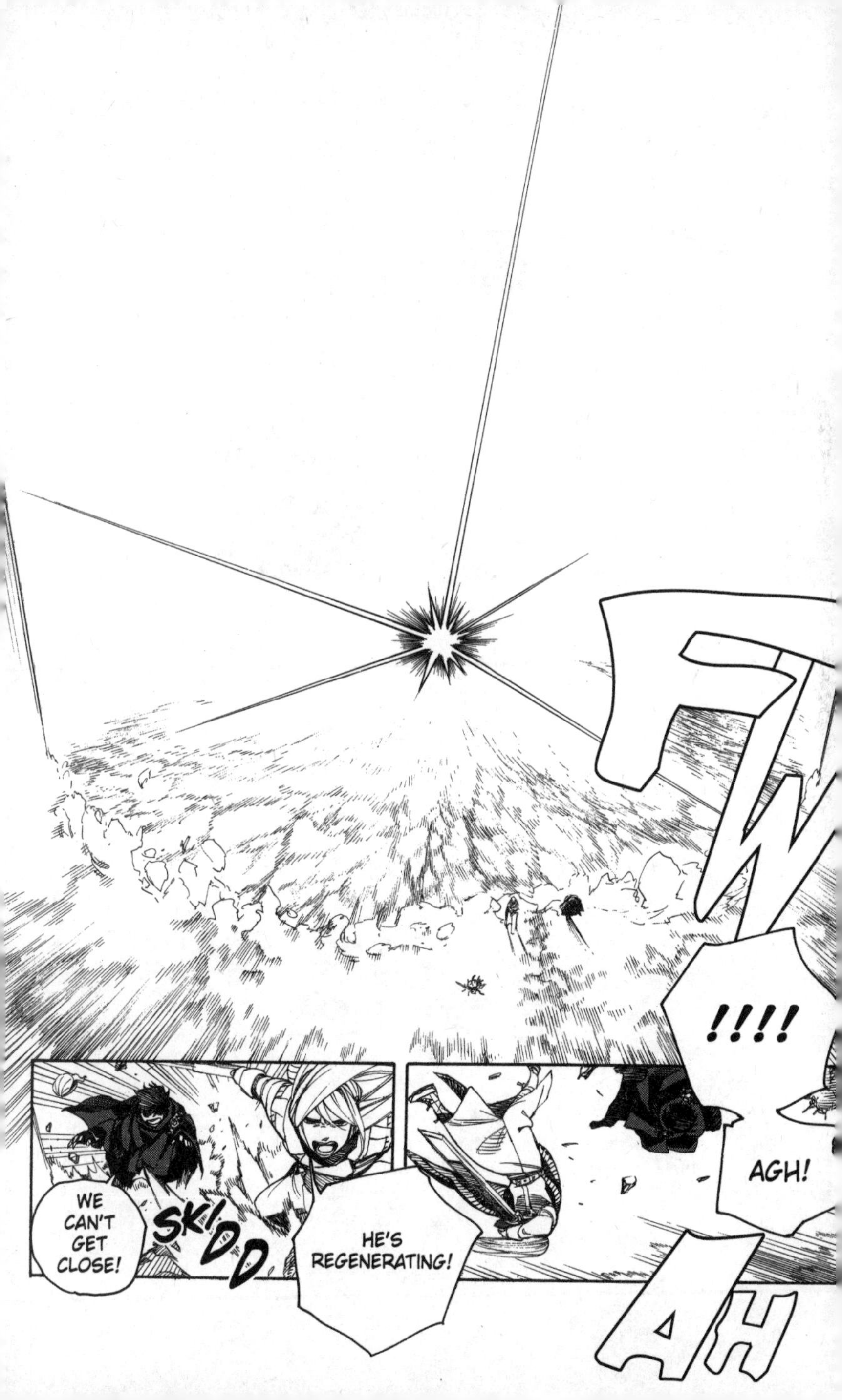
FW
!!!!
AGH!
HE'S REGENERATING!
AH
WE CAN'T GET CLOSE!
SKIDD

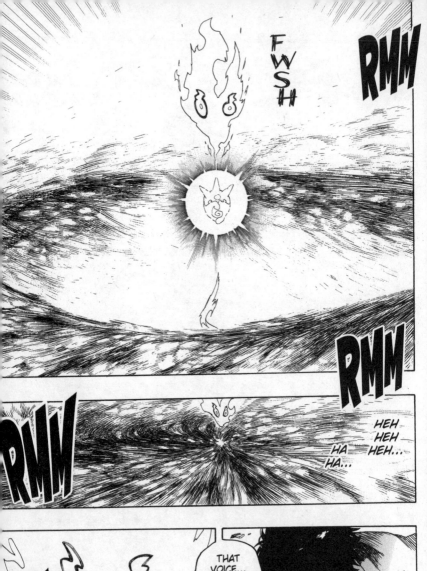

FWSH

RMM

RMM

RMM

HEH HEH...
HA HEH...
HA...

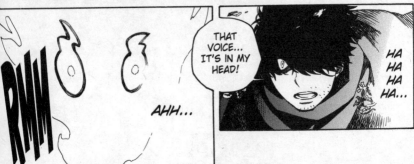

RMM

THAT VOICE... IT'S IN MY HEAD!

AHH...

HA
HA
HA
HA...

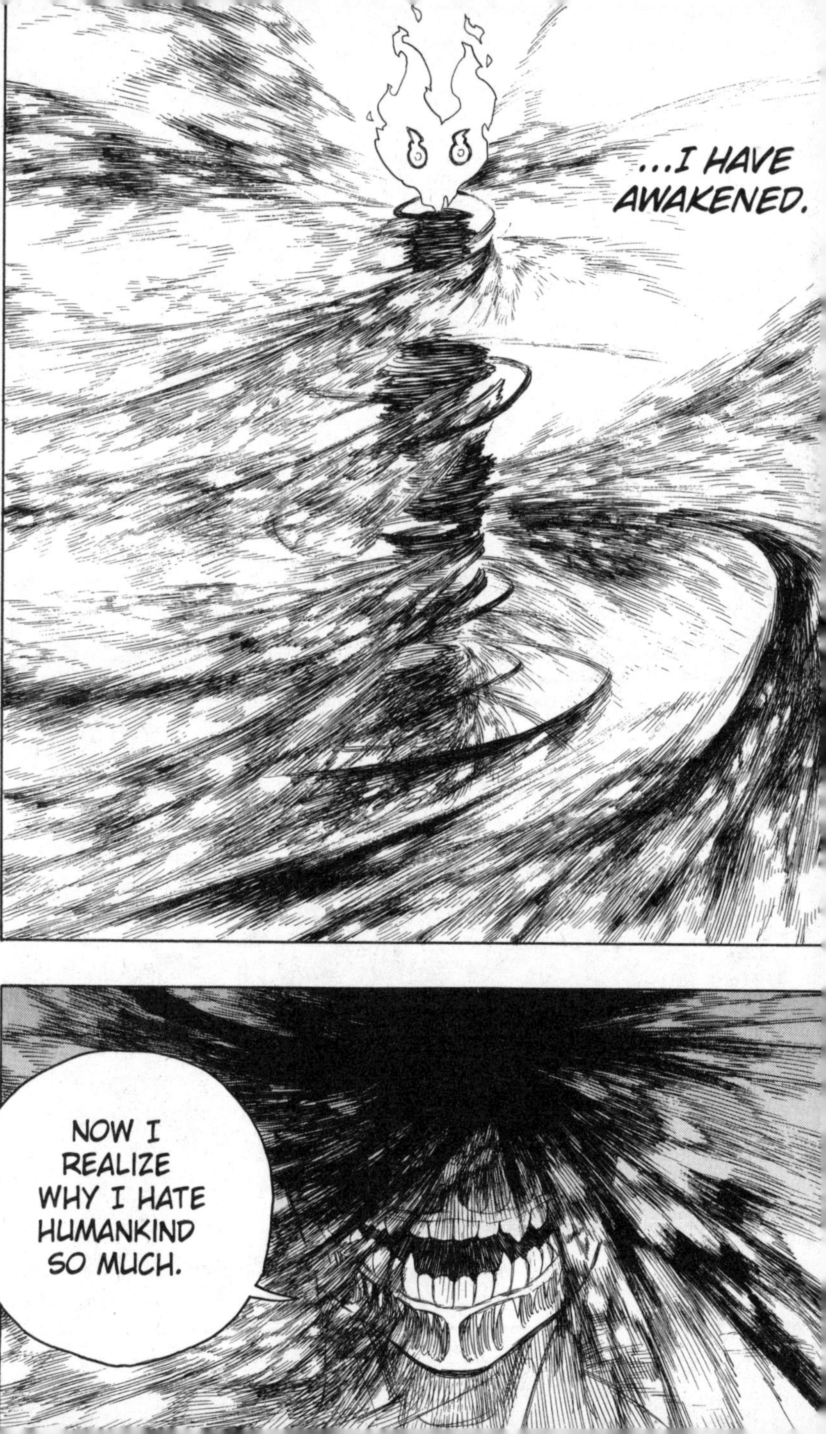
...I HAVE AWAKENED.
NOW I REALIZE WHY I HATE HUMANKIND SO MUCH.

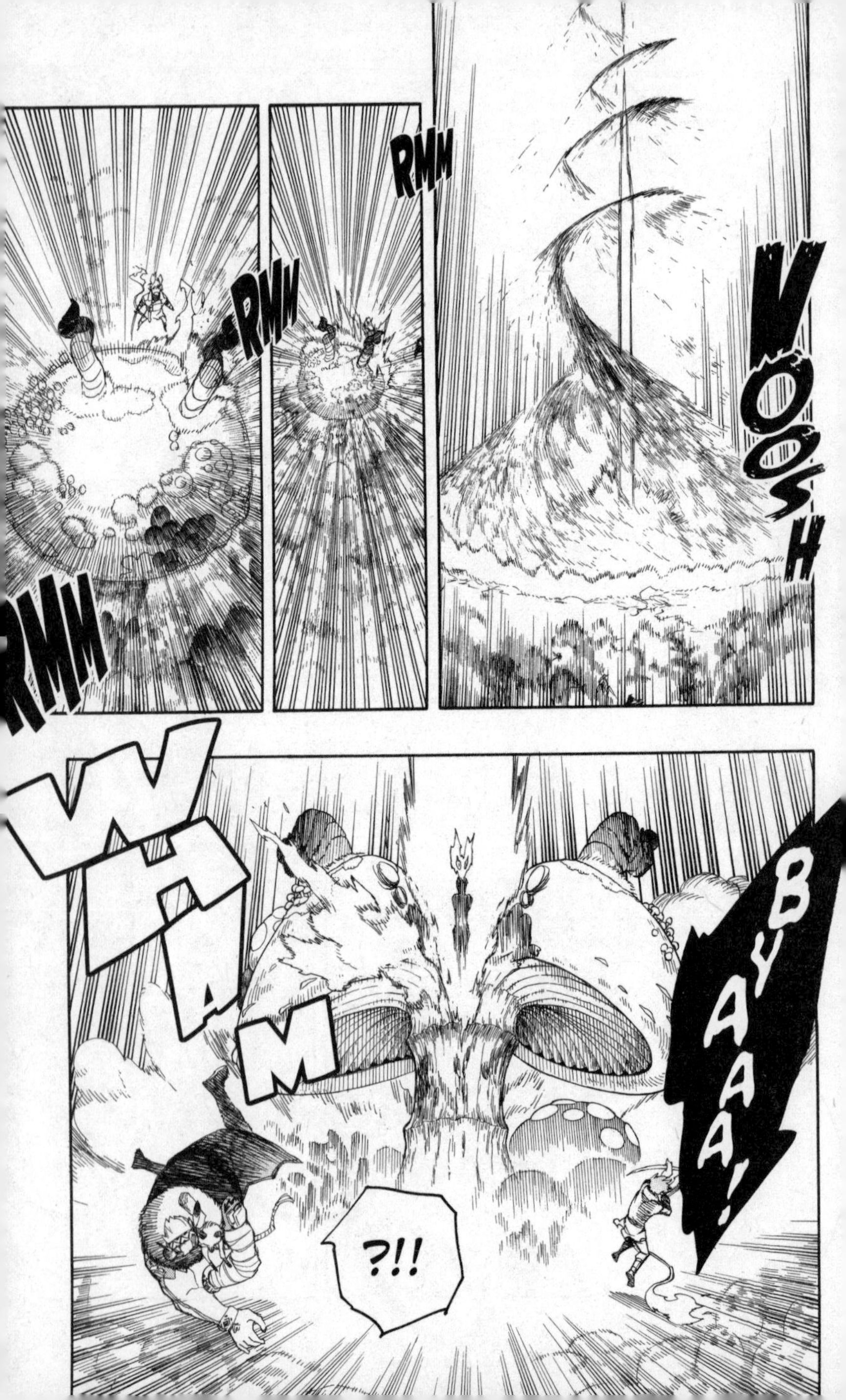
VOOSH
RMM
RMM
RMM
BYAAA!
WHAM
?!!

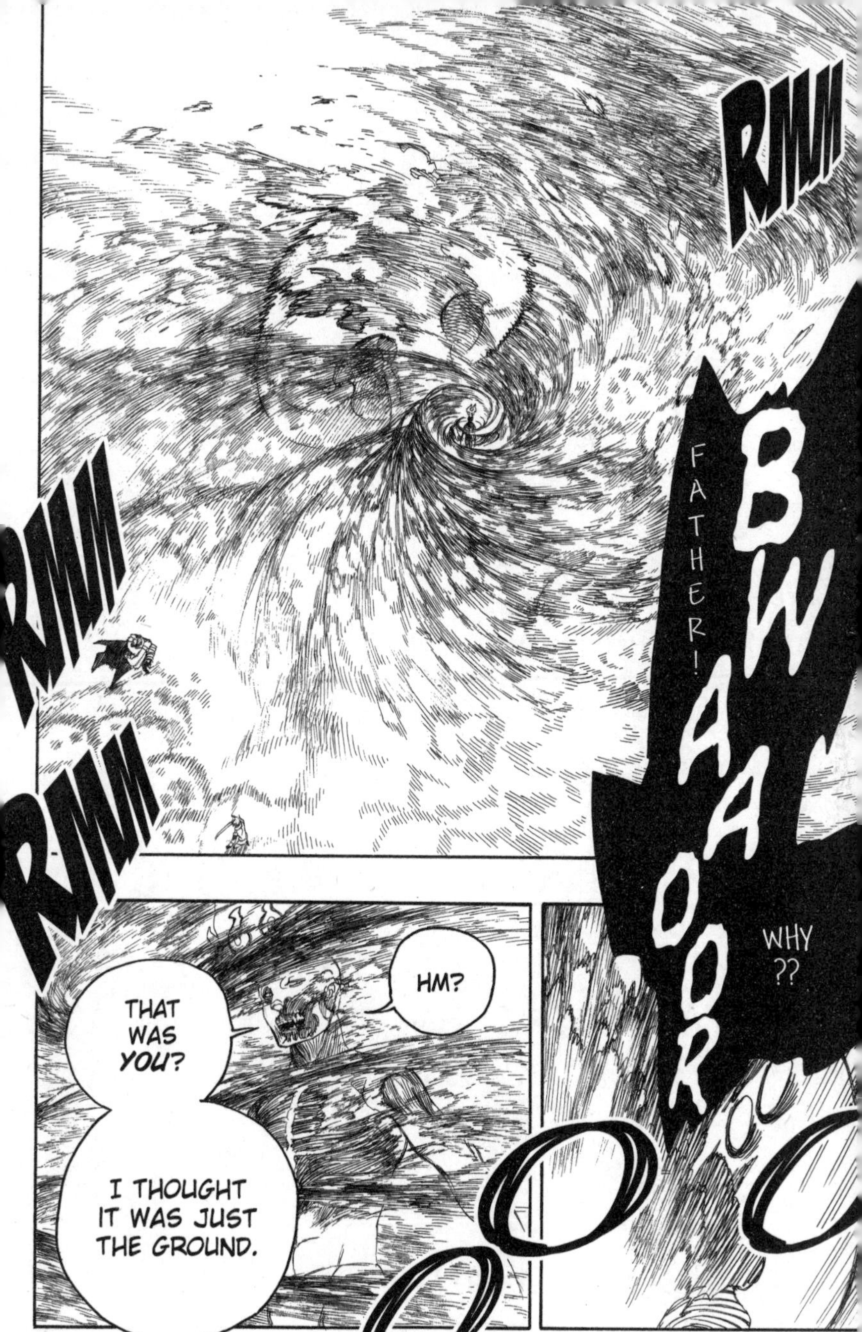
RMMM
RMMM
RMMM
FATHER!
BWAAOOR
WHY ??
HM?
THAT WAS YOU?
I THOUGHT IT WAS JUST THE GROUND.

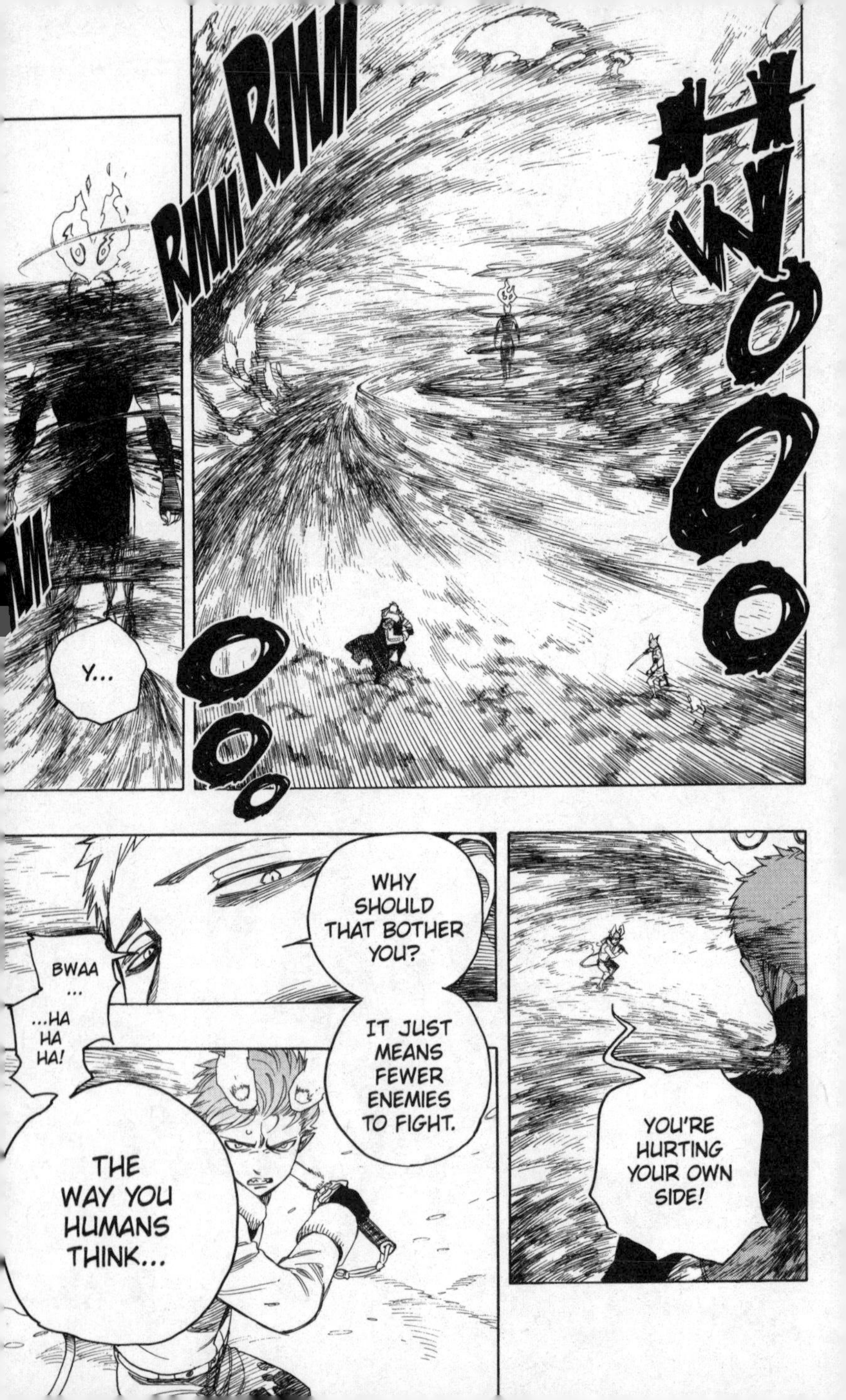
Y...
YOU'RE HURTING YOUR OWN SIDE!
WHY SHOULD THAT BOTHER YOU?
BWAA ... ...HA HA HA!
IT JUST MEANS FEWER ENEMIES TO FIGHT.
THE WAY YOU HUMANS THINK...

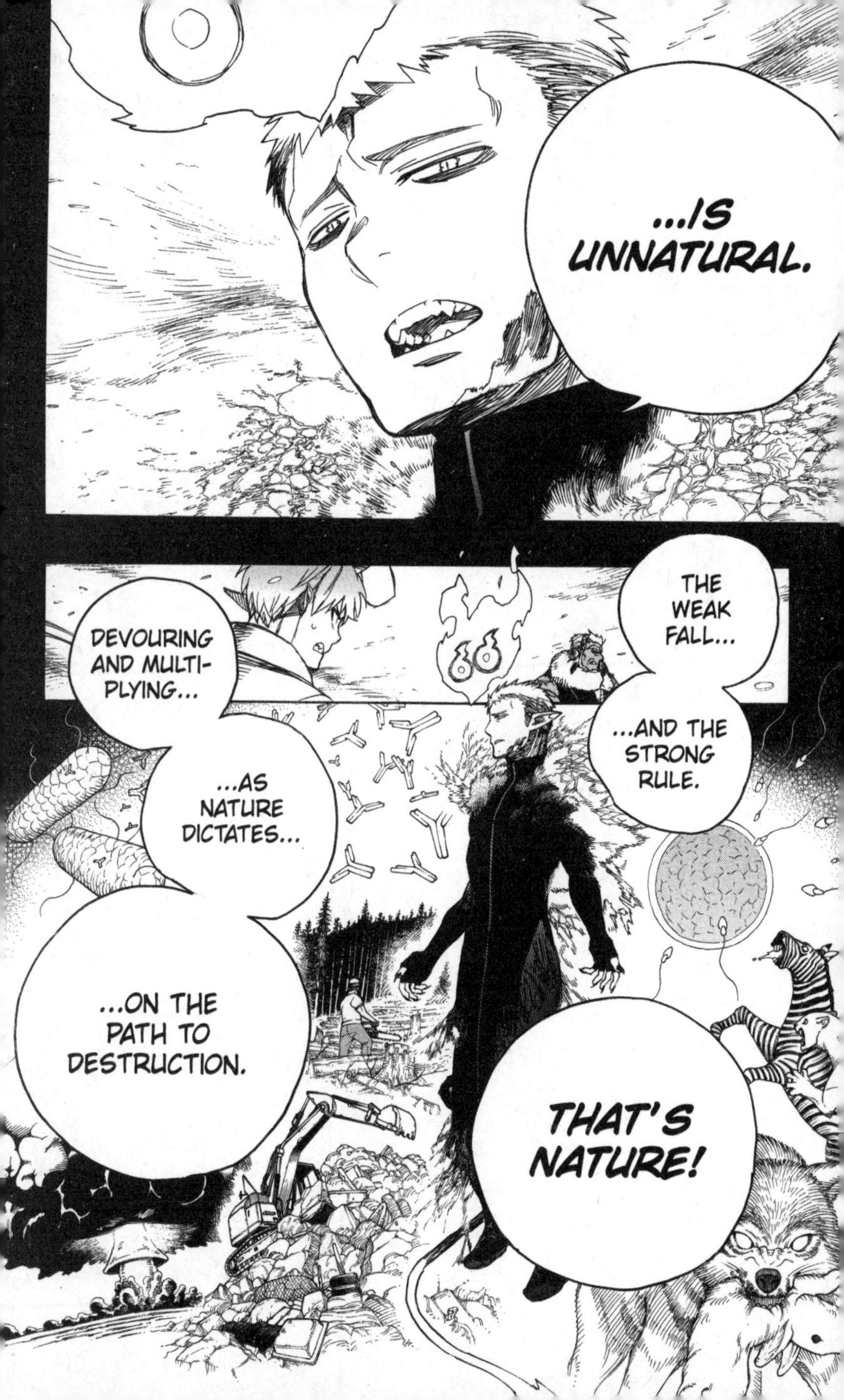
...IS UNNATURAL.
THE WEAK FALL...
...AND THE STRONG RULE.
DEVOURING AND MULTI-PLYING...
...AS NATURE DICTATES...
...ON THE PATH TO DESTRUCTION.
THAT'S NATURE!

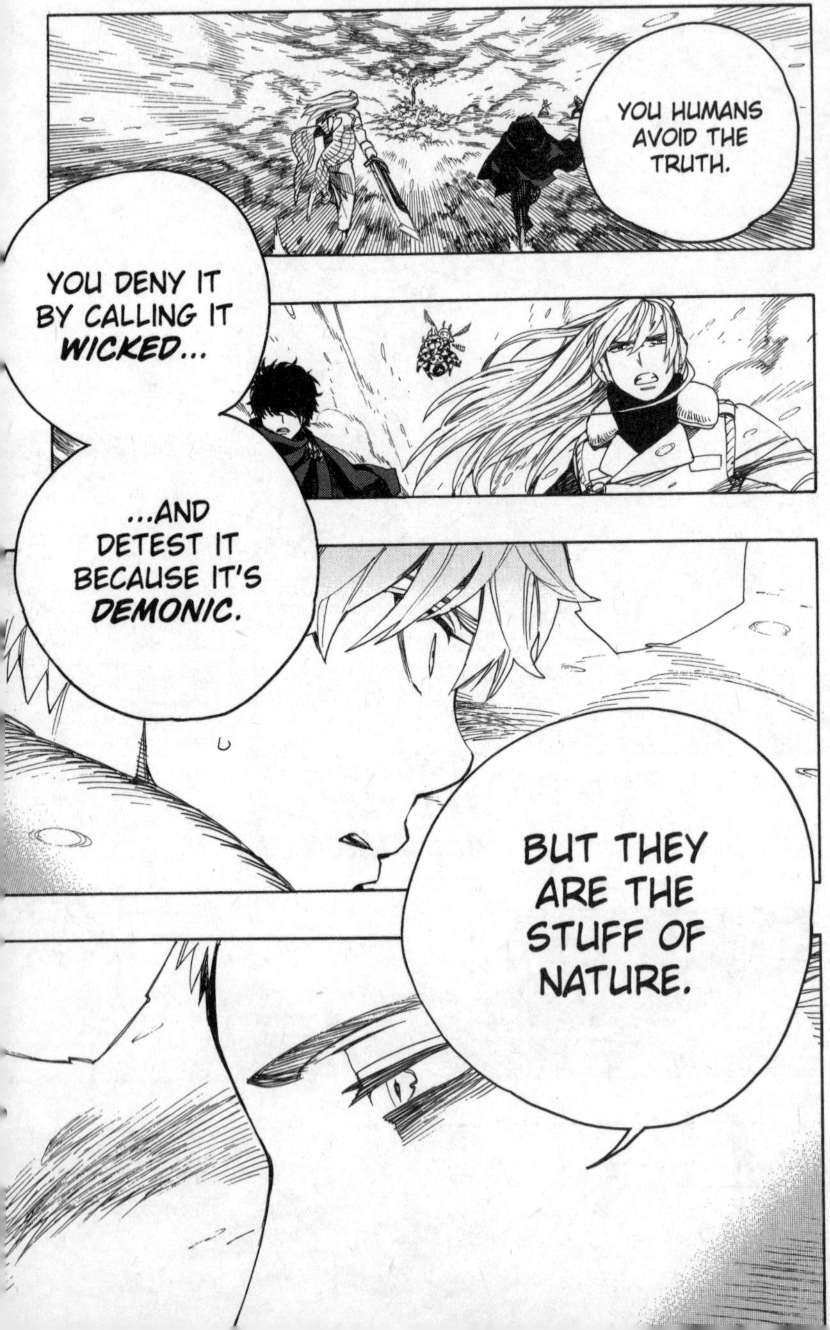
YOU HUMANS AVOID THE TRUTH.
YOU DENY IT BY CALLING IT *WICKED*...
...AND DETEST IT BECAUSE IT'S *DEMONIC*.
BUT THEY ARE THE STUFF OF NATURE.

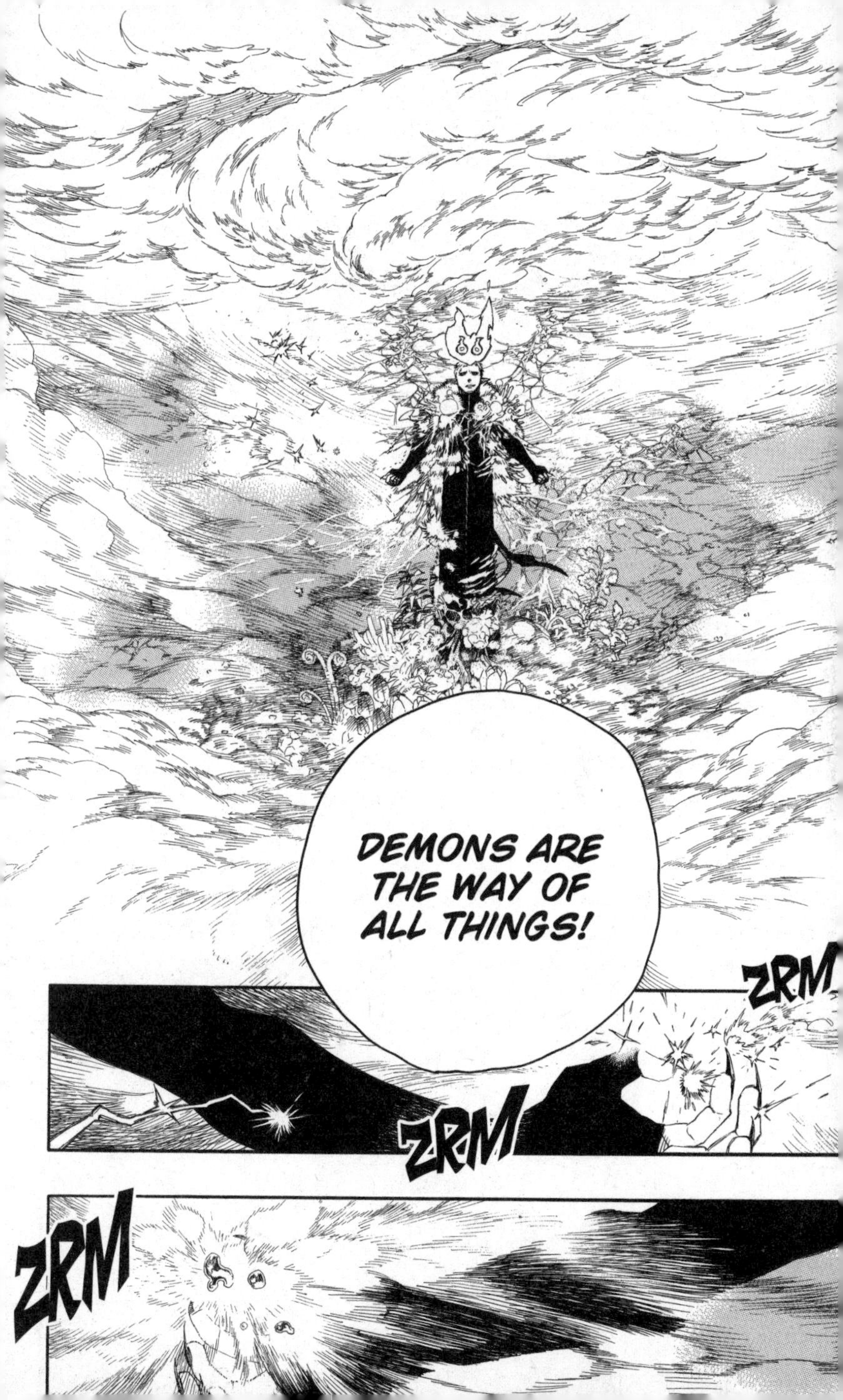
DEMONS ARE THE WAY OF ALL THINGS!
ZRM
ZRM
ZRM

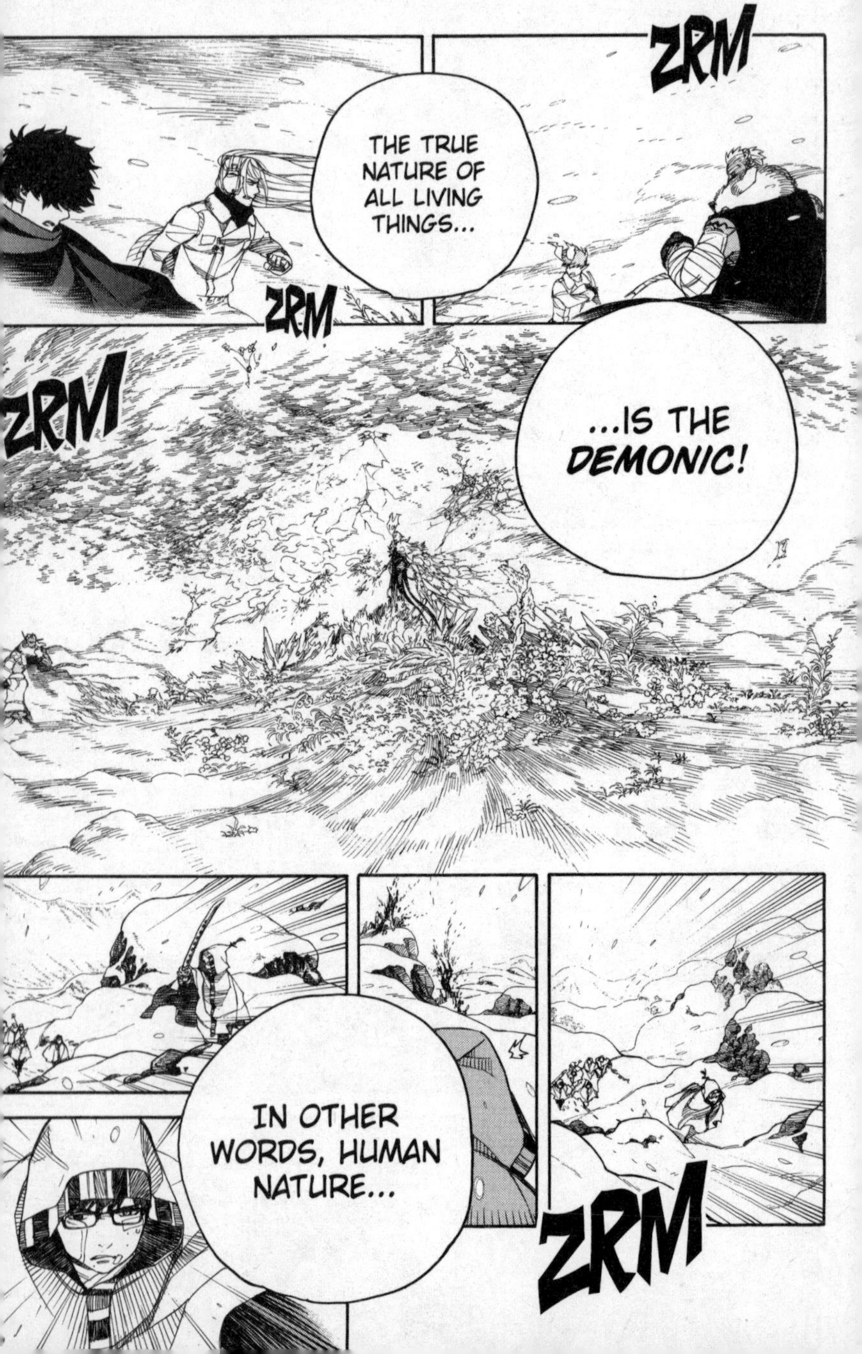
ZRM
THE TRUE NATURE OF ALL LIVING THINGS...
ZRM
...IS THE DEMONIC!
ZRM
IN OTHER WORDS, HUMAN NATURE...
ZRM

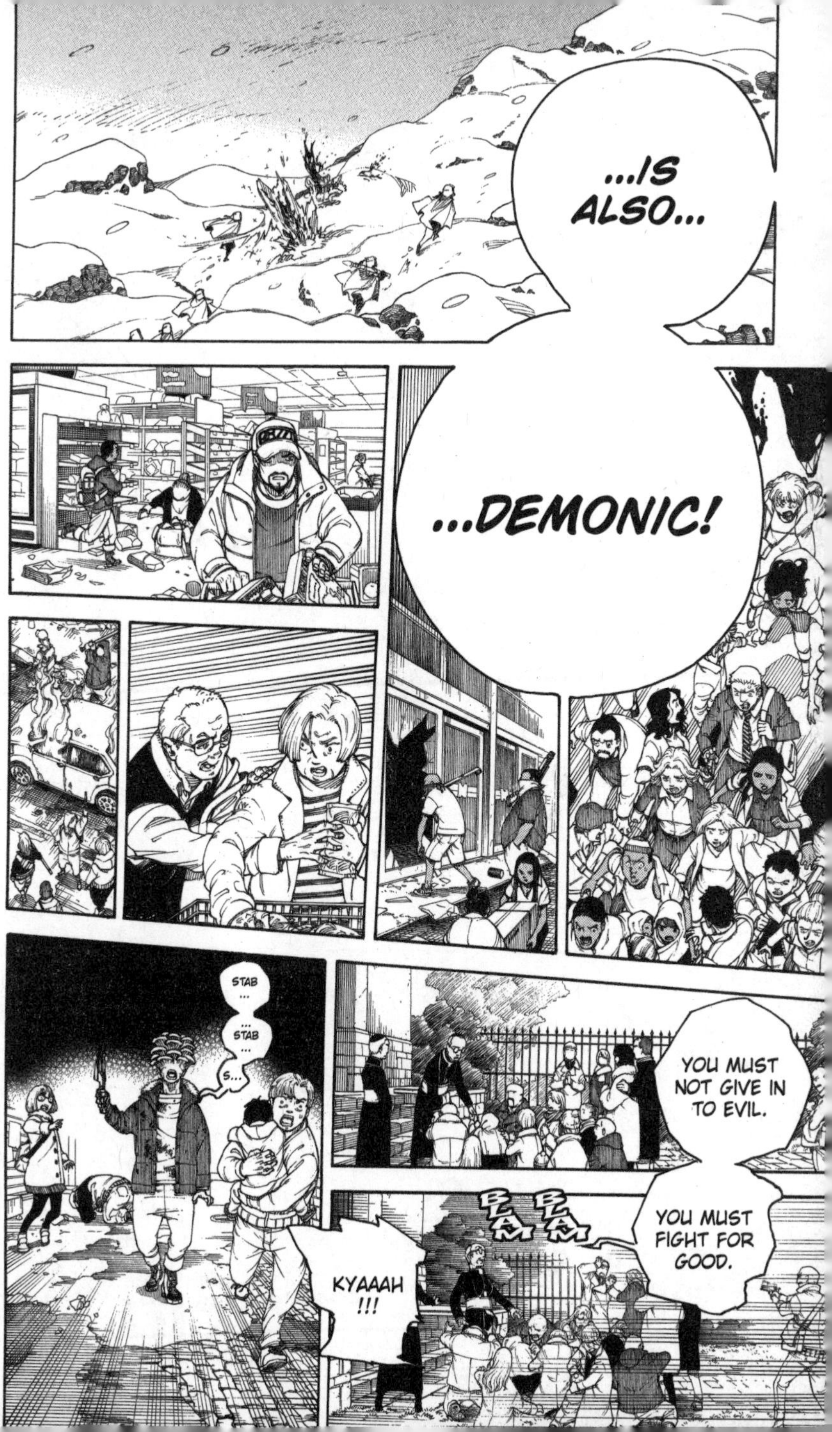
...IS ALSO...
...DEMONIC!
YOU MUST NOT GIVE IN TO EVIL.
YOU MUST FIGHT FOR GOOD.
BLAM BLAM
KYAAAH!!!
STAB... ...STAB... S...

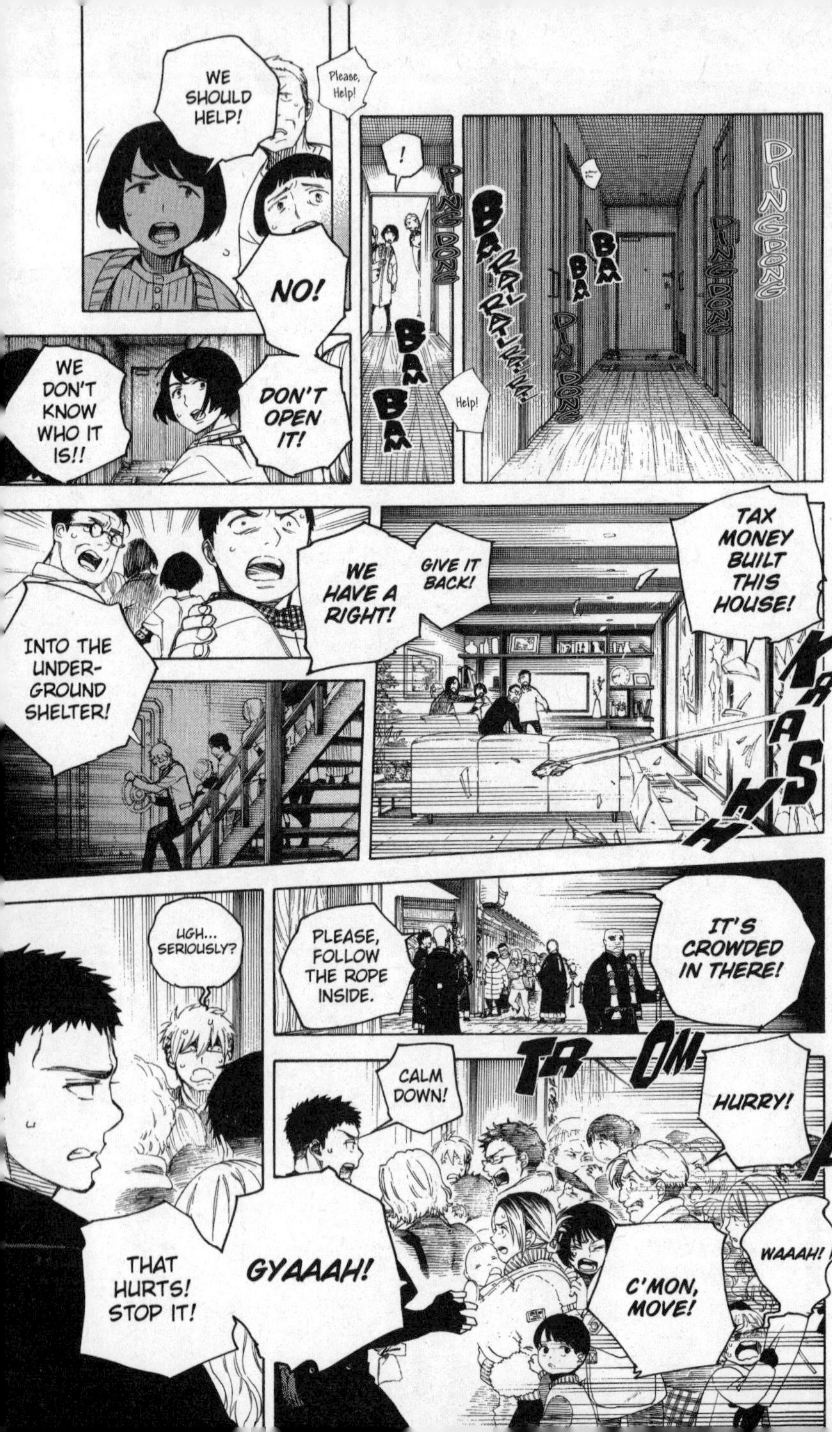
DINGDONG
BAM
BAM
DINGDONG
DING DONG
!
PING DONG
BAM
BAM
BAM
Help!
WE SHOULD HELP!
Please, Help!
NO!
WE DON'T KNOW WHO IT IS!!
DON'T OPEN IT!
TAX MONEY BUILT THIS HOUSE!
KRASHH
GIVE IT BACK!
WE HAVE A RIGHT!
INTO THE UNDERGROUND SHELTER!
IT'S CROWDED IN THERE!
PLEASE, FOLLOW THE ROPE INSIDE.
TROMP
HURRY!
CALM DOWN!
WAAAH!
C'MON, MOVE!
GYAAAH!
THAT HURTS! STOP IT!
UGH... SERIOUSLY?

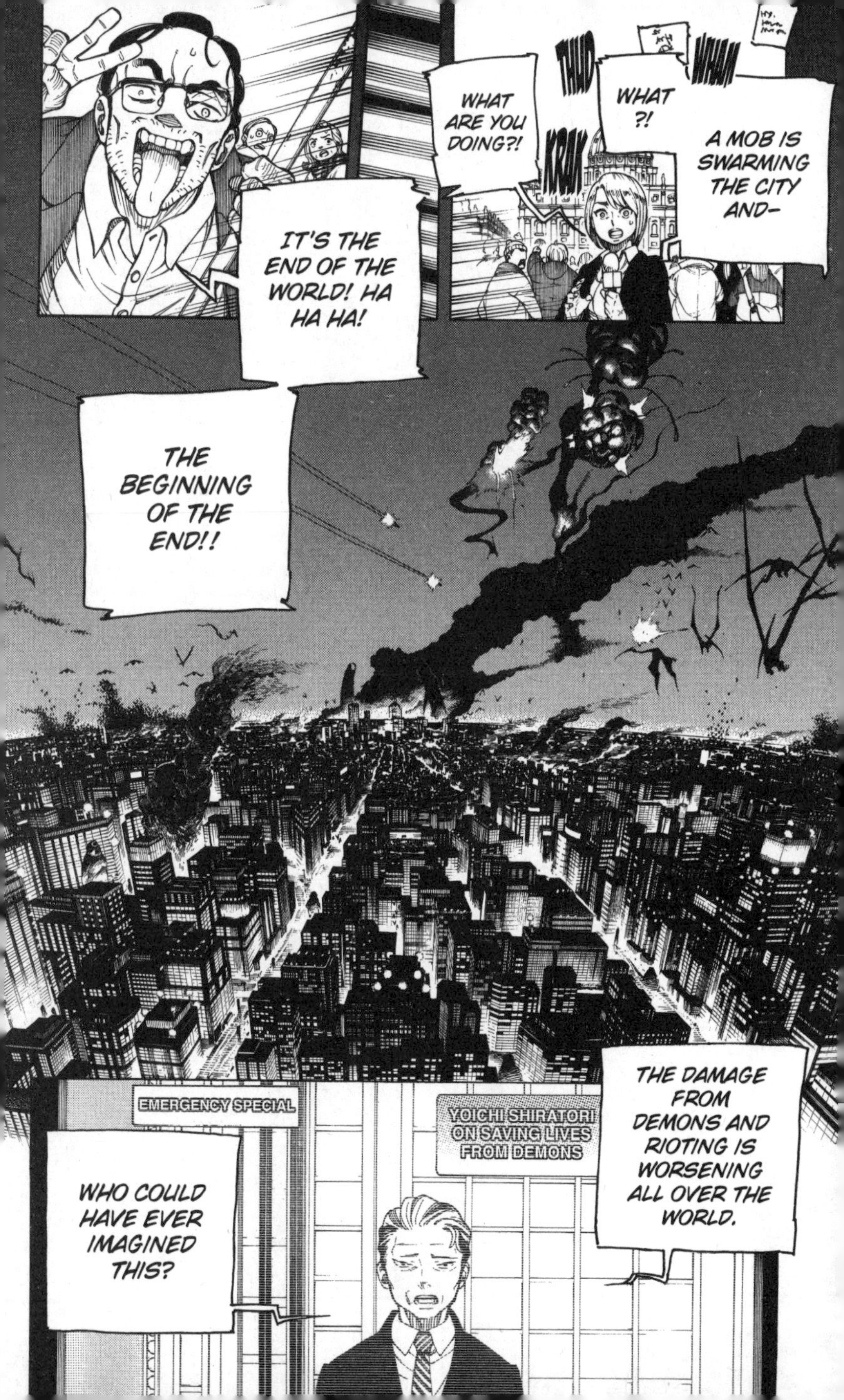
WHAM
WHAT ?!
A MOB IS SWARMING THE CITY AND–
THUD
WHAT ARE YOU DOING?!
KRAK
IT'S THE END OF THE WORLD! HA HA HA!
THE BEGINNING OF THE END!!
THE DAMAGE FROM DEMONS AND RIOTING IS WORSENING ALL OVER THE WORLD.
YOICHI SHIRATORI ON SAVING LIVES FROM DEMONS
EMERGENCY SPECIAL
WHO COULD HAVE EVER IMAGINED THIS?

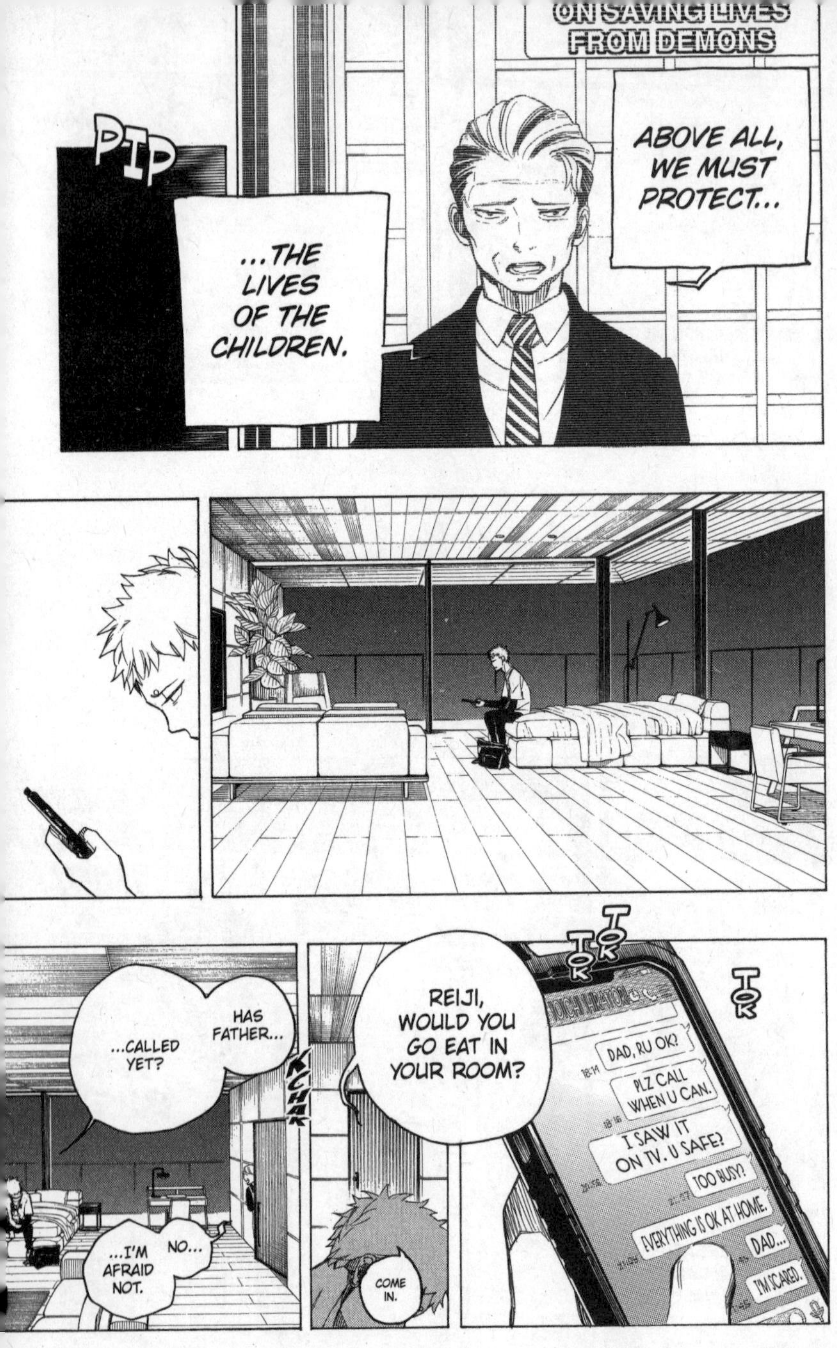
ON SAVING LIVES FROM DEMONS
ABOVE ALL, WE MUST PROTECT...
PIP
...THE LIVES OF THE CHILDREN.
TOK TOK
TOK
DAD, RU OK?
PLZ CALL WHEN U CAN.
I SAW IT ON TV. U SAFE?
TOO BUSY?
EVERYTHING IS OK AT HOME.
DAD...
I'M SCARED.
REIJI, WOULD YOU GO EAT IN YOUR ROOM?
COME IN.
KCHAK
HAS FATHER...
...CALLED YET?
NO...
...I'M AFRAID NOT.

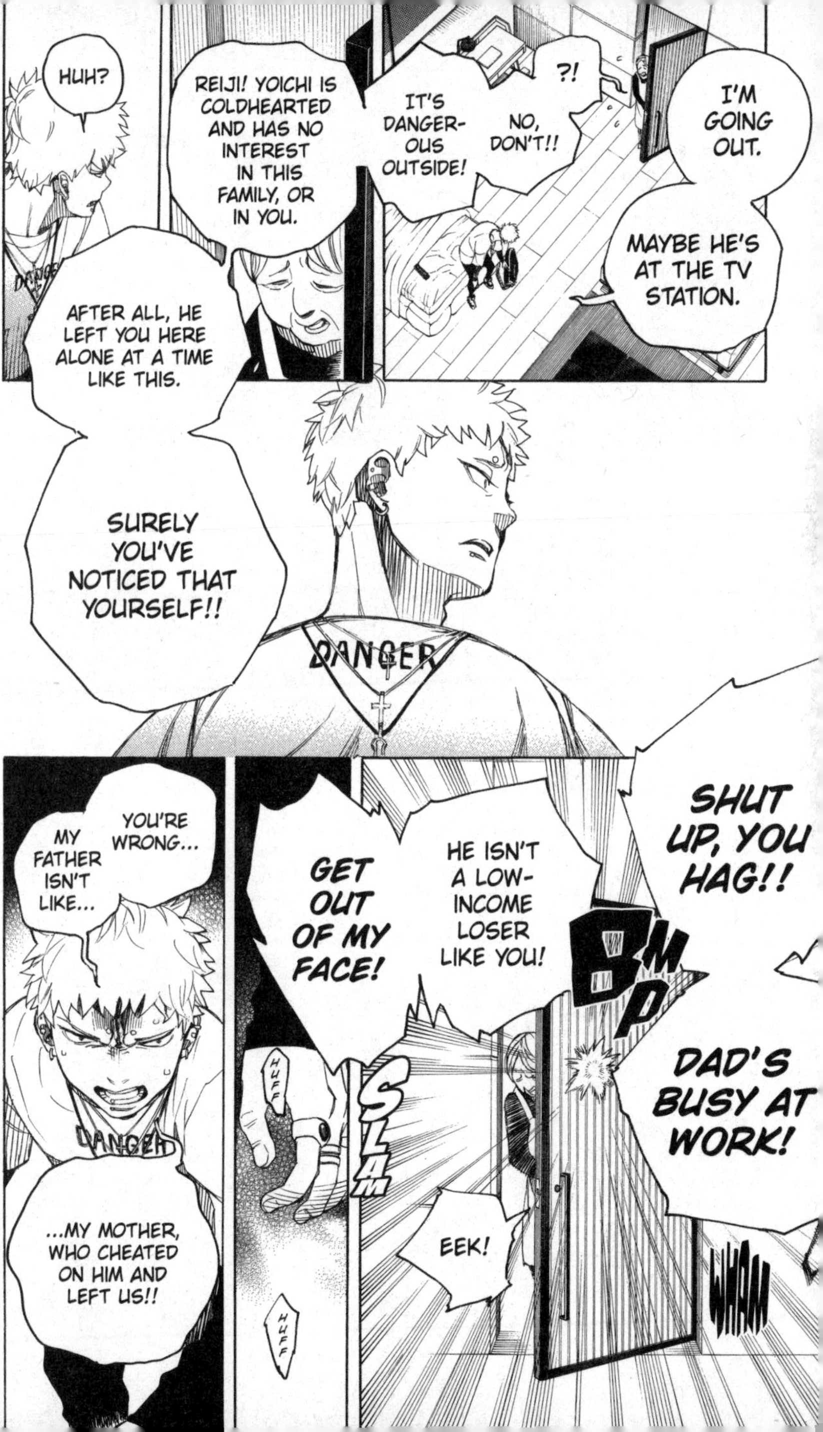
I'M GOING OUT.
MAYBE HE'S AT THE TV STATION.
?!
NO, DON'T!!
IT'S DANGER-OUS OUTSIDE!
REIJI! YOICHI IS COLDHEARTED AND HAS NO INTEREST IN THIS FAMILY, OR IN YOU.
HUH?
AFTER ALL, HE LEFT YOU HERE ALONE AT A TIME LIKE THIS.
SURELY YOU'VE NOTICED THAT YOURSELF!!
SHUT UP, YOU HAG!!
BMP
DAD'S BUSY AT WORK!
WHAM
HE ISN'T A LOW-INCOME LOSER LIKE YOU!
GET OUT OF MY FACE!
SLAM
EEK!
HUFF
HUFF
YOU'RE WRONG...
MY FATHER ISN'T LIKE...
...MY MOTHER, WHO CHEATED ON HIM AND LEFT US!!

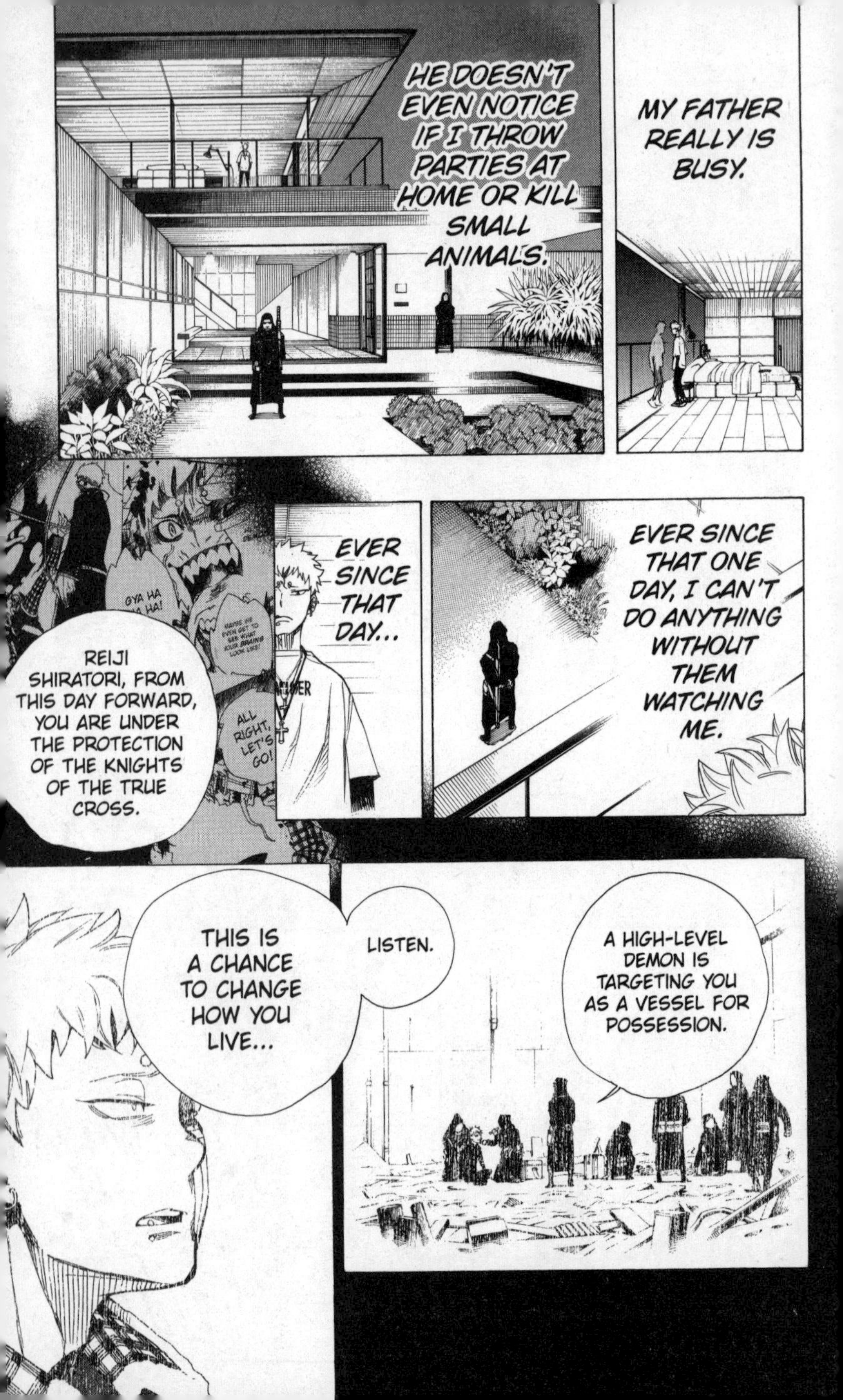
MY FATHER REALLY IS BUSY.
HE DOESN'T EVEN NOTICE IF I THROW PARTIES AT HOME OR KILL SMALL ANIMALS.
EVER SINCE THAT ONE DAY, I CAN'T DO ANYTHING WITHOUT THEM WATCHING ME.
EVER SINCE THAT DAY...
GYA HA
HA!
MAYBE WE EVEN GET TO SEE WHAT YOUR BRAINS LOOK LIKE!
ALL RIGHT, LET'S GO!
REIJI SHIRATORI, FROM THIS DAY FORWARD, YOU ARE UNDER THE PROTECTION OF THE KNIGHTS OF THE TRUE CROSS.
LISTEN.
A HIGH-LEVEL DEMON IS TARGETING YOU AS A VESSEL FOR POSSESSION.
THIS IS A CHANCE TO CHANGE HOW YOU LIVE...

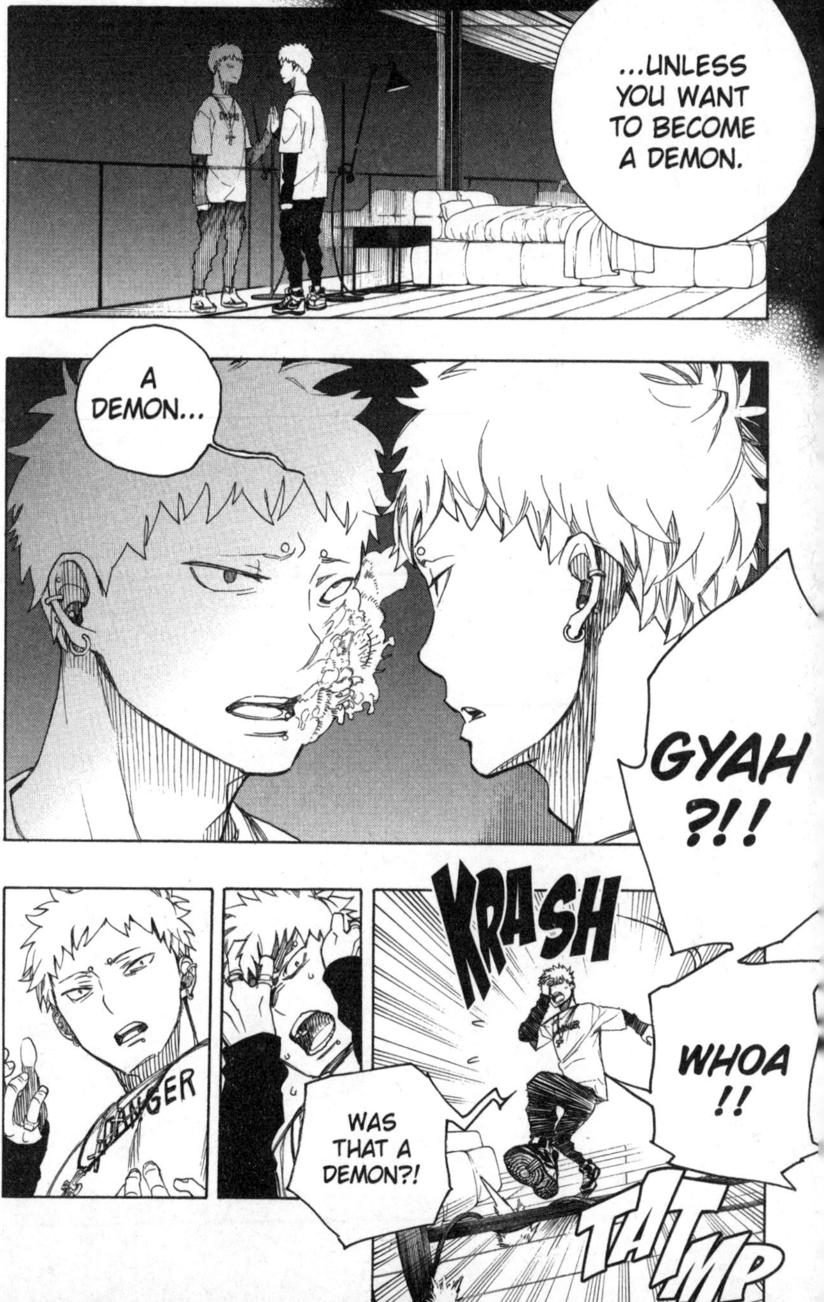
...UNLESS YOU WANT TO BECOME A DEMON.
A DEMON...
GYAH ?!!
KRASH
WHOA !!
TATMP
WAS THAT A DEMON?!

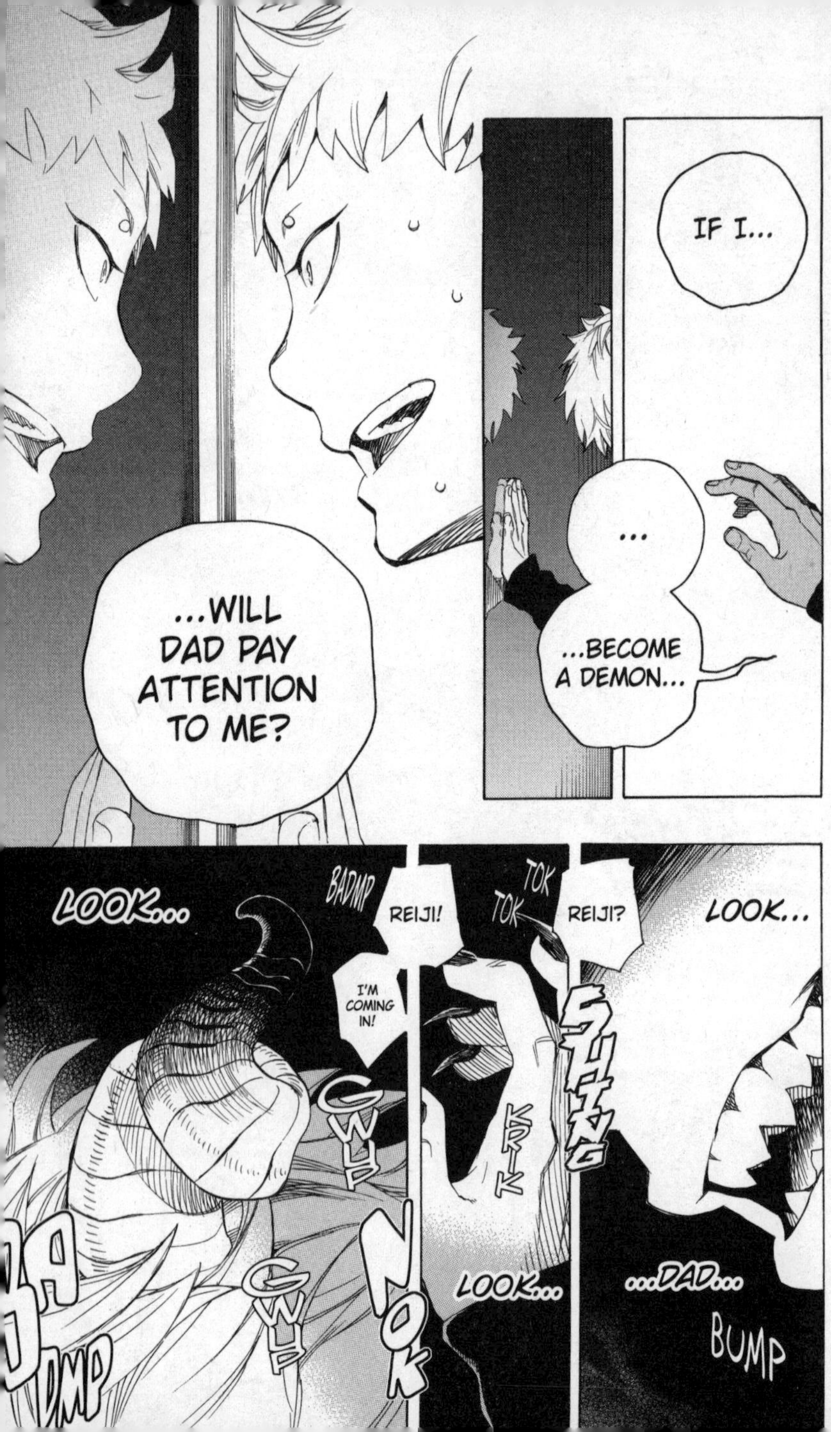
IF I...
...
...BECOME A DEMON...
...WILL DAD PAY ATTENTION TO ME?
LOOK...
...DAD...
BUMP
TOK TOK
REIJI?
SHING
KRIK
LOOK...
BADMP
REIJI!
I'M COMING IN!
LOOK...
GWUP
GWUP
NOK
BADMP

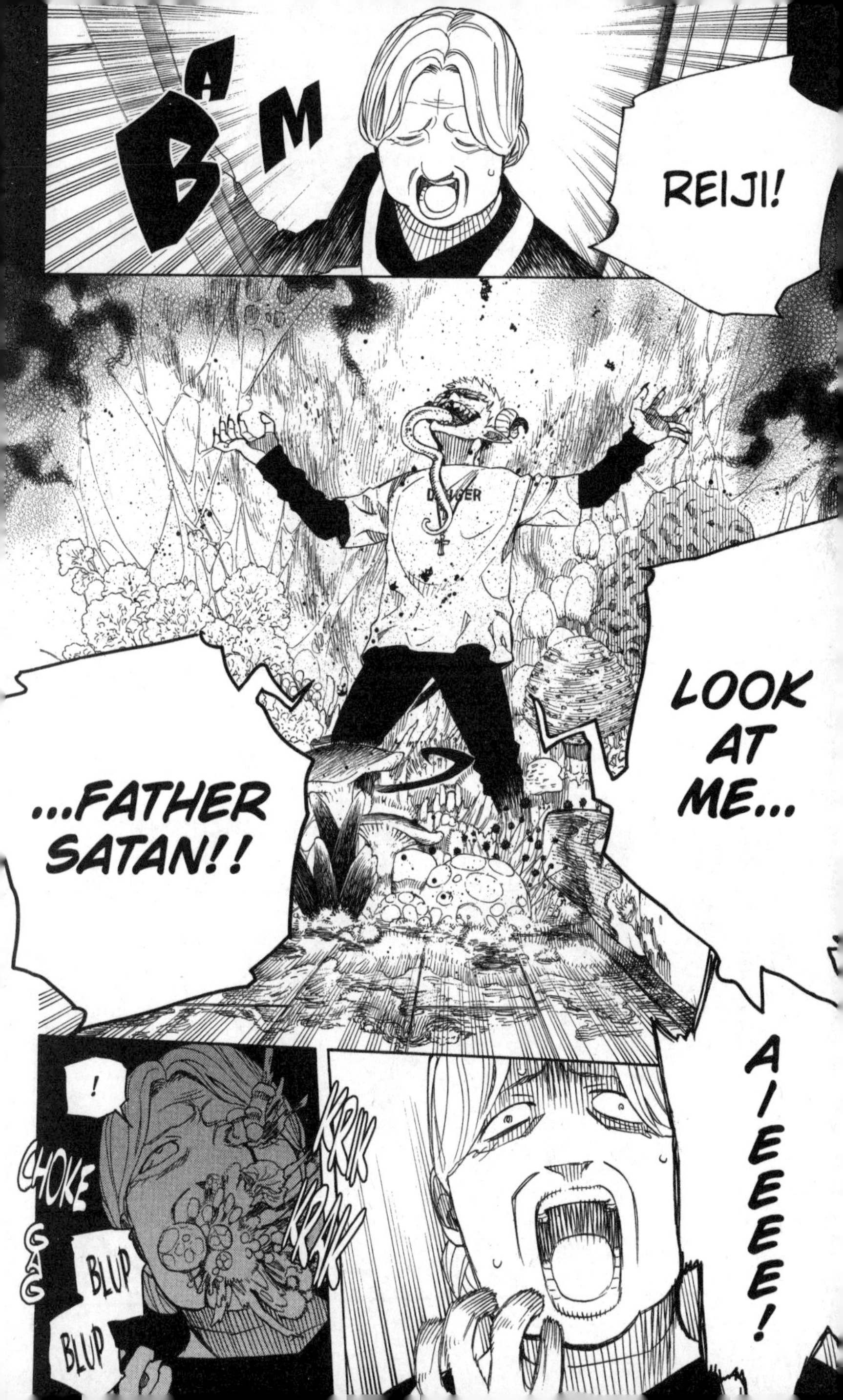
BAM
REIJI!
LOOK AT ME...
...FATHER SATAN!!
AIEEEEE!
!
KRIK KRAK
CHOKE GAG
BLUP BLUP

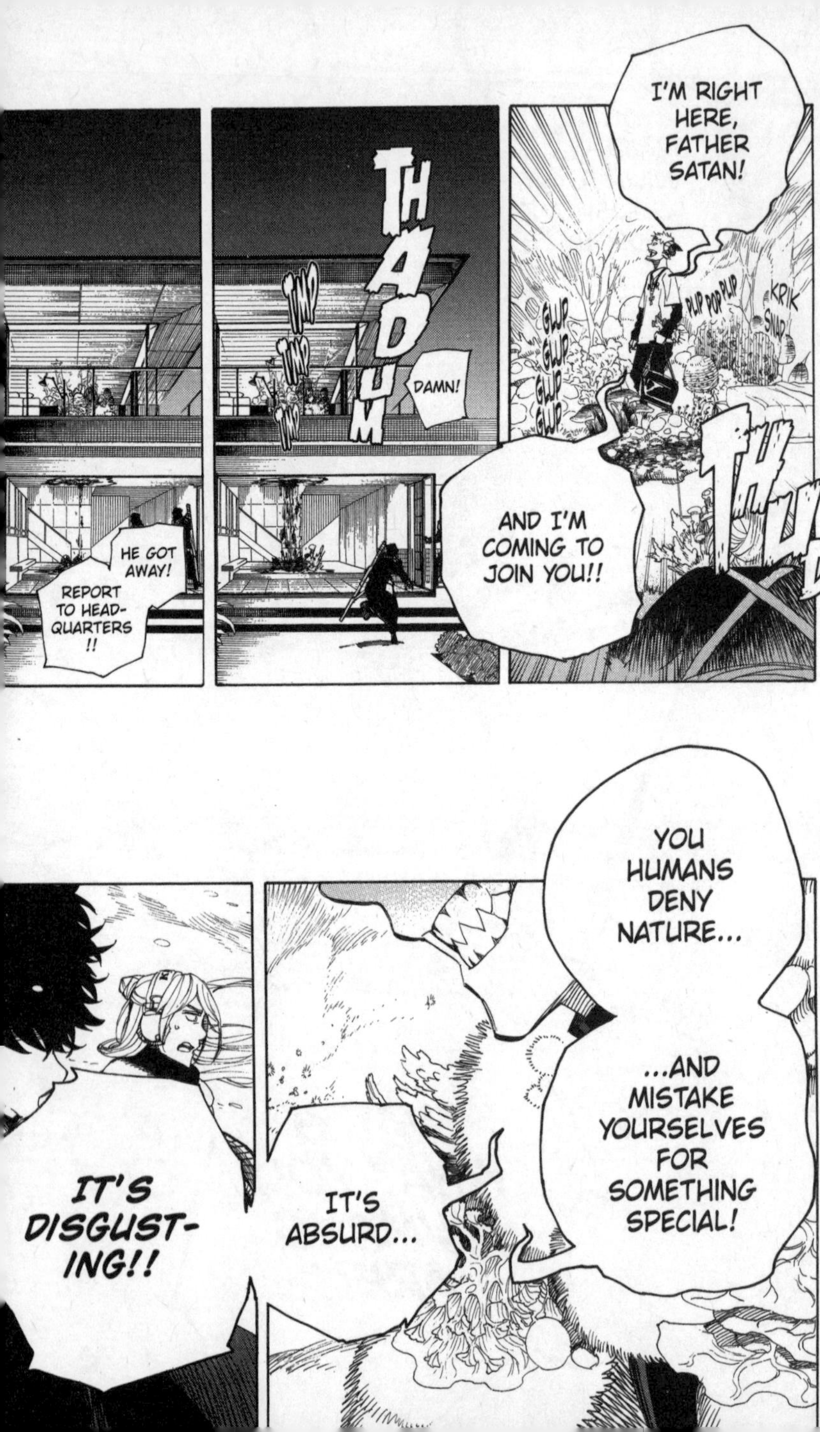
I'M RIGHT HERE, FATHER SATAN!
GLUP GLUP GLUP GLUP
PLIP POP PLIP
KRIK SNAP
AND I'M COMING TO JOIN YOU!!
THUD
THADUM
TMP TMP TMP
DAMN!
HE GOT AWAY!
REPORT TO HEAD-QUARTERS !!
YOU HUMANS DENY NATURE...
...AND MISTAKE YOURSELVES FOR SOMETHING SPECIAL!
IT'S ABSURD...
IT'S DISGUST-ING!!

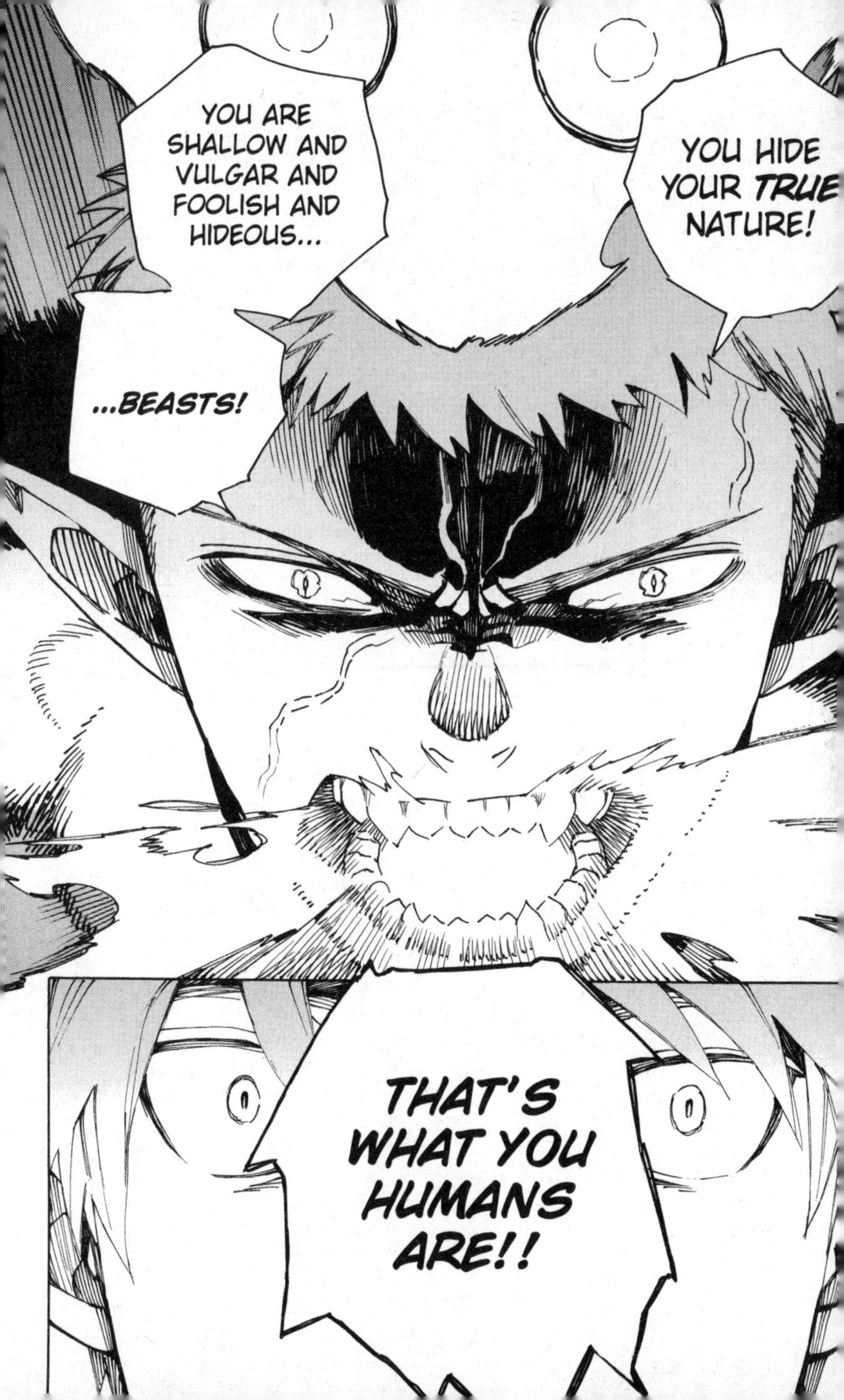
YOU HIDE YOUR TRUE NATURE!
YOU ARE SHALLOW AND VULGAR AND FOOLISH AND HIDEOUS...
...BEASTS!
THAT'S WHAT YOU HUMANS ARE!!

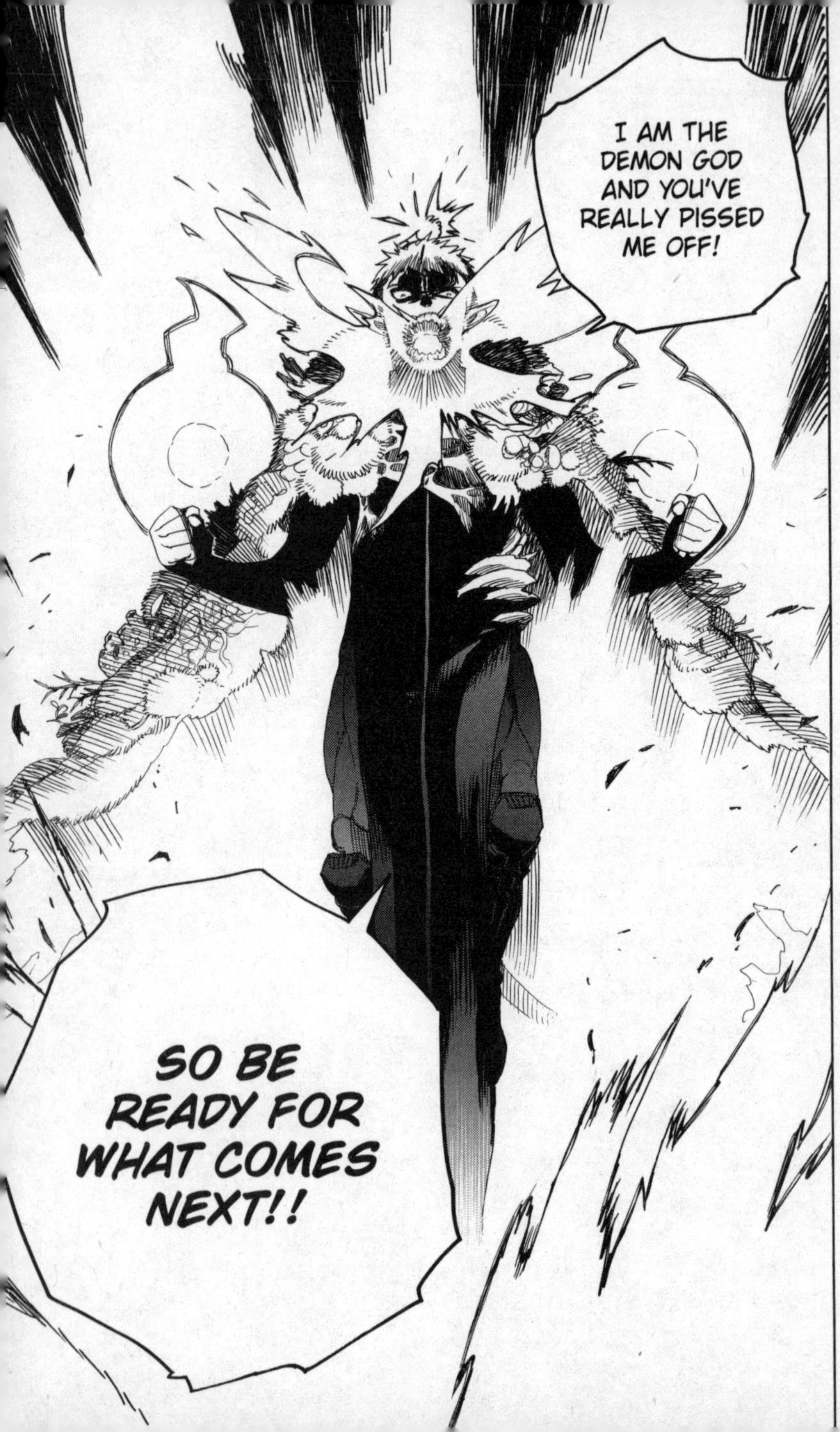
I AM THE DEMON GOD AND YOU'VE REALLY PISSED ME OFF!
SO BE READY FOR WHAT COMES NEXT!!

Blue Exorcist Chapter 134: Of One Cloth—Awakening

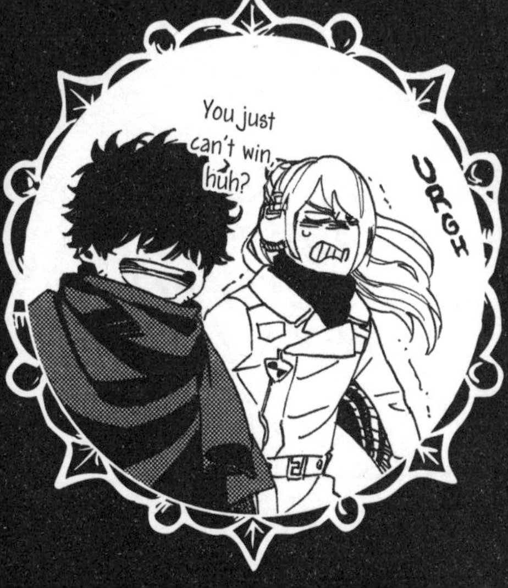
You just can't win, huh?
URGH

Chapter 135: Of One Cloth—Waking Up

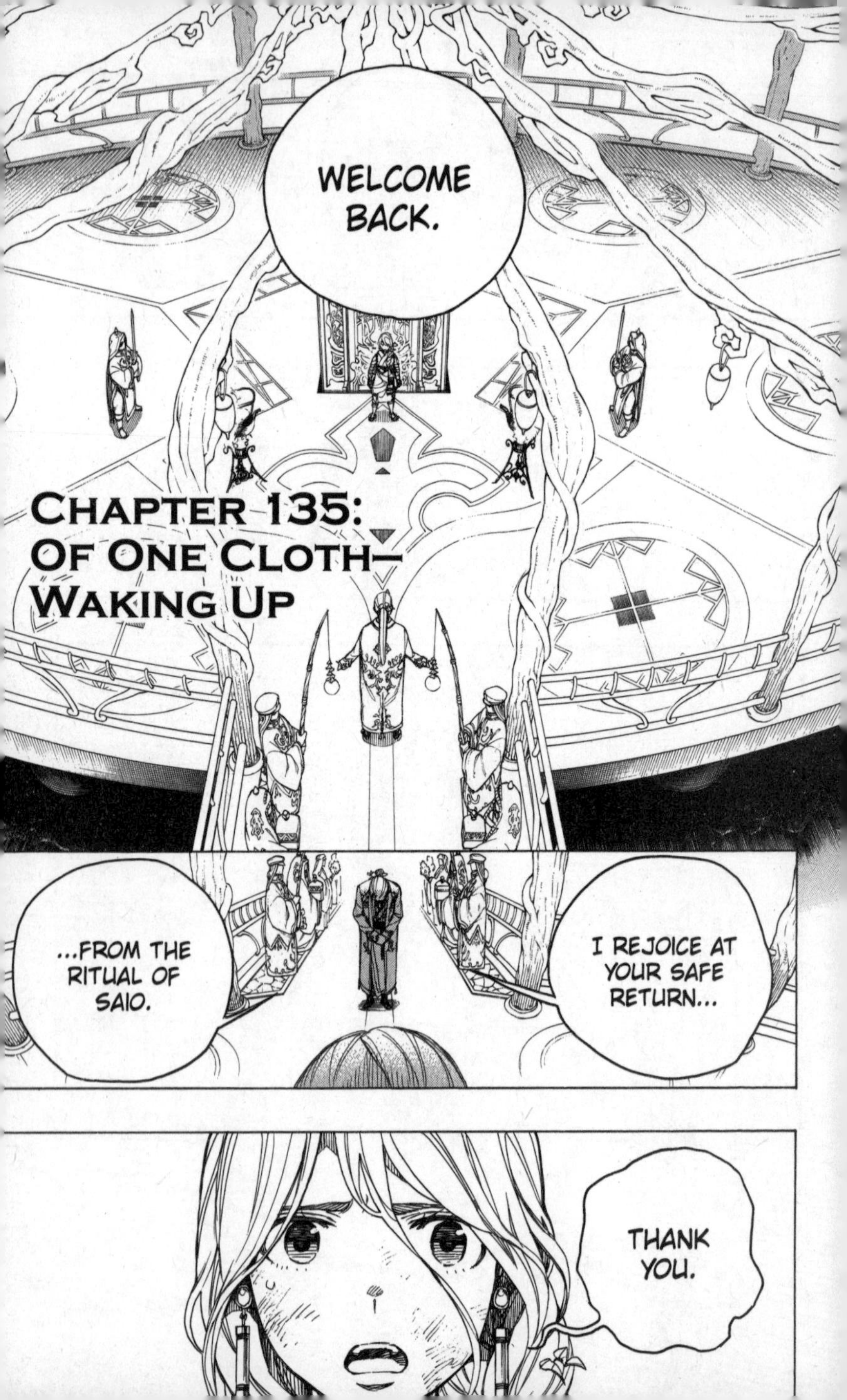
WELCOME BACK.
I REJOICE AT YOUR SAFE RETURN...
...FROM THE RITUAL OF SAIO.
THANK YOU.

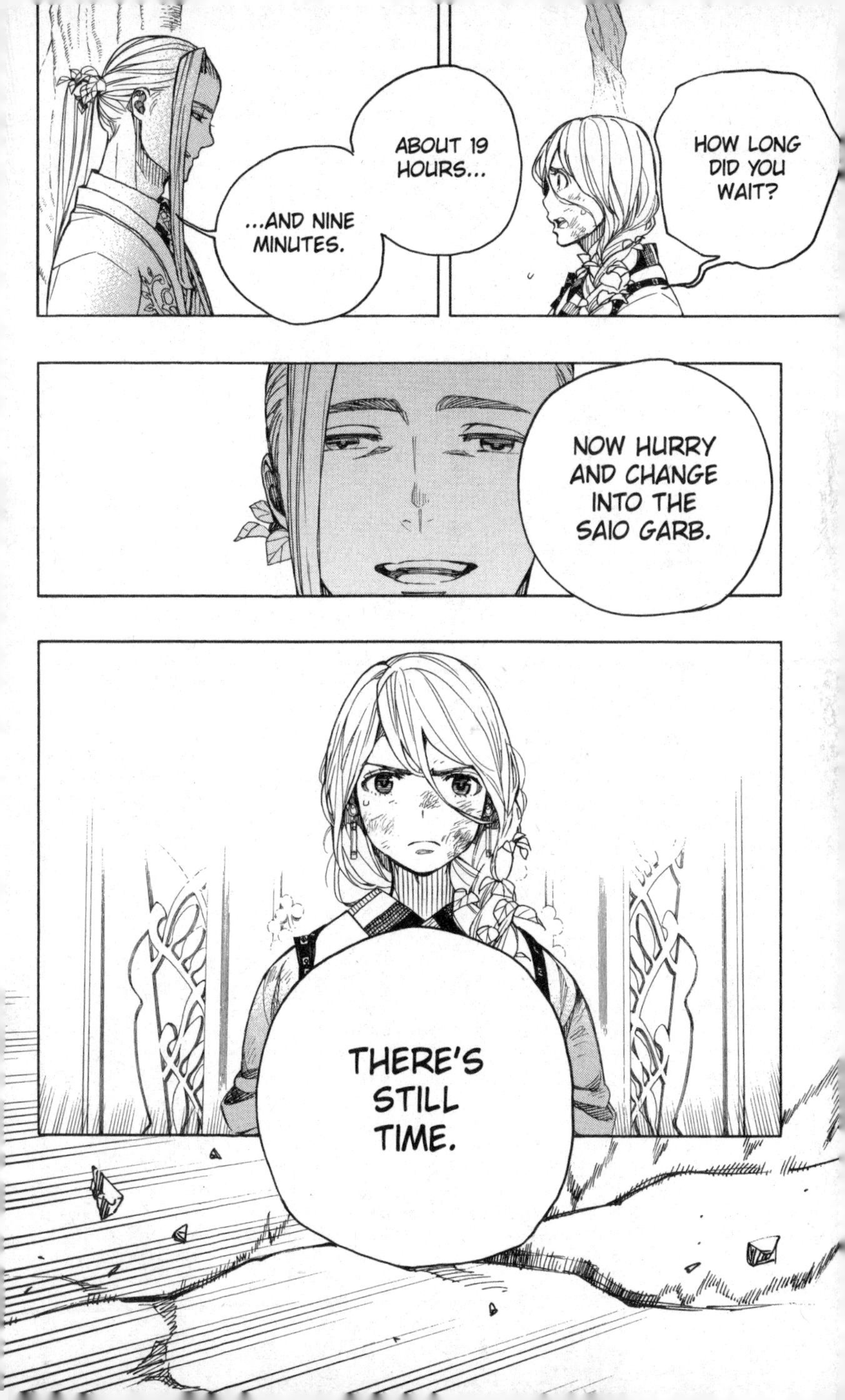
HOW LONG DID YOU WAIT?
ABOUT 19 HOURS...
...AND NINE MINUTES.
NOW HURRY AND CHANGE INTO THE SAIO GARB.
THERE'S STILL TIME.

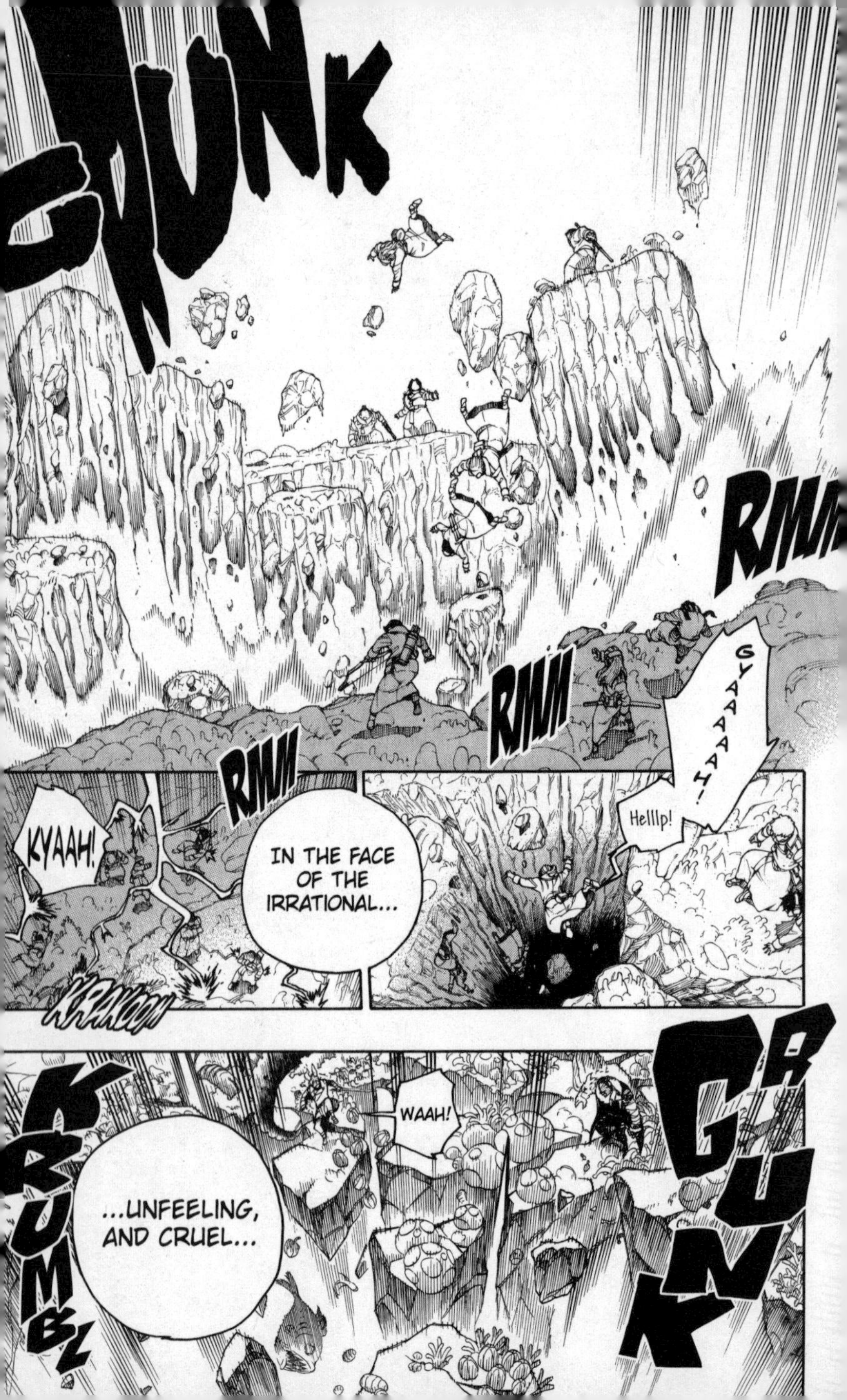
GRUNK
RMMM
RMM
GYAAAAAH!
Helllp!
RMM
KYAAH!
IN THE FACE OF THE IRRATIONAL...
KRAKOOM
GRUNK
WAAH!
...UNFEELING, AND CRUEL...
KRUMBL

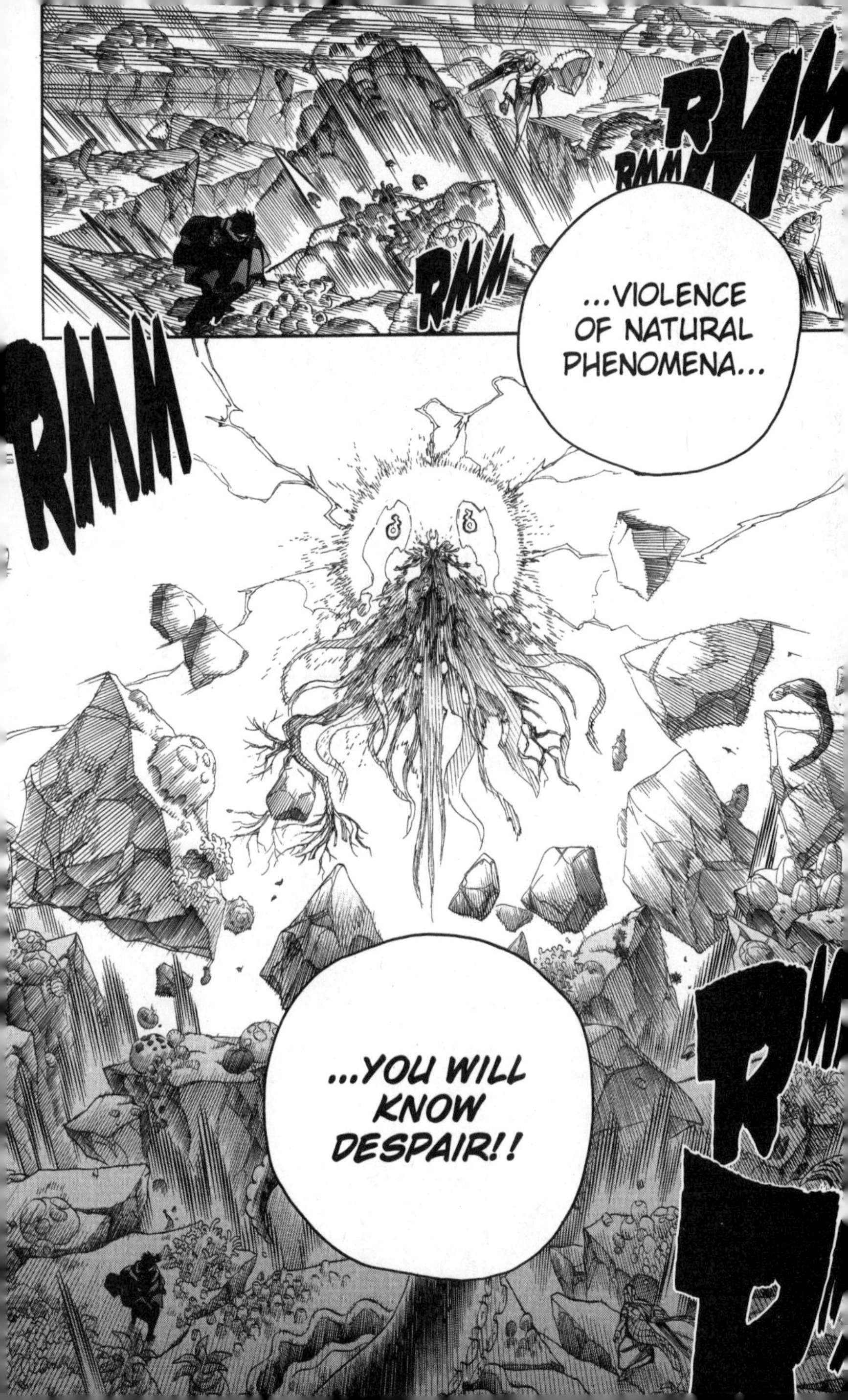
RMM
RMM
RMM
...VIOLENCE OF NATURAL PHENOMENA...
RMM
...YOU WILL KNOW DESPAIR!!

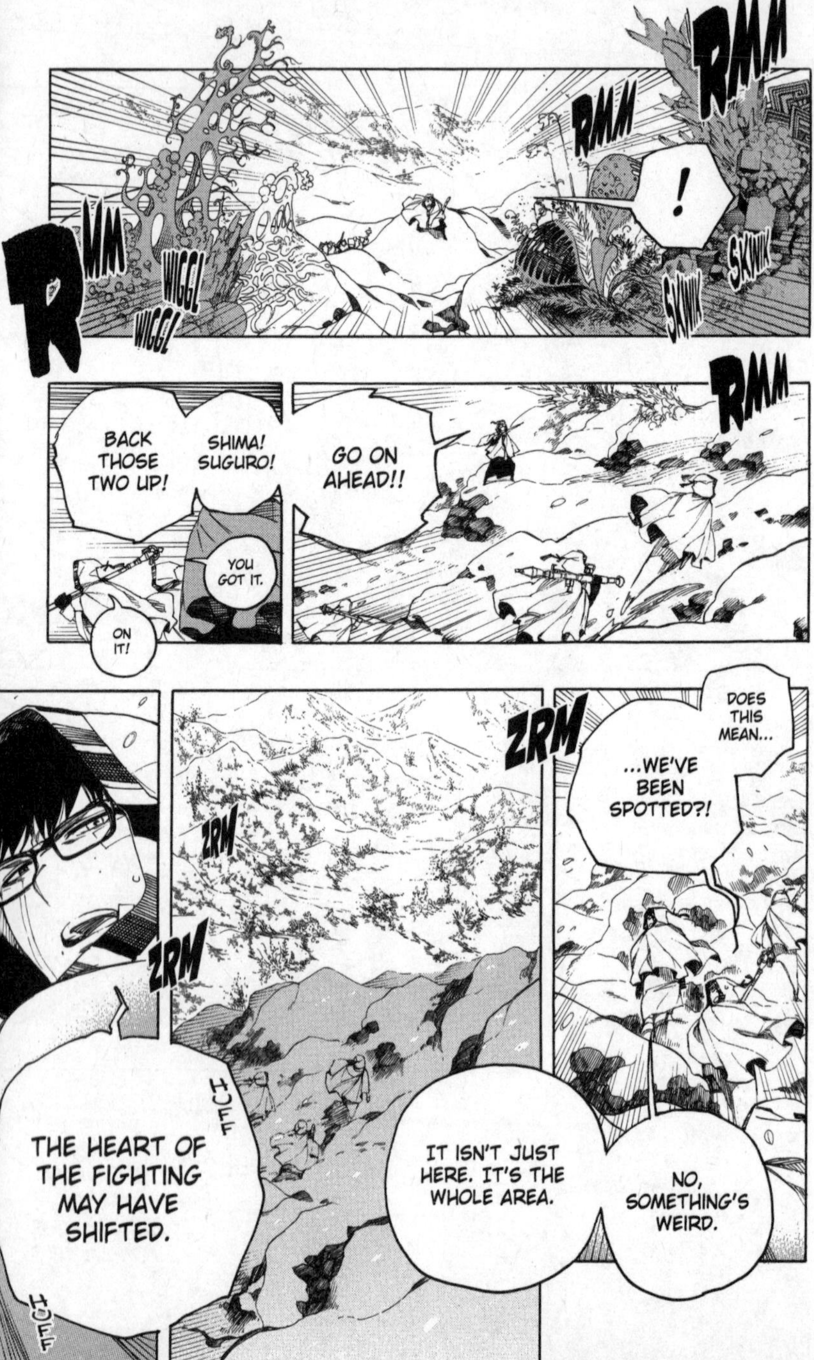
RMM
RMM
!
SKWIK
SKWIK
RMM
WIGGL
WIGGL
RMM
GO ON AHEAD!!
SHIMA! SUGURO!
BACK THOSE TWO UP!
YOU GOT IT.
ON IT!
ZRM
DOES THIS MEAN...
...WE'VE BEEN SPOTTED?!
NO, SOMETHING'S WEIRD.
IT ISN'T JUST HERE. IT'S THE WHOLE AREA.
ZRM
ZRM
HUFF
THE HEART OF THE FIGHTING MAY HAVE SHIFTED.
HUFF

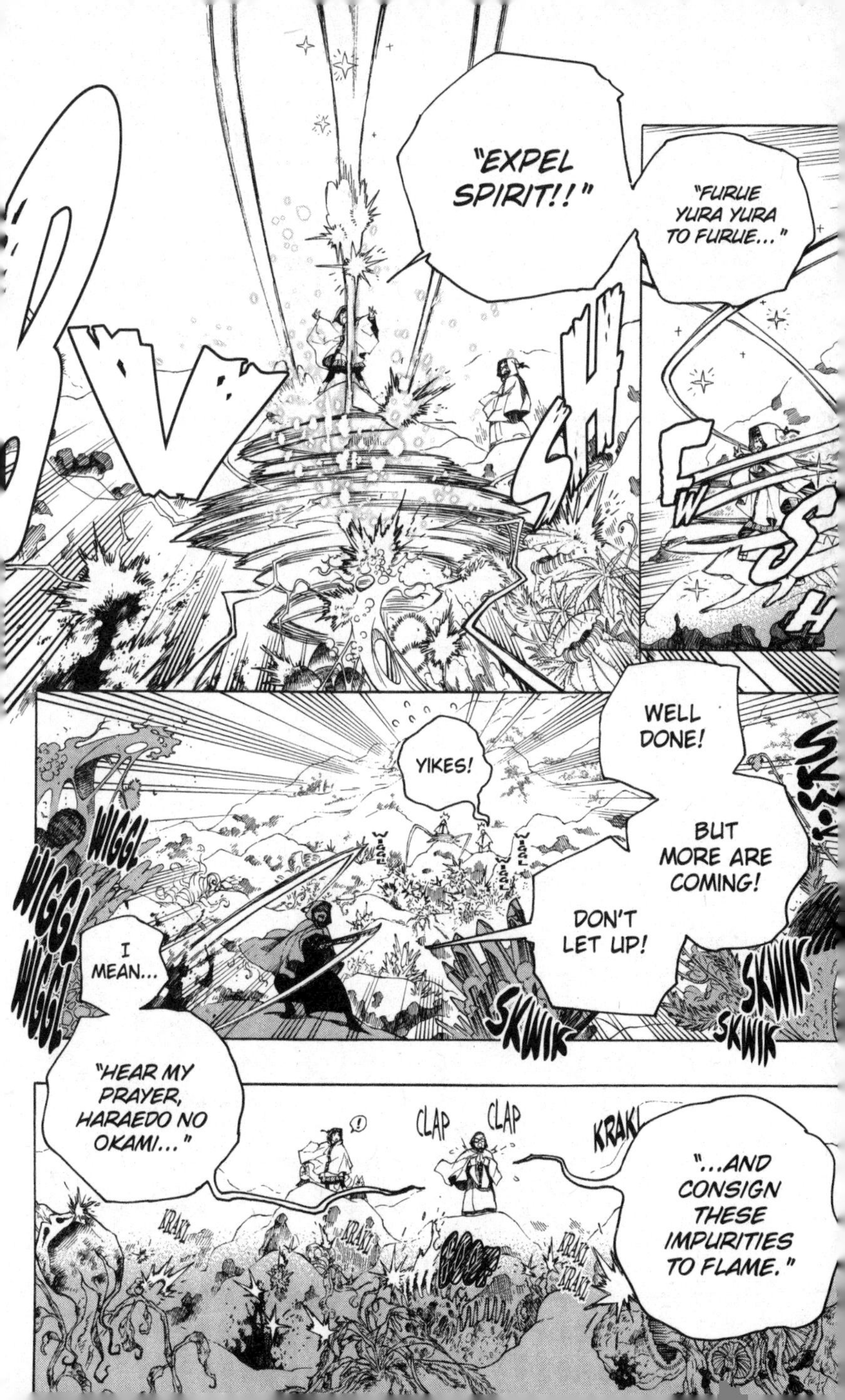
"FURUE YURA YURA TO FURUE..."
"EXPEL SPIRIT!!"
WELL DONE!
BUT MORE ARE COMING!
DON'T LET UP!
YIKES!
SKWIK
SKWIK
SKWIK
WIGGL
WIGGL
WIGGL
WIGGL
I MEAN...
"HEAR MY PRAYER, HARAEDO NO OKAMI..."
"...AND CONSIGN THESE IMPURITIES TO FLAME."
CLAP
CLAP
KRAK

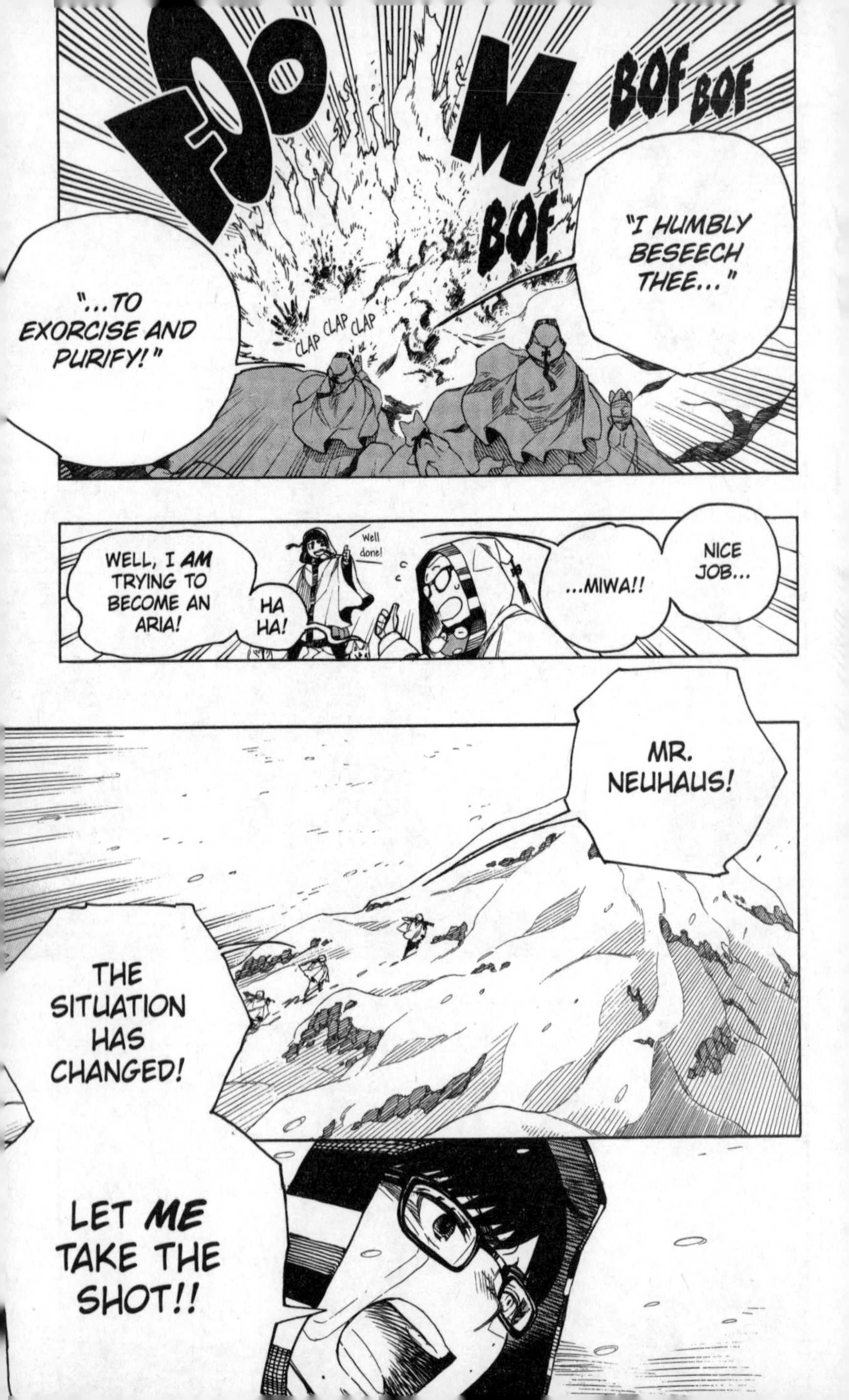
DOOM
BOF BOF
BOF
"I HUMBLY BESEECH THEE..."
CLAP CLAP CLAP
"...TO EXORCISE AND PURIFY!"
NICE JOB...
...MIWA!!
Well done!
HA HA!
WELL, I *AM* TRYING TO BECOME AN ARIA!
MR. NEUHAUS!
THE SITUATION HAS CHANGED!
LET *ME* TAKE THE SHOT!!

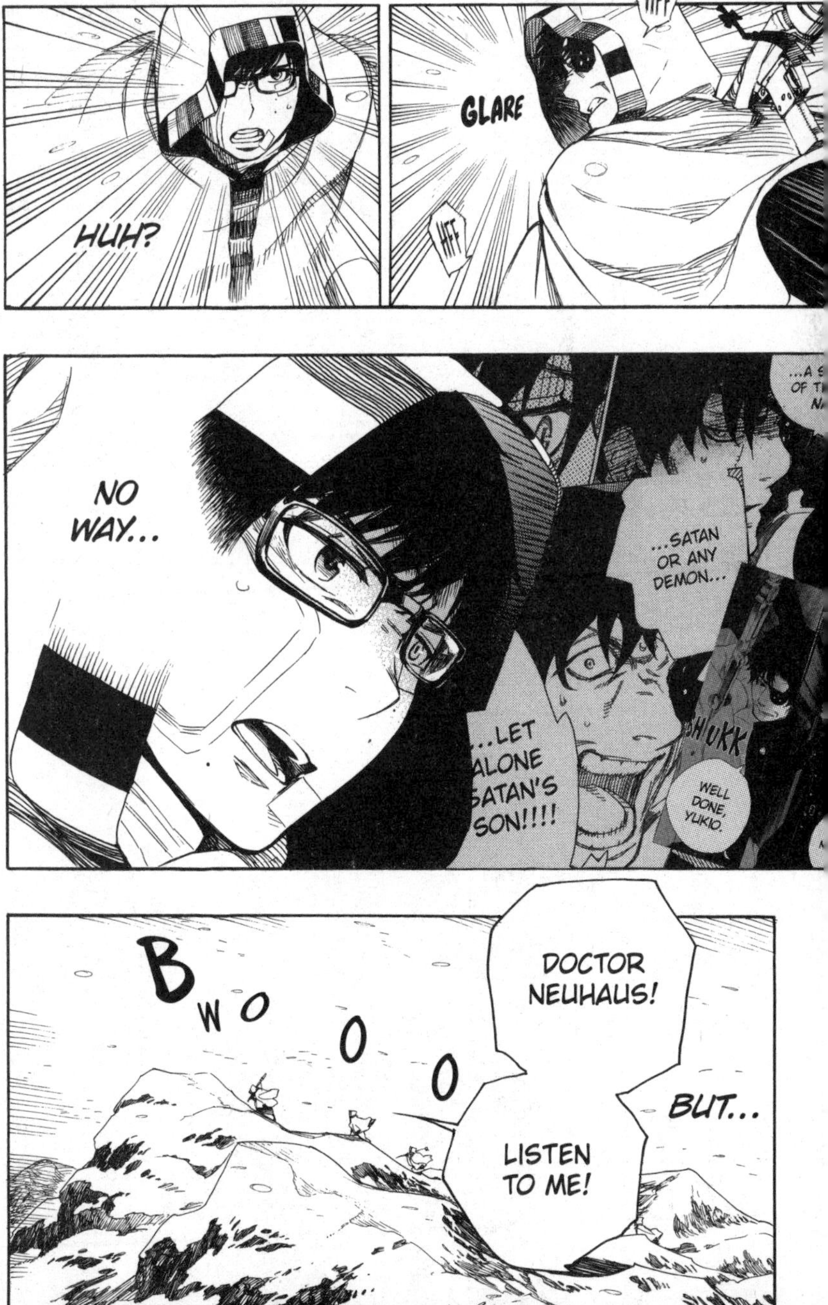
HFF
GLARE
HFF
HUH?
...SATAN OR ANY DEMON...
WELL DONE, YUKIO.
...LET ALONE SATAN'S SON!!!!
NO WAY...
DOCTOR NEUHAUS!
BUT...
LISTEN TO ME!
BWOOOO

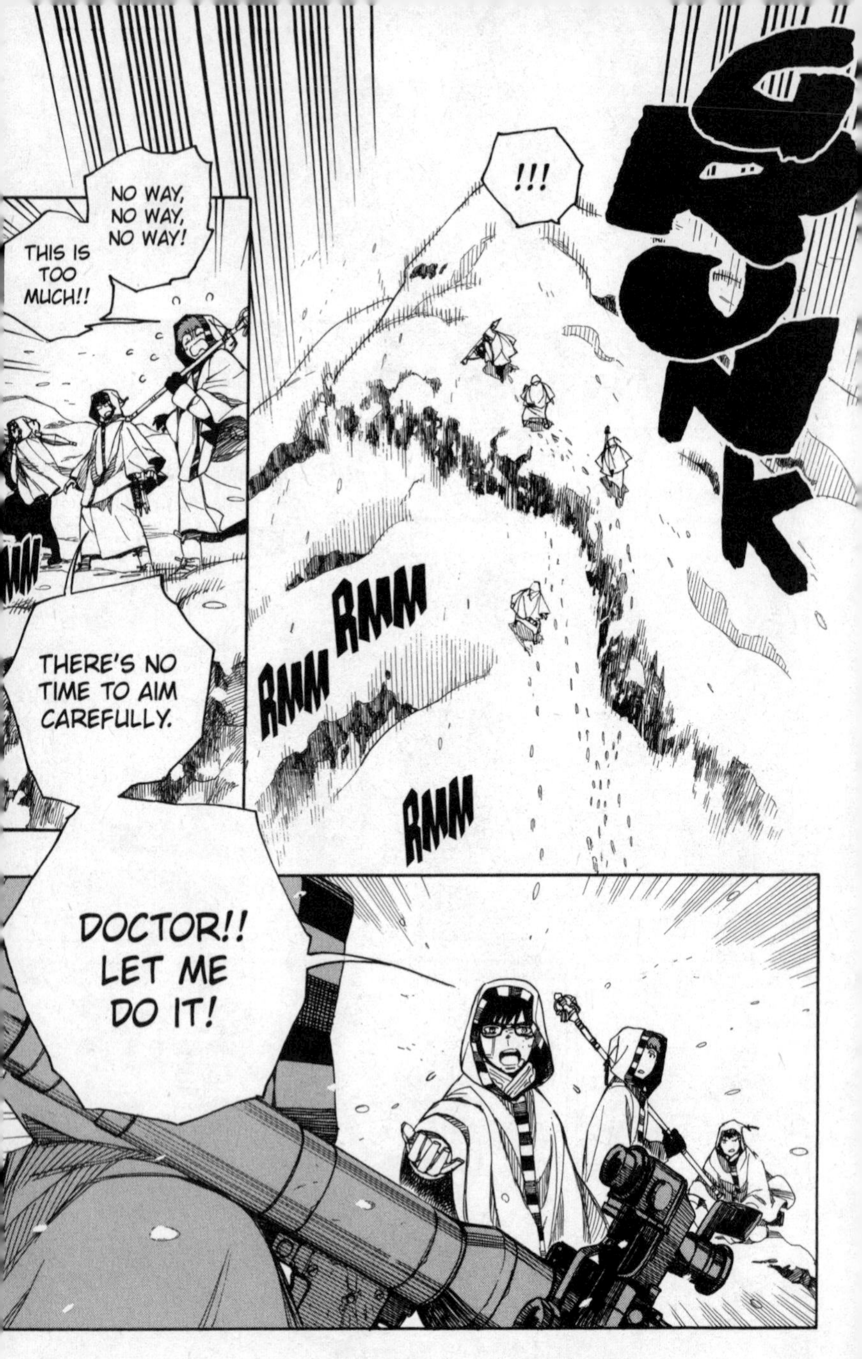
!!!
RMM
RMM
RMM
RMM
NO WAY, NO WAY, NO WAY!
THIS IS TOO MUCH!!
THERE'S NO TIME TO AIM CAREFULLY.
DOCTOR!! LET ME DO IT!

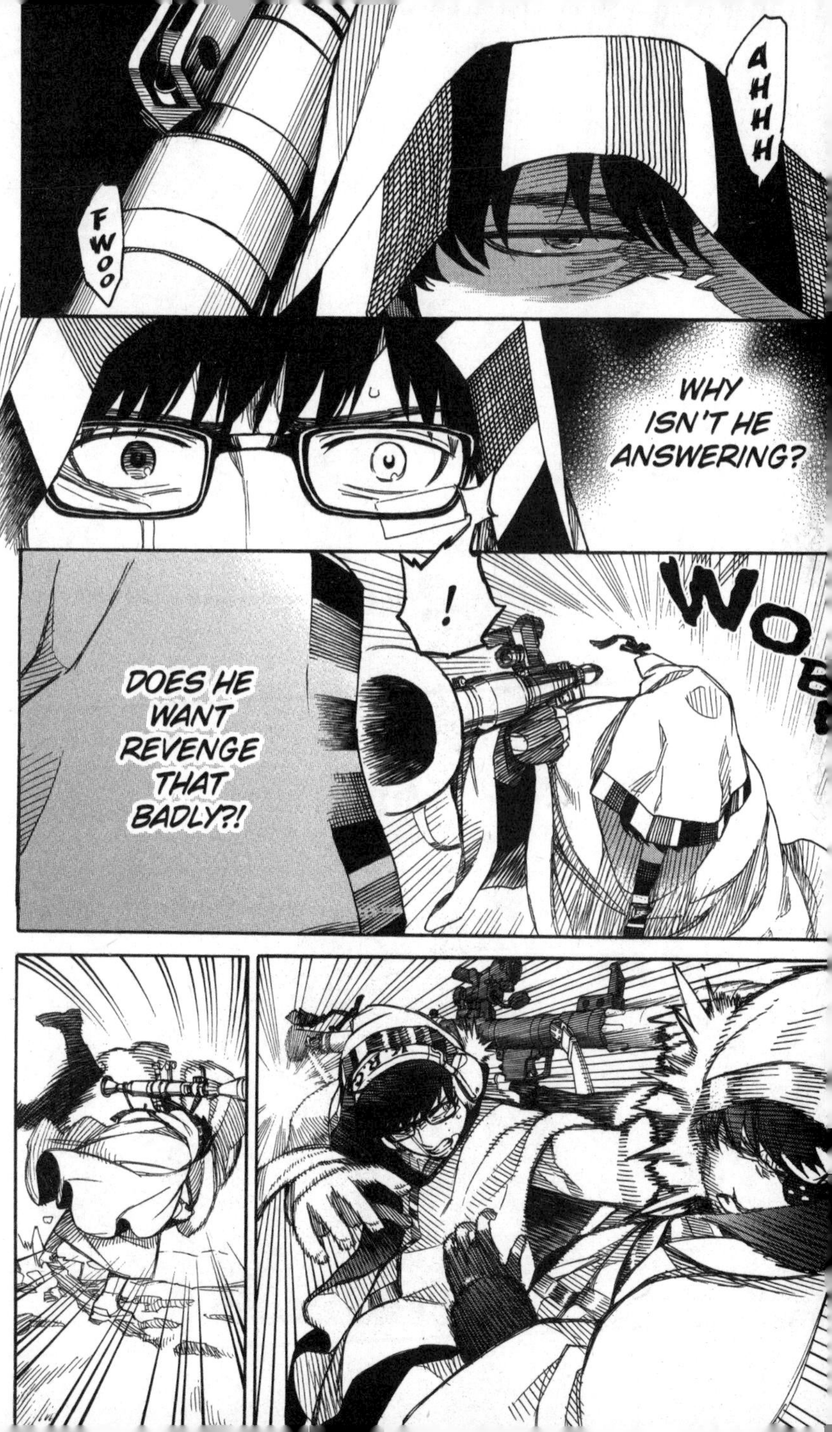
AHHH
FWOO
WHY ISN'T HE ANSWERING?
WOB
!
DOES HE WANT REVENGE THAT BADLY?!

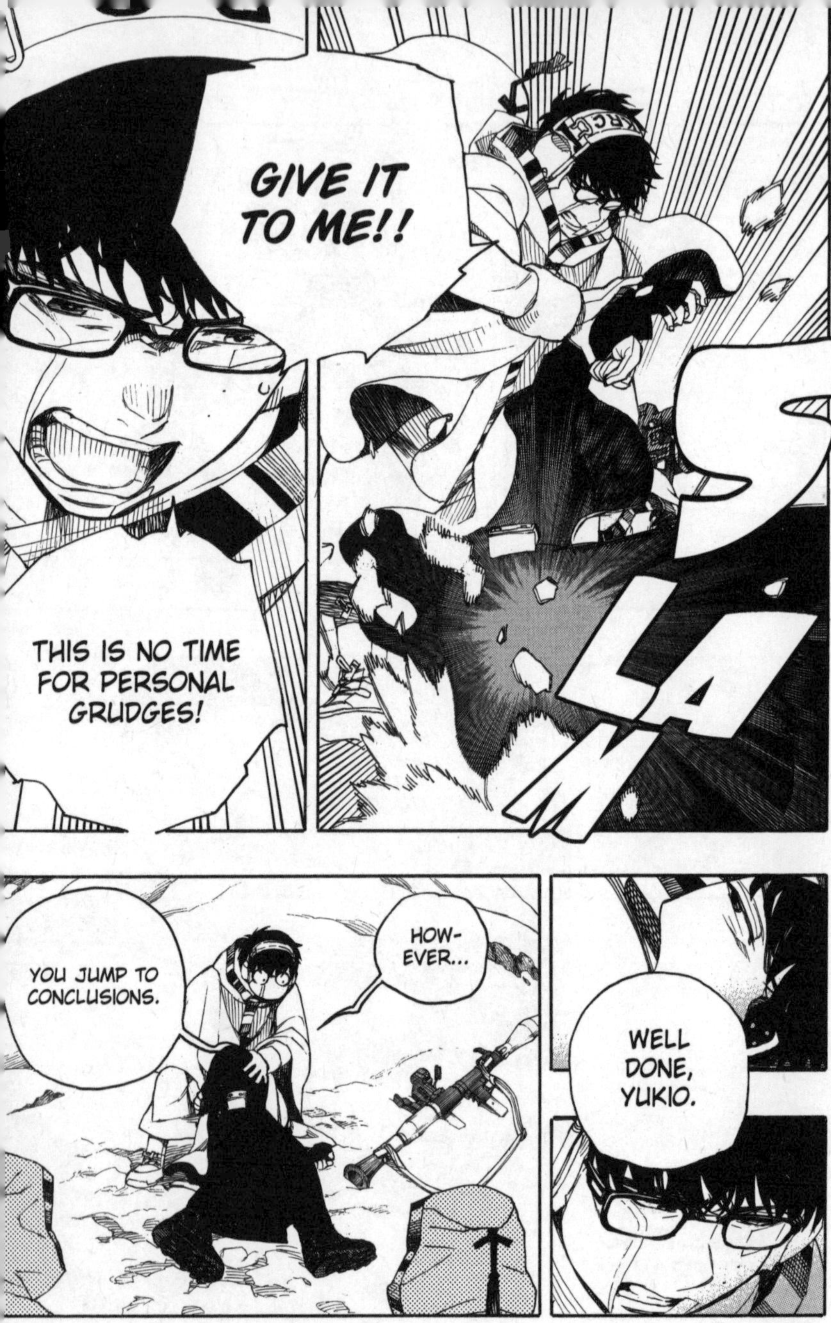
SLAM
GIVE IT TO ME!!
THIS IS NO TIME FOR PERSONAL GRUDGES!
WELL DONE, YUKIO.
HOW-EVER...
YOU JUMP TO CONCLUSIONS.

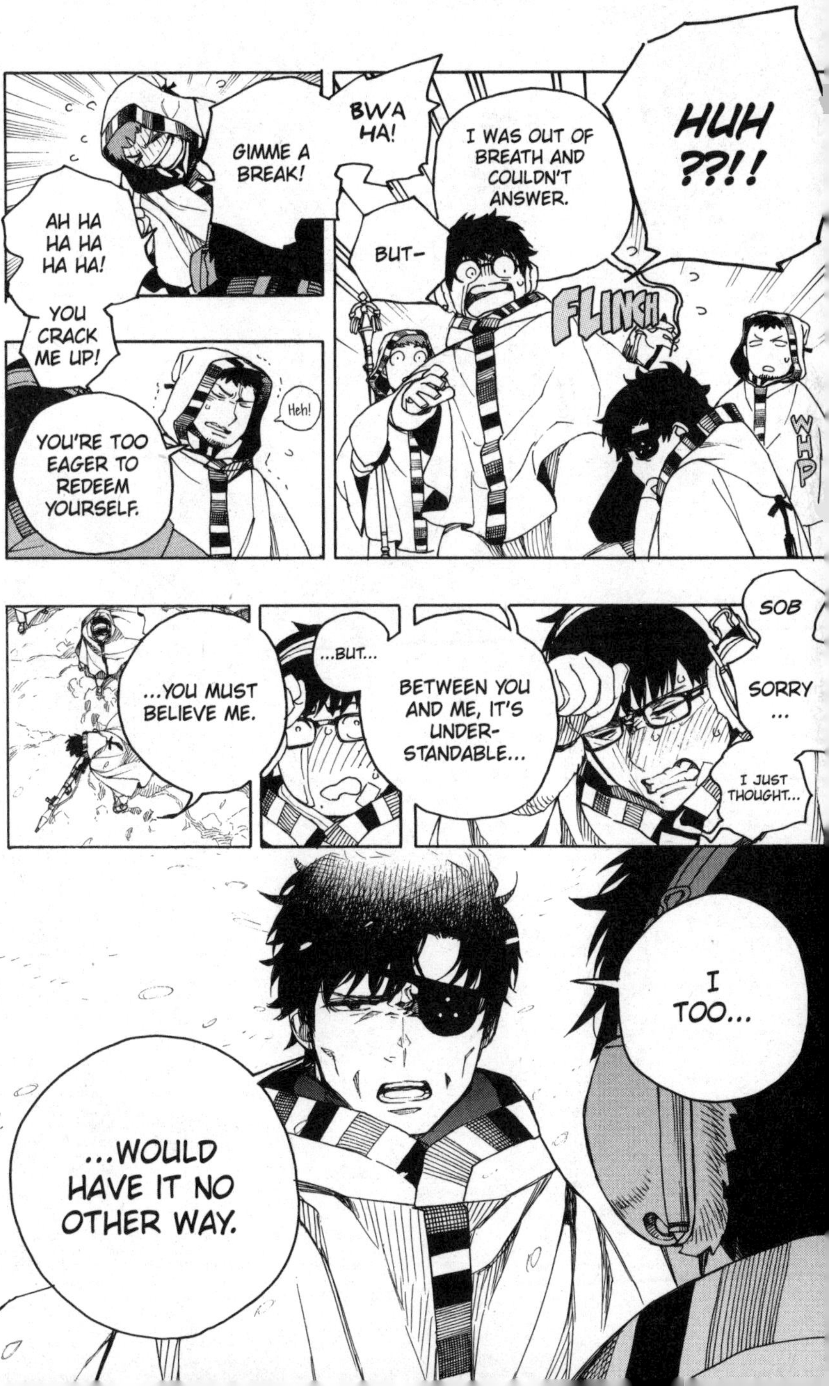
HUH ??!!
I WAS OUT OF BREATH AND COULDN'T ANSWER.
BWA HA!
BUT-
FLINCH
GIMME A BREAK!
AH HA HA HA HA HA!
YOU CRACK ME UP!
Heh!
YOU'RE TOO EAGER TO REDEEM YOURSELF.
SOB
SORRY ...
I JUST THOUGHT...
BETWEEN YOU AND ME, IT'S UNDER-STANDABLE...
...BUT...
...YOU MUST BELIEVE ME.
I TOO...
...WOULD HAVE IT NO OTHER WAY.

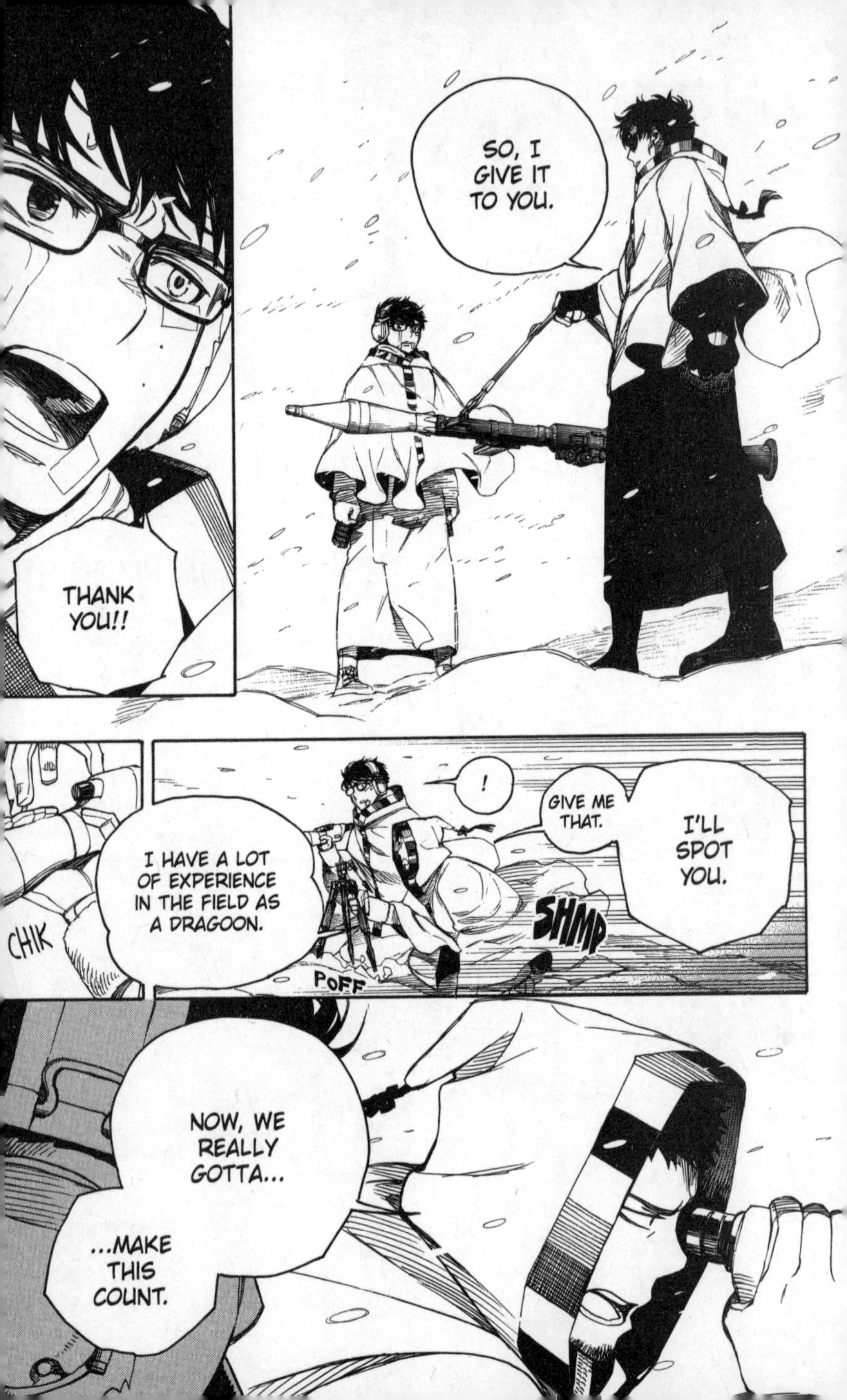
SO, I GIVE IT TO YOU.
THANK YOU!!
!
GIVE ME THAT.
I'LL SPOT YOU.
SHMP
I HAVE A LOT OF EXPERIENCE IN THE FIELD AS A DRAGOON.
POFF
CHIK
NOW, WE REALLY GOTTA...
...MAKE THIS COUNT.

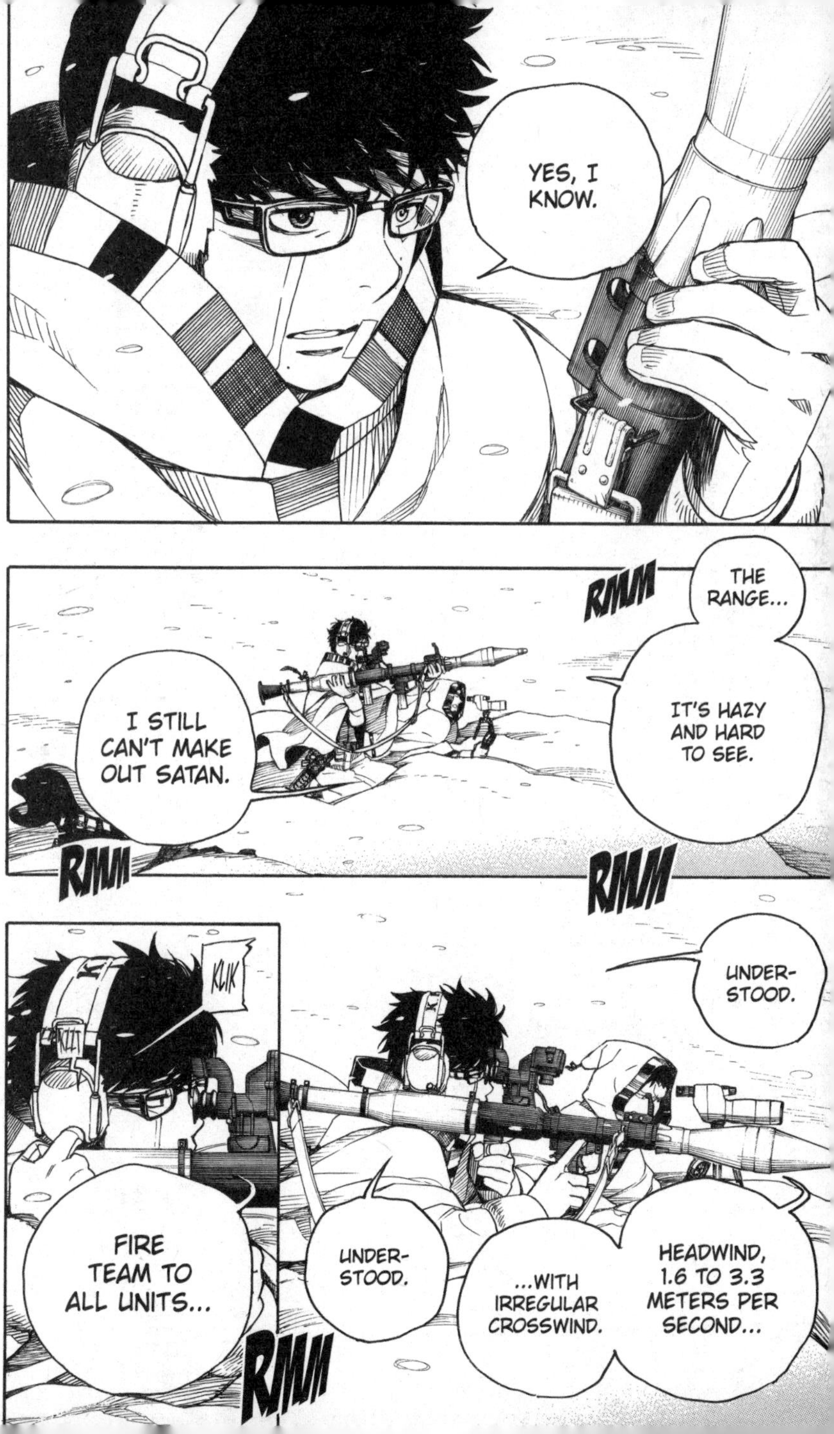
YES, I KNOW.
RMM
THE RANGE...
IT'S HAZY AND HARD TO SEE.
I STILL CAN'T MAKE OUT SATAN.
RMM
RMM
UNDER-STOOD.
KLIK
HEADWIND, 1.6 TO 3.3 METERS PER SECOND...
...WITH IRREGULAR CROSSWIND.
UNDER-STOOD.
FIRE TEAM TO ALL UNITS...
RMM

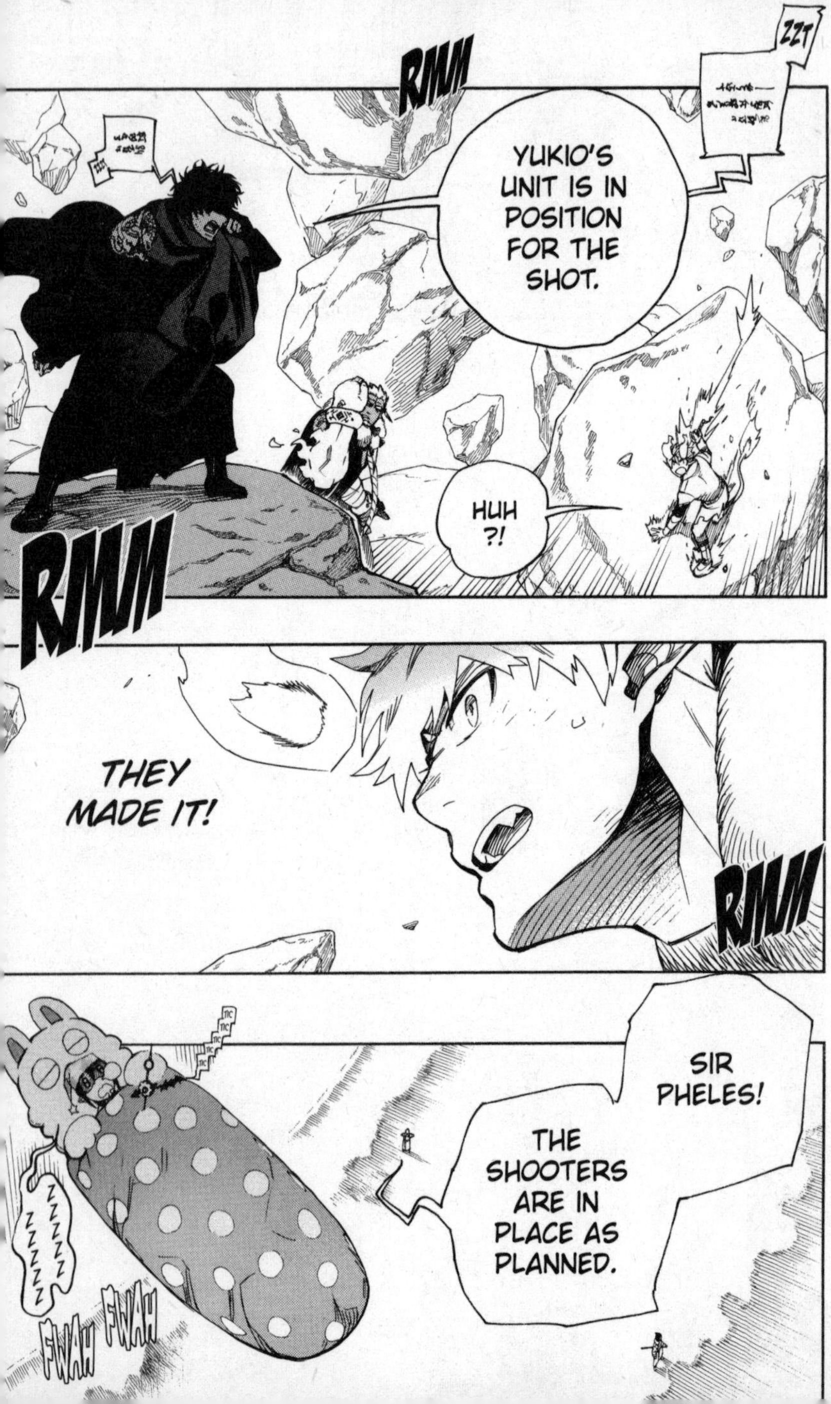
ZZT
YUKIO'S UNIT IS IN POSITION FOR THE SHOT.
RMM
HUH ?!
RMM
RMM
THEY MADE IT!
SIR PHELES!
THE SHOOTERS ARE IN PLACE AS PLANNED.
TIC TIC TIC TIC TIC
ZZZZZ ZZZZZ
FWAH FWAH

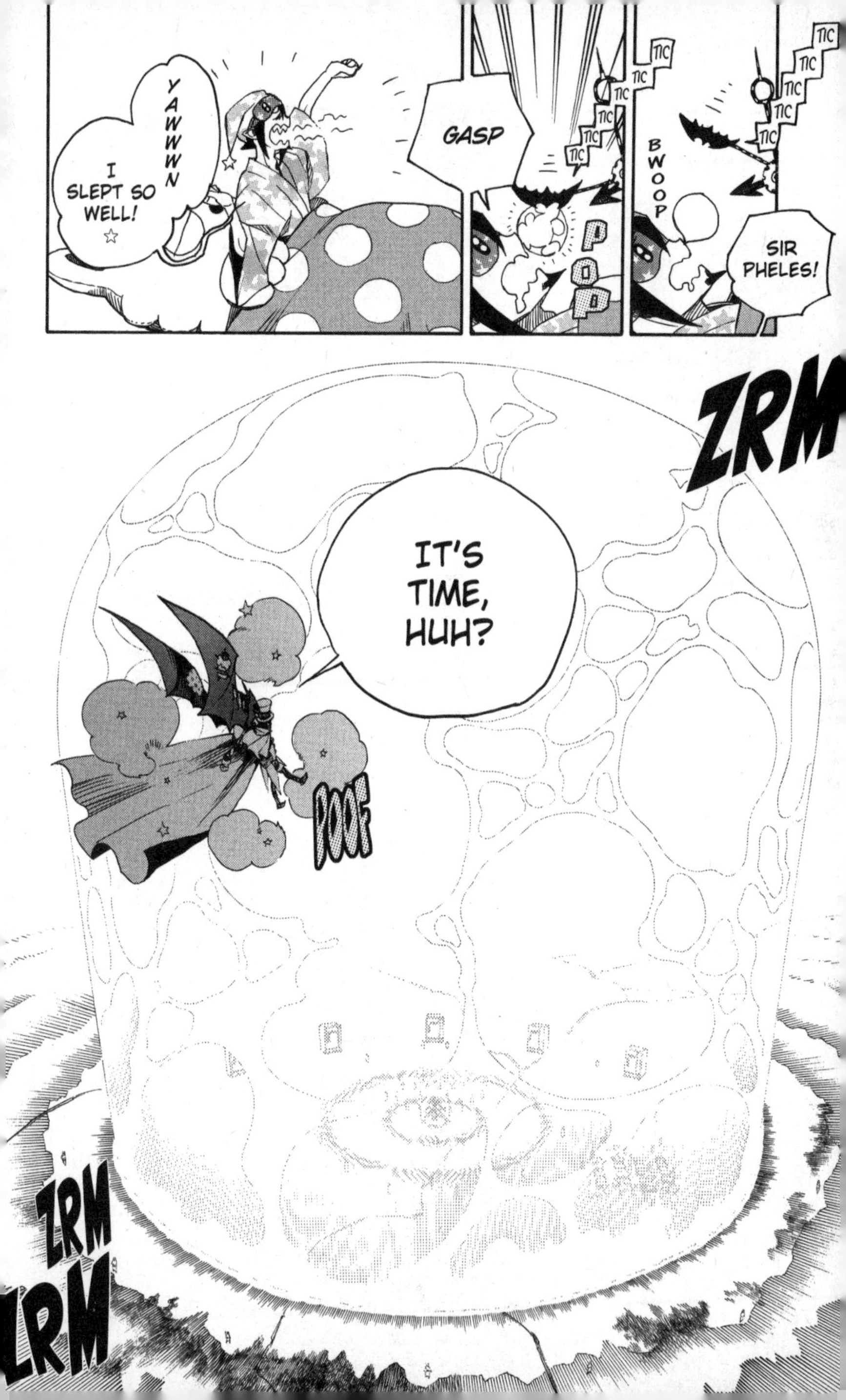
TIC TIC TIC TIC TIC
BWOOP
SIR PHELES!
TIC TIC TIC TIC
GASP
POP
YAWWWN
I SLEPT SO WELL! ☆
ZRM
IT'S TIME, HUH?
POOF
ZRM
ZRM

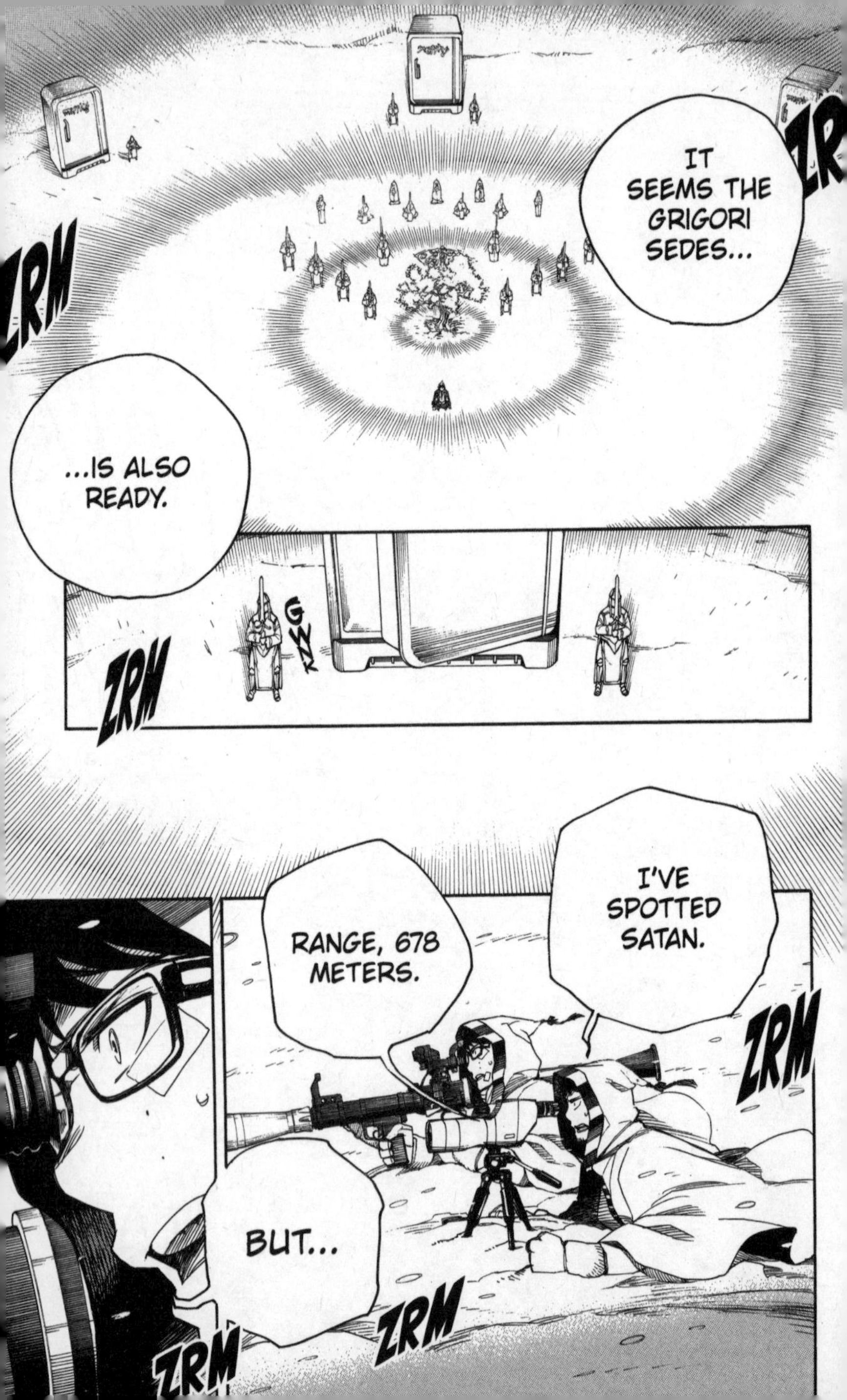
IT SEEMS THE GRIGORI SEDES...
ZR
ZRM
...IS ALSO READY.
GWNK
ZRM
I'VE SPOTTED SATAN.
RANGE, 678 METERS.
ZRM
BUT...
ZRM
ZRM

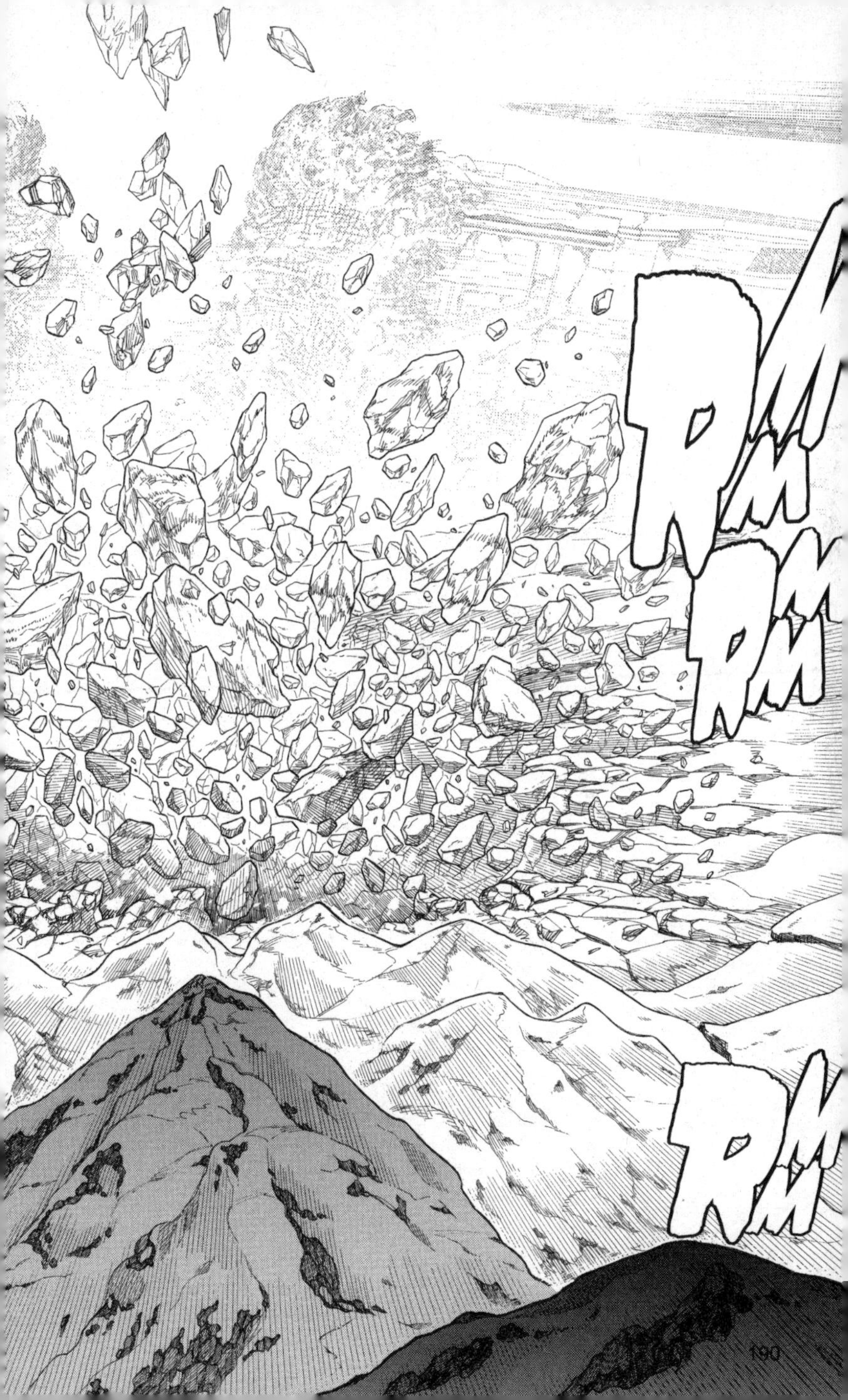
RMM
RMM
RMM

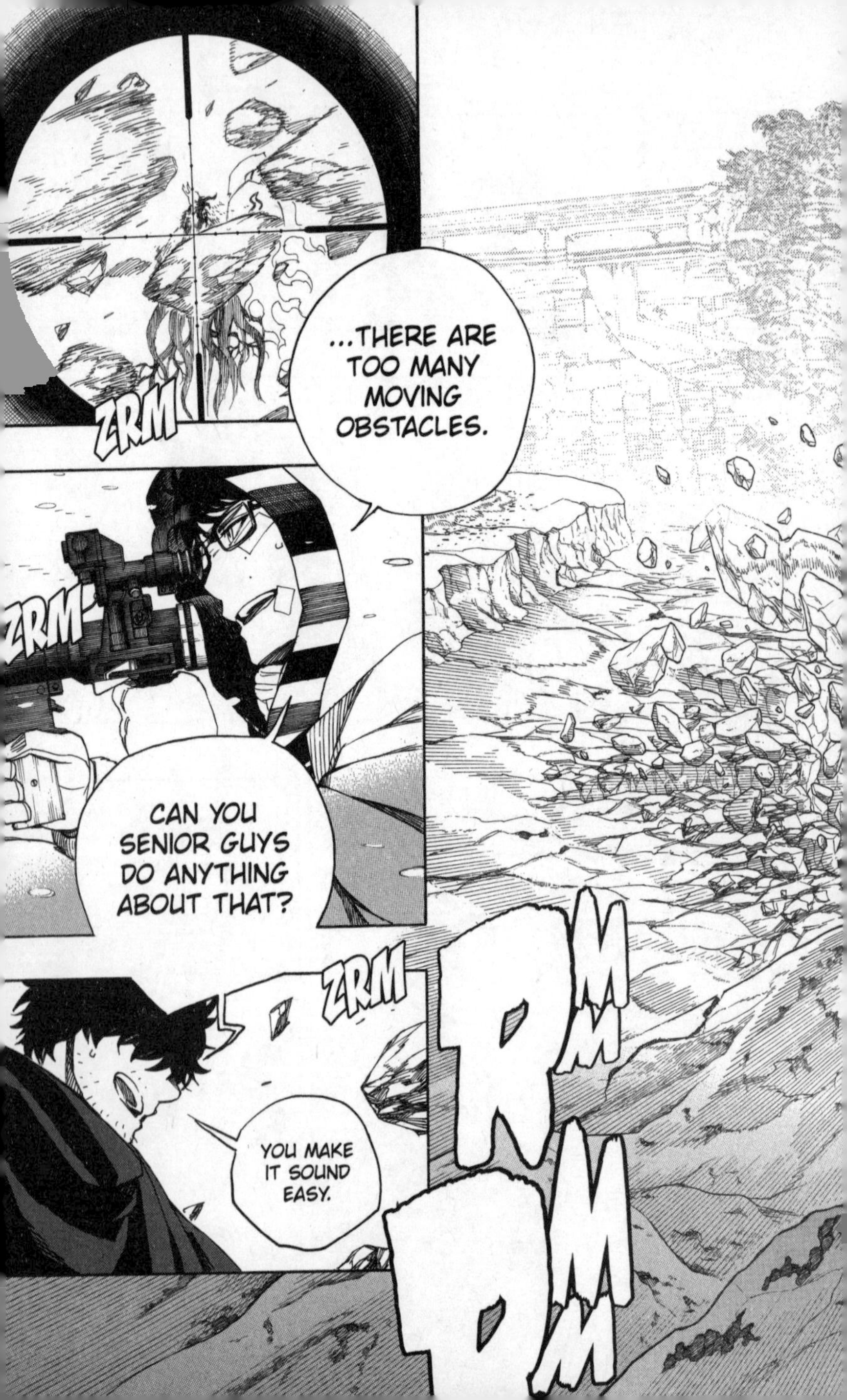
RMMM
DMMM
ZRM
...THERE ARE TOO MANY MOVING OBSTACLES.
ZRM
CAN YOU SENIOR GUYS DO ANYTHING ABOUT THAT?
ZRM
YOU MAKE IT SOUND EASY.

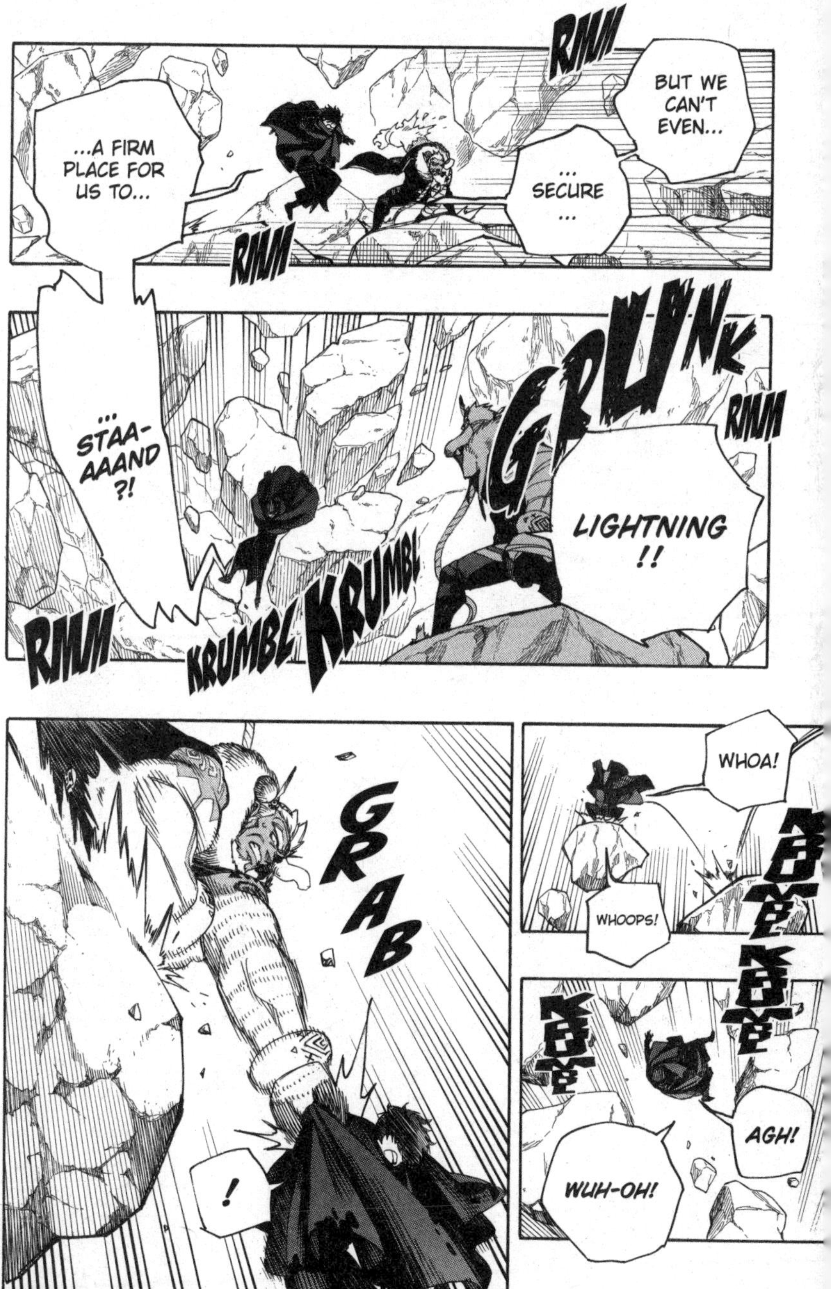
RMM
BUT WE CAN'T EVEN...
...SECURE...
...A FIRM PLACE FOR US TO...
RMM
GRUNK
RMM
LIGHTNING!!
...STAA-AAAND?!
KRUMBL
KRUMBL
RMM
WHOA!
WHOOPS!
AGH!
WUH-OH!
GRAB
!

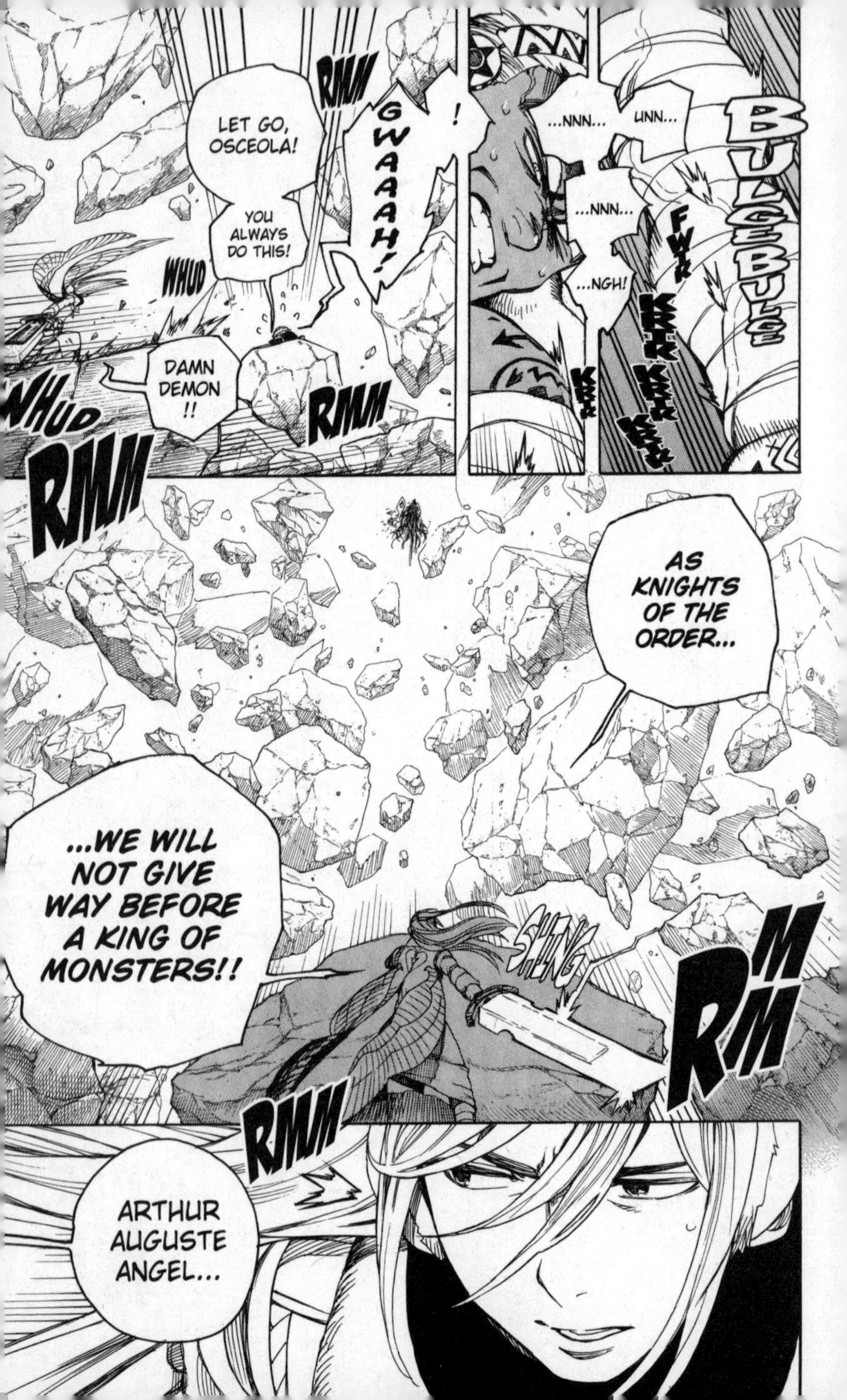
UNN...
BULGEBULGE
FWIR
KRIK
...NNN...
...NNN...
...NGH!
!
GWAAAAH!
RMM
LET GO, OSCEOLA!
YOU ALWAYS DO THIS!
WHUD
RMM
DAMN DEMON !!
WHUD
RMM
AS KNIGHTS OF THE ORDER...
...WE WILL NOT GIVE WAY BEFORE A KING OF MONSTERS!!
SHING
RMM
RMM
ARTHUR AUGUSTE ANGEL...

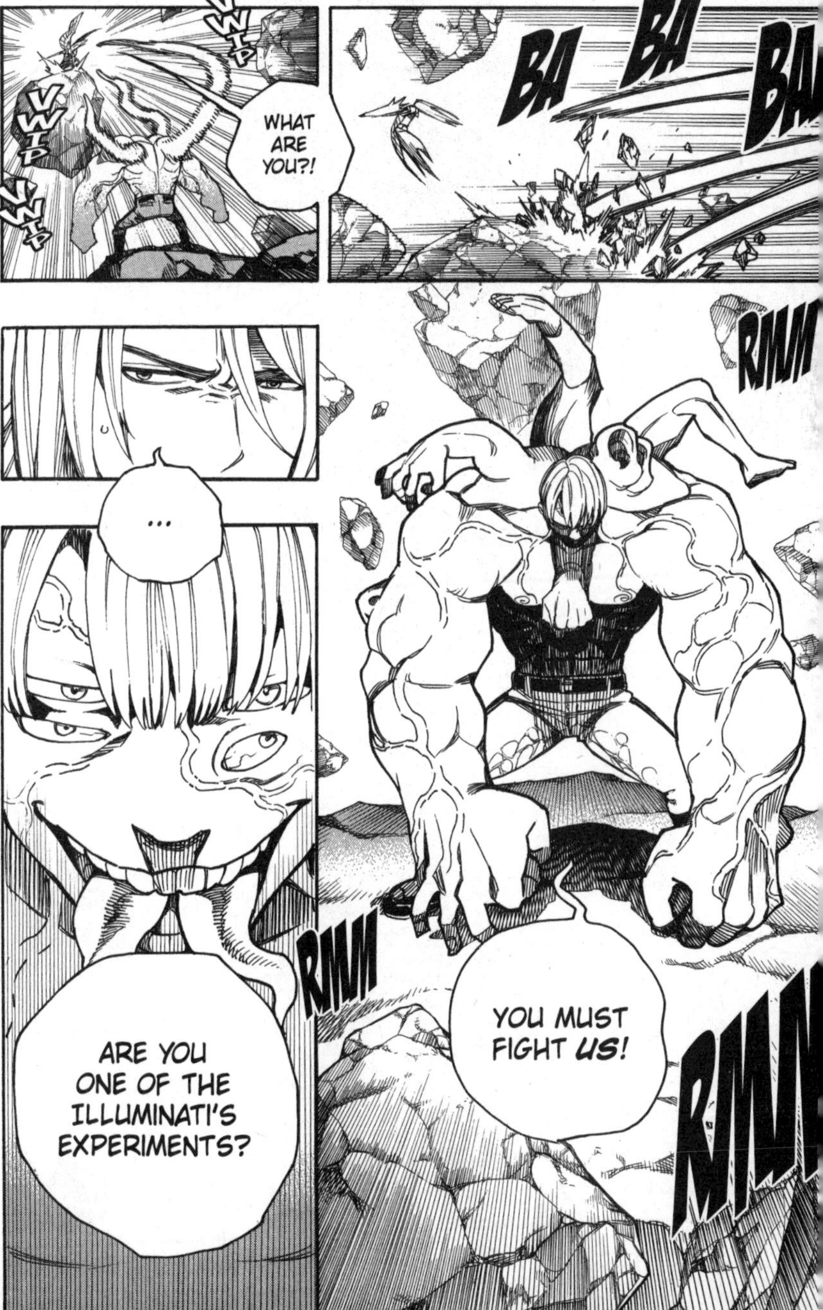
BA
BA
BA
VWIP
VWIP
VWIP
WHAT ARE YOU?!
RMM
RMM
YOU MUST FIGHT *US*!
RMM
...
ARE YOU ONE OF THE ILLUMINATI'S EXPERIMENTS?

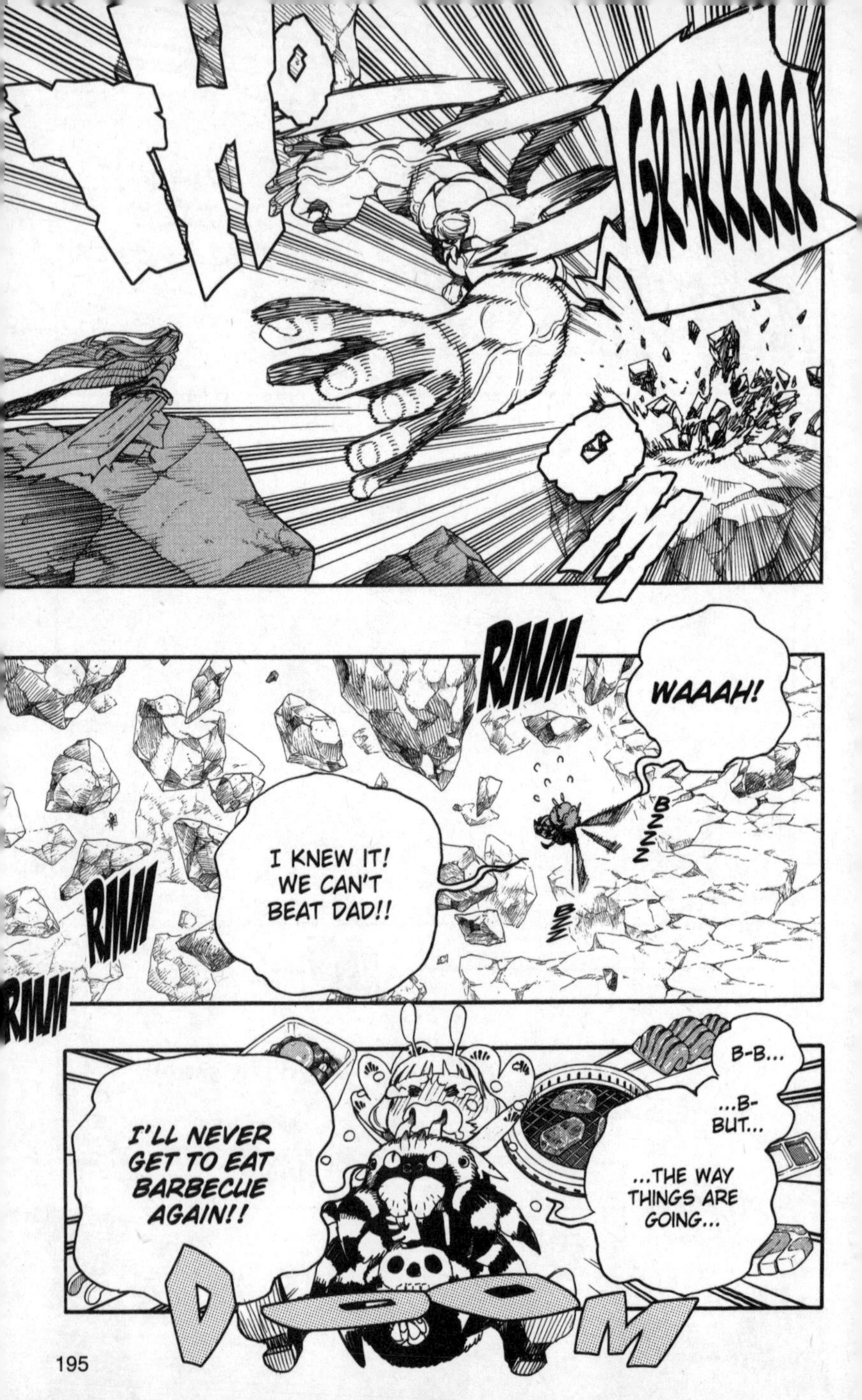
GRARRRRR
RMM
WAAAH!
BZZZ
I KNEW IT! WE CAN'T BEAT DAD!!
BZZ
RMM
RMM
B-B...
...B- BUT...
...THE WAY THINGS ARE GOING...
I'LL NEVER GET TO EAT BARBECUE AGAIN!!
DOOM

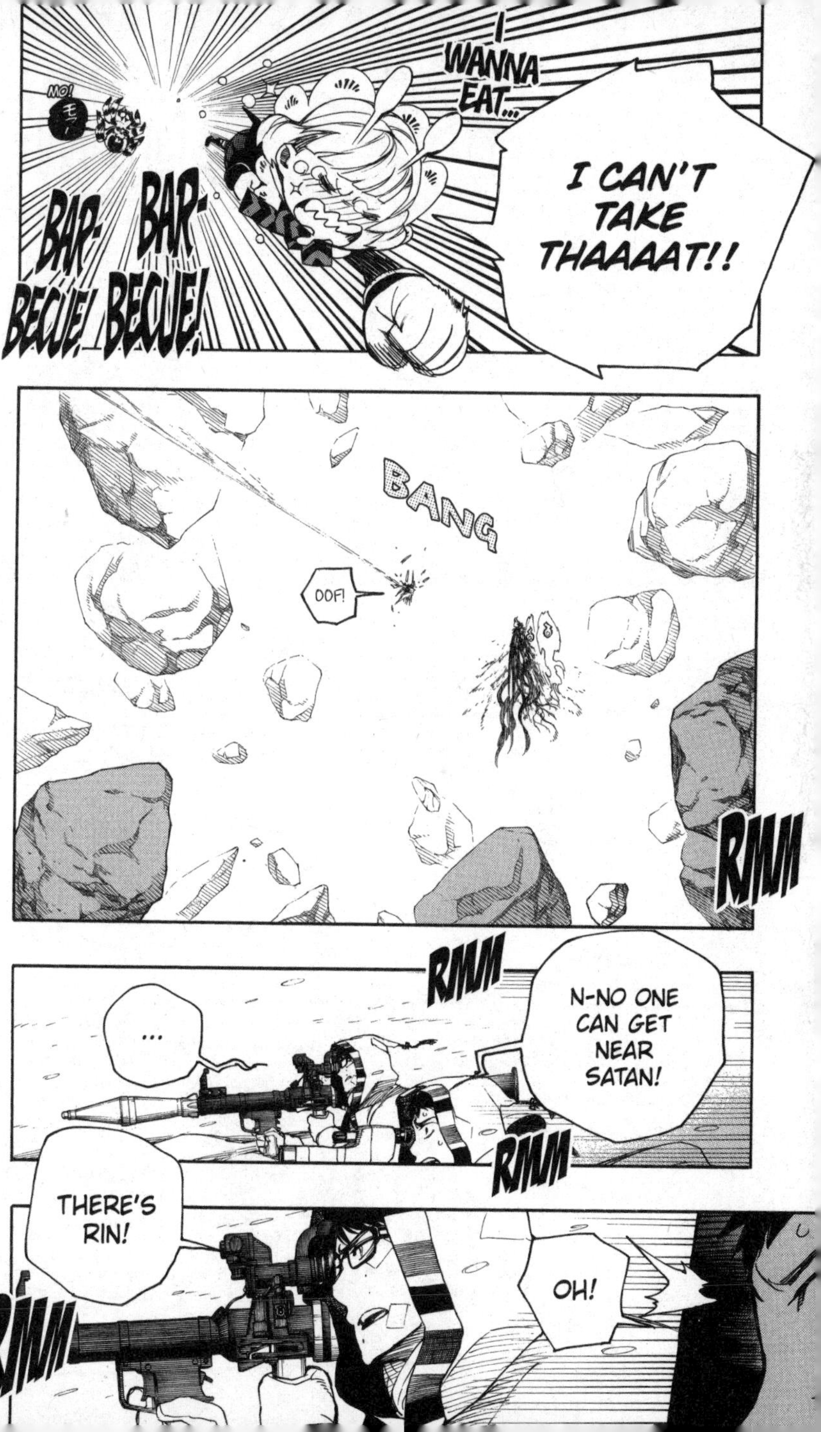
I CAN'T TAKE THAAAAT!!
I WANNA EAT...
MO!
BAR-BECUE! BAR-BECUE!
BANG
OOF!
RMM
RMM
N-NO ONE CAN GET NEAR SATAN!
...
RMM
OH!
THERE'S RIN!
RMM

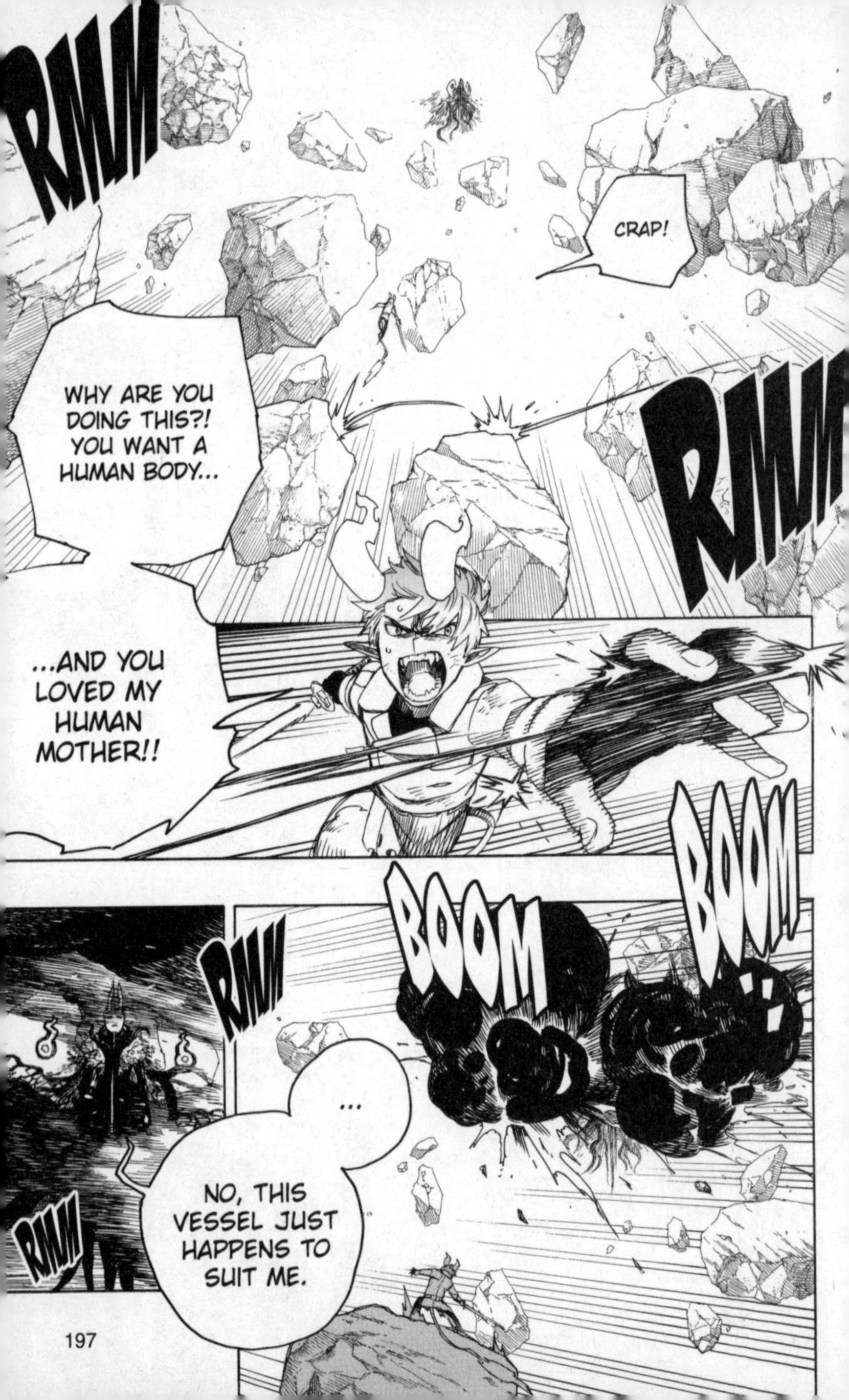
CRAP!
RMM
RMM
WHY ARE YOU DOING THIS?! YOU WANT A HUMAN BODY...
...AND YOU LOVED MY HUMAN MOTHER!!
BOOM
BOOM
...
NO, THIS VESSEL JUST HAPPENS TO SUIT ME.
RMM
RMM

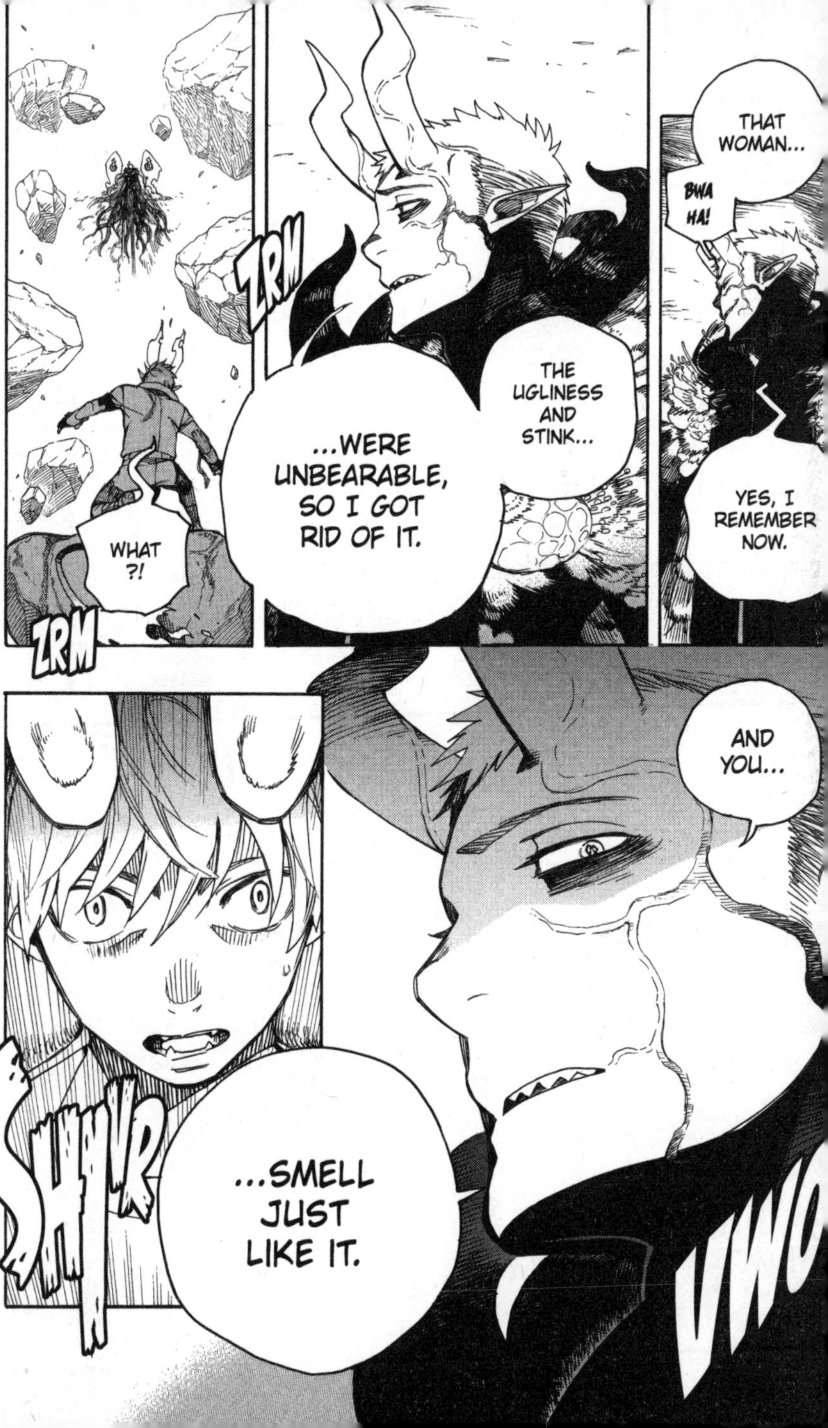
THAT WOMAN...
BWA HA!
YES, I REMEMBER NOW.
ZRM
THE UGLINESS AND STINK...
...WERE UNBEARABLE, SO I GOT RID OF IT.
WHAT ?!
ZRM
AND YOU...
...SMELL JUST LIKE IT.
VWO
SHIVR

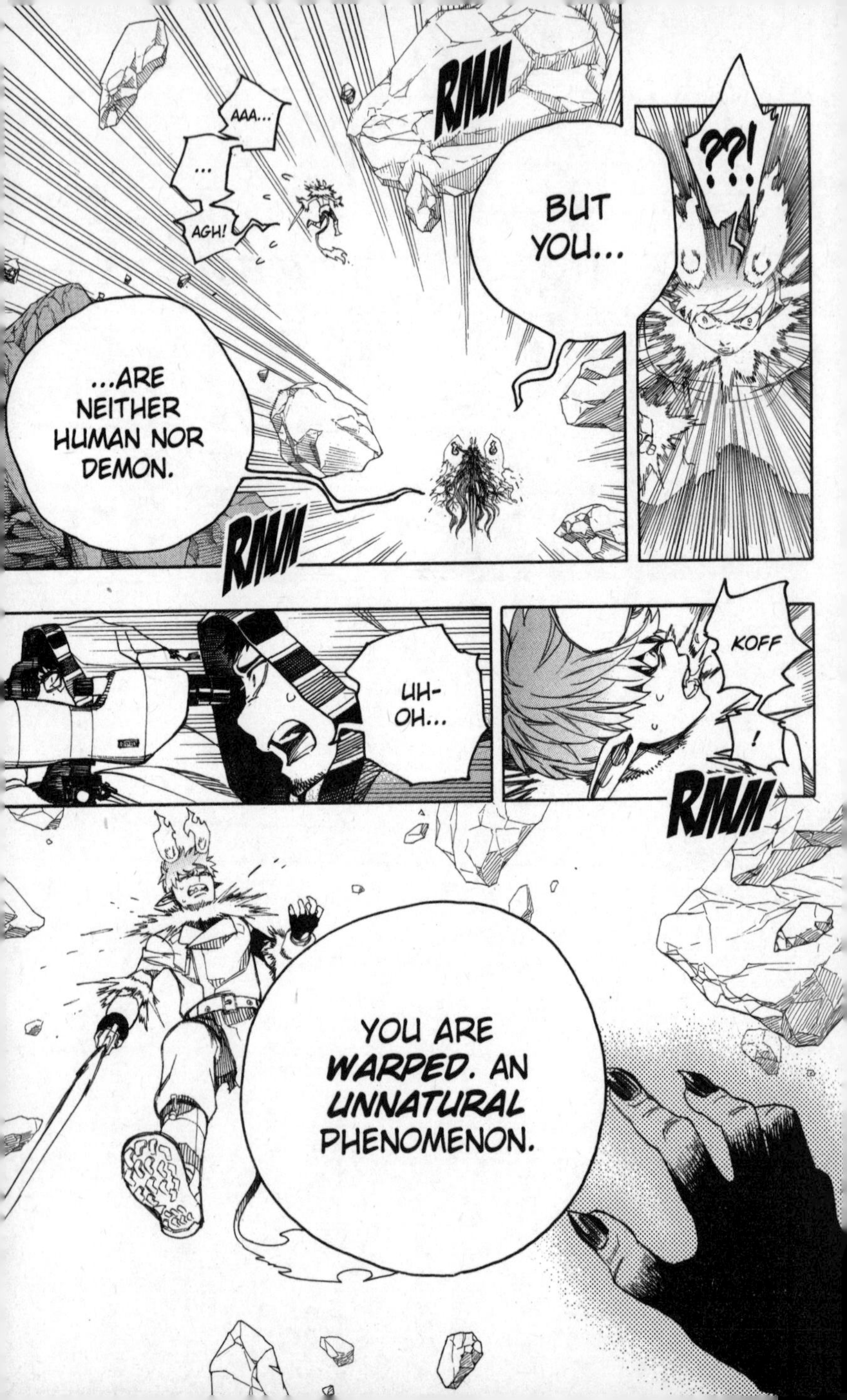
??!
RMM
BUT YOU...
AAA...
...
AGH!
...ARE NEITHER HUMAN NOR DEMON.
RMM
KOFF
!
RMM
UH-OH...
YOU ARE *WARPED*. AN *UNNATURAL* PHENOMENON.

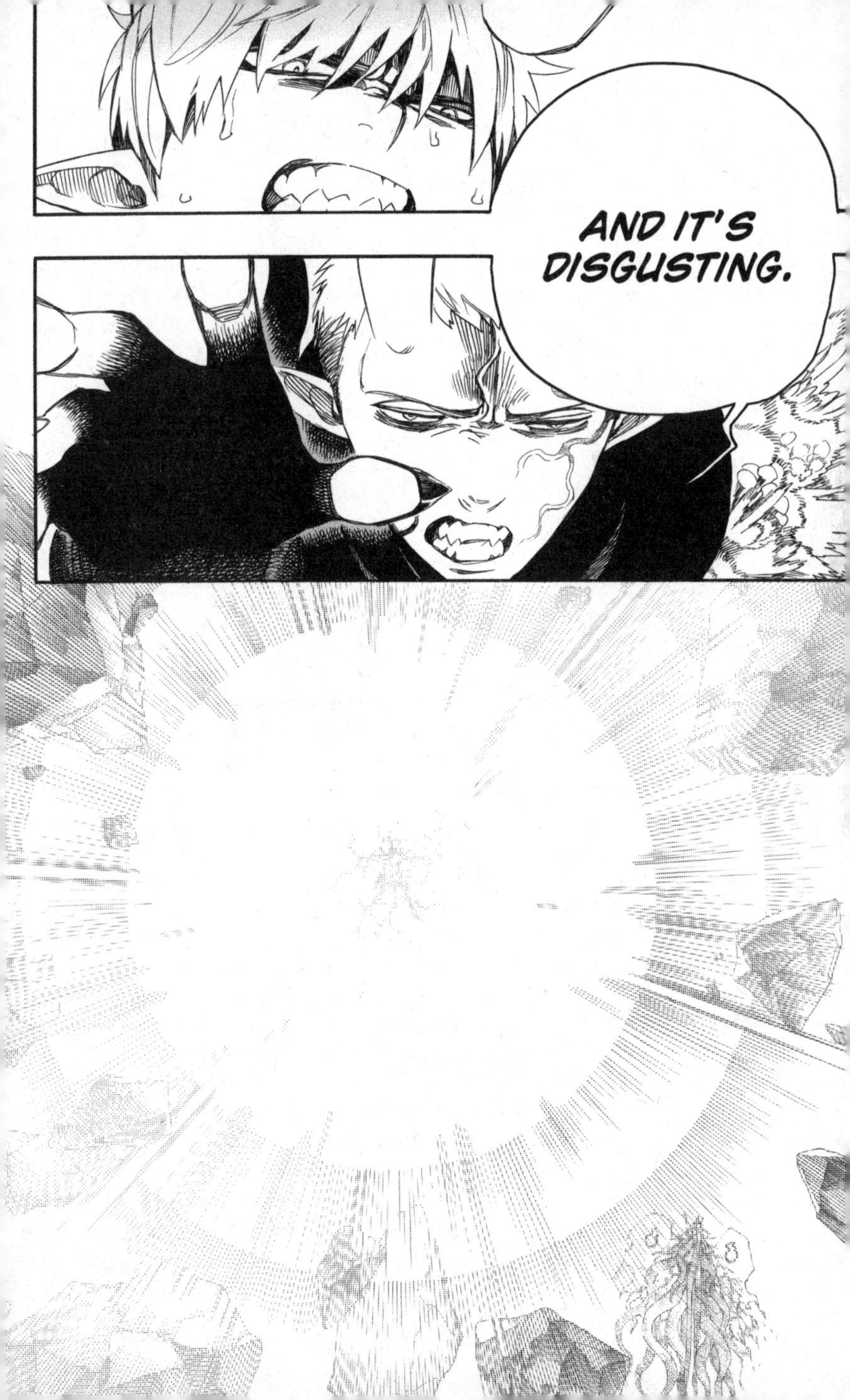
AND IT'S DISGUSTING.

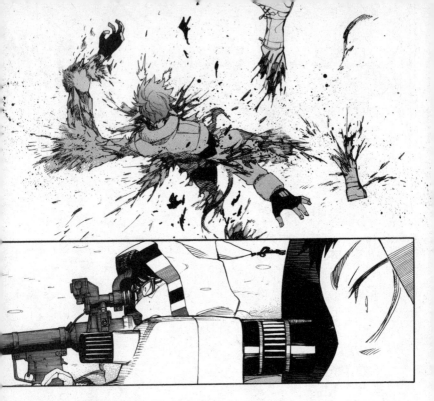

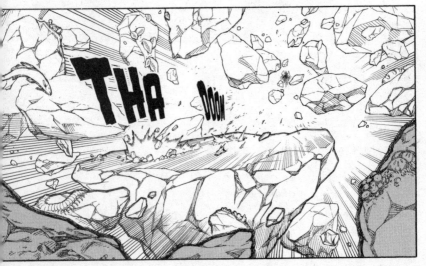

THA DOOM

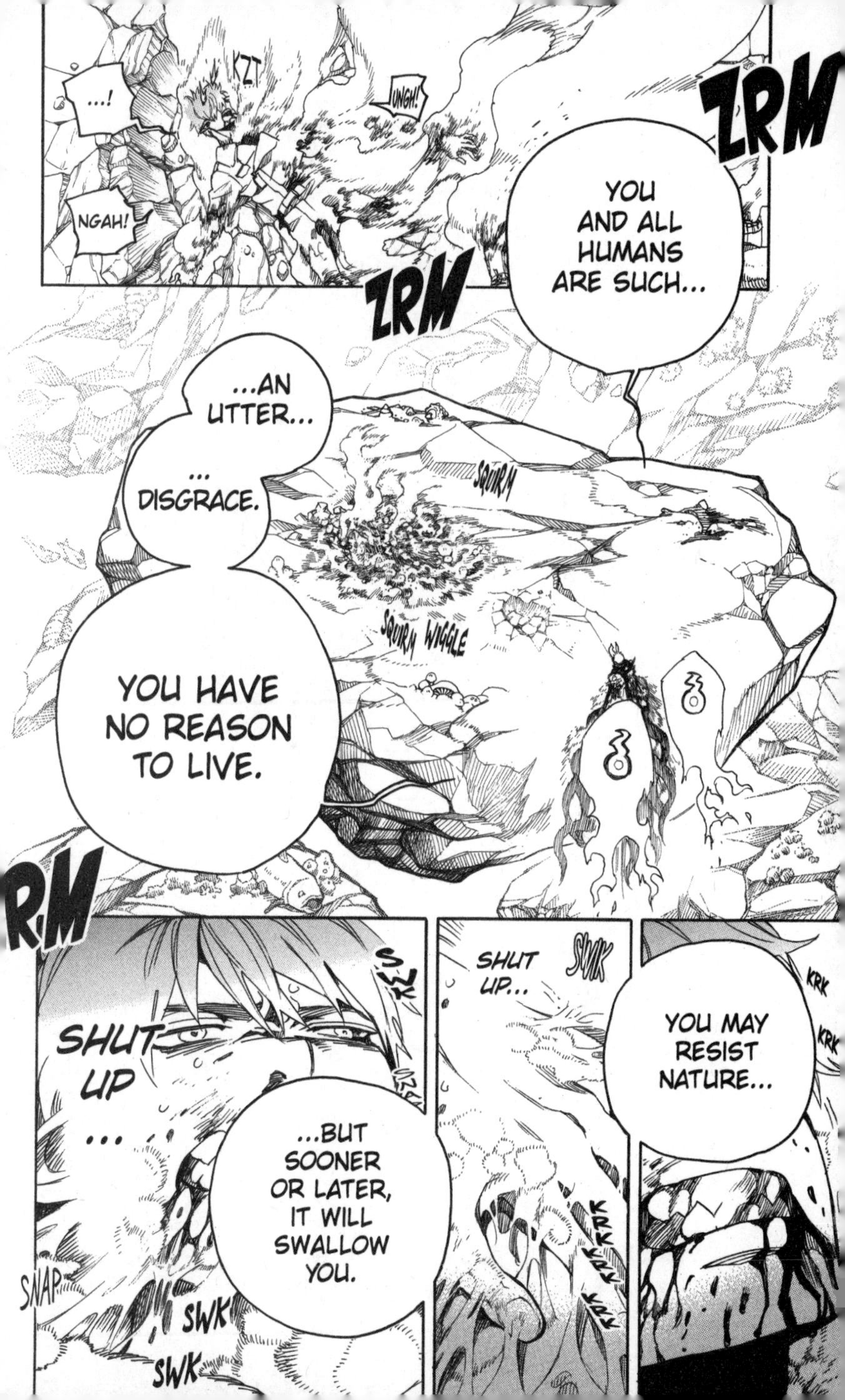
ZRM
KZT
UNGH!
...!
NGAH!
ZRM
YOU AND ALL HUMANS ARE SUCH...
...AN UTTER...
... DISGRACE.
SQUIRM
SQUIRM WIGGLE
YOU HAVE NO REASON TO LIVE.
R.M
KRK
KRK
YOU MAY RESIST NATURE...
SWK
SHUT UP...
KRK KRK KRK
SWK
SHUT UP ...
...BUT SOONER OR LATER, IT WILL SWALLOW YOU.
SNAP
SWK
SWK

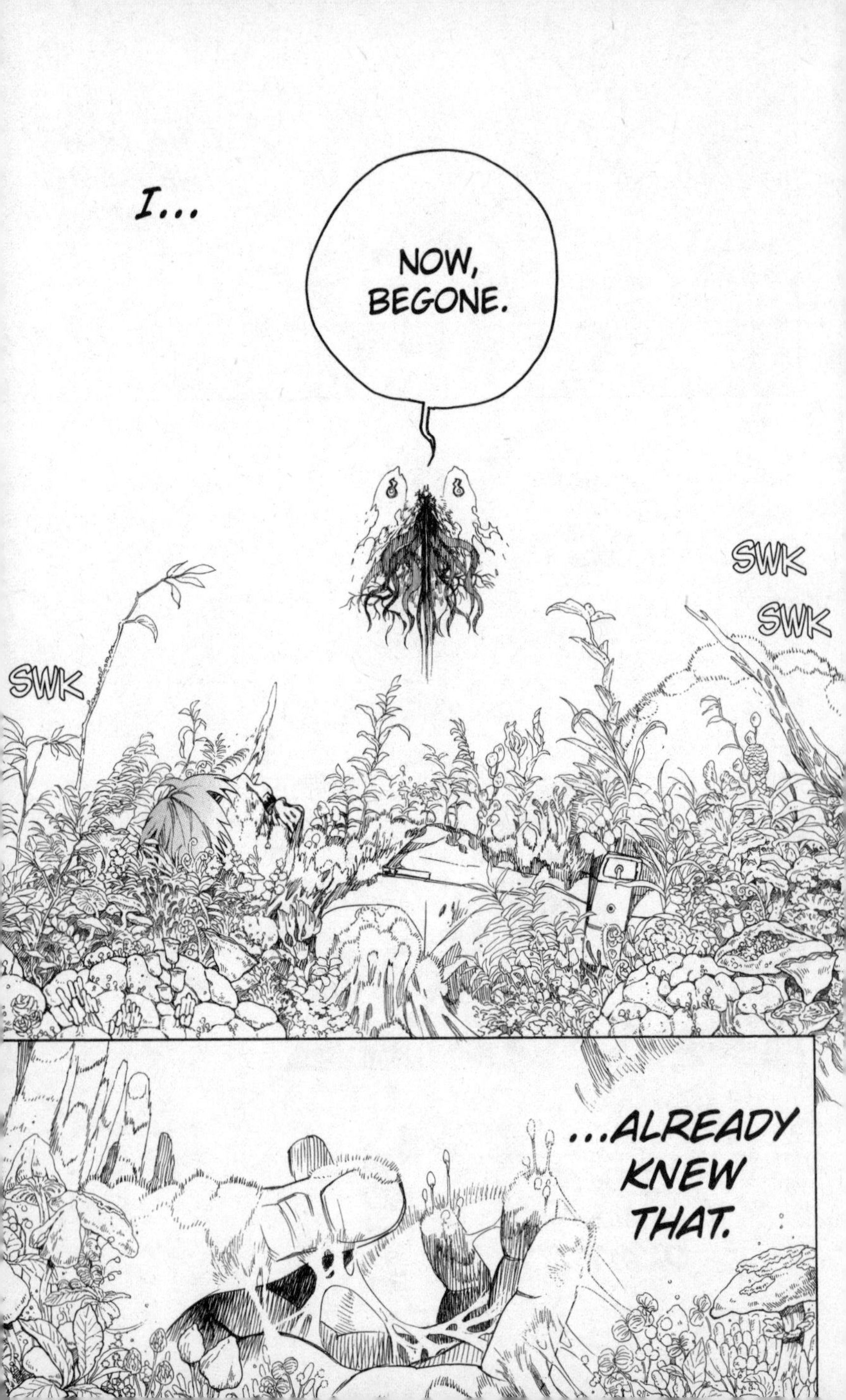
NOW, BEGONE.
I...
SWK
SWK
SWK
...ALREADY KNEW THAT.

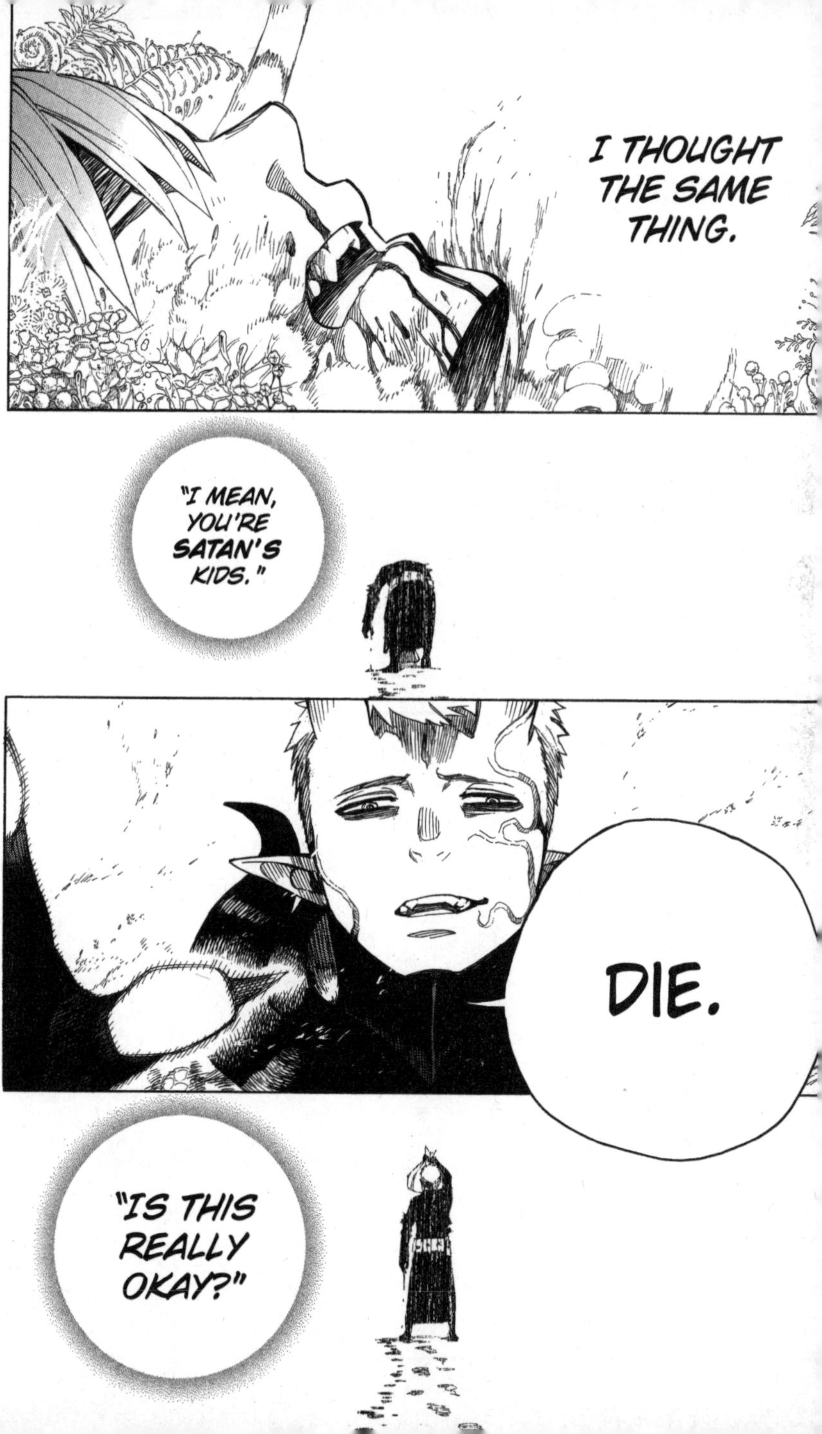
I THOUGHT THE SAME THING.
"I MEAN, YOU'RE SATAN'S KIDS."
DIE.
"IS THIS REALLY OKAY?"

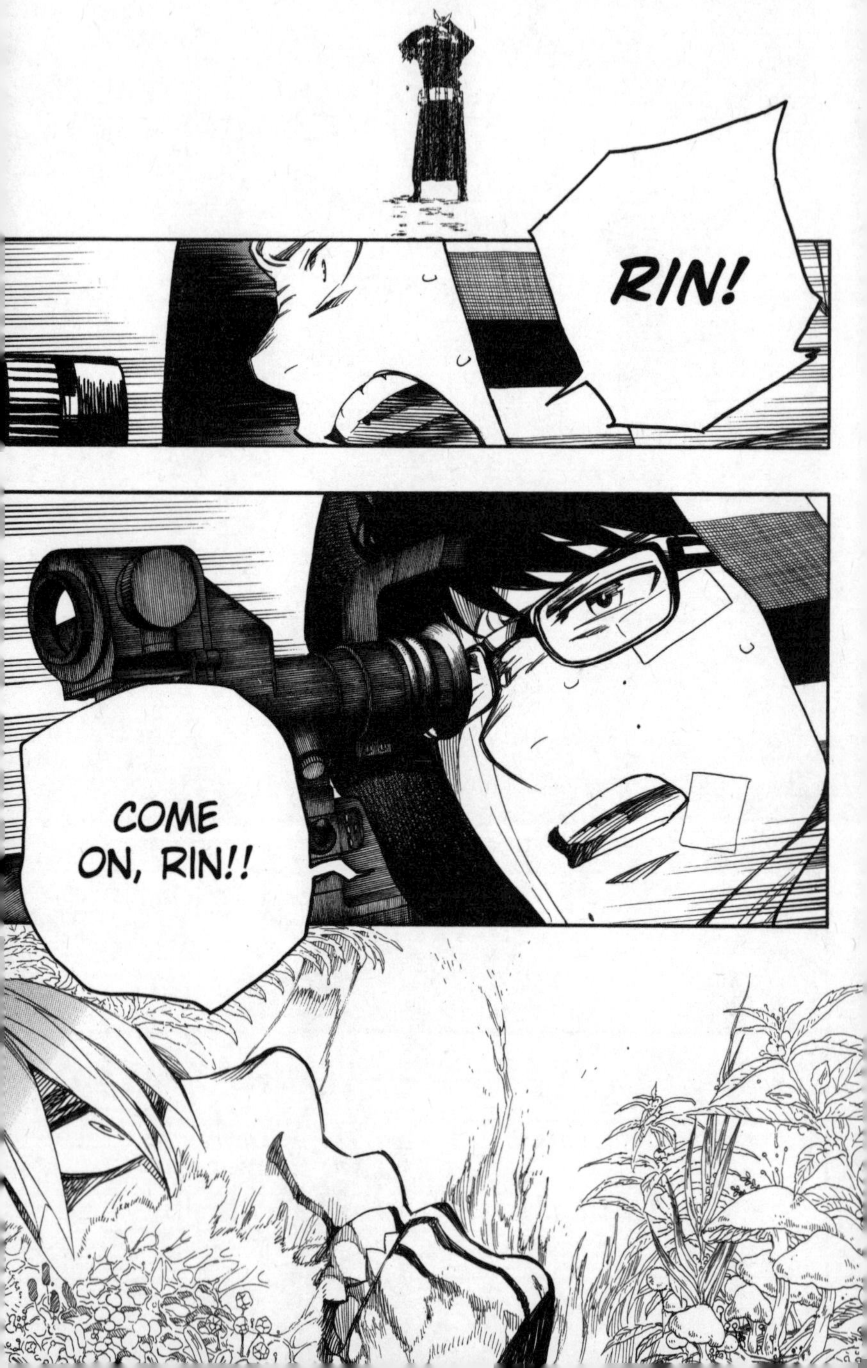
RIN!
COME ON, RIN!!

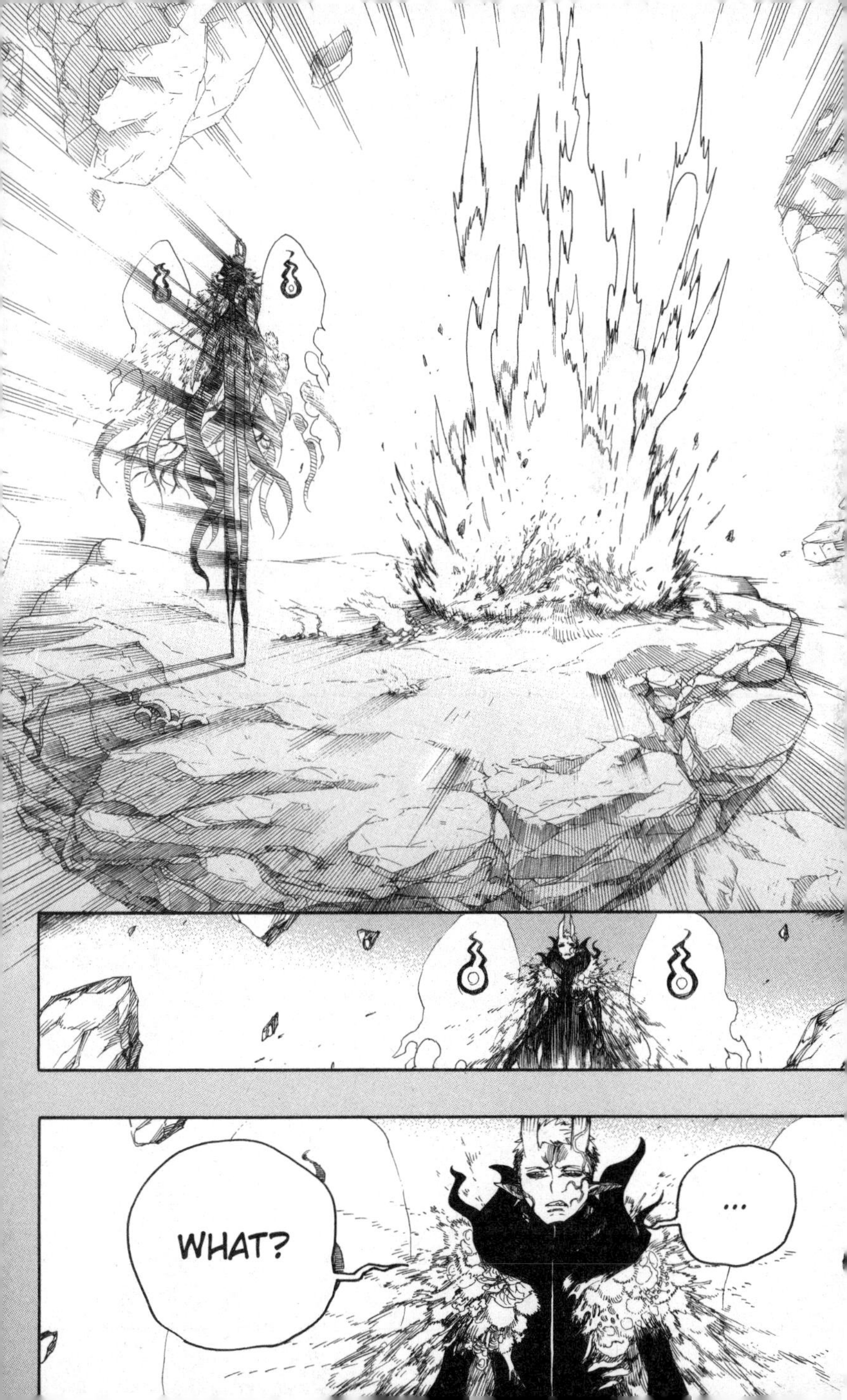
...
WHAT?

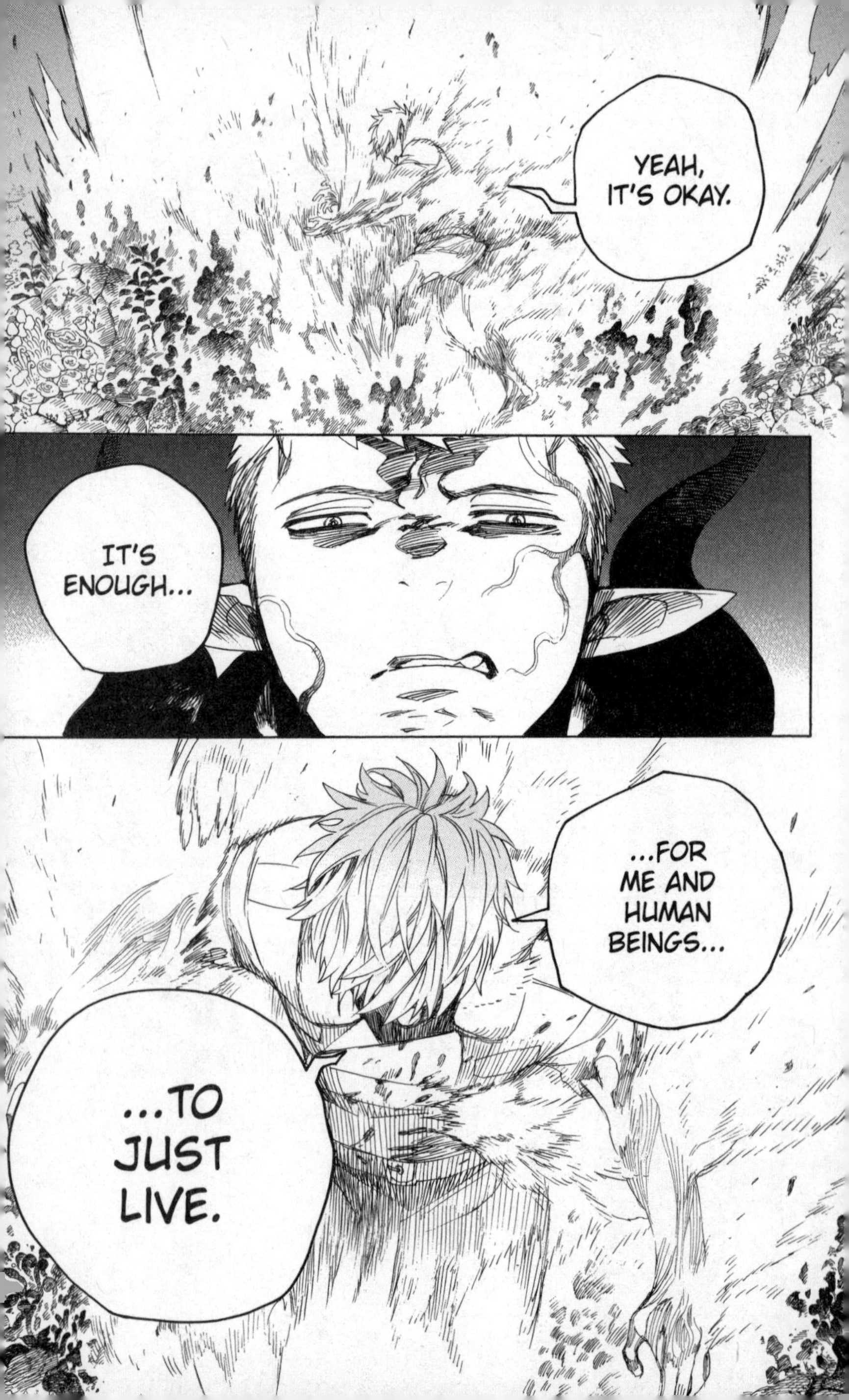
YEAH, IT'S OKAY.
IT'S ENOUGH...
...FOR ME AND HUMAN BEINGS...
...TO JUST LIVE.

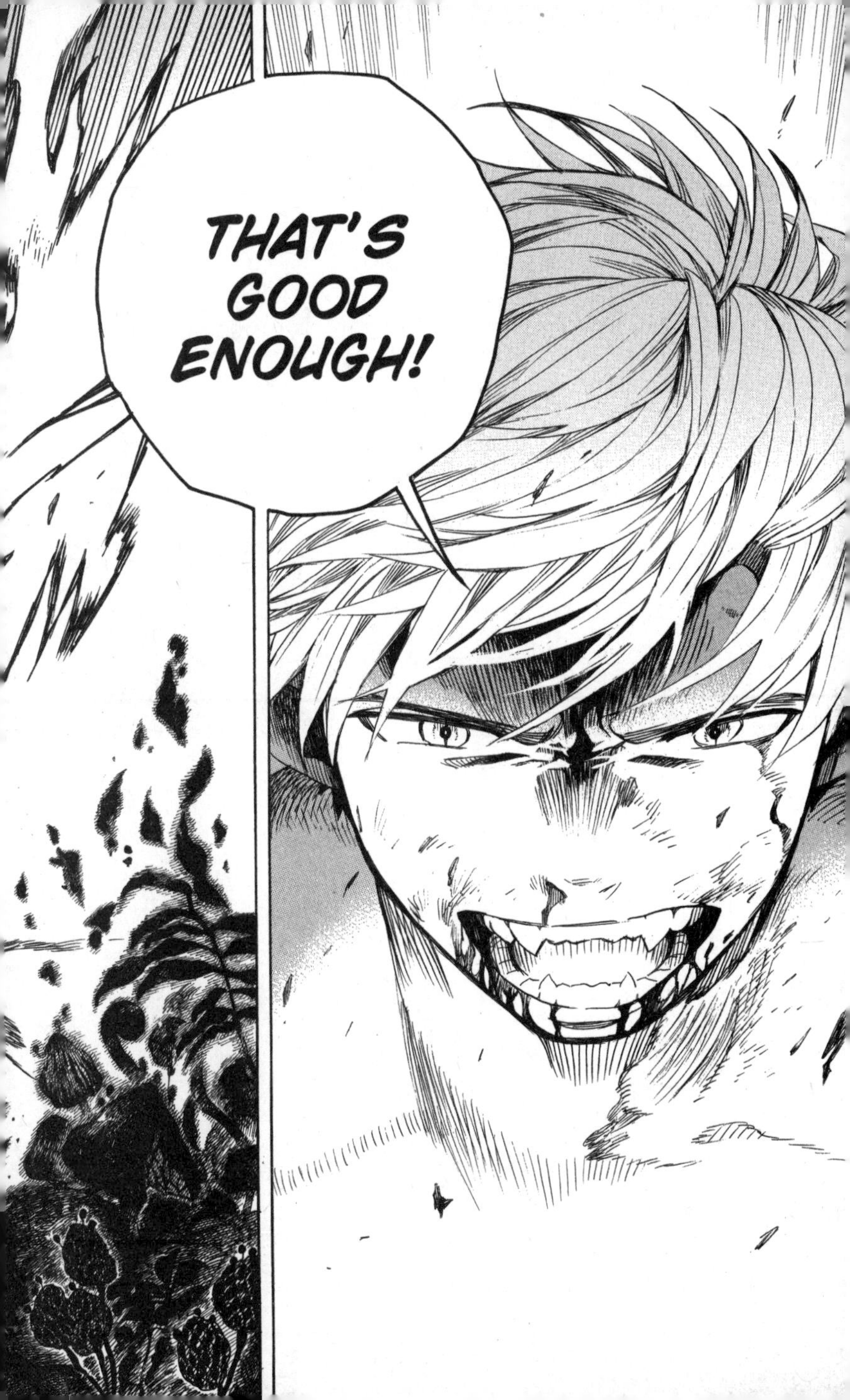
THAT'S GOOD ENOUGH!

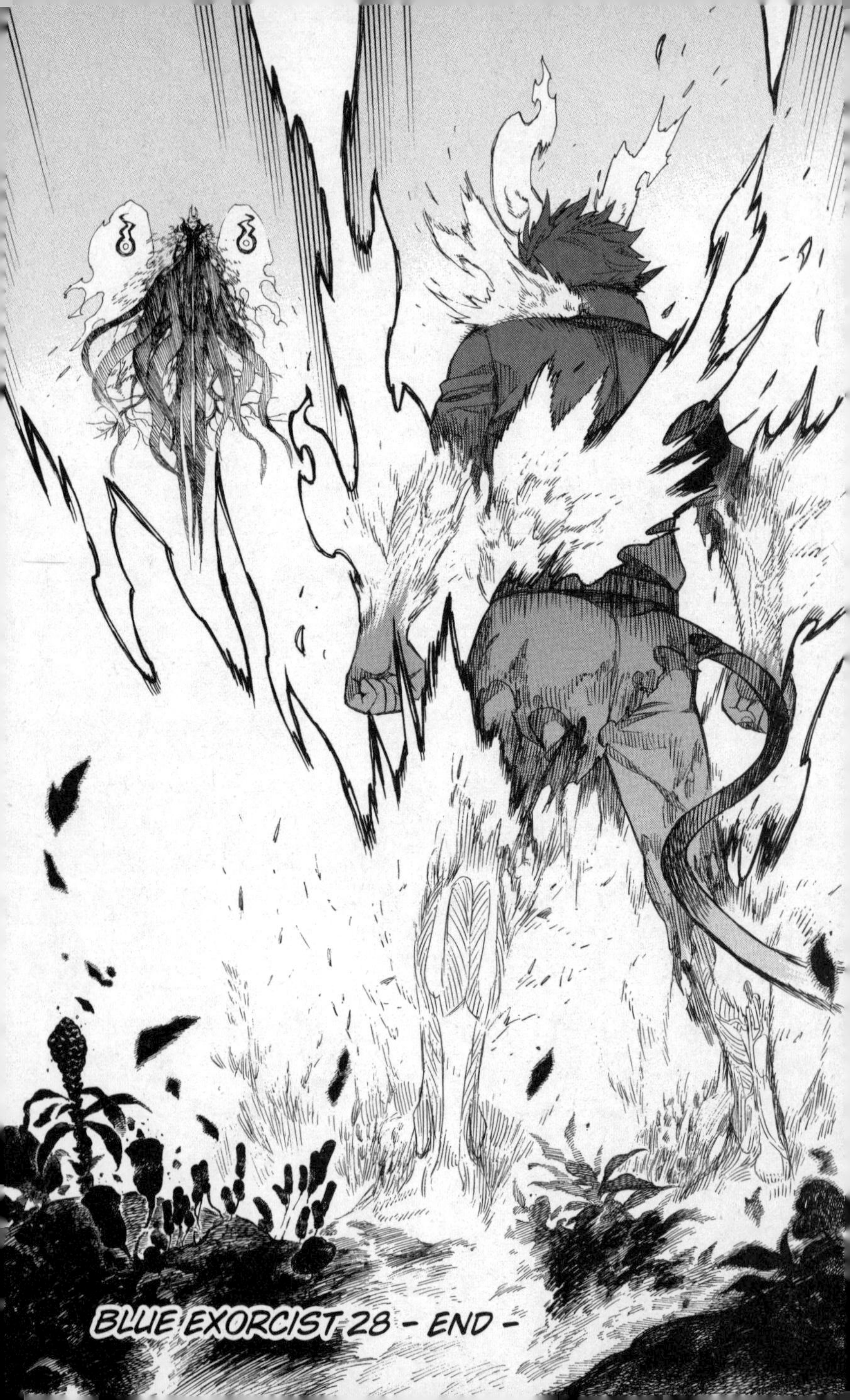
BLUE EXORCIST 28 - END -

Blue Exorcist Chapter 135: Of One Cloth—Waking Up

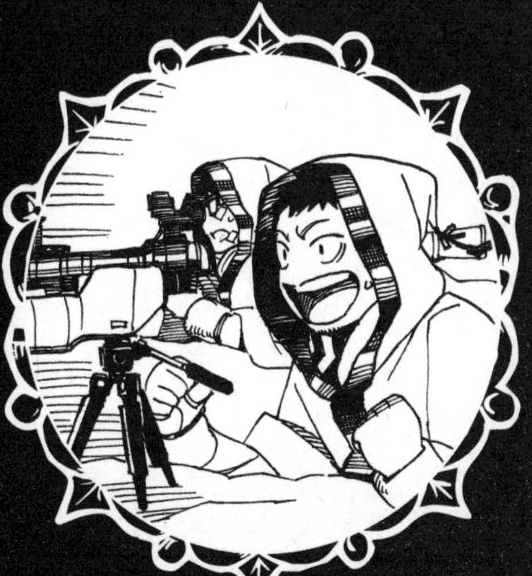

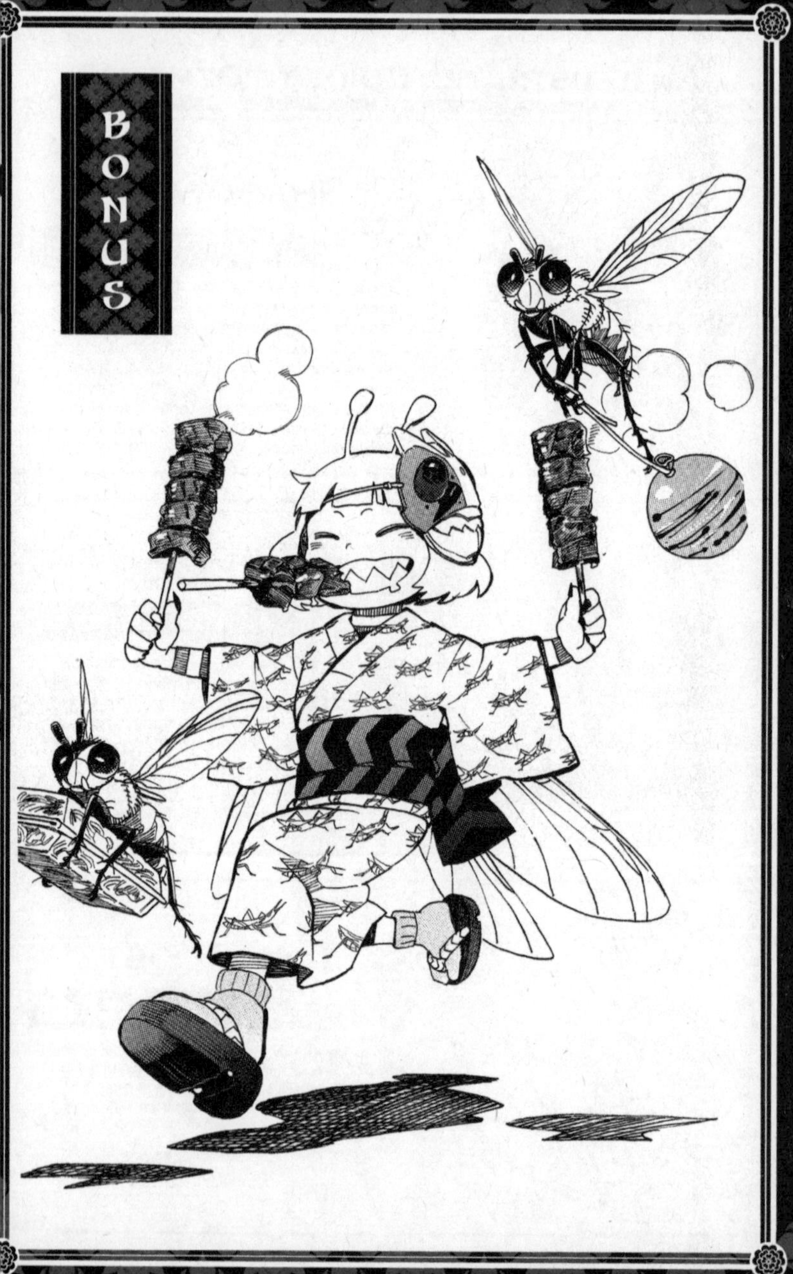
BONUS

BLUE EXORCIST BONUS

AN ILLUSTRATED GUIDE TO DEMONS

An Illustrated Guide to Satan

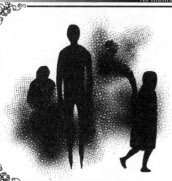

SHADOW

FILE 56

LOW TO MID LEVEL

Kin of Samael, King of Time. These demons possess unknown properties related to time and space. They mimic human forms and characteristics and lurk in various places. Most are weak and fleeting, but the strong ones are obsessed with human beings and are able to affect the nervous system. There have been sightings of them all over the world. Also known as Shadow People and Shadow Men.

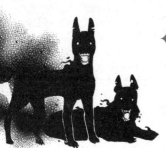

BLACK DOG

FILE 57

LOW TO HIGH LEVEL

Kin of Samael, King of Time. These demons possess unknown properties related to time and space. They appear when death is near and follow people around. They like people, so the Order captures and trains low- to mid-level black dogs for use in detecting traces of demons.

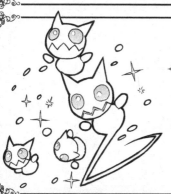

JACK FROST

FILE 58

LOW TO HIGH LEVEL

Kin of Azazel, King of Spirits. These are the smallest type of demons that possess ice crystals in the air. They're aggressive, mischievous, and especially active during winter and in cold places.

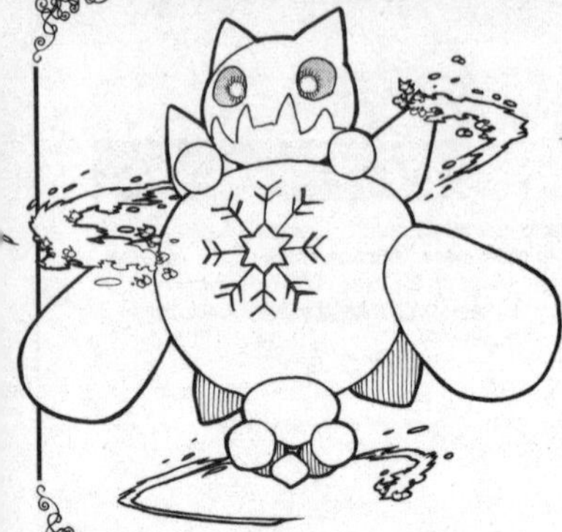

FILE 59

General Frost

High Level

Kin of Azazel, King of Spirits. These are large demons that possess ice crystals in the air. They're especially active during winter and in cold places. They can form and command large groups of Jack Frosts. When angered, they go wild and can instantaneously freeze a whole area.

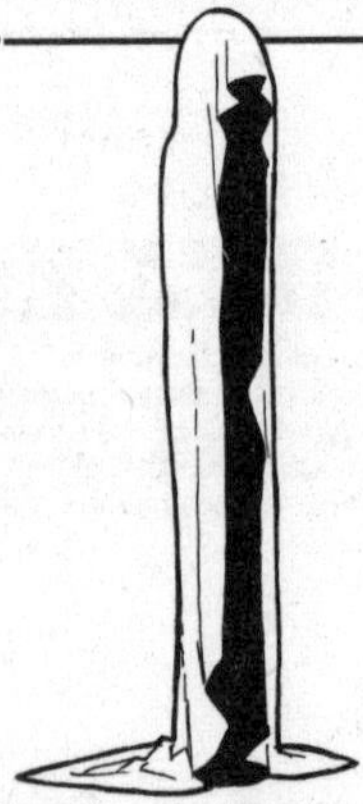

FILE 60

Death

High Level

Kin of Samael, King of Time. These demons possess unknown properties related to time and space. They appear to provide guidance when humans die in order to prevent demonic transformation into ghosts or evil spirits. The price of breaking a contract with one is obliteration.

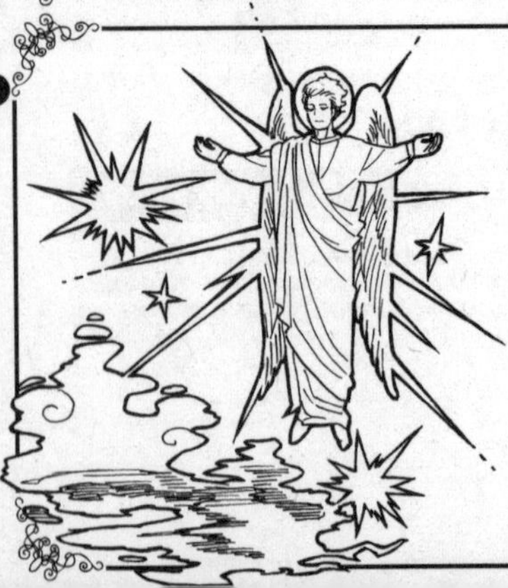

FILE 61

Phantasma

High Level

Kin of Lucifer, King of Light. These demons possess photons. They use the refraction of light to change into a wide variety of forms. They also cause mirages.

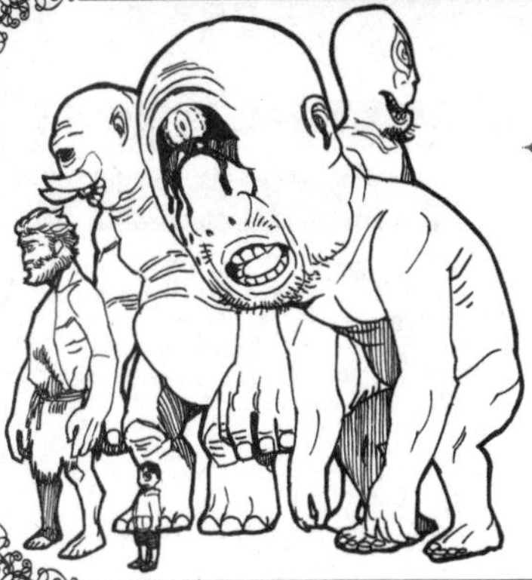

Cyclops

FILE 62

Mid to High Level

An old and legendary demon species. Large ones are rarely seen anymore. Giant ones are often related to fire or iron. Since so few exist, little is known about them. Some theories speculate they possess the corpses of elephants.

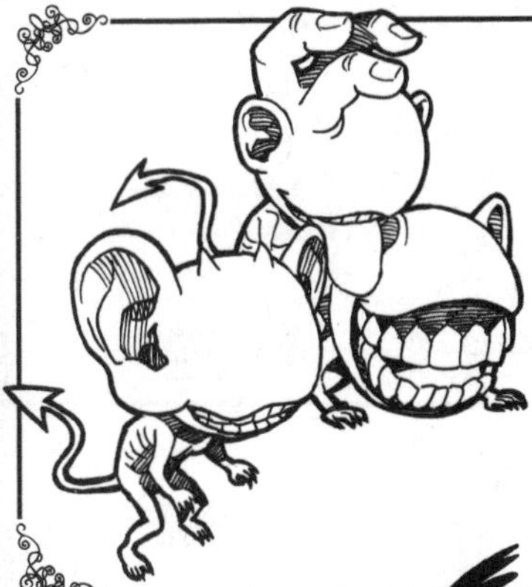

Gremlin

FILE 63

Low Level

No kinship. When human beings are injured in accidents or other incidents, these demons possess severed body parts. They love to cause man-made machines and mechanisms to malfunction. In the modern era, where machines are so prevalent, their mischief can prove fatal.

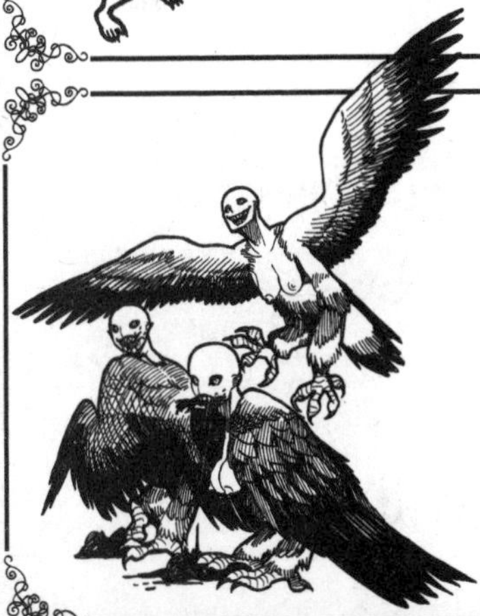

Harpy

FILE 64

Mid Level

No kinship. These demons possess the bodies of women who have died in suffering, such as during childbirth. Omnivorous and gluttonous, they eat anything, but they especially enjoy abducting infants and small children to devour.

AOEX! 28

Some Kinda Blue Exorcist

Art Staff

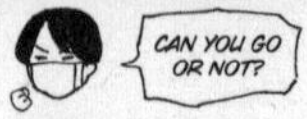
CAN YOU GO OR NOT?

Erika Uemura

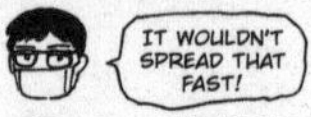
IT WOULDN'T SPREAD THAT FAST!

Ryoji Hayashi

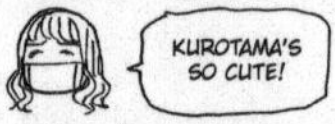
KUROTAMA'S SO CUTE!

Mari Oda

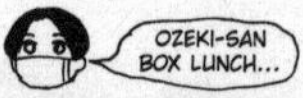
OZEKI-SAN BOX LUNCH...

Aki Shiina

Art Assistants

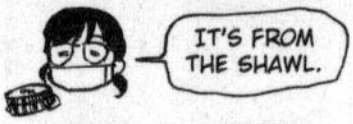
IT'S FROM THE SHAWL.

Yamanaka-san

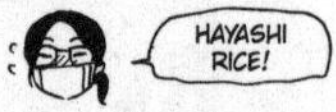
HAYASHI RICE!

Obata-san

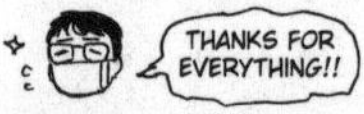
THANKS FOR EVERYTHING!!

Ito-kun

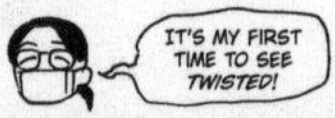
IT'S MY FIRST TIME TO SEE TWISTED!

Seo-san

Composition Assistant

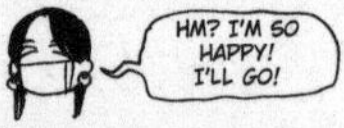
HM? I'M SO HAPPY! I'LL GO!

Minoru Sasaki

Editors

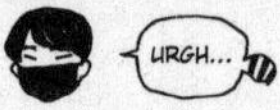
URGH...

Ippei Sawada

Graphic Novel Editor

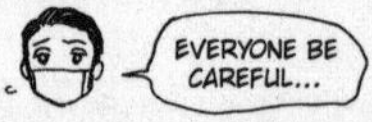
EVERYONE BE CAREFUL...

Ryusuke Kuroki

Graphic Novel Design

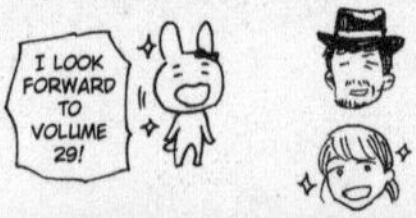
I LOOK FORWARD TO VOLUME 29!

Shimada Hideaki

Rie Akutsu (L.S.D.)

Manga

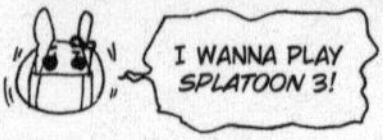
I WANNA PLAY SPLATOON 3!

Kazue Kato

(In no particular order)

(Note: The caricatures and statements are from memory!)

Sorry for volume 28 taking so long! See you in volume 29!

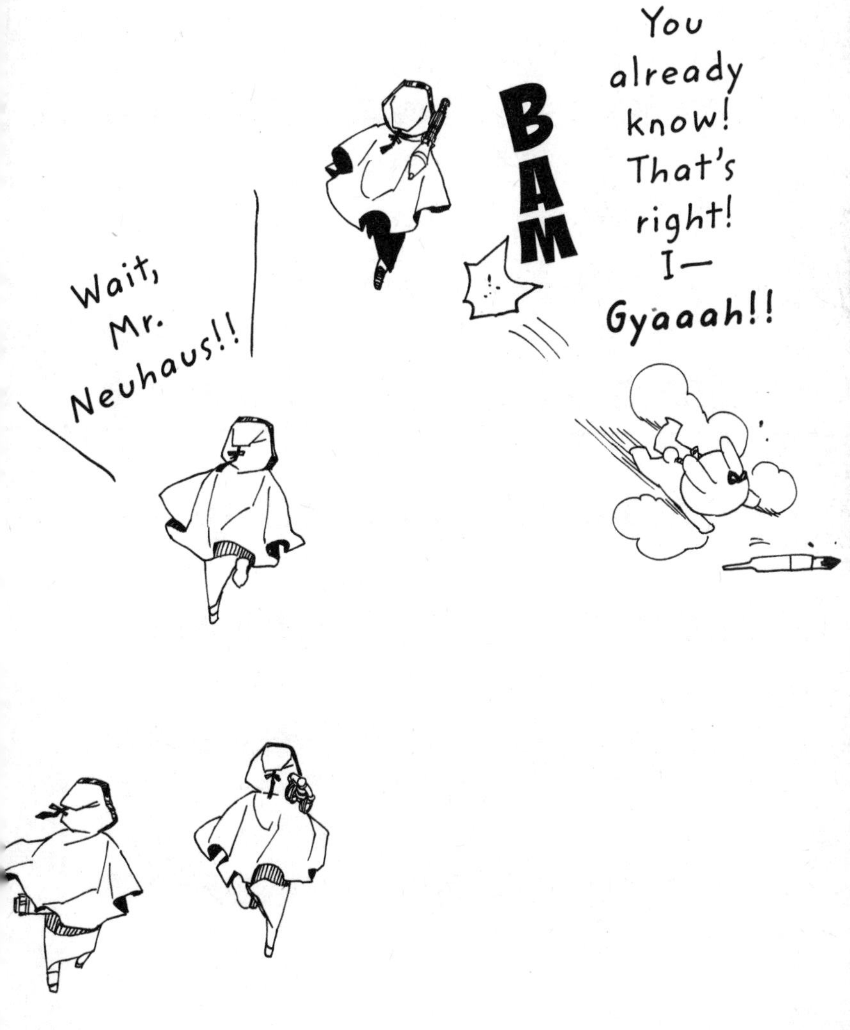
You already know! That's right! I— Gyaaah!!
BAM
Wait, Mr. Neuhaus!!

Suguro and Shima that one time...

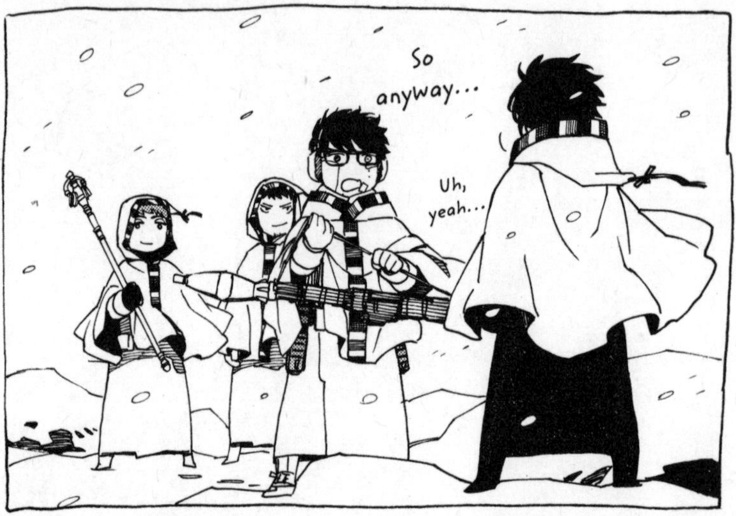
So anyway...
Uh, yeah...

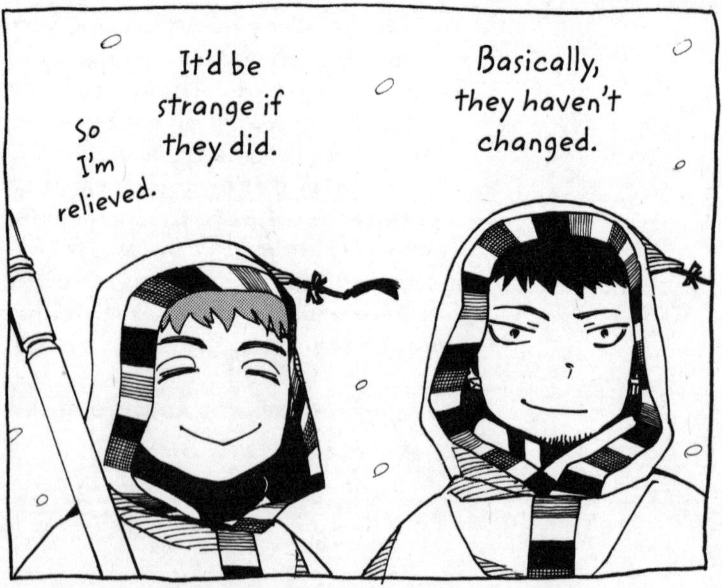
Basically, they haven't changed.
It'd be strange if they did.
So I'm relieved.

The pair watched over them warmly...

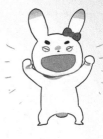

Kazue Kato

I took a break for about a year, so this is the first new volume in a long time! Thanks for waiting!! Thanks to that time off, I was able to recover from my mental exhaustion, but now I'm physically out of whack from lack of exercise. Yep. I hate to exercise. But my body's telling me I'll die early if I don't change, so I've started going to the gym. I really don't like it, but dying early would be worse, so I'll give it my best!

Hope you enjoyed volume 28!

BLUE EXORCIST

BLUE EXORCIST VOL. 28
SHONEN JUMP Edition

STORY & ART BY KAZUE KATO

Translation & English Adaptation/John Werry
Touch-Up Art & Lettering/John Hunt, Primary Graphix
Cover & Interior Design/Ian Miller
Editor/Mike Montesa

Printed in the U.S.A.

Published by VIZ Media, LLC
P.O. Box 77010
San Francisco, CA 94107

10 9 8 7 6 5 4 3 2 1
First printing, November 2023

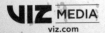

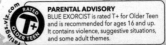

VIZ MEDIA
viz.com

In the next volume...

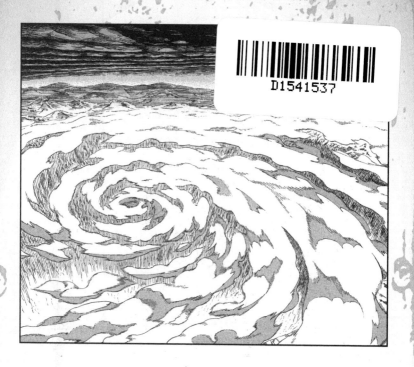

Although Rin is engaged in an epic battle with Satan, he's only buying time for the Grigori to arrive. When they do, Mephistopheles can start the ritual to seal away Satan. While Rin thinks back to his original pledge to defeat the demon lord, now he wonders if there can be any reconciliation between Assiah and Gehenna. But the enemy of all humanity is not so easily convinced, nor so easily defeated, and even if he can be sealed away by Shemihaza's ritual, the battle is far from over...

Coming soon!